BLOOD ROYAL

Issue of the Kings and Queens
of Medieval England
1066-1399

The Normans
and Plantagenets

BLOOD ROYAL

Issue of the Kings and Queens
of Medieval England
1066-1399

The Normans
and Plantagenets

T. Anna Leese

Heritage Books, Inc.

By the same author writing as T. A. Fuller:

THE SPEAR AND THE SPINDLE:
ANCESTORS OF SIR FRANCIS BRYAN (D. 1550), KT.

For my parents
Martha Elizabeth Price Leese
and
Grady Webster Leese
Vicksburg, Mississippi

Published 1996 by

HERITAGE BOOKS, INC.
1540E Pointer Ridge Place
Bowie, Maryland 20716
1-800-398-7709

ISBN 0-7884-0525-X

A Complete Catalog Listing Hundreds of Titles
On History, Genealogy, and Americana
Available Free Upon Request

Contents

Events and Instances

Tables and Lists

Tables

Map

Illustrations of Arms

Preface

Blood Royal: Issue of the Kings and Queens of England 1066-1399: The Normans and Plantagenets is the book I was hoping to find when I first became interested in medieval royal genealogy.

Here is compiled into one reference four generations of issue of each king and queen of England from 1066 to 1399. The first date is, of course, William the Conqueror's victory at Hastings. Though Edward III died in 1377, the time period of the book has been continued to 1399, the year of the death of Edward's son, John of Gaunt, a common ancestor of most American descendants of British royalty. Three generations of John of Gaunt's issue from his three marriages are listed in a separate chapter. His Beaufort family, though born out of wedlock, were later declared legitimate and played a major role in the history of medieval England.

The book is based on the family unit concept, which has been extended in this case to include the marriages of the children of the kings and queens and the resulting grandchildren, as well as marriages of the grandchildren and resulting great-grandchildren and their marriages and the resulting great-great-grandchildren, all *when known to your compiler*. In some cases, there may not have been four generations of issue, or, if there were, data simply may not have been located or may not have been available, or the records may not have survived the years.

Children who died at an early age or at birth are often ignored by some historians. Terminology such as *only daughter* or *only son* can sometimes be read as only *surviving* daughter or only *surving* son; and some sources, when indicating the number of sons or daughters, will total only the surviving

children. *All issue* that was located was included and counted in
this listing. Note that children are not necessarily listed in order
of birth.
    Immediate ancestors of many spouses are identified. The
previous marriages of many spouses are listed, sometimes with
issue of those marriages. Some illegitimate issue has been
included. The genealogist may find here interesting and
previously unknown collaterals who may very well become
ancestors as relationships are made evident.
    While some lines seemed to have a scarcity of data, other
lines offered so much historical data as to prove unusually
interesting. For example, Anne Boleyn, queen of England, left
an only child, Elizabeth I, who left no issue, but a line of
descent to Anne Boleyn is included in a separate chapter for the
value it holds as part of that particular family line. Individuals
in that line can be found on family trees of today.

    It is not unusual for an individual to be known by more than
one name—Matilda, Maud, Maude, the Empress Matilda, or
Matilda FitzEmpress, all referring to the daughter of Henry I,
king of England; Otho the Puer or Otto the Puer or Otto the
Child; or Hadwisa, Isabella, Avice, or Avisa, all referring to
the first wife of King John of England. Some names are seen in
two different forms: Guido is used by one source and Guy by
another, or Guillaume is used where another source uses
William. The name usage in this manuscript usually reflects that
used by the source consulted. The same may be said for such
seeming inconsistencies as Black Friars and black friars, and
Grey Friars and Greyfriars. Montagu is also seen Montague and
Montacute, though an attempt has been made to spell it as
Montagu for the sake of ease in indexing. And then there are
the common variants, such as Katherine and Catherine.
    In *The Complete Peerage*, Vol. 3, Appendix C, "Some
Observations on Mediæval Names," the editors remark that it is
sometimes impossible when reading old manuscripts and
documents to identify particular letters. The letters *u*, *n*, and *v*
are often difficult to read, and because of this, variations of the
same name are in use. Examples given include Alina and Oliva;

Hervico de Stauntone and Hernico de Stanton; Walter de Mauny and Walter de Manny; and Danvers, Daunvers, and Dauvers.

Another interesting feature of early names is discussed in *CP*, Vol. 6, Appendix A, "The Particle 'de' in Titles." Originally, *de* was used to differentiate the various families which had the same name, that is, the Greys of Codner, the Greys of Rotherfield, the Greys of Ruthin, and the Greys of Wilton. They were known as *de Codner, de Rotherfield, de Ruthin*, and *de Wilton*. The members of the families, however, were known simply as the Lords Grey, not the Lords de Grey. The use of the *de* was a kind of postal address necessary for sure identification. Later, when English became the common language, the *de* became *of*.

Every effort has been made to make the manuscript easy to use. The traditional *ibid*. and *op. cit*. have not been utilized. Rather, out of sympathy for the reader, the source names are repeated in shortened forms for ready reference. These shortened forms are included in the section, "Abbreviations."

Further genealogical information is often given in footnotes and can include ancestors of a spouse or information on other marriages and issue the spouse might have had. The fact that there is a large number of footnotes may require an apology. Some readers feel that a large number of footnotes and lengthy footnotes interrupt the flow of the text and should be grouped together at the end of the chapter or section. Others readers are of the opinion that having to stop and locate footnotes placed elsewhere in the book is equally disruptive to text and thought. I have used footnotes to note sources and to add additional information which does not necessarily fit into the body text. It would seem that having the additional information is worth the inconvenience of putting up with footnotes. For that reason, the footnotes have been made readily accessible to the reader on the page where they are referenced. The reader, with a minimum of disruption to reading, can glance down and quickly decide if a particular footnote is to be perused now or later.

Effort has been made to include every name in the index. The only conscious exceptions are the names of children who died young.

In the same spirit of passing on information, it was decided to include the burial places of individuals when that information was seen in sources, despite the fact that often simply the name of a religious house would be given as a burial place, with no identity on the location.

It is not to be assumed that such graves are extant: Henry VIII was responsible for despoiling and destroying many religious houses. In the words of Scarisbrick, "hundreds of glorious buildings ... disappeared off the face of the land ... soaring stone, the vaults, towers and spires ... glass and statue, choirstalls and rood-screens, plate and vestments—the flower of a dozen minor arts."[1] This destruction, begun in 1536, included tombs, many of them being those of the individuals mentioned herein. Nor did shrines escape the dissolution: St. Thomas Becket's shrine at Canterbury, St. Swithin's shrine at Winchester, St. Cuthbert's shrine at Durham—these and others were utterly destroyed. Today, only a marker might indicate where the body at one time rested.

Though many sources were used, the information was gathered mainly from the following:

Burke's Peerage, *Burke's Guide to the Royal Family*, Burke's
   Peerage Limited, 1973.

Cokayne, G. E., *The Complete Peerage*, St Catherine Press,
   London.

Green, Mary Anne Everett, *Lives of the Princesses of England*,
   Vols. I-III, Henry Colburn, Pub., London, 1849.

Previte-Orton, C. W., *The Shorter Cambridge Medieval
   History*, The University Press, Cambridge, 1962.

Stephen, Sir Leslie, and Lee, Sir Sidney, eds., *Dictionary of
   National Biography*, Oxford University Press, London,
   1964.

---

[1] Scarisbrick, *Henry VIII*, pgs. 509-510.

Tauté, Anne, compiler, Kings and Queens of Great Britain wall
    chart, 1990.
Weis, Frederick Lewis, *Ancestral Roots of Sixty Colonists Who
    Came to New England between 1623 and 1650*, 6th ed.,
    Genealogical Publishing Co., Inc., Baltimore, MD, 1988.
Williamson, David, *Debrett's Kings and Queens of Britain*,
    Dorset Press, New York, 1992.
Williamson, David, *DeBrett's Kings and Queens of Europe*,
    Salem House Publishers, Mass., 1988.

For the reader's convenience, "Bibliography and
References" includes books that may not have been specifically
referenced in this manuscript but may be of interest to the
reader in search of titles for his own research.

The differences in what we might call the numbering system
applied to Earls can cause confusion. For example, an Earl may
be the 2nd Earl of the creation or the 6th Earl of that title or the
3rd Earl of his house to hold the title. The Percy family
illustrates that situation.

⸴ Henry de Percy (d. 19 Feb 1407/1408) was created the
1st Earl of Northumberland at the coronation of Richard II
16 Jul 1377. He was, however, the fourth man to hold this title.
In 1406 he was charged with treason and "his honours and
estates...forfeited."

His son, known as Hotspur, died 21 Jul 1403 (in the
lifetime of his father) and thus did not succeed to the earldom.
In fact, his activities were declared treasonous, and "forfeiture
followed thereupon." [1]

Hotspur's son, Henry de Percy (k. 22 May 1455), was on
16 Mar 1415/1416 *created* the Earl of Northumberland and thus
became the 1st Earl of Northumberland of the 1415/1416
creation or, because four other men had held the title before
him, actually the 5th Earl of Northumberland; but because he

---

[1] *CP*, Northumberland section.

was the second *of his house* to hold that title, he is called by Lodge[1] the 2nd Earl of Northumberland.

His son became the 2nd or 6th Earl; Lodge calls him the 3rd Earl. In 1461, he was attainted,[2] and in 1464 John Neville was created the 1st or 7th Earl of Northumberland. This John Neville was in 1470 created the Marquess of Montagu (a higher dignity), and he released the Earldom to Hotspur's grandson, who became the 3rd or 8th or 4th Earl, depending on how you choose to count your Earls.

Unless the reader is familiar with the various creations, identifying the Earls can be very confusing; thus, less emphasis is put on who is which Earl of which creation. Rather, for the majority of titles herein, the death date is used as an identifying factor. Hotspur's son can be identified simply as Henry de Percy (d. 1455), Earl of Northumberland.

Historians, researchers, and writers do not always agree, and it is common to come upon two or more views of a situation. Even in dealing with source material, such a disparity is not unusual. Charles Ross comments concerning the wars of the Roses that "Such accounts as do exist often conflict on essential points of evidence."[3] Modern writers offer disparity as well. When reading of Malcolm III Canmore, I came across the following three particular opinions concerning the meaning of the king's name:

Scotland's Kings & Queens, Pitkin Guide, 1980, pg. 9, states that Canmore (Gaelic *Ceann Mor*) means "bighead" or "great chief" but enlightens us no further on the meaning of these names.

---

[1] Lodge, *The Genealogy of the Existing British Peerage with Brief Sketches of the Family Histories of the Nobility*, pgs. 274-275.

[2] An attainder was an act of Parliament that in effect was the legal end of a family. The guilty person was to be hanged, drawn, and quartered. His estate was to be confiscated and his heirs disinherited. Such a violent execution could be commuted to beheading when royal blood was involved. Attainders could be later reversed and property restored to heirs of the attainted.

[3] Ross, *The Wars of the Roses*, pg. 109.

The Kings & Queens of Scotland by Caroline Bingham, pg. 15, states, "King Malcolm III was known as Ceann Mor, which is customarily translated as 'Bighead'. Only one historian has suggested that 'head' in this context bears the same meaning as in 'headman', so that *Ceann Mor* ought to be translated as 'Great Chief'. This suggestion appears to have the merit of inherent probability."

Monarchs of Scotland by Stewart Ross, 1990, pg. 43, states that Ceann Mor or Canmore literally translated means Big Head and that this term "most probably refers to the king's imposing physiognomy but it may be a more laudatory epithet, metaphorically signifying the fact that Duncan I's son was regarded as a Great Leader. Tne first explanation is more likely as Malcolm's government does not appear all that remarkable."

Headman or big-headed man? Drawing even educated conclusions is a risky business.

There are varying modern opinions on contemporary chroniclers. For example, Edward II is traditionally believed to have been homosexual. However, each writer might have his own opinion on a chronicler's remarks on this subject. Hutchinson, *Edward II*, pg. 147, states, "Only one chronicle specifically refers to sodomy between Edward and Gaveston — the Cistercian monk, of the abbey of Meaux in the East Riding of Yorkshire — and his knife is somewhat blunted in that he does not complain of sodomy, but of 'too much' sodomy." Chaplais, author of *Piers Gaveston*, pg. 8, writes, "But all this is more likely to have been just malicious gossip, no more trustworthy than the gratuitous assertion of the late Meaux chronicle that Edward indulged in the vice of sodomy 'excessively'."

Hutchinson refers to *Chronica monasterii de Melsa* (Meaux), ed. W. D. Macray (Rolls Series, 1863), ii, 355; Chaplais refers to the same reference but having ed. E. A. Bond and being Rolls Series, 1867.

And then Mairin Mitchell, author of *Berengaria, Enigmatic Queen of England*, reminds us that history is not static. She includes in her writing such phrases as "no evidence of this has yet been made known" and "so far no document has come to light." Neither are the opinions of historians static. Mitchell remarks, for example, that it was long believed that after Richard the Lion-Heart disappeared on his way home from the Holy Land, his wife, Berengaria, found his belt in Rome, a discovery that enabled others to locate him. Mitchell writes that this story, so long accepted by scholars, was eventually disregarded by some historians as a "pretty but romantic fiction." Now, however, many historians are beginning to "regard the story as not wholly fictional."[1] Sir Ivan de la Bere writes, concerning the origin of the garter for the Most Noble Order of the Garter, "One thing is sure, namely that it is as arrogant and unsafe to reject all such legends absolutely as it would be rash and unintelligent to accept them implicitly and blindly."[2]

Researchers, historians, and writers of all eras are not always in agreement. Barbara Tuchman states that "any statement of fact about the Middle Ages may (and probably will) be met by a statement of the opposite or a different version" and that "the Middle Ages change color depending on who is looking at them."[3] Despite extensive examination and study, the truth in some cases may never be known.

The medieval age stands with one booted foot nudging the Renaissance and the other just stepping from an age of Viking barbarity. Medieval man's mindset is not the modern man's mindset. Desmond Seward writes that the mentality of medieval man was "immeasurably remote" from that of today's man.[4] In pondering the lives of the people of the medieval time, the reader is urged to remember that the deciding factors regarding their motives, priorities, reasoning, and survival may not always be within our comprehension.

---

[1] Mitchell, *Berengaria, Enigmatic Queen of England*, pgs. 72, 74, and 81.

[2] *The Queen's Orders of Chivalry*, Spring Books, London, 1964, pg. 62.

[3] Tuchman, *A Distant Mirror: The Calamitous 14th Century*, pg. xvii. Her foreword details other "hazards" faced when researching the Middle Ages.

[4] Seward, *The Wars of the Roses*, pg. 9.

Occasionally throughout the manuscript, a year will be written with a slash, for example, 1407/1408. Until 1752, the English legal year (Julian) began March 25 rather than January 1. Therefore, dates from January 1 to March 25 may commonly be seen with both years indicated.

In September 1752, the British Empire switched from the Julian to the Gregorian calendar. That month, the calendar appeared thus:

```
                September 1752
        S   M   Tu  W   Th  F   S
                1   2   14  15  16
        17  18  19  20  21  22  23
        24  25  26  27  28  29  30
```

Historians today will usually use the new style (NS) calendar or will use the old style (OS) for the months and days and the new style for the year. The OS/NS format for the year is preferred in this manuscript: John de Montagu, 3rd Earl of Salisbury, was beheaded 5 Jan 1399/1400, that is, in 1399 by the Julian or Old Style (OS) calendar in effect at that time, or in 1400 by the Gregorian or New Style (NS) calendar.

Dates are given as seen in sources. Different calendar usages among historians and authors may cause a date to be off by several days or by one or two years.

It was not the intent of this book to draw conclusions but to present information. The remarks in the footnotes and the articles of the **Events and Instances** section are written to give the reader an idea of the lives led by these people and the times they lived in, to make them persons rather than simply names and dates, and to be a guide in determining where the reader would like to begin reading and researching his own line.

"Abbreviations" contains the most common Latin abbreviations encountered in research; though they are not used in this book, they are included because they were used in some of the sources which were researched for this material.

The reader who would undertake his own research is encouraged to refer to as many works and authors as possible and to remember the words of Henry Grove, written 25 Jul 1896 in his *Alienated Tithes*: "A Work of this kind, consisting principally of names, dates, and figures, cannot in the nature of things be free from mistakes." [1]

Special Thanks

Special thanks to Dr. Roelof Oostingh for his translations of research material, particularly those selections concerning the Lusignan family. His expert insights were most helpful and enlightening.

---

[1] Grove, Henry, *Alienated Tithes In Appropriated and Impropriated Parishes, Commuted or Merged under Local Statutes and the Tithe Acts: Together with all Crown Grants of Tithes, from Henry viii to William iii*, Printed for the Author's Subscribers, London, 1896, pg. 16.

Numbering System

Each chapter is introduced with the data of a king and queen. When a king has married more than once, each queen is recognized separately and her issue listed.

The numbering system used is a common one. Numbers represent the generation of descent from the king and queen.

Issue of king and queen:

1 — Child A, issue of king and queen.
   2 — Child B, issue of Child A.
   2 — Child C, further issue of Child A.
      3 — Child D, issue of Child C.
         4 — Child E, issue of Child D.
      3 — Child F, further issue of Child C.
1 — Child G, further issue of king and queen.
   2 — Child H, issue of Child G.
      3 — Child I, issue of Child H.
1 — Child J, further issue of king and queen.

An example of issue from William the Conqueror and Matilda:

1 — **Adela** (b. abt 1062; d. 8 Mar 1137/1138; bur. in Abbey of the Holy Trinity in Caen with her mother and sister **Cecilia**) m. at Chartres 1081 **Stephen II** (d. 1102 Battle of Ascalon), Count of Blois and Chartres. Issue:
   2 — **William of Champagne**, eldest son; m. **Agnes**, daughter and heiress of **Giles de Sully** and became founder of house of Sully Champagne. Issue:

3 — **Margaret de Champagne** (d. 15 Dec 1145)
m. (3) **Henry**, Count of Eu, Lord of Hastings, a
descendant of **Richard I**, Duke of Normandy. Issue:
    4 — **John** (d 26 Jun 1170), Count of Eu, Lord of
Hastings; m. 11 Sep 1188 **Alice**, daughter of
William d'Aubigny, Earl of Arundel, and his wife
Adeliza of Louvain.

Adela is one generation from William the Conqueror and is
mother of William of Champagne. William of Champagne is
two generations from William the Conqueror and is father of
Margaret de Champagne. Margaret de Champagne is three
generations from William the Conqueror and is mother of John,
who is four generations from William the Conqueror. This
example shows child, grandchild, great-grandchild, and great-
great-grandchild of William the Conqueror and Matilda.

Abbreviations

abt	about
aft	after
appt.	appointed
b.	born
bef	before
bet.	between
bur.	buried
d.	died
da.	daughter
diss.	dissolved
div.	divorced
ex.	executed
inf.	infant
k.	killed
K.B.	Knight of the Bath
K.G.	Knight of the Garter
Kt.	knight
liv.	living
m.	married
nr	near
unm.	unmarried
yng	young

Shortened book titles:

Ancestral — *Ancestral Roots of Sixty Colonists* by Weis (numbers following this shortened book title refer to genealogical lines in the book)

Beltz — *Memorials of the Most Noble Order of the Garter from Its Foundation to the Present Time*

Burke's Peerage — *Burke's Genealogical and Heraldic History of the Peerage: Baronetage & Knightage*

CP — *Complete Peerage* by Cokayne

DNB — *Dictionary of National Biography* edited by Stephen and Lee

Enc. Brit. — *Encyclopedia Britannia*

KQB — *DeBrett's Kings and Queens of Britain* by Williamson

KQE — *DeBrett's Kings and Queens of Europe* by Williamson

Lives — *Lives of the Queens of England* by Strickland

Living Descendants — *Living Descendants of Blood Royal (in America)* by Count d'Angerville

Peerage and Baronetage — *Peerage and Baronetage* by Burke, 1907

Previté-Orton — *The Shorter Cambridge Medieval History* by Previté-Orton

Royal Family — *Guide to the Royal Family* by Burke

Sureties — *The Magna Charta Sureties, 1215* by Weis and Adams

Tauté — Kings and Queens of Great Britain wall chart, published by Penguin Group, London, 1990

Abbreviations frequently encountered in research:

d.		died
ob.	*obit*	died
o.s.p.	*obit sine prole*	died without issue
s.p.	*sine prole*	without issue
s.p.l.	*sine prole legitima*	without legitimate issue
s.p.m.	*sine prole mascula*	without male issue
s.p.m.s.	*sine prole mascula superstite*	
		without surviving male issue
s.p.s.	*sine prole superstite*	without surviving issue
v.p.	*vita patris*	in the lifetime of the father
v.f.	*vita fratris*	in the lifetime of the brother
v.m.	*vita matris*	in the lifetime of the mother

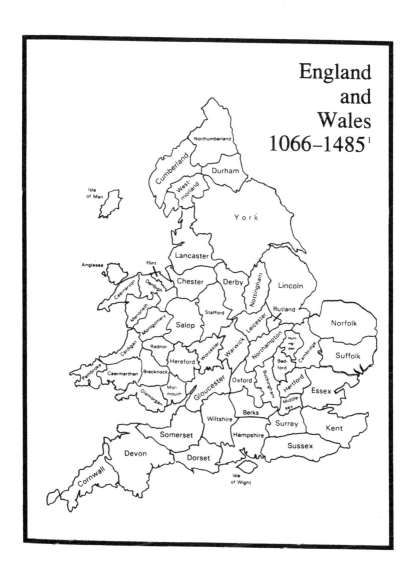

England
and
Wales
1066–1485[1]

[1] After Montgomery, *Leading Facts in English History*; Sanford, *The Great Governing Families of England*, Vol. I; Turner, *King John*; and Breasted, Huth, and Harding, *European History Atlas*.

Issue of the Kings and Queens
of England 1066–1399

William I the Conqueror
1066-1087
m. Matilda of Flanders

William I the Conqueror, [1] illegitimate son of **Robert I the Magnificent** (d. 1/2/3 Jul 1035), Duke of Normandy, and his mistress, **Arlette/Herleve**, daughter of **Fulbert the Tanner** of Falaise; *b.* 1027/1028, Falaise, Normandy; *crowned* 25 Dec 1066, Westminster Abbey; *m.* at Eu abt 1051/1053 **Matilda of Flanders**; *d.* 9 Sep 1087, Priory of St. Gervais, nr Rouen; *bur.* Abbey of St. Stephen, Caen, which he had founded. [2]

---

[1] Sometimes called **William the Bastard**. It should be noted that the word *bastard* was not a derogatory term during the Middle Ages. Rather, it was used to indicate that the child's parents were not married to each other, thus the child would not inherit *by right*. He could inherit, however, if his father, having no legitimate heirs, acknowledged him as his heir, which is exactly what **William's** father did. For more information on the state of bastardy, see *The Royal Bastards of Medieval England* by Chris Given-Wilson and Alice Curteis.

Aubrey, *The Rise and Growth of the English Nation*, pg. 96, states that, concerning the lack of marriage between **Robert** and **Arlette/Herleve**, "The accommodating morals of the period made no trouble of this, and attached no stigma to the offspring."

See also chapters, "The Papal Prohibition of the Marriage of William the Conqueror" and "Other Relations of William the Conqueror."

[2] **William the Conqueror's** heart was left to Rouen Cathedral, and his entrails were interred at the church in Chalus (*Enc. Brit.*, Macropaedia, Vol. 5, "Death Rites and Customs," pg. 536). His burial place has been often disturbed: in 1522, Rome instructed an examination of the grave contents; in 1562, Calvinists caused "complete devastation"

(continued...)

Matilda of Flanders, daughter of **Baldwin V** (b. 1012; d. 1 Sep 1067[1]), Count of Flanders, and **Adela of France** (d. 8 Jan 1079)[2]; *b*. abt 1031/1032, Flanders; *crowned* 11 May 1068 (Whit Sunday), Winchester Cathedral; *d*. 2 or 3 Nov 1083, Caen; *bur*. Abbey of Holy Trinity, Caen, which she had founded.

Ancestors of Matilda of Flanders

```
                      ┌─Baldwin IV, Count of Flanders (d. 1036)³
            ┌─Baldwin V, Count of Flanders (d. 1067)
            │         └─Ogiva/Ogive of Luxembourg (d. 1030)
Matilda/Maud of Flanders (d. 1083)
            │         ┌─Robert II the Pious, King of France (d. 1031)
            └─Adela of France (d. 1079)
                      └─Constance of Toulouse (d. 1032)
```

---

[2] (...continued)
of the tomb, in which the only bit of remains of the **Conqueror** was a thigh bone (it was reburied under a new monument); the grave was again demolished in the riots of the revolution of 1793. What was the grave of **William the Conqueror** is today marked with a stone slab (Douglas, *William the Conqueror*, pg. 363).

[1] *Ancestral* 162-22.

[2] **Baldwin V** was a descendant of **Alfred the Great** (d. 899). His wife, **Adela**, was sister of **Henry I**, King of France 1031-1060.

[3] After the death of **Ogiva**, **Baldwin IV** m. the sister **(Eleanor?)** of **Robert I**, father of **William the Conqueror**. (Douglas, *William the Conqueror*, pg. 77)

Issue

1 — **Robert Curthose**[1] (b. abt 1054, Normandy; d. 3/
10[2] Feb 1134, Cardiff Castle; bur. Gloucester Cathedral),
Duke of Normandy; affianced (1061) **Margaret** (d. yng
abt 1063), daughter of **Hugh IV** (d. 1051),[3] Count of Maine,
but she died before they were marriage[4]; m. at Ampulia 1100
Sybilla of Conversano (d. Feb/Mar 1103; bur. Caen
Cathedral), daughter of **Geoffrey**, Count of Conversano. Issue:
    2 — **William Clito**[5] (b. 1101; d. 27 Jul 1128, battle of
Alost/Abbey of St. Bertin, St. Omer; bur. Abbey of
St. Bertin), Count of Flanders 1127-1128; m. (1) (annulled

---

[1] It is believed he was called **Curthose** because of his short legs. The
eldest of **William the Conqueror's** sons, **Robert Curthose**, received at
his father's death the duchy of Normandy. **William Rufus**, was his
father's heir to the throne of England. **Curthose** rebelled against his
brother when he became **William II Rufus**, KING OF ENGLAND, and
later against his youngest brother, **Henry**, when he became **Henry I**,
KING OF ENGLAND. In 1106, **Henry I** captured the troublesome
Robert Curthose at the Battle of Tinchebrai (29 Sep). As a result,
Robert Curthose spent his last twenty-eight years in prison, dying in
Cardiff Castle at age eighty.

    Churchill, *The Birth of Britain*, pg. 134, remarks on the
psychological importance of Tinchebrai: "The Saxons, who had fought
heartily for Henry, regarded this battle as their military revenge for
Hastings." This victory, along with **Henry's** marriage to the Saxon
Edith Matilda, released them "from some at least of the pangs of being
conquered," and "a certain broad measure of unity was re-established in
the Island."

    Politically, the Battle of Tinchebrai reunited Normandy and England
under **Henry I**.

[2] *KQB*, pg. 43, states **Robert Curthose** died 10 Feb; *Living
Descendants*, pg. xiii, gives the date as 3 Feb.

[3] Douglas, *William the Conqueror*, Table 7.

[4] Duncan, *The Dukes of Normandy*, pg. 181; *DNB*, "Robert, Duke of
Normandy (1054?-1134)."

[5] *Clito*, meaning *prince*. Like his father, he plotted against **Henry I**,
KING OF ENGLAND.

1124) 1123 **Sybil**[1] (b. 1112; d. 1165, as a nun in the
Abbey of St. Lazarus, Bethlehem), daughter of **Fulk V**
(d. 1143), Count of Anjou and Maine, King of Jerusalem,
and his first wife (m. 1110), **Heremburge/Ermentrude**
(d. 1126) (daughter of **Hélie I**, Count of Maine). No issue.
William Clito, as above, m. (2) Jan 1128 **Joan/Giovanna**,
daughter of **Reiner/Regnier**, Marquis of Montferrat, and
Giséle (widow of **Umberto II**, Count of Savoy and
Maurienne, and daughter of **Guillaume I**, Count of
Burgundy). No issue.

    2 – **Henry** (b. 1102; k. in the New Forest[2]). Unm.[3]

1 — **Richard** (b. abt 1055/1056, Normandy; k. while hunting
in the New Forest abt 1075/1081; bur. Winchester Cathedral),
Duke of Bernay.

1 — **William II**, KING OF ENGLAND.

1 — **Cecily/Cecilia** (b. abt 1055, Normandy; d. 30 Jul 1126,

---

[1] **Sybil** m. (2) 1134 **Thierry of Alsace**, Count of Flanders (d. 1168).

[2] Tauté. The New Forest was 75,000 or more acres in southern
England that **William the Conqueror** reserved as royal hunting land.
The villages were emptied, cultivated land was claimed by the king, and
severe forest laws were put into effect. Any subject caught poaching in
the New Forest could be maimed or put to death.
    The New Forest was not a lucky place for the Normans. Two of
Robert Curthose's illegitimate sons, **Richard** and **Henry**, died in the
New Forest, as did two of **William the Conqueror's** sons, **Richard** and
William II Rufus, KING OF ENGLAND (see chapter, "The Death of
William Rufus"). Douglas, *William the Conqueror*, pg. 371, states that
twelfth century chroniclers attributed the deaths to "divine vengeance"
for **William's** eviction of the inhabitants of the land.

[3] *DNB*, "Robert, Duke of Normandy (1054?–1134)," does not
mention this **Henry** but does list the three illegitimate issue: an
illegitimate daughter m. 1089 **Elias of Saint-Saëns**; an illegitimate son,
Richard, was "accidentally shot dead in the New Forest in May 1100";
an illegitimate son, **William**, went to the Holy Land after the capture of
his father at the battle of Tinchebrai (29 Sep 1106). Duncan, *The Dukes
of Normandy*, pg. 181, states that the three illegitimate issue were "by
the daughter of a priest in the French Vexin," adding only that "the
eldest was killed at the chase, the second died in the Holy Land, and the
third was married to Hélier of Saint-Saëns."

Caen; bur. Abbey of the Holy Trinity), abbess of Holy Trinity
(Benedictine convent), Caen.

1 — **Constance** (b. abt 1066, Normandy[1]; d. 13 Aug 1090,
St. Melans, Rhedon; bur. St. Melans, Rhedon[2]) m. at Caen
1086 **Alan IV**, Count of Brittany[3]/**Alan Fergant** (d. 13 Oct
1119), Duke of Brittany. No issue.

1 — **Adeliza/Adelaide** (d. abt 1065), a nun.

1 — **Adela** (b. abt 1062, Normandy; d. 8 Mar 1137/1138,
Cluniac Priory of Marcigny-sur-Loire; bur. Abbey of the Holy
Trinity in Caen with her mother and sister, **Cecilia**) m. at
Breteuil and Chartres[4] 1080/1081/bef 1085 **Stephen II**
(k. 19 May 1102, Battle of Ramlah[5]), Count of Blois and
Chartres, son of **Thibaut III/Theobald III** (d. 1089/1090),
Count of Blois and Champagne, and his second wife, **Alix de
Crepi**[6] (daughter of **Raoul III**). Issue (five sons, three
daughters[7]):

> 2 — **William of Champagne**, eldest son, did not succeed to
> his father's earldom because he was "wholly unfit to
> rule"[8]; m. **Agnes**, daughter and heiress of **Giles de Sully**
> and his wife, **Eldeburge** (sister of **Etienne**, Viscount of

[1] According to Green, *Lives of the Princesses of England*, **Constance**
was born abt 1057.

[2] Green, *Lives of the Princesses of England*, Vol. I, pg. 31.

[3] *KQB*, pg. 43; Green, *Lives of the Princesses of England*, Vol. I,
pg. 32. **Alan Fergant** was a descendant of **Geoffrey I**, Duke of
Bretagne. **Alan's** son and heir, **Conan III**, was issue by his second wife,
Ermengarde, daughter of **Foulk Rechin**, Earl of Anjou (Green, *Lives of
the Princesses of England*, Vol. I, pgs. 32-33). **Alan's** great-grandson,
Conan IV, m. **Margaret of Huntingdon**, daughter of **Henry of
Huntingdon** (d. 1152), son of **David I** (d. 1153), King of Scots.

[4] *DNB*, "Adela (1062?-1137)."

[5] Davis, *King Stephen*, pg. 4.

[6] *Ancestral* 137-22.

[7] Davis, *King Stephen*, pg. 4.

[8] Green, *Lives of the Princesses of England*, Vol. I, pg. 69. Davis in
King Stephen, pg. 4, informs us that exactly why **William** was not made
his father's heir is not known but adds that it is known that "in 1103
[William] went into Chartres Cathedral and took a solemn oath to kill the
bishop."

Bourges), and became founder of house of Sully Champagne. Issue:

    3 — **Henry de Sully**, Abbot of Fécamp 1140–1189.[1]

    3 — **Margaret de Champagne** (d. 15 Dec "about" 1145; bur. Abbey of Foucarmont) m. as his third wife **Henry** (became a monk at Foucarmont, d. 12 Jul 1140; bur. Abbey of Foucarmont), Count of Eu, Lord of Hastings, a descendant of **Richard I**, Duke of Normandy. Issue:[2]

        4 — **John** (d. 26 Jun 1170, as a monk at Foucarmont; bur. Abbey of Foucarmont), Count of Eu, Lord of Hastings; m. **Alice** (d. on or bef 11 Sep 1188; bur. Abbey of Foucarmont), daughter of **William d'Aubigny** (d. 12 Oct 1176), Earl of Arundel, and his wife, **Adela of Louvain** (b. abt 1105, Louvain; d. 23 Mar/Apr 1151, Afflighem, Flanders; bur. Afflighem) (widow of **Henry I**, KING OF ENGLAND). For historical interest, they were parents of:

            5 — **Henry** (d. 16/17 Mar 1183; bur. Abbey of Foucarmont), Count of Eu, Lord of Hastings; m. as her first husband, **Maud de Warenne** (d. abt 1212; bur. "it is said" in the Abbey of Foucarmont "but, perhaps, in that of Valmont"), daughter of **Hameline Plantagenet** (d. 7 May 1202), Earl of Warenne or of Surrey, and half-brother of **Henry II**, KING OF ENGLAND.[3]

2 — **Theobald/Thibaut IV** (b. abt 1085; d. 8 Jan 1152), second son, Earl of Blois/Count of Blois and Chartres and Champagne, his father's heir; m. 1123/1126 **Maud/Matilda of Carinthia** (b. abt 1105; d. 1160), daughter of **Engelbert II**, Duke of Carinthia, and his wife, **Uta**

---

[1] Davis, *King Stephen*, pgs. 148–149.

[2] *CP*, Eu section, in which is noted that the number of issue of **Henry** and **Margaret de Champagne** is uncertain and inconsistent among chroniclers.

[3] *Ancestral* 123-26, 123-27; *CP*, Eu section.

(daughter of **Udalrich**, Count of Passau); "progenitor of long line of noble descendants." [1] Issue [2]:

    3 — **Theobald V** (d. 1190, seige of Acre), Count of Blois and Chartres 1152–1191; m. **Alice of France**, daughter of **Louis VII** of France and his first wife, **Eleanor of Aquitaine**. Issue [3]:

        4 — A daughter, Countess of Blois; m. **John of Chastillon** (d. Apr 1201), Lord of Avesnes, Count of Blois. No issue.

        4 — **Lewis** ("slain in Battel at Adrianaple 1205"), Count of Charters and Blois. No issue.

        4 — **Theobald** (d. 1219), Count of Charters and Blois. No issue.

        4 — **Margaret** m. **Otto I**, Palatine of Burgundy, youngest son of **Frederick Barbarossa**.

        4 — Another daughter, Countess of Blois; m. **Gauthier**, Lord of Avesnes in Hainault, Count of Blois.

    3 — **Henry I** (d. in the Holy Land soon after 1181), Count of Champagne 1152–1181 and Brie; m. **Marie of France** (b. 1145; d. 11 Mar 1198), daughter of **Louis VII** of France and his first wife, **Eleanor of Aquitaine**. [4] Issue [5]:

        4 — **Henry II of Champagne** (d. 1196, "at his palace at Acre"), Palatine of Champagne and Brie, King of Jerusalem; m. 1191 **Isabella of Jerusalem**, widow of **Conrad**, margrave of Montserrat, and daughter of **Almeric I** (d. 1174) and **Maria Comena**.

        4 — **Mary/Marie of Champagne** m. **Baldwin VI**,

---

[1] Green, *Lives of the Princesses of England*, Vol. I, pg. 70.

[2] Anderson, *Royal Genealogies*, Table CCCXCII; Appleby, *Henry II: The Vanquished King*, Table "The House of Blois," pg. 69.

[3] Anderson, *Royal Genealogies*, Table CCCXCII; the table on pg. viii of Meade, *Eleanor of Aquitaine*, shows a daughter, **Isabel**, and a son, **Louis**.

[4] See also chapter, "The Marriages of Louis VII of France."

[5] Warren, *Henry II*, Table 7; Anderson, *Royal Genealogies*, Table CCCXCII.

Count of Hainault and Flanders, Emperor of
Constantinople.

4 — **Theobald** (d. 1201), Palatin of Champaign;
m. **Blanca of Navarre**, sister and heiress of
Santius VI, King of Navarre.[1]

3 — **Stephen**, Count of Sancerre; m. daughter of
Geoffrey, Count of Gien.

3 — **William**, Bishop of Sens and Archbishop Rheims.[2]

3 — **Adela of Champagne and Blois** m. as his third
wife **Louis VII**, King of France. For issue see chapter,
"The Marriages of Louis VII of France."

3 — **Mary** m. **Ivo II**, Duke of Burgundy.

3 — A daughter m. the Count of Bar. Issue:
    4 — **Theobald**, Count of Bar.

3 — A daughter m. (1) Duke of Apulia; m. **William
Goeth** (d. on his way to the Holy Land), Lord of
MontMiran.

3 — A daughter m. **Geoffrey**, Count of Perche.

2 — **Stephen**, third son, KING OF ENGLAND.

2 — **Henry of Blois** (b. 1099; d. 6 Aug 1171;
bur. Winchester Cathedral), youngest son, Bishop of
Winchester, Abbot of Glastonbury.[3]

2 — **Humbert** (d. yng).

2 — **Philip**, Bishop of Chalons.

2 — **Eudo**.[4]

2 — **Matilda/Lucia** (d. 25 Nov 1120, drowned in the wreck
of the *White Ship*) m. 1115 **Richard/Ralph d'Avranches**

---

[1] The great-granddaughter of **Theobald** and **Blanca**, **Joanna/Jeanne
of Navarre** (b. 1273; d. 1305), was the queen of **Philip IV**, King of
France. (Anderson, *Royal Genealogies*, Table CCCXCII, pg. 637;
Wismes, *Genealogy of the Kings of France*, main table)

[2] "William, Bishop of Charters, Archbishop of Sens then Cardinal
and Archbishop of Rheims" crowned his nephew, **Philip Augustus**, King
of France. (Anderson, *Royal Genealogies*, Table CCCXCII, pg. 637)

[3] Green, *Lives of the Princesses of England*, Vol. I, pg. 69. *DNB*,
"Henry of Blois (d. 1171)," states that he died 8 Aug 1171.

[4] **Eudo** is mentioned in charters, but, aside from his name, nothing is
known of him. (*DNB*, "Adela (1062?–1137)")

(d. 25 Nov 1120, drowned in the wreck of the *White Ship*[1]), Earl of Chester, only son of **Hugh d'Avranches** (d. 27 Jul 1101) and his wife, **Ermentrude** (daughter of **Hugues**, Count of Clermont in Beauvaisis).[2] No issue.

2 — **Adela** m. (annulled[3]) **Milo de Brai**, Lord of Montlheri and Viscount of Troyes.

2 — **Agnes** m. **Hugues III**, Seigneur de Puiset. Issue:

3 — **Hugh du Puiset** (b. 1102; d. 1128), Treasurer of York 1143–1153, Bishop of Durham 1153–1195.[4]

2 — **Alice**, possible daughter; m. **Reynald III**, Earl of Joigni.

2 — **Eleanor**, possible daughter; m. **Raoul**, Earl of Vermandois.[5]

1 — **Matilda** (d. bef 1080; bur. in cathedral church of St. Mary's, Bayeux), betrothed (1) to **Edwin** (murdered), Earl of Chester, a Saxon noble; betrothed (2) to **Alphonso VI the Valiant** of Leon and Castile and Gallicia. Unm.

1 — **Agatha**.[6]

---

[1] *CP*, Chester section. See chapter, "The Wreck of the *White Ship*."

[2] *CP*, Chester section.

[3] "...to the great grief of the bridegroom, the marriage was annulled" at the instigation of **Ivo**, Bishop of Chartres, who "found or framed a plea of illegality in the union, and appealed to the Pope." It is interesting to note that the bride's brother, **William**, at one time attempted unsuccessfully "to murder Bishop Ivo and all the clergy of Chartres, while they were officiating in the church." (Green, *Lives of the Princesses of England*, Vol. I, pgs. 59, 69–70)

[4] Burke's *Royal Family*; Davis, *King Stephen*, pgs. 148–149.

[5] The relationships of possible daughters, **Alice** and **Eleanor**, to **Stephen** and **Adela** is not certain. (Green, *Lives of the Princesses of England*, Vol. I, pgs. 70–71)

[6] Some authorities question whether **Agatha** belongs in this family; Tauté includes **Agatha** in this family. It may have been **Agatha** who was betrothed first to **Harold**, Earl of Wessex, and then to **Alphonso**, King of Gallicia. Douglas in *William the Conqueror*, pgs. 393–394, discusses the daughters of **William the Conqueror** and **Matilda**, adding that *Ordericus Vitalis* mentions five daughters, one being **Agatha**, who was betrothed to **Harold Godwinson** of Wessex and **Alphonso of Spain** and

(continued...)

1 — **Henry I, KING OF ENGLAND.**
1 — **Gundred** (d. 26 May 1085 in childbed; bur. chapter house, Lewes Priory[1]), believed by some historians to be the daughter of **William the Conqueror** and his wife **Matilda of Flanders**, though not certain[2]; m. bef 1078 **William** (d. 1088), Earl Warenne, a descendant of a sister of **Countess Gunnora**, wife of **Duke Richard I** of Normandy. Despite the uncertainty of **Gundred's** parentage, her issue with **William** (d. 1088) is presented for its information:

2 — **William de Warenne** (d. 1138), Earl of Surrey, his father's heir and ancestor of "many noble earls of that family"[3]; m. 1118 as her second husband[4] **Isabel de Vermandois** (d. 13 Feb 1131; bur. Lewes), daughter of **Hugh Magnus** (d. 1101), Duke of France, Count of Vermandois (son of **Henry I**, King of France, and a

---

[6] (...continued)
who died unmarried.

While the careers of daughters **Cecily**, **Adela**, and **Constance** are well known, less is known concerning the lives (or even existence) of **Agatha**, **Adeliza**, and **Matilda**. "The separate existence of **Agatha** and **Adeliza** is not certain, and the evidence about **Matilda** is less than satisfactory." (Douglas, *William the Conqueror*, pg. 395)

[1] **Gundred's** tomb was discovered at a later time in Isfield Church, Sussex, where it had been moved on the dissolution of the monasteries in the late 1530s.

[2] Green, *Lives of the Princesses of England*, Vol. I, pgs. 72-74, discusses the reasons **Gundred** is thought to be the daughter of either **Matilda** or of **William** and **Matilda**. Douglas in *William the Conqueror*, pg. 392, does not believe her to be the daughter of either **William** or **Matilda**.

[3] Green, *Lives of the Princesses of England*, Vol. I, pg. 78.

[4] **Isabel de Vermandois** m. (1) 1096 **Robert de Beaumont** (b. abt 1049; d. 5 Jun 1118), Lord Beaumont, Pont-Audemer and Brionne, Count of Meulan, Earl of Leicester, and had issue, including **Waleran de Beaumont** (b. 1104; d. 10 Apr 1166, Earl of Worcester) (*Ancestral* 50-24). The *DNB*, "Warenne or Warren, William de, second earl of Surrey (d. 1138)," reports that **William de Warenne** (d. 11 May 1138), her second husband, "carried her off while Robert was still living, though she was the mother of eight children."

descendant of **Charlemagne**).[1] Issue:

   3 — **William de Warenne III** (b. "probably" 1119;
   d. 19 Jan 1147/1148, "being slain when the rearguard of
   the French King's army was cut to pieces in the defiles
   of Laodicea"[2]), Earl of Surrey; m. **Ela Talvas**[3]
   (d. 4 Oct 1174), daughter of **William Talvas**, Count of
   Ponthieu, and his wife **Ela** (daughter of **Eudes Borel**,
   Duke of Burgundy, and widow of **Bertrand**, Count of
   Toulouse). Issue ("an only daughter"[4]):

      4 — **Isabel de Warenne** (b. abt 1137; liv. Apr 1203;
      d. "possibly" 12 Jul 1203[5]; bur. Chapter House,
      Lewes Priory) m. (1) **William II/William of Blois**[6]
      (b. abt 1134/bet. 1132 and 1137[7]; k. 11 Oct
      1159/1160, siege of Toulouse; bur. hospital of
      Montmorillon, Poitou), Count of Mortain/Boulogne,
      Earl of Warenne and Surrey, son of **Stephen**, KING
      OF ENGLAND, and his wife, **Matilda of Boulogne**;
      no issue; m. (2) 1164 **Hameline Plantagenet**
      (d. 7 May 1202; bur. Chapter House at Lewes),
      illegitimate son of **Geoffrey V Plantagenet** (d. 1151)
      and half brother of **Henry II**, KING OF ENGLAND.
   3 — **Gundred de Warenne**[8] (liv. 1166) m. bef 1130

---

[1] *Ancestral* 140-24.

[2] *CP*, Surrey section.

[3] **Ela Talvas** m. (2) in or bef 1152 **Patrick de Salisbury** (k. abt Apr 1168, in battle in Poitou, by **Geoffrey de Lusignan**; bur. Abbey of St. Hilaire, Poitiers), 1st Earl of Wiltshire or Salisbury, by whom she was mother of **William FitzPatrick of Salisbury**, Earl of Wiltshire, Earl of Salisbury (d. 1196; bur. Bradenstoke). **William FitzPatrick's** only daughter and heir, **Ela** (b. 1187/abt 1191; d. 24 Aug 1261; bur. Lacock Abbey), m. **William Longespée** (d. 7 Mar 1225/1226, Salisbury Castle; bur. Salisbury Cathedral), illegitimate son of **Henry II**, KING OF ENGLAND. (*CP*, Salisbury section)

[4] *CP*, Surrey section.

[5] *CP*, Surrey section.

[6] *Ancestral* 83-26.

[7] *CP*, Surrey section.

[8] *Ancestral* 84-25.

(1) **Roger de Newburg** (d. 1153), first son of **Henry de Beaumont** (d. "probably" 20 Jun 1119; bur. Préaux), Earl of Warwick, and **Margaret** (liv. 1156) (daughter of **Geoffrey**, Count of Perche). [1] Issue (three sons, three daughters [2]):

4 — **William de Newburg** (d. 1184 "it is said on 15 Nov. in the Holy Land"), Earl of Warwick, first son; m. (1) **Margery d'Eivile** (d. bet. Michaelmas 1202 and 13 Oct 1204; bur. Fountains Abbey), daughter of **John d'Eivile**; no issue; m. (2) bef 28 Dec 1175 **Maud de Percy** [3] (b. Catton, nr. Stamford Bridge), daughter of **William de Percy** (d. bef Easter 1175) and his first wife, **Alice de Tonbridge** (liv. 1148 [4]) ("probably da. of Richard FitzGilbert, (de Clare)"); no issue.

4 — **Waleran de Newburg** (b. bef 1153; d. bef 13 Oct 1204, "it is said" on 24 Dec 1203 [5]), Earl of Warwick, [6] second son; m. (1) **Margery de Bohun**, daughter of **Humphrey III de Bohun** (d. 6 Apr 1187) and his wife, **Margaret of Gloucester** (daughter of **Miles of Gloucester**); m. (2) abt 1196 **Alice de Harcourt** (liv. Sep 1212), daughter of **Robert de Harcourt** of Bosworth, co. Leicester, and Stanton, Oxon., and his wife, **Isabel de Camville** (daughter of **Richard de Camville**).

4 — **Henry de Newburg.**

4 — **Agnes** m. **Geoffrey de Clinton**, Chamberlain.

---

[1] *CP*, Warwick section.

[2] *CP*, Warwick section, in which the reader is referred to Clay's *Early Yorks Charters*, vol. viii, pg. 10, for information concerning daughters, **Margaret** and **Gundred**. Your compiler has not seen this volume.

[3] Her sister was **Agnes de Percy**, who married after 1154 **Joceline of Louvain**, brother of **Adela**, second queen of **Henry I**, KING OF ENGLAND. (*CP*, Percy section)

[4] *CP*, Percy section.

[5] *CP*, Warwick section.

[6] *Ancestral* 84-26.

4 — **Margaret**.

4 — **Gundred**.

Gundred de Warenne, as above, wife of **Roger de Newburg**, m. (2) **William de Lancaster I** (d. 1170), 5th Baron Kendal, Governor of the Castle of Lancaster. Issue:

    4 — **William de Lancaster II** (d. 1184), 6th Baron Kendal; m. **Helwise de Stouteville**, daughter of **Robert de Stouteville** and **Helwise**.[1]

3 — **Ada de Warenne** (d. 1178) m. 1139 **Henry of Huntingdon**[2] (b. abt 1114; d. 12 Jun 1152; bur. Kelso), Earl of Huntingdon and Northumberland, only son of **David I the Saint** (d. 1153), King of Scots. Issue (three sons, three daughters[3]):

    4 — **Malcolm IV the Maiden**[4] (b. 1141; d. 9 Dec 1165, Jedburgh,[5] aged 23 years), Earl of Huntingdon, King of Scots. Unm.

    4 — **William the Lion/Lyon** (b. 1143; d. 4 Dec 1214, Stirling; bur. Arbroath Abbey, Scotland), second son, Earl of Huntingdon, King of Scots; m. 1186 **Ermengarde de Beaumont**, daughter of **Richard**, Viscount de Beaumont.[6] Some further generations are listed here for historical interest. **William the Lion** and **Ermengarde de Beaumont** were parents of:

        5 — **Alexander II** (b. 24 Aug 1198, Haddington, East Lothian; d. 6 Jul 1249, Kerrara; bur. Melrose

---

[1] *Ancestral* 88-26.

[2] During a visit to England, he "fell in love with and married" her. (*DNB*, "Henry of Scotland (1114?–1152)")

[3] *CP*, Huntingdon section.

[4] Called the Maiden because he supposedly took a vow of celibacy; however, Ross in *Monarchs of Scotland*, pg. 55, says that **Malcolm IV** "probably" fathered an illegitimate son.

[5] *DNB*, "Malcolm IV (The Maiden) (1141–1165)."

[6] According to the *CP*, Pembroke section, the mother of **Richard**, Vicomte de Beaumont, was an illegitimate daughter of **Henry I**, KING OF ENGLAND.

Abbey, Roxburghshire), King of Scots; m. at York
Minster 18/25 Jun 1221 **Joan** (b. 22 Jul 1210,
Normandy; d. Mar 1238, Havering-atte-Bower,
Essex; bur. Tarrant Crawford Abbey, Dorset),
daughter of **John**, KING OF ENGLAND; no issue;
m. (2) at Roxburgh 15 May 1239 **Marie de Coucy**
(bur. Newbottle, Scotland), daughter of
Enguerrand III de Coucy, a French baron, and
his wife **Mary**, (daughter of **John**, Lord of
Montmirel-en-Brie). (After her husband's death,
Marie de Coucy returned to France in 1251 and
married **John de Brienne**, also called **John of
Acre**, son of the king of Jerusalem.[1]) Issue (an
only son):
> 6 — **Alexander III** (b. 1241; d. 1286).

5 — **Margaret of Scotland** (b. abt 1193; d. 1259;
bur. Church of the Black Friars, London)
m. 19 Jun 1221 as his third wife **Hubert de Burgh**
(d. 1243), 1st Earl of Kent. (Issue "a daughter"):
> 6 — **Margaret de Burgh** (d. in the lifetime of
> her father/Nov 1237; her body rested "a night at
> St. Albans on the way to burial") m. **Richard
> de Clare** (b. 4 Aug 1222; d. (poisoned?) 15 Jul
> 1262, Ashenfield in Waltham, nr Canterbury;
> bowels bur. Canterbury "before the altar of
> St. Edward; his body bur. (1) Tonbridge,
> (2) 28 Jul 1262 Tewkesbury "at his father's
> right hand"), Earl of Gloucester.[2]

5 — **Isabella** (bur. Church of the Black Friars,
London) m. at Alnwick, Northumberland, May
1225 **Roger Bigod** (b. 1212(?); d. 3 or 4 Jul 1270;
bur. 10 Jul 1270, church of St. Mary of Thetford),
4th Earl of Norfolk. No issue.[3]

5 — **Majorie** (sometimes called **Margaret**)

---

[1] Bingham, *Kings and Queens of Scotland*, pgs. 29, 30.

[2] *CP*, Kent section, Gloucester section.

[3] *CP*, Norfolk section.

(d. 17 Nov 1244; bur. Church of the Black Friars, London) m. at Berwick 1 Aug 1235 **Gilbert Marshal** (d. 27 Jun 1241, Hertford Priory, from injuries received in a tournament[1]; entrails bur. Hertford Priory; body bur. New Temple Church, London), 4th Earl of Pembroke, third son of **William the Marshal** the Regent (d. 1219) and **Isabel de Clare**. No issue.[2]

4 — **David of Huntingdon** (b. 1144; d. 17 Jun 1219, Yardley, Northamptonshire; bur. Sawtrey Abbey), Earl of Huntingdon, youngest son; m. 26 Aug 1190 **Maud of Chester** (b. 1171; d. abt 6 Jan 1233), daughter of **Hugh of Kevelioc**, Earl of Chester.[3] Issue:

    5 — **Margaret of Huntingdon** m. 1209 **Alan** (d. 1234), Lord of Galloway.

    5 — **Isabella of Huntingdon** m. **Robert the Bruce**, Lord of Annandale.

    5 — **Ada of Huntingdon** m. **Henry de Hastings** (d. 1250), son of **William de Hastings** and **Margaret Bigod** and grandson of **Roger Bigod** (d. 1220), **Magna Charta Surety**.

    5 — **John the Scot** (b. abt 1207; d. bef 6 Jun 1237), only surviving son, Earl of Chester, Earl of Huntingdon. No issue.

    5 — **Robert** (d. yng).

    5 — **Henry** (d. unm.).

4 — **Margaret de Huntingdon** (d. 1201; bur. Sawtrey Abbey, Hunts.) m. (1) 1159 or 1160 **Conan IV** le Petit, (d. 20 Feb 1171), Duke of Brittany, Earl of Richmond. Issue (an only daughter):

---

[1] According to the *CP*, Pembroke section, **Gilbert Marshal** sustained serious injuries when the reins of his Italian charger broke ("not without suspicion of foul play") and the horse bolted. **Gilbert** fell and was dragged by the horse. He later died from severe internal injuries.

[2] *CP*, Pembroke section.

[3] *CP*, Huntingdon section.

>   5 — **Constance of Brittany** (d. 1201) m. **Geoffrey**
>   (k. in tournament in Paris, 1186), son of **Henry II,**
>   KING OF ENGLAND. [1]
>
> **Margaret de Huntingdon**, as above, wife of
> **Conan IV**, m. (2) bef Easter 1175 **Humphrey IV de
> Bohun** (d. 1182), son of **Humphrey III de Bohun**
> (d. 6 Apr 1187) and his wife, **Margaret of
> Gloucester**. [2] They were parents of:
>
>>   5 — **Henry de Bohun** (d. 1 Jun 1220,
>>   bur. "chapter house of Llanthony Priory outside
>>   Gloucester" [3]), Earl of Hereford, **Magna Charta
>>   Surety**; m. **Maude FitzPiers FitzGeoffrey**,
>>   daughter of **Geoffrey FitzPiers** (d. 14 Oct 1213 [4]),
>>   Earl of Essex.
>
>   4 — **Ada de Warenne** (d. 1206) m. 1162 **Florent III**
>   (d. 1190), Count of Holland, Earl of Ros. [5]
>   4 — **Maud de Warenne** (d. 1152). Unm.
>
> 2 — **Renald de Warenne**, second son. No issue.
> 2 — A married daughter, **Edith**.
> 2 — Another married daughter, name not known.

Illegitimate Issue

It is believed that **William the Conqueror** had no illegitimate
issue. His reputation was one of faithfulness to his wife.

---

[1] **Arthur of Brittany**, son of **Geoffrey** and **Constance**, is believed to
have been murdered by his uncle, **John**, KING OF ENGLAND. Their
daughter, **Eleanor**, was kept by **John** in honourable confinement until
her death. See chapter, "The Disappearance of Arthur."

[2] *DNB*, "Bohun, Humphrey III de (d. 1187)"; *CP*, Richmond
section.

[3] *CP*, Hereford section.

[4] *CP*, Essex section.

[5] *Ancestral* 100-26.

William II Rufus
1087–1100

William II Rufus, [1] third son of **William I the Conqueror** and his wife, **Matilda of Flanders**; *b.* abt 1056/1060, Normandy; *crowned* 26 Sep 1087, Westminster Abbey; *killed* [2] 2 Aug 1100 while hunting in the New Forest; *bur.* Winchester Cathedral.

William II was never married.

Illegitimate Issue

One **Berstrand** may have been an illegitimate son, but it is doubtful. [3]

---

[1] Called **Rufus** because of his red coloring; also called **William the Red**.

[2] Possibly assassinated. See chapter, "The Death of William Rufus."

[3] Given-Wilson and Curteis, pg. 178.

Henry I
1100–1135
m. (1) Matilda of Scotland
m. (2) Adela of Louvain

Henry I Beauclerc,[1] youngest son of **William I the Conqueror** and his wife, **Matilda of Flanders**; Duke of Normandy 1106–1135; *b.* abt Sep 1068/1070, Selby, Yorkshire; *crowned* 6 Aug 1100, Westminster Abbey, the only one of his father's children to be born in England, youngest son[2]; *m.* (1) at Westminster Abbey 11 Nov 1100 **Edith Matilda of Scotland**; *m.* (2) at Windsor Castle 24/29 Jan 1120/1121 **Adela of Louvain** (no issue); *d.* 1 Dec 1135, St. Denis-le-Fermont, nr Rouen; *bur.* Reading Abbey, which he had founded.[3]

Edith Matilda of Scotland,[4] elder daughter of **Malcolm III Canmore** (d. 13 Nov 1093), King of Scots, and his second wife, **St. Margaret of Scotland** (d. 16 Nov 1093); *b.* 1079/1080, Dunfermline; *crowned* 11 Nov 1100,

---

[1] **Henry I** was called Beauclerc because of his love of learning and knowledge. Concerning the name, Henry: according to *CP*, Vol. 3, Appendix C, "Before Hen. VII the name Henry appeared almost invariably in the forms 'Harry' or 'Herry' in English Privy Seals."

[2] *KQB*, pg. 47.

[3] His bowels were buried in the church of St. Mary de Pre at Emandreville (*DNB*, "Henry I (1068–1135)"). According to *KQB*, pg. 48, nothing remains today of **Henry's** tomb, its location now "covered by a car park."

[4] She was born **Eadgyth**, but her name was changed to **Matilda**. To avoid confusion with other Matildas, she is herein referred to as **Edith Matilda**.

Westminster Abbey; *d.* 1 May 1118, Palace of Westminster; *bur.* Westminster Abbey.[1]

Ancestors of Edith Matilda of Scotland

```
                          ┌Duncan I, King of Scots (d. 1040)
            ┌Malcolm III, King of Scots (d. 1093)
            │             └Sibylla
Edith Matilda of Scotland (d. 1118)
            │             ┌Edward the Exile (d. 1057)
            └Princess Margaret (d. 1093)
                          └Agatha
```

Adela,[2] daughter of **Godfrey I the Bearded** of Brabant, Duke of Lower Lorraine, Marquis of Antwerp, and Count of Louvain[3]; *b.* abt 1103/1105, Louvain; crowned 3 Feb 1121/1122, Westminster Abbey; *d.* 23/24 Mar or 23 Apr 1151, Afflighem, Flanders; *bur.* Afflighem, Flanders. No issue.

Ancestors of Adela of Brabant

```
                          ┌Henry II, Count of Lorraine and Louvain
            ┌Godfrey I the Bearded of Brabant (d. 1139/1140)
            │             └Adelaide of Orlamunda (d. aft 1086)
Adela of Brabant (d. 1151)
            │             ┌Otto II, Count of Chiny (d. 1124-1131)
            └Ida de Chiny and de Namur (d. aft 1125)
                          └Adelaide of Namur (d. 1124)
```

---

[1] "All trace of her tomb has disappeared." (*KQB*, pg. 50)

[2] **Adeliza** m. (2) 1138 **William d'Aubigny** (d. 12 Oct 1176), 1st Earl of Arundel. *DNB*, "Adeliza of Louvain (d. 1151)," calls him **William de Albini** and states that in this second marriage, she had issue of seven children. Their grandson, **William d'Aubigny** (d. 1220/1221), Earl of Arundel, was named in the **Magna Charta** (*Ancestral* 149-24, 149-26; *CP*, Arundel section).

[3] According to the *DNB*, "Adeliza of Louvain (d. 1151)," **Godfrey** was "descended in the male line from Charles the Great."

* * *
Issue by Edith Matilda of Scotland

1 — **Euphemia** (d. yng).[1]
1 — **William Audelin/William the Atheling** (b. bef 5 Aug 1103, Winchester; d. 25 Nov 1120, drowned in the wreck of the *White Ship*), Duke of Normandy; m. at Lisieux June 1119 **Alice/Matilda of Anjou** (b. 1107; d. 1154), Abbess of Fontévrault, daughter of **Fulk V** (b. 1092; d. 10 Nov 1143, Jerusalem), Count of Anjou and Maine, King of Jerusalem, and his first wife (m. 1110), **Heremburge/Ermentrude** (d. 1126) (daughter of **Hélie I**, Count of Maine)[2]. No issue.
1 — **Matilda FitzEmpress/the Empress Matilda**[3] (b. abt 1102/1104,[4] Winchester; d. 9[5]/10 Sep[6] 1167, Rouen; bur. Abbey of Bec[7]) m. (1) at Mainz 7 Jan 1114 **Henry V,**

---

[1] Tauté.

[2] Burke's *Royal Family*, pg. 194.

[3] Though she was never a crowned English monarch, she was in April 1141 proclaimed the Sovereign Lady of the English and had received the homage of her father's barons.

[4] Green, *Lives of the Princesses of England*, Vol. 1, pg. 84, gives a birth year of 1102 for **Matilda**; *Ancestral* 1-24 gives 1104; *KQB* gives a date of abt 1103/1104. Both *KQB* and Burke's *Royal Family* suggest **Matilda** could have been a twin with **William**. *Living Descendants* gives a birth year of 1103.

[5] Pain, *Empress Matilda*, pg. 177.

[6] *KQB*, pg. 47; *Living Descendants*, pg. xiv.

[7] Her remains were reinterred in 1282 before the high altar; during the revolution, her grave was destroyed (Green, *Lives of the Princesses of England*, Vol. 1, pg. 188). According to *DNB*, "Matilda, Maud, Mold, Æthelic, Aaliz (1102–1167)," the church and tomb were destroyed by fire in 1263; when it was restored in 1282, her remains were found, "wrapped in an ox-hide." Her new tomb was stripped of its decorations by the English in 1421; a brass plate marking her grave in 1684 was lost in 1793; and the church was demolished in 1841. In 1846, her lead coffin was re-discovered and moved to the cathedral church of Rouen. The *DNB*'s source for this information is an 1847 publication, *Revue de Rouen*. Green in *Lives of the Princesses of England*, Vol. I,

(continued...)

Holy Roman Emperor and King/Emperor of Germany
(d. 22/23 May 1125, Utrecht; bur. Speyer); she was crowned
Empress on the same day as her marriage[1]; no issue[2];
m. (2) at Le Mans 22 May 1127[3] **Geoffrey V Plantagenet**[4]

---

[7] (...continued)
pg. 187, offers a literal translation of the epitaph found on **Matilda's**
tomb, part of which reads, "Here lies the daughter, wife, and parent of
Henry."

[1] Burke's *Royal Family*, pg. 194.

[2] According to Anderson's *Royal Genealogies*, Tables CCXVIII and
CCLXXXVI, **Matilda** had by **Henry V** a daughter, **Christina**, "the only
child of the Emperor Henry V by Maud the Empress, from whom are
descended the Dukes of Silesia." **Christina** married **Vladislaus II**
(d. 1159, Oldenburg) of Poland, son of **Boleslaus III**, King of Poland.
They had three sons:
1 — **Boleslaus I Altus** (d. 1201) m. (1) **Wenceiliva** (sp?), a Russian
princess. Issue:
  2 — **Jaroslaus** (d. 23 Jan 1201), "a wicked Son," Bishop of
  Breslau.
Boleslaus I Altus m. (2) **Adelheid**, daughter of **Beringerus**, Count of
Sultzbach, and sister of **Gertraut**, the Empress of **Conrad III**. Issue:
  2 — **Adeheid** m. **Theobald II** (d. 1212), Duke of Bohemia.
  2 — **Henry I Barbatus** (d. 1238), Duke of Breslau; m. **St. Hedwig**
  (d. 1263; canonized 1297), and they were parents of **Henry II**, from
  whom descended dukes of Bresslau, Liegnitz, and Glogan.
1 — **Conrad** (d. 1179); no issue.
1 — **Miecislaus I** (d. 15 May 1211) m. **Ludoihilla** (sp?) and had issue.
  NOTE: This is the only mention seen by your compiler of issue of
Matilda FitzEmpress and her husband, **Henry V**. Pain, *Empress
Matilda: Uncrowned Queen of England*, pg. 16, states, "She had borne
her husband no child; he left behind him no heir." This is the common
belief. Your compiler does not know if inclusion of this issue by
Anderson is an error on his part, if he is repeating traditional or
erroneous information, or if such issue has since been disproven.

[3] *Ancestral* 118-25 and 1-24 give 3 Apr 1127 as marriage date for
Geoffrey and **Matilda**. *KQB* gives a date of 22 May 1127, Le Mans.

[4] *Ancestral* 1-24. **Geoffrey, Count of Anjou**, was also called
Geoffrey Plantagenet because of the sprig of broom or *planta genista*
which he was said to have worn in his hat. His son, **Henry II**, became
the first of the **Plantagenet** kings.

(b. 24 Aug 1113; d. 7 Sep 1151, Château-du-Loir; bur. church of St. Julian at Mans[1]/bur. Le Mans Cathedral[2]), Count of Anjou and Maine and Touraine, Duke of Normandy, and brother of **Alice/Matilda of Anjou**, wife of **William Audelin** (d. 1120). **Geoffrey V** was the son of **Fulk V** (d. 1143), Count of Anjou and Maine and Touraine, and King of Jerusalem 1131–1143, and his first wife, **Eremberga**, daughter of **Elias**, Count of Maine.[3] Issue[4]:

2 — **Henry II**, KING OF ENGLAND.
2 — **Geoffrey Martel** (b. 1 Mar[5]/1 Jun[6] 1134, Rouen; d. 1158; bur. Nantes), Count of Nantes. Unm.
2 — **William** (b. 21 Jul 1136, Argentan; d. 1164, Rouen; bur. on the left of the high altar in the cathedral of Notre

---

[1] Green, *Lives of the Princesses of England*, Vol. 1, pg. 188.

[2] Burke's *Royal Family*, pg. 194.

[3] **Fulk V**'s mother was **Bertrada of Montfort**. **Bertrada** deserted her husband, **Fulk IV le Rechin** (d. 1109), and married **Philip I**, King of France. Popes **Urbain II** and **Pascal II** considered this a "scandalous alliance" and excommunicated **Philip**. It was to no avail: **Philip** would not put **Bertrada** aside. In 1104, **Philip** received absolution for his marriage. Bush reports that **Bertrada** attempted to arrange the death of **Philip's** son and heir, **Louis**, so that her son by **Philip** would be elevated to the throne. The attempts failed. Despite this, **Philip** apparently retained affection for **Bertrada** until his death in 1108. She retired to a convent and died in 1117. (Bush, *Memoirs of the Queens of France*, pgs. 110–114; Douglas, *The Norman Fate 1100–1154*, Table V)

[4] **Geoffrey V Plantagenet** had an illegitimate son, **Hameline** (d. 7 May 1202), Earl of Warenne or Surrey (*Ancestral* 123-26). It is also believed he had two illegitimate daughters, **Aldewide** and **Emma** (Green, *Lives of the Princesses of England*, Vol. 1, pg. 168). **Hameline** m. 1164 as her second husband **Isabel de Warenne** (liv. Apr 1203, but d. "probably soon afterwards, possibly 12 July 1203"), daughter of **William de Warenne** (*Ancestral* 83-26). Her first husband (m. bef. 1153; no issue) was **William of Blois**, younger son of **Stephen**, KING OF ENGLAND. (*CP*, Surrey section)

[5] Green, *Lives of the Princesses of England*, Vol. 1.

[6] Burke's *Royal Family*, pg. 194; *DNB*, "Matilda, Maud, Mold, Aethelic, Aaliz (1102–1167)."

Dame, Rouen[1]), Count of Poitou.

2 — **Emma**[2] m. 1173 **David** (d. 1204), son of **Owen Gwynedd**, Prince of Wales.

1 — **Richard**[3] (b. abt.1101; d. 25 Nov 1120, drowned in the wreck of the *White Ship*), betrothed 1120 to **Amice de Gael**, daughter of **Ralph de Gael** (d. 25 Nov 1120, also drowned in the wreck of the *White Ship*).

---

[1] Green, *Lives of the Princesses of England*, Vol. 1, pgs. 179.

[2] *Living Descendants*, pg. xiv.

[3] "He is often described as an illegitimate son of King Henry I, but the *Anglo-Saxon Chronicle* implies his legitimacy and Piers of Langtoft and Robert of Gloucester both refer to him specifically as a son of Queen Matilda" (Burke's *Royal Family*, pg. 194). According to Given-Wilson and Curteis, pg. 63, and *CP*, Vol. 11, Appendix D, **Richard** (b. bef 1100) was the son of **Ansfride**, "a lady of unknown parentage," widow of **Anskill**. (**Anskill** was a knight and tenant of Abingdon Abbey. He was imprisoned by **King William II** and so ill-treated that he died. His young son, **William**, regained part of his inheritance, which the king had taken, by marrying into the family to which the king had given the properties. (*CP*, Vol. 11, Appendix D))

The Descent of Edith Matilda of Scotland
from the Saxon Kings
(Names of kings and queens are in uppercase letters.)

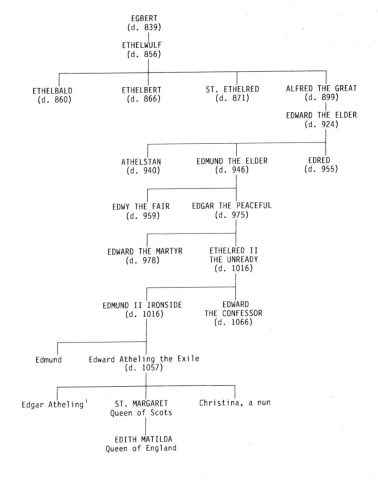

---

[1] Edgar, "the last male member of the House of Wessex," was elected king in 1066 after the death of Harold II, but he submitted to William the Conqueror, who treated him well. (Pitkin, *Britain's Kings and Queens*, pg. 7)

Some Illegitimate Issue of Henry I

According to the *CP*, Vol. 11, Appendix D, "it seems fairly certain that [Henry I] was the father of at least 9 sons and 11 daughters." It adds, however, "there is no satisfactory modern list of Henry's bastards." Given-Wilson and Curteis (pg. 60) state that Henry was father of "at least twenty royal bastards, more than any other king in English history."

There were advantages to a king's having bastards. The marriages of bastards could be used to cement alliances, and, most importantly, bastards were greatly loyal: "Being illegitimate, they were almost entirely dependent on the king for advancement." [1]

Following is a list of those individuals who can be identified with a fair amount of certainty as being issue of Henry I. Information is drawn mainly from Given-Wilson and Curteis and the *CP*, Vol. 11, Appendix D, "Henry I's Illegitimate Children." Detailed discussion of other possible illegitimate issue can be found in Given-Wilson and Curteis. Where particular issue of further generations proves historically interesting, information has been included but should not be considered inclusive.

1 — Robert of Gloucester/Robert de Caen the Consul, [2] (b. abt 1090, "probably at Caen" [3]; d. 31 Oct 1147, of fever, Bristol Castle; bur. St. James Church, Bristol, which he

---

[1] Given-Wilson and Curteis, pg. 57.

[2] *Ancestral* 124-26 and 125-26. According to the *DNB*, "Henry 1 (1068–1135)," **Robert** was reported "on insufficient grounds to have been the son of Nesta, daughter of Rhys sp Tewdwr (d. 1093)..." Given-Wilson and Curteis state that **Robert of Caen's** mother was "a woman of Caen."

[3] *DNB*, "Henry I (1068–1135)." *CP*, Vol. 11, Appendix D, adds that "it is impossible to set out the names of the children in the order in which they were born, as the date of birth is not known for any of them; nor is it possible to arrange them according to their maternal parentage, for in most instances this is not recorded."

founded[1]), Earl of Gloucester, son "probably by Sibyl," daughter of **Robert Corbet**, burgess of Caen; m. 1119 **Mabel/Maud** (d. 1157),[2] heiress of Gloucester, daughter of **Robert FitzHamon**, Lord of Glamorgan, Baron of Thoringni, and **Sybil** (daughter of **Roger de Montgomery** (d. 27 Jul 1094), Earl of Shrewsbury).[3] Their issue included[4]:

2 — **William FitzRobert** (d. "on his birthday"[5] 23 Nov 1183), 2nd Earl of Gloucester; m. 1150 **Hawise de Beaumont** (d. 24 Apr 1197), daughter of **Robert de Beaumont** (b. 1104; d. 5 Apr 1168[6]), Earl of Leicester, Justice of England, and his wife, **Amice de Montfort**. Issue ("three daughters and coheirs"[7]):

   3 — **Mabel FitzRobert** m. abt 1170 **Aumarie de Montfort** (d. 1191), Count of Evreux.

   3 — **Amice FitzRobert** (d. 1 Jan 1224/1225), Countess of Gloucester; m. **Richard de Clare** (d. abt 28 Nov 1217), 6th Earl of Clare, Hertford, and Gloucester, **Magna Charta Surety**, son of **Roger de Clare**[8] (d. 1173) and **Maud St. Hilary** (daughter of **James de St. Hilary**).

   3 — **Hawise/Isabella FitzRobert**[9] (d. 14 Oct 1217; bur. Canterbury Cathedral) m. (1) as his first wife **John, KING OF ENGLAND**; no issue; m. (2) **Geoffrey de Mandeville** (d. 23 Feb 1215/1216); no issue; m. (3) abt Oct 1217 as his second wife **Hubert de Burgh** (d. 1243), Earl of Kent. No issue.

2 — **Roger**, Bishop of Worcester 1163–1179.

2 — **Hamon** (d. 1159).

2 — **Richard** (d. 1175), ancestor of barons of Creully.

---

[1] Green, *Lives of the Princesses of England*, Vol. 1, pg. 164.
[2] *CP*, Gloucester section.
[3] *Ancestral* 124-26; *CP*, Shrewsbury section.
[4] *CP*, Gloucester section.
[5] *CP*, Gloucester section.
[6] *Ancestral* 63-25; *CP*, Gloucester section, Leicester section.
[7] *CP*, Gloucester section.
[8] *Ancestral* 246B-26; *CP*, Hertford section.
[9] *Ancestral* 124-27.

2 — **Richard**, Bishop of Bayeux 1135-1142.

2 — **Philip** (liv. 1147).

2 — **Robert**, Castellan of Gloucester.

2 — **Maud** m. **Ranulph des Gernons**, Earl of Chester.

2 — **Mabel** m. **Aubrey de Vere**.

1 — **Fulk** (d. yng(?)), believed to be son of **Ansfride**; "probably" a monk at Abingdon Abbey.[1]

1 — **Juliana**, "not unlikely"[2] that she was the daughter of **Ansfride**; m. 1103 **Eustace of Pacy** (d. 1136), Lord of Breteuil.

1 — **Sibylla** (b. in 1090s; d. 12 or 13 Jul 1122, island of Loch Tay), daughter of **Sibyl Corbet**[3]; m. **Alexander I the Fierce** (d. 23 Apr 1124; bur. Dunfermline Abbey), King of Scots, and son of **Malcolm III Canmore** and his second wife, **St. Margaret**.

1 — **Rohese**,[4] a daughter of **Sibyl Corbet**; m. 1146 **Henry de la Pomerai** (d. by 1167), "a great Devonshire baron."[5]

1 — **William** (liv. 1187), son of **Sibyl Corbet**, brother of **Sibyl**, Queen of Scotland (wife of **Alexander I**, King of Scotland); m. **Alice**.[6]

1 — **Reginald FitzRoy/FitzHenry de Dunstanville**[7] or **Reynold de Dunstanville** (d. 1 Jul 1175, Chertsey, Surrey; bur. Reading Abbey[8]), son of **Sibyl Corbet**, Earl of Cornwall, Sheriff of Devon 1173-1175[9]; m. 1140[10] **Beatrice de Mortain**, daughter of **William FitzRichard** and granddaughter of **Robert de Mortain**,[11] a half-brother of **William I the Conqueror**.

---

[1] *CP*, Vol. 11, Appendix D.

[2] *CP*, Vol. 11, Appendix D.

[3] Given-Wilson and Curteis, pg. 63; *DNB*, "Henry I (1068-1135)," identifies her mother as a sister of **Waleran**, Count of Meulan.

[4] *Ancestral* 195-26.

[5] *CP*, Vol. 11, Appendix D.

[6] *CP*, Vol. 11, Appendix D.

[7] *Ancestral* 121-26.

[8] *CP*, Vol. 11, Appendix D.

[9] *CP*, Cornwall section.

[10] Given-Wilson and Curteis, pg. 63.

[11] *Ancestral* 185-1.

1 — **Gundred**, sister of **Rainald de Dunstanville**.

1 — **Matilda/Maud**, abbess of Montvilliers, daughter or sister of the Earl of Mellent. [1]

1 — **Henry FitzHenry** [2] (b. abt 1105; d. 1157, Anglesey), son of **Nest/Nesta**, [3] daughter of **Rhys ap Tewdr/Tewdwr**, Prince of South Wales.

    2 — **Meiler FitzHenry** (d. 1220) m. the niece of **Hugh de Lacy**, justiciar of Ireland.

        3 — **Meiler FitzHenry**, "who in 1206 was old enough to dispossess William de Braose of Limerick." [4]

1 — **Constance** [5] m. **Roscelin de Beaumont** (d. aft 1145), Viscount of Maine. They were parents of:

    2 — **Richard**. [6]

        3 — **Ermengard** m. at Woodstock 5 Sep 1186 **William the Lion**, King of Scotland.

1 — **Maud/Matilda** m. **Conan III** (d. 1148), Duke of Brittany, son of **Alan Fergant** [7] (d. 1119) and his second wife, **Ermengard of Anjou** (d. 1147 [8]). [9]

1 — **Matilda** (b. 1086; d. 25 Nov 1120, drowned in the wreck of the *White Ship* [10]), Countess of Perche, daughter of

---

[1] Green, *Lives of the Princesses of England*, Vol. 1, pg. 176.

[2] *Ancestral* 33A-24.

[3] *Ancestral* 178-2.

[4] *DNB*, "FitzHenry, Meiler (d. 1220)."

[5] *Ancestral* 98-25.

[6] A descendant of **Richard**, **Agnes**, m. abt 1253 **Louis de Brienne**, Viscount Beaumont in Maine, son of **John**, King of Jerusalem and Emperor of Constantinople. "From this marriage descended the English Barons and Viscounts Beaumont...who did not adopt the arms of Beaumont...but retained those of Brienne...." (*CP*, Vol. 11, Appendix D)

[7] *CP*, Vol. 11, Appendix D; *Ancestral* 119-25.

[8] *Ancestral* 39-25.

[9] **Conan III** was the great-grandfather of **Constance of Brittany** who married **Geoffrey**, son of **Henry II**, KING OF ENGLAND. (Given-Wilson and Curteis, pg. 69)

[10] *Ancestral* 153-24A.

Edith[1]; m. 1103 **Routrou II** (d. Apr 1144), Count of Perche.
2 — **Maude de Perche**[2] (b. 1105; d. 1143) m. **Raymond I**
(d. abt 1122), Viscount of Turenne. Issue:
3 — **Marguerite de Turenne**[3] (d. 1120)
m. (3) **William IV** (d. 1178), Count of Angoulême.
Issue:
4 — **Aymer de Valence/Tallifer**[4] (d. 1218), Count
of Angoulême; m. **Alice de Courtenay**, daughter of
Pierre de Courtenay/Peter of France (d. bef 1183)
and **Elizabeth de Courtenay** (liv. 1205).[5] Issue:
5 — **Isabelle of Angoulême**, QUEEN OF
ENGLAND (b. 1188, Angoulême; d. 31 May
1246, Fontévrault Abbey, bur. Fontévrault Abbey);
m. (1) at Bordeaux 24 Aug 1200 **John**, KING OF
ENGLAND; m. (2) bef 22 May 1220 **Hugh X de
Lusignan**[6] (d. 1246).
1 — **William de Tracy**[7] (b. aft 1090; d. abt 1135)
m. unknown. They were parents of:
2 — **William de Tracy** (liv. 1170).[8]
2 — A daughter (**Grace**?) m. **Gervase de Courtenay** or

---

[1] Given-Wilson and Curteis, pg. 63, emphasize that this **Edith** was not **Edith of Greystoke**.
[2] *Ancestral* 153-25.
[3] *Ancestral* 153 26.
[4] *Ancestral* 153-27.
[5] *Ancestral* 117-26.
[6] *Ancestral* 117-27.
[7] *Ancestral* 222-26.
[8] *Ancestral* 222-26 states that **William de Tracy**, the son, was one of the men who in 1170 murdered **Thomas Becket**, Archbishop of Canterbury. However, *CP*, Vol. 11, Appendix D, states that the father, **William de Tracy** (d. 1135), "d. soon after his father [Henry I], leaving (by an unknown wife) a daughter and heir." No mention is made of a son. The *DNB*, "Tracy, William de (d. 1173)," states that there were two William de Tracys living at this time and that is it "impossible to distinguish with certainty between them...."

John de Sudeley. [1]
1 — A daughter possibly named **Eustacia of England**
m. **William III Gouet de Montmirail (de Gault).** [2]
1 — **Robert**, son of **Ede** or **Edith**, "apparently" daughter of
Forn Sigulfson, Lord of Greystoke; m. **Maud de Avranches**,
widow of **William de Courcy.**
1 — **Alice** or **Aline** m. **Matthew de Montmorenci,** [3] Constable
of France, son of **Bouchard de Montmorenci.**
1 — **Isabel**, daughter of **Isabel/Elizabeth de Beaumont** [4]
(daughter of **Robert de Beaumont** (d. 1118), Count of Meulan,
1st Earl of Leicester).
1 — **Gilbert** "still young and unmarried in (?) 1142." [5]
1 — **Elizabeth** [6] m. **Fergus** [7] (d. 12 May 1166), Lord of
Galloway. They were ancestors of **Robert I** (d. 1329), King of
Scots.

---

[1] *Ancestral* 222-26 has no name for the daughter but states she
married **de Courtenay**. *CP*, Vol. 11, Appendix D, names the daughter
as **Grace** who married **John de Sudeley** of Sudeley Castle and
Toddington, co. Gloucester.
[2] Turton, pg. 203; Given-Wilson and Curteis, pg. 63.
[3] **Matthew de Montmorenci** m. (2) **Adelaide**, widow of **Louis VI
the Fat**, King of France. No issue.
[4] **Henry I's** mistress, **Isabel/Elizabeth de Beaumont**, m. (1) **Gilbert
de Clare** (d. "probably" 6 Jan 1147/1148), Earl of Pembroke.
[5] *CP*, Vol. 11, Appendix D.
[6] *Ancestral* 121B-26 (referencing James Balfour's *Scots Peerage*,
1904–1914); Given-Wilson and Curteis, pg. 63.
[7] *Ancestral* 38-24.

Stephen
1135–1154
m. Matilda of Boulogne

Stephen of Blois, third son of **Adela** (d. 1137) (daughter of **William the Conqueror**) and **Stephen II** of Blois and Chartres (k. 1102, Battle of Ascalon); Count of Mortain, Count of Boulogne; *b.* abt 1096, Blois; *crowned* 26 Dec 1135, Westminster Abbey, and 25 Dec 1141 [1]; *m.* abt 1125 **Matilda of Boulogne;** *d.* 25 Oct 1154, St. Martin's Priory; *bur.* Faversham Abbey, which he had founded. [2]

    Matilda of Boulogne, only daughter of **Eustace III** (d. 1125), Count of Boulogne, and **Mary of Scotland** (d. 31 May 1116; bur. Abbey of St. Savior, Bermondsey, London) (daughter of **Malcolm III Canmore** and **St. Margaret**); *b.* abt 1105; *crowned* 22 Mar 1136, Westminster Abbey; *d.* 3 May 1152, Hedingham Castle, Essex; *bur.* Faversham Abbey. [3]

---

[1] After his capture and release by **Matilda the Empress** (whose throne, some believed, he had usurped), **Stephen** was recrowned but not reconsecrated, insisting "that he had never been deposed." (David, *King Stephen*, pg. 66)

[2] *DNB*, "Stephen (1097?–1154), king of England."

[3] *Ancestral* 158-24, 169-25.

Ancestors of Matilda of Boulogne

```
                          ┌Eustace II, Count of Boulogne (d. abt 1080)
              ┌Eustace III (d. 1125)
              │           └Ida (d. 1113), da. of Geoffrey the Bearded
Matilda of Boulogne
              │           ┌Malcolm III, King of Scots (d. 1093)
              └Princess Mary (d. 1116)
                          └Princess Margaret (d. 1093)
```

Issue

1 — **Baldwin** (b. abt 1126; d. bef 2 Dec 1135, London;
bur. Holy Trinity Church, Aldgate[1]).

1 — **Eustace IV** (b. abt 1120[2]/1130 or 1131[3]; d. 17 Aug
1153,[4] Rheims; bur. Faversham Abbey), Count of Bologne;
m. in Paris aft Feb 1140 (when they were betrothed[5])
Constance of Toulouse/France[6] (d. 1176/abt 1180), only
daughter of **Louis VI**, King of France, and his second wife,
Adelaide (daughter of **Umberto II**, Count of Savoy and
Maurienne). **Constance** was sister of **Louis VII**, King of
France. No issue.[7]

---

[1] Burke's *Royal Family*, pg. 194.

[2] *Ancestral* 169A-26.

[3] *KQB*, pg. 50; Warren, *Henry II*, pg. 35; *Royal Family*, pg. 194.

[4] Gervase of Canterbury, chronicler, remarks that **Eustace** died on
the day that **Henry II's** first legitimate son was born. (Appleby, *The
Troubled Reign of King Stephen 1135-1154*, pg. 191)

[5] Appleby, *The Troubled Reign of King Stephen 1135-1154*, pg. 79.

[6] **Constance** m. (2) **Raymond V** (d. 1194), Count of Toulouse, and
had issue, **Raymond VI**, and "another son." (Warren, *Henry II*,
pg. 107)

[7] *Ancestral* 169A-26 and *CP*, Essex section, indicate that **Eustace**
had illegitimate issue, **Eustachie de Champagne**, who m. (1) **Geoffrey
de Mandeville** (d. 21 Oct 1166), Earl of Essex; the marriage ended in
divorce; no issue (the *CP*, Essex section, reports that he refused to live
with her, and the king had them divorced); m. (2) **Anselme Candavaine**
(d. 1174), Count of Saint-Pol (*CP*, Essex section). Along with three
sons, **Hugh**, Count of St. Pol, **Engerrand**, and **Guy**, she had **Beatrice
Candavaine de St. Pol** who m. as his third wife, **John I**, Count of
Ponthieu (d. 1191) (*Ancestral* 109-27). **John I** and **Beatrice** were parents
of **William III** (b. 1179; d. 1221), Count of Ponthieu, who m. **Alice/
Adela of France**, daughter of **Louis VII**, King of France.

1 — **Matilda** (b. abt 1133/1134; d. abt 1134/bef 1137; bur.
beside her brother **Baldwin** in Christ's Church, Aldgate, which
at that time was called priory of the Holy Trinity[1]), second
child, she had been promised in 1136 to **Waleran**, Earl/Count
of Mellent/Meulan.[2]

1 — **William II/William of Blois** (b. abt 1134[3]; k. 11 Oct
1159/1160, seige of Toulouse), Count of Mortain/Boulogne,
Earl of Warenne and Surrey; m. abt 1149 **Isabella/Isabelle**[4]
(b. abt 1137; liv. Apr 1203; d. "probably soon afterwards,
possibly 12 July 1203"[5]; bur. Chapter House, Lewes Priory),
only daughter and heiress of **William de Warenne**, Earl of
Warenne and Surrey. No issue.

1 — **Mary/Marie of Blois** (b. abt 1136; d. abt 1181/1182;
bur. nunnery of St. Austrebert), nun at Stratford, prioress at
Lillechurch, abbess of Rumsey/Romsey,[6] Countess of
Boulogne; m. abt 1160 (annulled 1169[7]) **Matthew I of
Alsace**[8] (d. 25 Jul 1173, seige of Driencourt), Count of
Boulogne,[9] son of **Theodore/Thierry**, Count of Flanders, and

---

[1] *Lives*, Vol. I, pg. 192.

[2] *DNB*, "Matilda of Boulogne (1103?–1152), wife of Stephen, king of
England."

[3] Warren, *Henry II*, pg. 35, gives **William's** birth date as between
1132 and 1137.

[4] **Isabella** m. (2) 1164 **Hameline** (d. 7 May 1202), illegitimate son of
Geoffrey V Plantagenet, Count of Anjou (husband of **Matilda the
Empress**, daughter of **Henry I**, KING OF ENGLAND).

[5] *CP*, Surrey section.

[6] *Lives*, Vol. I, pg. 196.

[7] *KQB*, pg. 50.

[8] *Ancestral* 169-26; **Matthew** m. (2) **Eleanor of Vermandois**, sister
of **Elizabeth**, his brother's wife; there was no surviving issue of this
marriage. **Matthew** died St. James' Day 1173 (*Lives*, Vol. I, pgs. 209-
211).

[9] *KQB*, pg. 50, states that the marriage was annulled in 1169. In
Lives of the Princesses of England, Vol. I, pgs. 196–212, Green writes
how **Mary** was used as the political tool of **Henry II** of England to help
secure his continental possessions: **Mary's** only brother **William** died,
leaving her countess of Boulogne and Mortagne. The king, despite her

(continued...)

his second wife, **Sybil of Anjou** (daughter of **Fulk V** (d. 1143), Count of Anjou and Maine, King of Jerusalem). Issue (two daughters[1]):

    2 — **Ida of Bologne** m.[2] (1) 1181 **Gerard**, Earl of Geldres/Count of Guelders and Zutphen (d. a few months after the marriage), son of **Henry** (d. 1162), Count of Gelders and Zutphen, and **Mary** (daughter of **Geoffrey of Bouillon**); m. (2) **Bertold of Saringes**; issue[3]:

        3 — **Berthold** (d. inf.).

        3 — **Frideric** (d. inf.).

Ida of Bologne, as above, m. (3) **Reginald de Trie/ Reginald de Dammartin**, Lord of Dammartin, Count of Dammartin. Issue:

        3 — **Matilda** (d. 1262), Countess of Boulogne, her mother's heir; m. (2) (repudiated 1245) in France 1235 **Alfonso III** (b. 5 May 1210; d. 16 Feb 1279), King of Portugal. Issue[4]:

           4 — **Robert** (b. 1239; d. 1239).

---

[9] (...continued)
vows, "then considered so sacred, which bound her to a life of perpetual virginity," had her taken from the monastery and married against her will to **Matthew of Alsace**. The nun found herself "the innocent object of execration to the whole Catholic world" and her marriage described as "execrable nuptials." **Matthew** was excommunicated; his bride was not, indicating she was held faultless in the matter. Bologne was placed under an interdict, which was followed by "an interdict of fire and water, by which any one who assisted the earl in procuring even the ordinary necessaries of life was subjected to the same penalties as he himself had incurred." Eventually, her husband allowed **Mary** to return to the cloister, and in 1169 she entered the Benedictine nunnery of St. Austrebert near Montreuil, where she remained until her death thirteen years later.

   [1] *DNB*, "Matilda of Boulogne (1103?–1152)."

   [2] Anderson, *Royal Genealogies*, shows four marriages, making her first husband to be **Matthew of Tulli**.

   [3] Anderson, *Royal Genealogies*, Table CCCVIII.

   [4] *KQE*, pgs. 7, 181. Green, *Lives of the Princesses of England*, Vol. I, pg. 212, states, "but her line failed on the death of her daughter and only child without issue."

4 — A son (b. 1240; d. 1240).

2 — **Matilda/Maud of Boulogne** (d. 1240[1]) m. 1179 as his first wife **Henry I** or **IV** (d. 5 Sep 1235[2]), Duke of Louvaine and Brabant, son of **Godfrey III** (d. 1186), Duke of Brabant and Count of Louvain.[3] Issue (three sons, four daughters[4]):

    3 — **Henry II** or **V** (d. 1 Feb 1247/1248[5]), Duke of Brabant; m. (1) **Marie of Swabia/Mary of Hohenstauffen** (d. abt 1240[6]), daughter of **Philip II** (murdered 21 Jun 1208), Emperor of Germany, Duke of Swabia, Margrave of Tuscany, and **Irene Angelica**. Issue[7]:

        4 — **Matilda of Brabant** (d. 29 Sep 1288) m. (1) 1237 **Robert I** (b. 1216; d. 1250), Count of Artois, son of **Louis VIII** (b. 1187; d. 1226), King of France, and **Blanche of Castile** (d. 1253).[8]

        4 — **Henry III** or **VI** (d. 28 Feb 1260/1261), Duke of Brabant; m. **Alice of Burgundy** (d. 1273), daughter of **Hugh IV** (b. 1212; d. 1272), Duke of Burgundy, and **Yolande de Dreux** (d. 1255) (daughter of

---

[1] *Ancestral* 155-26, 165-27.

[2] *Ancestral* 155-26.

[3] *Ancestral* 155-25, 155-26.

[4] Green, *Lives of the Princesses of England*, Vol I, pg. 213, in which is stated, "her posterity succeeded to the earldom of Boulogne."
Henry IV or **I** m. (2) **Mary**, daughter of **Philip II**, King of France, and was father of **Isabel**, who m. **Theodoric VI**, Count of Cleve (Anderson, *Royal Genealogies*, Table CCCLV).

[5] *Ancestral* 155-27.

[6] *Ancestral* 45-28.

[7] Anderson, *Royal Genealogies*, Table CCCLV.

[8] Their daughter, **Blanche of Artois** (b. abt 1245–1250; d. 2 May 1302, Paris), as the widow of **Henry** (d. 22 Jul 1274), King of Navarre, married 29 Oct 1276 (according to the *CP*, Lancaster section, bet. 27 Jul and 29 Oct 1276) as his second wife **Edmund Crouchback** (d. 5 Jun 1296), Earl of Lancaster, Earl of Leicester, son of **Henry III**, KING OF ENGLAND.

Robert III (d. 1234[1]), Count of Dreux).[2]

4 — **Mary** (beheaded 1256 by her husband "thro'
Jealousy") m. as his first wife **Lewis Severus**
(b. 1229; d. 1294), Duke of Upper Bavaria and
Elector Palatine of the Rhine, son of **Otto the
Illustrious** (d. 1253), Duke of Bavaria and Elector
Palatine of the Rhine.[3] No issue.

4 — **Beatrice** m. (1) **Herman** (d. 1241), Langrave of
Thuringia; m. (2) **William** (d. 1251), Count of
Flanders.

4 — **Elizabeth** m. **Albert I** (b. 1236; d. 15 Aug
1279), Duke of Brunswick/Braunschweig, son of
Otho the Puer. No issue.[4]

Henry II or **V**, husband of **Marie of Swabia**,
m. (2) **Sophia** (b. 1224), daughter of **Lewis VI** (b. 1200;
d. 11 Sep 1227), Landgrave of Thuringia and Hesse, and
his wife, **Elizabeth** (d. 1231) (daughter of **Andrew II**
(d. 1235), King of Hungary). Issue[5]:

4 — **Henry I the Kind** (b. 1245; d. 8 Sep 1308),
Landgrave of Hesse; m. (1) 1265 **Adelaid** (d. 1280),
daughter of **Otho the Puer** (b. 1204; d. 9 Jun 1252),
Duke of Brunswick-Luneburg and a great-grandson of
Henry II, KING OF ENGLAND; m. (2) 1280
Mechtild, daughter of **Theodoric V**, Count of Cleve;
m. (3) **Ann**, daughter of **Lewis Severus** (d. 1294),
Elector Palatine; no issue of third marriage.[6]

---

[1] Painter, *Peter of Dreux*, Genealogical Chart 1.

[2] **Henry III** and **Alice of Burgundy** were parents of **Marie of
Brabant** (b. abt 1260, Liege; d. 12 Jan 1322, Murel) who m. (2) as his
second wife at Vincennes 21 Aug 1274 **Philip III the Bold** (b. 1 May
1245, Poissy; crowned 15 Aug 1271, Rheims; d. 5 Oct 1285, Perpignan;
bur. St. Denis), King of France 1270-1285. **Philip III's** daughter,
Marguerite of France, became the second wife of **Edward I**, KING OF
ENGLAND.

[3] Anderson, *Royal Genealogies*, Table CCLXVI.

[4] Anderson, *Royal Genealogies*, Table CCLXXVIII.

[5] Anderson, *Royal Genealogies*, Table CCXLVI.

[6] Anderson, *Royal Genealogies*, Table CCXCIV.

4 — **Isabel** m. **Theodoric VI/Theobald VI** (d. 1261), Count of Cleve. [1]

3 — **Godfrey**, Count of Louvain.

3 — **Mary** m. 1214 **Otto IV** (d. 15 May 1218, "much afflicted and without issue"[2]) of the House of Brunswick, Emperor, son of **Henry the Lion** (d. 1195) and **Matilda** (d. 1189) (daughter of **Henry II**, KING OF ENGLAND). No issue.

3 — **Adelaide** m. **William** (d. 1247), Count of Auvergne.

3 — **Margaret** m. as his second wife **Gerhard III** (d. 1229), Count of Guelders. Issue:

> 4 — **Otto III Claudus** (d. 1271), Count of Gelders and Zutphen; m. (1) **Margaret** (d. 1251), daughter of **Theodoric VI**, Count of Cleve; m. (2) **Philippa**, Countess of Aumale. [3]

> 4 — **Henry** (d. 1282), Bishop of Liege.

3 — **Matilda/Mechtild** m. bef Dec 1224 **Florent IV** (d. 1245), Count of Holland. [4] Issue:

> 4 — **William II** (d. 1256), Count of Holland, Emperor; m. 1251 **Elizabeth** (d. 1266), daughter of **Otho the Puer** (b. 1204; d. 9 Jun 1252), Duke of Brunswick-Luneburg and a great-grandson of **Henry II**, KING OF ENGLAND. [5]

> 4 — **Florence** (d. 1258, "slain at a tournament").

> 4 — **Margaret** (d. 1276) m. **Herman**, Count of Henneburg(?). [6]

> 4 — **Richardis**.

> 4 — **Adelaide of Holland** (d. abt 1284) m. **John I**

---

[1] Anderson, *Royal Genealogies*, Tables CCXCIV and CCCXLVII.

[2] Anderson, *Royal Genealogies*, Table CCLXXVI.

[3] Anderson, *Royal Genealogies*, Table CCCXLIX.

[4] *Ancestral* 100-28.

[5] Anderson, *Royal Genealogies*, Tables CCCLI, CCLXXVII.

[6] "...to whom she bore 1276, at one Birth 365 Children, the one half Males baptiz'd John the other half Females baptiz'd Elizabeth; the odd one was an Hermaphrodite." Your compiler does not know the story behind this remark from Anderson, *Royal Genealogies*, Table CCCLI.

d'Avesnes (d. 1256), Count of Holland, son of
Bouchard d'Avenes (d. abt 1243/1244) and
Margaret (d. abt 1280), Countess of Hainault and
Flanders (daughter of **Baldwin VI** (d. 1205 or 1206),
Count of Hainault and Flanders),[1] from whom
descend the counts of Holland of the House of
Flanders.[2]

1 — **Eufemia**(?) m. **Alberic** or **Aubrey de Vere**, 1st Earl of
Oxford(?)[3]

Illegitimate Issue

1 — **Gervase** (b. abt 1115–1120; d. abt 1160/1161;
bur. Westminster Abbey), Abbot of Westminster 1138–1158,
son of **Dameta**.[4]

---

[1] *Ancestral* 100-29; 168-28, 168-29, 168-30.

[2] Anderson, *Royal Genealogies*, Tables CCCLI and CCCLII.

[3] *Lives*, Vol. I, pg. 213. This individual has not yet been confirmed
by definite evidence as being a daughter of **Stephen**, KING OF
ENGLAND. According to the *CP*, Oxford section, **Aubrey de Vere**
(b. abt 1110; d. 26 Dec 1126, bur. Colne), 1st Earl of Oxford, m. in or
bef 1152 **Eufeme** (d. 1152–1154), "said to be da. of William de
Cauntelo."

It is interesting to note in Furtado's *Castles in Britain*, pg. 150, that
the 1st Earl of Oxford built Hedingham Castle in 1140, and it was there
in 1152 that **Matilda of Boulogne** (**Eufemia's** mother?) died.

The *CP*, Vere or Veer section, states that Vere was originally
spelled Ver, and that was later modified to Veer, then Vere. The name
refers to Ver in the Cotentin, a region of Normandy in northern France.

[4] Warren, *Henry II*, pg. 35; Davis, *King Stephen*, pgs. 148–149;
listed by Given-Wilson and Curteis (pgs. 94–96, 179) as an identifiable
bastard of **Stephen**, KING OF ENGLAND.

Henry II
1154–1189
m. Eleanor of Aquitaine

Henry II Curtmantle,[1] son of **Matilda FitzEmpress** (daughter of **Henry I, KING OF ENGLAND**) and **Geoffrey V Plantagenet** (b. Aug 24 1113; d. 7 Sep 1151, Le Mans, Maine), Count of Anjou, Maine, and Touraine[2]; *b.* 5 Mar 1132/1133, Le Mans[3]; *crowned* 19 Dec 1154, Westminster Abbey; *m.* at Poitiers 18 May 1152 **Eleanor of Aquitaine**; *d.* 6 Jul 1189, Chinon; *bur.* Fontévrault Abbey, Saumur in Maine-et-Loire, France.

Eleanor of Aquitaine,[4] daughter of **William X**, Duke of

---

[1] **Henry** was called **Curtmantle** because of the short capes he preferred over the stylish longer capes.

[2] *Ancestral* 118-25. **Geoffrey Plantagenet** was son of **Fulk V** (d. 1143) of Anjou by his first wife, **Ermentrude**. **Geoffrey's** sister, **Matilda**, m. **William Audelin** (d. 1120), son of **Henry I, KING OF ENGLAND**. **Geoffrey** had another sister, **Sibyl**.

Fulk V m. (2) **Melisenda** and had issue of **Baldwin III** (d. 1163), King of Jerusalem, and **Amalric I** (d. 1174), King of Jerusalem. **Sibyl**, the daughter of **Amalric I** and **Agnes de Courtenay**, m. **Guy of Lusignan** (d. 1192). (Barber, *The Devil's Crown*, Table 1, Table 3; Riley-Smith, *The Crusades: A Short History*, pgs. 74–76)

[3] Burke's *Royal Family*, pg. 194; *Ancestral* 1-25; *DNB*, "Matilda, Maud, Mold, Aethelic, Aaliz (1102–1167)"; *DNB*, "Henry II (1133–1189)."

[4] *Ancestral* 110-26. **Eleanor** was distantly related to **Henry**; her great-great-grandfather, **Robert**, Count of Mortain (d. 1091), was a half-brother of **Henry's** great-grandfather, **William the Conqueror**. (*DNB*,

(continued...)

Aquitaine, Count of Poitou (b. 1099; d. 8 or 9 Apr 1137[1]) and
Aenor/Eleanor de Chastellerault (d. aft Mar 1130) (daughter
of **Aimery I/Almeric**, Viscount of Châtellerault, and
Dangereuse[2]); *b.* abt 1122, Bordeaux or Belin; *crowned* with
her husband 19 Dec 1154, Westminster Abbey;
d. 31 Mar/1 Apr 1204, Poitiers or Fontévrault; *bur.* Fontévrault
Abbey, nr Saumur in Maine-et-Loire, France.

Ancestors of Eleanor of Aquitaine

```
                        ┌William IX, Duke of Aquitaine (d. 1126)
              ┌William X, Duke of Aquitaine (d. 1137)
              │         └Philippa of Toulouse (d. 1118)³
Eleanor of Aquitaine (d. 1204)
              │         ┌Viscount Aimery of Châtellerault
              └Aenor de Châtellerault (d. 1130)
                        └Dangereuse
```

---

[4] (…continued)
"Eleanor, Alienor, or Aenor, Duchess of Aquitaine, Queen of France
and Queen of England (1122?–1204)")

[1] Meade, *Eleanor of Aquitaine*, pg. 31.

[2] **Dangereuse**, after having had three children by her husband,
became the mistress of **Eleanor's** grandfather, **William IX**. After
William IX brought **Dangereuse** to live in the ducal palace in Poitiers,
his wife, **Philippa of Toulouse**, withdrew to the Abbey of Fontévrault,
where on 28 Nov 1118 she died "whether from illness or wretchedness
there is no way of knowing." To secure her position with the Duke,
Dangereuse reportedly arranged for her daughter, **Aenor**, to marry the
Duke's son, **William**, in 1121. (Meade, *Eleanor of Aquitaine*,
pgs. 15–17)

[3] Fontévrault Abbey was founded in 1099 by **Robert d'Abrissel**, a
Breton hermit, who believed that women made better administrators than
men. Monks and nuns from the highest families inhabited Fontévrault
under the leadership of an abbess. **Philippa of Toulouse** (d. 1118) was a
passionate follower of **d'Abrissel** and more than likely assisted in the
founding and works of the abbey. Burials in the abbey church include
Henry II and **Eleanor of Aquitaine**, their daughter, **Joanna**, and their
son, **Richard I**. **Isabel of Angoulême**, wife of **John**, King of England,
is also buried there. The abbey was suppressed in 1792 and became,
under **Napolean**, a prison. In 1963, the prison was closed and
restoration work was begun. (*Enc. Brit.*, "Fontevrault-l'Abbaye";
Meade, *Eleanor of Aquitaine*, pg. 14; Green, *Lives of the Princesses of
England*, Vol. I, pgs. 367–368)

Issue

1 — **William** (b. 17 Aug 1152, Normandy; d. abt Apr 1156, Wallingford Castle, Berkshire; bur. Reading Abbey).

1 — **Henry the Young King** (b. 28 Feb 1155, Bermondsey; crowned 14 Jun 1170, Westminster Abbey, and again when his wife was crowned, 27 Aug 1172, Winchester; d. 11 Jun 1183, Martel; bur. (1) LeMans, (2) Rouen), Duke of Normandy, Count of Anjou; m. at Newburgh/Neubourg, Normandy, 2 Nov 1160 **Margaret of France**[1] (six months old in September 1158 when she was chosen as young **Henry's** bride[2]; d. 1197/1198, Acre), daughter of **Louis VII**,[3] King of France, and his second wife, **Constance of Castile** (d. 1160) (daughter of **Alfonso VII**, King of Castile). Issue (one son):

2 — **William** (b. 19 Jun 1177, Paris; d. 22 Jun 1177).

1 — **Matilda/Maud** (b. 1156, London; d. 28 Jun 1189, Brunswick, eight days before the death of her father; bur. cathedral church of St. Blasius, Brunswick, of which she had been co-founder[4]), eldest daughter, third child,[5] and ancestor of the house of Brunswick; betrothed 1165[6] and m. at Minden "at the altar of St. Peter's in the cathedral church"[7] 1 Feb 1168 as his second wife[8] **Henry V the Lion** of Saxony

---

[1] **Margaret** m. (2) 1185 **Béla III** (d. 1196), King of Hungary. (*Ancestral* 242-10)

[2] Moore, *The Young King, Henry Plantagenet (1155–1183)*, pg. 30.

[3] *Ancestral* 101-29.

[4] Green, *Lives of the Princesses of England*, Vol. I, pg. 257.

[5] Green, *Lives of the Princesses of England*, Vol. I, pg. 216.

[6] Jordan, *Henry the Lion: A Biography*, pg. 147.

[7] Green, *Lives of the Princesses of England*, Vol. I, pg. 236.

[8] **Henry the Lion** m. (1) 1147 **Clementia of Zähringen** (Previté-Orton, Table 16). This marriage was dissolved 1162. There was a son (d. yng) and "probably two daughters" of the marriage: **Gertrude** m. (1) **Frederick IV** (d. 1167, Rome) of Swabia/Rothenburg, son of **Conrad III**; m. (2) **Knut VI** (d. 1202), King of Denmark (no issue); and a daughter (d. yng), "whose name is not certain but may have been Richenza" and who was betrothed to **Knut**, son of **Valdemar** of

(continued...)

(b. 1129; d. 6 Aug[1]/1 Apr 1195; bur. with his wife), Duke of
Saxony (1142–1180) and Bavaria (1156–1180), son of **Henry
the Proud**.[2] Issue ("four sons, one daughter"[3]):

   2 — **Henry I** (b. prob. 1193; d. 28 Apr 1227/5 May
   1227[4]), heir, Duke of Brunswick, Count Palatine of the
   Rhine; m. (1) 1194 **Agnes of Staufen** (d. 1204), only child
   and heiress of **Conrad**, Earl/Count Palatine of the Rhine
   (brother of Emperor **Frederick I**); no male issue[5];
   m. (2) abt 1209 **Agnes of Wettin**, a Countess of
   Landsberg.[6] Issue (no surviving male issue[7]):

      3 — **Irmingardis** (d. 1259) m. **Herman IV** (d. 1243),
      Margrave of Baden. Issue[8]:

         4 — **Herman V** (d. 1250), Margrave of Baden; m. ?
         [Gertraut(?) — name difficult to read[9]] daughter of
         Henry III, Duke of Austria, and widow of
         Vladislaus, Duke of Bohemia.

         4 — **Rudolph I** (d. 19 Nov 1288) of Baden;
         m. **Cunigunda**, daughter of **Otto**, Count of Eberstein.

         4 — **Elizabeth** m. **Lewis**, Lord of Lichtenberg.

      3 — **Agnes** (b. 1201; d. 1262) m. **Otto the Illustrious**

---

[8] (…continued)
Denmark. **Henry the Lion** had an illegitimate daughter, **Matilda** (d. abt
1155/1156; d. bef 1219), who married after 1167 **Henry Borwin I** of
Mecklenburg, eldest son of **Pribislav**. (Jordan, *Henry the Lion: A
Biography*, pgs. 64, 80, 83)

   [1] Burke's *Royal Family*, pg. 195; Anderson, *Royal Genealogies*,
Table CCXLII.

   [2] Jordan, *Henry the Lion: A Biography*, pg. 158.

   [3] Burke's *Royal Family*, pg. 195; Green, *Lives of the Princesses of
England*, Vol. I, pgs. 215–262; Jordan, *Henry the Lion: A Biography*,
pgs. 258–259.

   [4] Anderson, *Royal Genealogies*, Table CCXLII.

   [5] Green, *Lives of the Princesses of England*, Vol. I, pgs. 242, 259.

   [6] Anderson, *Royal Genealogies*, Table CCLXXVI.

   [7] Anderson, *Royal Genealogies*, Table CCLXXVI.

   [8] Anderson, *Royal Genealogies*, Tables CCCVIII, CCCIX.

   [9] Compiler's note: The typeface of Anderson's *Royal Genealogies*
(seen in microfilm) was in many places rather difficult to read. Data has
been extracted as carefully as possible and spelled as written.

(d. 1253), Duke of Bavaria, Elector Palatine of the
Rhine. Issue:
    4 — **Henry** (b. 1235; d. 1290), Duke of Lower
Bavaria; m. (1) **Elizabeth** (d. 1271), daughter of
Bela IV (d. 1270), King of Hungary[1];
m. (2) **Elizabeth of Poland.**
    4 — **Lewis Severus** (d. 1294, aged 65[2]), Duke of
Upper Bavaria, Elector Palatine of the Rhine;
m. (1) **Mary** (beheaded 1256), daughter of **Henry V**
or **II** the Magnanimus (d. 1247), Duke of Brabant; no
issue; m. (2) **Ann** (d. 1275), daughter of **Conrade**,
Duke of Glogan; m. (3) 1276 **Matilda/Mechtild**
(d. 1304), daughter of **Rudolph of Hapsburg,**
Emperor.
    4 — **Elizabeth** (d. 1273) m. (1) **Conrade IV**
(d. 1254), son of the Emperor, **Frederick II**;
m. (2) as his first wife **Mainhard III** (d. 1296),
Count of Tyrol, Duke of Carinthia, son of
Mainhard II (d. 1258), Count of Tyrol.[3]
    4 — **Sophia** m. **Gebhard**, Count of Hirschberg.[4]
  3 — **Henry** (b. 1197; d. 1212/1213).
2 — **Richenza**, who was renamed **Matilda**[5] (b. 1172;
d. 1208/1209); m. (1) 1189 **Geoffrey II** (d. 1202), Earl of

---

[1] Previté-Orton, Table 26; Anderson, *Royal Genealogies*,
Table CCLXVI. Henry and his first wife, **Elizabeth**, were parents of
Otto (b. 1261), King of Hungary. Previté-Orton gives a death date of
1308 for **Otto**; Anderson gives a death date of 1312.
    [2] Anderson, *Royal Genealogies*, Table CCLXVI.
    [3] Anderson, *Royal Genealogies*, Table CCXXIX. According to
Anderson, Table CCLXXXIV, **Elizabeth's** line descends into kings of
Sicily, Arragon, Castile, Spain, Portugal, and France.
    [4] Anderson, *Royal Genealogies*, Table CCLXVI.
    [5] In 1182, **Henry the Lion**, **Matilda**, and their daughter, **Richenza**,
travelled to England. That seems to be the time that **Richenza's** name
was changed. "The name Richenza being quite unfamiliar in the Anglo-
Norman realm, she was henceforth known by her mother's name
Matilda." (Jordan, *Henry the Lion: A Biography*, pg. 183; Genealogical
Tables).

Perche in southern Normandy; m. (2) 1204 **Ingelram III de Coucy** (d. abt 1242).

2 — **Lothaire** (b. 1174/1175; d. 15 Oct 1190, Augsburg).[1]

2 — **Otho IV/Otto of Brunswick** (b. 1177; d. 19 May 1218), second son, crowned Emperor 1209 (deposed 1215), King of Germany; m. (1) 1212 **Beatrix** (d. 1212), daughter of **Philip II** (k. 1208), Duke of Swabia; no issue; m. (2) 1214 **Mary of Brabant**, daughter of **Henry I** (d. 1235[2]), Duke of Brabant; no surviving issue.[3]

2 — **William of Lüneburg/William of Winchester** (b. 11 Apr 1184, Winchester; d. 13 Dec 1213), youngest son, progenitor of the house of Brunswick; m. 1200/1202 **Helen of Denmark** (d. 1233), daughter of **Waldemar I** and sister of **Waldemar II** and **Canute VI**, kings of Denmark.[4] Issue (only an son[5]):

3 — **Otto** or **Otho** (b. 1204; d. 9 Jun 1252), also known as **Otho the Puer** or **Otho the Child**; ancestor of the house of Brunswick-Lüneburgh, first duke of Brunswick-Lüneburg[6]; m. **Matilda** (d. 1261), sister of **John I**, Elector of Brandenburg. Issue (five sons, five daughters[7]):

4 — **Albert the Great** (b. 1236; d. 15 Aug 1279), Duke of Braunschweig; m. **Elizabeth**, daughter of **Henry II** or **V** (d. 1 Feb 1247/1248), Duke of Brabant; no issue.[8]

4 — **Otto** (d. 1279), Bishop of Hildesheim.

4 — **Conrad** (d. 1303), Bishop of Verden.

4 — **Ulric** (d. yng).

---

[1] Jordan, *Henry the Lion: A Biography*, pg. 192.

[2] Anderson, *Royal Genealogies*, Table CCCLV.

[3] Green, *Lives of the Princesses of England*, Vol. I, pg. 261.

[4] Anderson, *Royal Genealogies*, Table CCLXXVII; Previté-Orton, Table 16.

[5] Anderson, *Royal Genealogies*, Table CCLXXVII.

[6] Green, *Lives of the Princesses of England*, Vol. I, pgs. 253, 262; Jordan, *Henry the Lion: A Biography*, pgs. 184, 265.

[7] Anderson, *Royal Genealogies*, Table CCLXXVII.

[8] Anderson, *Royal Genealogies*, Table CCLXXVIII.

4 — **Matilda** or **Helen** (d. 1270 or 1280) m. **Henry
Pinguis**, Count of Ascania.
4 — **Helen** or **Matilda** (d. 1270 or 1273)
m. (1) **Herman**, called a Landgrave of Hesse;
m. (2) **Albert I** (d. 1262), Elector of Saxony.
4 — **Adelaide** (d. 1280) m. 1265 as his first wife
Henry I the Kind (b. 1245; d. 8 Apr 1308),
Landgrave of Hesse.[1]
4 — **Agnes** m. **Wenceslaus/Wencelm**, Prince of
Rugen.
4 — **Elizabeth** (d. 1266) m. **William II** (slain 1256),
Count of Holland, Emperor.
4 — **John the Handsome** (d. 13 Sep 1277) m. 1265
Lutgarde or **Agnes**, daughter of **Gerhard I**, Count of
Holstein.
1 — **Richard I the Lion-Heart**, KING OF ENGLAND.
1 — **Geoffrey** (b. 23 Sep 1158; d. 19 Aug 1186, Paris[2];
bur. Nôtre Dame Cathedral), fourth son, Count of Brittany,
Duke of Brittany 1171-1186, Earl of Richmond; m. Jul 1181
Constance of Brittany[3] (b. abt 1161; d. 4 or 5 Sep 1201,

---

[1] Anderson, *Royal Genealogies*, Table CCXCIV.

[2] "Being killed, according to some accounts, in a [jousting]
tournament...according to others, dying of disease" (*DNB*, "Geoffrey
(1158-1186)"). According to the *CP*, Richmond section, he was "killed
in a tournament at Paris on 19 Aug 1186." A footnote adds, "In the
obituary of Notre-Dame his death is given as 21 Aug."

[3] **Constance** m. (2) 1186/1188 (diss./div. 1199) **Ranulph de
Blundevile** (b. abt 1172, Oswestry in Powys; d. 28 Oct 1231,
Wallingford; bur. 3 Nov 1232, St. Werburg's, Chester), Earl of Chester,
only son and heir of **Hugh de Kevelioc** (d. 1181), Earl of Chester and
Vicomte d'Avranches; no issue; m. (3) 1199 **Guy de Thours**, Viscount
of Thouars, brother of **Aimery**, Vicomte of Thouars. **Constance** and
Guy were the parents of:
1 — **Alice** (b. 1203; d. 1221), Duchess of Brittany; m. 1212 **Pierre de
Dreux/Peter of Dreux/Piers de Braine/Pierre Mauclerc** (d. May
1240/1250), Count of Brittany/Duke of Brittany. They were parents of:
2 — **Yolande de Dreux** (b. 1218; d. 10/16 Oct 1272) m. Jan
1235/1236 **Hugh XI de Lusignan** (b. 1220; d. 1260), son of

(continued...)

Nantes; bur. 24 Nov 1225, Villeneuve [1]), daughter of
Conan IV the Little (d. 1171), [2] Duke of Brittany, and his
wife, **Margaret de Huntingdon**, (daughter of **Henry of
Huntingdon** (d. 1152) and a granddaughter of **David I the
Saint** [3] (d. 1153), King of Scots). Issue:

    2 — **Eleanor, Maid of Brittany** (b. 1184; d. 10 Aug 1241,
Bristol Castle; bur. (1) St. Jame's Church, Bristol,
(2) Amesbury, Wiltshire). No issue. Unm.

    2 — **Matilda** (b. 1185/1186; d. yng).

    2 — **Arthur** (b. 29 Mar or 29/30 Apr 1187; k. 3 Apr 1203,

---

[3] (...continued)

Hugh X de Lusignan (d. 1246/1249, fighting in the Crusades) and
his wife, **Isabelle of Angoulême** (widow of John, KING OF
ENGLAND).

    2 — **John de Dreux** (b. 1221; d. 1286), Duke of Brittany;
m. **Blanche of Navarre**, daughter of **Thibaud IV**, Comte of
Champagne. They were parents of:

        3 — **John II de Dreux** (b. Jan 1239; d. 18 Nov 1305), Duke of
Brittany, Earl of Richmond; m. **Beatrice**, daughter of **Henry III**,
KING OF ENGLAND, and **Eleanor of Provence**.

        3 — **Peter** (b. 1241; d. 1268).

        3 — **Alice** (b. 6 Jun 1243; d. 1288) m. **John I** (d. 2 Aug 1268),
Count of Blois.

        3 — Four sons, a daughter (d. yng).

    2 — **Arthur** (d. yng).

1 — **Catherine** m. **André III**, Lord of Vitré.

(*Ancestral* 96-27, 96-28, 135-29 through 135-31, 117-28, 117-30, 63-30;
KQB, pg. 68; Painter, *The Scourge of the Clergy: Peter of Dreux, Duke
of Brittany*, Chart II; *CP*, Richmond section, Chester section; Anderson,
Royal Genealogies, Table CCCLXXVIII; Galliou and Jones, *The
Bretons*, Table I "The ducal family: the descendants of Count Eudes,
brother of Alain III (1008–40)")

  [1] "The church not being built at the time of her death...." The
church was dedicated 24 Nov 1225. On that day, she, her third husband,
and their daughter **Alice** were buried together. (*CP*, Richmond section)

  [2] *Ancestral* 119-27.

  [3] *Ancestral* 170-22.

Rouen[1]; bur. perhaps Abbey of Bec), Duke of Brittany
1186-1203, Prince of Brittany, heir of **Richard I**, KING
OF ENGLAND. No issue.
1 — **Eleanor of England** (b. 13 Oct 1161/1162, Domfront/
Damfront, Normandy; d. 31 Oct 1214, Burgos; bur. in
monastery of Las Huelgas) m. at Burgos/Taragona in Spain Sep
1177/1179 **Alfonso VIII** (b. 11 Nov 1155; d. 6 Oct 1214,
Galcear Meynos; bur. in monastery of Las Huelgas), King of
Castile, only surviving son of **King Sancho III** (d. 31 Aug
1158), King of Castile.[2] Issue (four sons, eight daughters[3]):
   2 — **Berengaria of Castile** (b. 1171[4]/1181; d. 8 Nov
   1245) m. (2) (div. 1209) as his second wife[5] at Valladolid
   1197 **Alfonso IX** (b. 1166; d. 23 Sep 1230, Villanueva de
   Saria), King of Leon 1188-1230, son of **Ferdinand II**
   (d. 1188), King of Leon, and **Urraca of Portugal**
   (d. abt 1188) (daughter of **Alfonso I**, King of Portugal).
   Issue (two sons, three daughters[6]):
      3 — **Ferdinand III the Saint** (b. 1200, nr Salamanca;
      d. 30 May 1252, Seville; bur. Seville Cathedral), King
      of Castile 1217-1252, King of Leon 1230-1252,
      canonized 1671; m. (1) at Burgos 27 Nov 1219 **Beatrice/
      Elizabeth of Swabia** (b. abt 1202; d. 30 Nov 1235,
      Toro), daughter of **Philip II** (b. abt 1177; k. 1208),
      Duke of Swabia, King of the Romans, and (m. 1197)

---

[1] "The victim of his uncle **King John's** ambition, **Arthur** was
believed murdered by him" (*DNB*, "Geoffrey (1155-1186)"). See
chapter, "The Disappearance of Arthur."
  [2] *KQE*, pg. 67.
  [3] Burke's *Royal Family*, pg. 195; *KQE*, pg. 42; Previté-Orton, Table
22(a); Márquez-Villanueva and Vega, *Alfonso X of Castile, The Learned
King*, pg. 57.
  [4] Socarras, *Alfonso X of Castile: A Study on Imperialistic Frustration*,
Appendix I.
  [5] **Alfonso IX** m. (1) (diss. 1198) 1190 **St. Teresa** (b. 1181;
d. 18 Jun 1250, Coimbra), daughter of **Sancho I**, King of Portugal, and
Dulce of Barcelona (d. 1198); **Teresa** was canonized in 1705. (*KQE*,
pg. 42)
  [6] *KQE*, pg. 42.

Irene Angelica/Angela (d. 1252), (daughter of **Isaac II of Byzantium**).[1] Issue (seven sons, two daughters[2]):[3]

4 — **Alfonso X** (b. 23 Nov 1220/1221, Toledo; d. 4 Apr 1284, Seville), eldest son, King of Castile and Leon 1252-1284, King of the Romans 1257; m. 26 Nov 1246 **Yolande/Violante** (d. 1300, Roncesvalles), daughter of **James I the Conqueror** (b. 1/2 Feb 1208, Montpellier; d. 25 Jul 1276, Valencia), King of Aragon,[4] and his second wife, **Yolande/Violante of Hungary**[5] (d. 1255).

4 — **Fadrique** (k. 1277, "slain at Burgis by the command of his br. K. Alfonso") m. the "daughter of a Roman despot."[6]

4 — **Enrique** (b. 1224; d. 1304), guardian of **Ferdinand IV.**

4 — **Felipe** (d. 1274) m. (1) **Cristina of Norway/Christiana of Denmark**; m. (2) **Leonor Roderigues de Castro.**

---

[1] Previté-Orton, Table 16(b); *Columbia-Viking Desk Encyclopedia*, 1953, "Philip of Swabia."

[2] *KQE*, pg. 43; O'Callaghan, *The Learned King: The Reign of Alfonso X of Castile*, Table "The Family of Alfonso X of Castile."

[3] A **Beatrix of Swabia**, daughter of **Philip of Swabia**, is shown in some sources (Previté-Orton, Tables 16a and 16b; Anderson's *Royal Genealogies*, Table CCXIX) as being married to **Otto IV** of Brunswick, Emperor, and dying in 1212 without issue. Socarro, *Alfonso X of Castile: A Study Imperialistic Frustration*, Appendix V, explains that another daughter of **Philip of Swabia**, **Elizabeth**, was "known in Spanish history as Beatrix," and it was this **Beatrix/Elizabeth** who married **Ferdinand III the Saint**. She died in 1235.

[4] *Ancestral* 105A-29.

[5] This second wife (m. 8 Sep 1235), **Yolande/Violante of Hungary** (d. 1255/abt 1251), was the daughter of **Andrew II** (d. 1235), King of Hungary, and **Yolande de Courtenay**. **Yolande/Violante's** sister, **Isabella** (d. 1271), m. **Philip III**, King of France. (*KQE*, pg. 38, 67; *Ancestral* 105-29; Bisson, Table IV)

[6] Anderson, *Royal Genealogies*, Table CCCLIX.

4 — **Sancho** (d. 1261[1]/"slain by the Maurs" 1262 or 1268[2]).

4 — **Berengaria**, nun.

4 — **John Emmanuel of Pennafiel** (d. 1283) m. (1) **Constanza**, daughter of **James I**, King of Aragon; no male issue; m. (2) **Beatrix**, daughter of **Amadeus IV**, Count of Savoy.[3]

4 — **Mary** (d. 1272).

4 — **Fernando** (d. yng).

4 — **Eleanora** (d. yng).

Ferdinand III the Saint, as above, m. (2) at Burgos 1237 **Joanna/Joan/Jeanne de Dammartin**[4] (d. 16 May 1279), Countess of Ponthieu, daughter of **Simon de Dammartin**,[5] Count of Aumale/Count of Dammartin and Boulogne, and **Marie** (d. 1250), Countess of Ponthieu (granddaughter of **Louis VII)**. Issue (two sons, one daughter[6]):

4 — **Fernando** (d. 1260), Count of Aumale.

4 — **Eleanor of Castile**[7] (d. 28 Nov 1290, Grantham) m. 1254 as his first wife **Edward I**, KING OF ENGLAND.

4 — **Luis**.

4 — **Simón**.

4 — **Juan**.

3 — **Constanza**, a nun.

3 — **Eleanora** (d. 1210).

---

[1] O'Callaghan, *The Learned King: The Reign of Alfonso X of Castile*, Table "The Family of Alfonso X of Castile."

[2] Anderson, *Royal Genealogies*, Table CCCCLIX.

[3] Anderson, *Royal Genealogies*, Table CCCCLXVI.

[4] According to *KQE*, pg. 43, **Jeanne**, Countess of Ponthieu, m. (2) 1260 **Jean de Nesle** (d. 16 Mar 1278).

[5] *Ancestral* 144-27.

[6] *KQE*, pg. 43; O'Callaghan, *The Learned King: The Reign of Alfonso X of Castile*, Table "The Family of Alfonso X of Castile"; Socarras, *Alfonso X of Castile: A Study on Imperialistic Frustration*, Appendix II.

[7] *Ancestral* 110-30.

3 — **Berengaria of Leon**[1] (d. 12 Apr 1237)
m. (2) 1212 as his third wife **John/Jean of Brienne**[2]
(d. 1237), Emperor of Constantinople, King of
Jerusalem. Issue[3]:
  4 — **Jean de Brienne** (d. 1296) m. (1) **Marie de
  Coucy** (bur. Newbottle, Scotland), daughter of
  Enguerrand III de Coucy, and widow of
  Alexander II, King of Scots; m. (2) 1251 **Jeanne,
  Dame de Chateau du Loir**, daughter of **Geoffrey IV**,
  Vicomte de Chateaudun.
  4 — **Yolanda of Brienne/Jolanta** (d. Apr 1228[4]),
  "the last heiress of the kingdom of Jerusalem"[5];
  m. 1225[6] **Frederick II** of Hohenstaufen (b. 26 Dec
  1194, Jesi nr Ancona; d. Dec 1250; bur. Palermo),
  Emperor, King of Naples and Sicily.
  4 — **Louis de Brienne**,[7] Viscount of Beaumont in
  Maine; m. **Agnes de Beaumont**, daughter of **Raoul**,
  Viscount of Beaumont. They were parents of:
    5 — **Henry de Beaumont** (d. 10 Mar 1339/1340),
    Lord Beaumont, Kt., Earl of Buchan; m. abt 1310/
    by 14 Jul 1310 **Alice Comyn**[8] (d. bef 10 Aug
    1349) of Buchan, daughter of **Alexander Comyn**,
    Sheriff of Aberdeen, and his wife, **Joan Latimer**.
    They were parents of:
      6 — **John de Beaumont** (b. abt 1318; d. May
      1342), Kt., Earl of Buchan, Lord Beaumont;

---

[1] *Ancestral* 114-28.

[2] *Ancestral* 114-28; 120-29.

[3] *Ancestral* 120-30. This is a portion of an interesting line leading to
Elizabeth I, QUEEN OF ENGLAND, and containing many prominent
names of old English families who played pertinent roles in the history
of England. See "Some Ancestors of Anne Boleyn and Elizabeth I."

[4] Andrewes, *Frederick II of Hohenstaufen*, pg. 19.

[5] Anderson, *Royal Genealogies*, Table CLIX.

[6] Andrewes, *Frederick II of Hohenstaufen*, pg. 55.

[7] *Ancestral* 114-29.

[8] **Alice Comyn** was a descendant of **Magna Charta Surety Saher de
Quincy**. (*Ancestral* 114-29, 53-28, and 53-27)

m. bef Jun 1337 **Eleanor Plantagenet**[1]
(d. 11 Jan 1372, Arundel), daughter of **Henry
Plantagenet** (d. 1345), Earl of Lancaster, and
his wife, **Maud de Chaworth** (d. bef 3 Dec
1322), and the great-granddaughter of
Henry III, KING OF ENGLAND.
3 — **Alfonso of Molina** (d. 1272) m. (1) **Malora**;
m. (2) **Monfalda Perez**, Lady of Molina; m. (3) **Teresia
Perez**, daughter of **Peter Fernandez**, Lord of
Bragançon. Issue of third marriage[2]:
    4 — **Mary** m. **Sancho IV**, King of Castile and Leon.
    4 — **Johanna** m. the Count of Lupo, Lord of Biscay.
    4 — **Alphonso**, Infant de Molina; m. **Teresia
    Alvarez**, daughter of **Peter Alvarez** de Asturias.
    4 — **Blanca**, Lady of Molina; m. **Alphonso
    Fernandez** de Castile.
    4 — **Berenguela**, mistress of **James II**, King of
    Aragon.
    4 — **Leonora** m. **Alfonso Garcias** de Celada.
2 — **Blanca/Blanche of Castile** (b. bef 4 Mar 1188,
Palencia; d. 27 Nov 1252; bur. Abbey of Maubuisson,
which she founded) m. 23 May 1200 **Louis VIII the Lion**
(b. 5/3 Sep 1187, Paris; d. 8 Nov 1226; bur. St. Denis),
King of France 1223–1226. (For issue, see under "The
Marriages of Louis VII of France.")
2 — **Constance**, became abbess in 1205 of nunnery at
Huelgas.
2 — **Ferdinand** (b. 29 Nov 1189, Cuenca; d. 14 Oct
1209/1211, Madrid; bur. in the monastery of St. Mary's at
Huelgas, Burgos).

---

[1] **Eleanor Plantagenet** m. (2) 5 Feb 1344/1345 **Richard II Copped
Hat FitzAlan** (b. abt 1313; d. 24 Jan 1375/1376), Earl of Arundel and
Warenne. He had previously married 9 Feb 1320/1321 **Isabel
Despenser**, daughter of **Hugh Despenser** (ex. 24 Nov 1326, Hereford)
and his wife, **Eleanor/Alianore de Clare** (b. Oct 1292; d. 30 Jun 1337).
(*Ancestral* 17-30, 8-30, 8-31, 60-32)
[2] Anderson, *Royal Genealogies*, Table CCCLIX.

2 — **Urraca** (b. 1190; d. 3 Nov 1220) m. 1206 **Alfonso II the Fat** (b. 23 Apr 1185; d. 25 Mar 1223, Santarém; bur. Alcobaça), King of Portugal 1211-1223, son of **Sancho I** (d. 1211), King of Portugal, and **Dulce of Barcelona** (d. 1198). Issue (four sons, one daughter[1]):

   3 — **Sancho II** (b. 8 Sep 1207; d. 8 Jan 1248/1246, Toledo, in exile), eldest son, King of Portugal, "...giving himself to all manner of Sloth, the Porguese depos'd him 1244"[2]; m. abt 1245 **Mencia** (d. aft 1270), daughter of **Diego Lopes de Haro** and **Urraca** (natural daughter of **Alfonso IX**, King of Leon).

   3 — **Alfonso III** (b. 5/10 May 1210; d. 16 Feb/20 Mar 1279; bur. Alcobaça), second son; m. (1) (repudiated 1245) in France 1235 **Matilda** (d. 1258/1262), Countess of Boulogne, daughter of **Renaud**, Count of Dammartin, and his wife **Ida of Boulogne**. Issue (two sons[3]):

     4 — **Robert** (b. 1239; d. yng).

     4 — Another son (b. 1240; d. yng).

Alfonso III, as above, m. (2) abt 3 Jun 1254 **Beatrice** (b. 1242; d. 27 Oct 1303), illegitimate daughter of **Alfonso X**, King of Castile, and **Maria de Guzman**. Issue (four sons, four daughters[4]):

     4 — **Blanca** (b. 18 Feb 1259; d. 1322), Abbess of Lorrain, then Huelgas de Burgos.

     4 — **Denis/Dionysius** (b. 9 Oct 1261; d. 7 Jan 1323[5]/1325), King of Portugal; m. 1281 **Isabel/ St. Elizabeth of Aragon** (d. 1336), daughter of **Peter/Pedro III** (d. 1285), King of Aragon.

     4 — **Ferdinand** (b. 1262; d. 1262).

     4 — **Alfonso** (b. 8 Feb 1263; d. 1312), Lord of Portalegre; m. **Yolande of Castile**, daughter of

---

[1] *KQE*, pg. 7.

[2] Anderson, *Royal Genealogies*, Table CCCCLXVIII.

[3] *KQE*, pg. 7.

[4] *KQE*, pgs. 7, 181; Anderson, *Royal Genealogies*, Table CCCCLXVIII.

[5] Anderson, *Royal Genealogies*, Table CCCCLXVIII.

Emanuel, Infant of Castile.
4 — **Sancha** (b. 1264; d. 1302).
4 — **Maria** (b. 1264; d. 1304).
4 — **Constance** (b. 1266; d. 1271).
4 — **Vincent** (b. 1268; d. 1271).
3 — **Leonor** (b. 1211; d. 1231) m. 1229 **Waldemar III**, King of Denmark, son of **Waldemar II**, King of Denmark. No issue.[1]
3 — **Ferdinand** (d. 1217; d. 1246), Lord of Leira; m. **Sancha Fernandez de Leira**, daughter of **Ferdinand**, Count of Lara. Issue:
4 — **Eleanora** "by some call'd the Wife of Waldemar Prince of Denmark."[2]
3 — **Vincent** (b. abt 1219; d. yng).
2 — **Eleanor/Leonor** (b. 1205[3]; d. 1244) m. (1) (div. 1229) 1221 as his first wife **James I the Conqueror**, King of Aragon (b. 1204; d. 1276). Issue (one son[4]):
3 — **Alfonso** (d. 1260).
2 — **Henry I** (b. 14 Apr 1204, Cuenca; d. 6 Jun 1217 after accident, Placentia), youngest child, King of Castile 1214–1217; reigned two years, ten months. No issue.
2 — Four children (d. yng).[5]
1 — **Joan/Joanna** (b. Oct 1165, Angers, Anjou; d. 4 Sep 1199; bur. at Fontévrault, with her brother, **Richard I**, and father[6]), third daughter; m. (1) 13 Feb 1177[7] **William II the Good**

---

[1] Anderson, *Royal Genealogies*, Table CLXXXVII.

[2] Anderson, *Royal Genealogies*, Table CCCCLXVIII.

[3] Socarras, *Alfonso X of Castile: A Study on Imperialistic Frustration*, Appendix I.

[4] *KQE*, pg. 38; Anderson, *Royal Genealogies*, Table CCCCLVII; Bisson, *The Medieval Crown of Aragon*, Table IV. **James I** m. (2) **Yolanda of Hungary**, and their issue included **Isabel**, who m. **Philip III**, King of France.

[5] Green, *Lives of the Princesses of England*, Vol. I.

[6] Green, *Lives of the Princesses of England*, Vol. I, pgs. 367-368.

[7] She was crowned Queen of Sicily the same day. (Green, *Lives of the Princesses of England*, Vol. I, pg. 310)

(d. 18 Nov 1189, Palermo; bur. church of Monreale), King of
Sicily. Issue (an only son): .

    2 — **Boemond** (b. 1181; d. 1181).

Joan/Joanna, as above, wife of **William II the Good**, m. (2)
at Rouen Oct 1196 as his fourth wife **Raymond VI**[1] of
St. Giles (d. Aug 1222), Count of Toulouse, son of
Raymond V (d. 1194) and his wife, **Constance** (sister of
Louis VII of France and widow of **Eustace IV**, son of
Stephen, KING OF ENGLAND). Issue (two sons[2]):

    2 — **Raymond VII** (b. 1197, Beaucondrieu), last Earl of
    Toulouse. Issue (one daughter):

        3 — **Joanna** (d. 1271) m. **Alphonso** (d. 1271), Count of
        Toulouse (1249), Count of Poitou (1241), son of
        Louis VIII the Lion and **Blanche**,[3] Queen of France.
        No issue.

    2 — Child (d. at birth).

1 — **John Lackland**, KING OF ENGLAND.

Illegitimate Issue of Henry II

1 — **William Longespée**[4] (b. "prob. bef 1173"; d. 7 Mar
1225/1226, Salisbury castle[5]; bur. cathedral of Salisbury), Earl
of Salisbury, mother unknown; m. 1198 **Ela/Isabel**[6] (b. 1187-

---

[1] According to Green, *Lives of the Princesses of England*, Vol. I,
pg. 376, **Raymond VI** had several natural children, including a son
Bertrand and a daughter **Wilhelmina**.

[2] Burke's *Royal Family*, pg. 195.

[3] **Blanche** was granddaughter of **Henry II**, KING OF ENGLAND,
and **Eleanor of Aquitaine**.

[4] *Ancestral* 30-26; *DNB*, "Longespée or Lungespée (Longsword),
William de, third Earl of Salisbury (d. 1226)"; **William Longsword** has
been thought by some to be the son of **Henry II's** mistress, **Rosamunde
Clifford**. However, the *DNB*, "Clifford, Rosamond (Fair Rosamond)
(d. 1176?)," states that there is "no positive evidence in favour of
William Longsword's being the son of Rosamond."

[5] *CP*, Salisbury section.

[6] *Ancestral* 108-28; *CP*, Salisbury section; Hallam, *The Plantagenet
Encyclopedia*, pg. 124.

1191, Amesbury, Wiltshire; d. 24 Aug 1261; bur. in monastery she built for nuns at Lacock, Wiltshire), Countess of Salisbury, only daughter and heir of **William FitzPatrick** (d. 1196; bur. Bradenstoke) of Salisbury, Earl of Salisbury. Issue (four sons, four daughters[1]):

    2 — **William Longespée** (b. abt 1212; d. 7 Feb 1249/1250, as a Crusader fighting at Mansura on the Nile; later bur. in Acre), eldest son; m. in or aft Apr 1216 **Idoine de Camville** (d. bet 1 Jan 1250/1251 and 21 Sep 1252), daughter and heir of **Richard de Camville** and **Eustache Basset** (daughter of **Gilbert Basset**).

    2 — **Richard Longespée**, described as a canon of Salisbury.

    2 — **Stephen Longespée** (d. 1260/d. by 23 Jan 1274/1275[2]), Seneschal of Gascony, Justiciary of Ireland; m. **Emmeline** (d. 1276), daughter of **Walter de Ridelisford/Rydeleford** (d. by 12 Dec 1244) and widow of **Henry de Lacy** (d. 1242), Earl of Ulster.

    2 — **Nicholas Longespée** (d. 1297; bur. "in the cathedral at the foot of his father's tomb"[3]), Bishop of Salisbury 1291–1297.

    2 — **Isabella Longespée** m. **William de Vesey**.

    2 — **Petronilla Longespée** (d. unm.)

    2 — **Ela Longespée** (d. 9 Feb 1297/1298; bur. Oseney Abbey, Oxon[4]) m. (1) **Thomas de Beaumont** (d. 26 or 27 Jun 1242; bur. St. Mary's, Warwick), Earl of Warwick, son of **Henry de Beaumont** (d. bef 17 Oct 1229) and his wife, **Margery de Oilly** (daughter of **Henry de Oilly** and **Maud de Bohun**); no issue; m. (2) bet 25 Nov 1254 and 23 Mar 1254/1255 as his second wife **Philip Basset** (d. 29 Oct 1271; bur. Stanley, Wiltshire); no issue.

---

[1] *CP*, Salisbury section.
[2] *Ancestral* 31-27, 33A-26.
[3] *CP*, Salisbury section.
[4] *CP*, Warwick section.

2 — **Ida/Idonea de Longespée.** [1]

1 — **Geoffrey** (b. "probably." 1151; d. 18 Dec 1212, monastery of Notre-Dame-du-Parc, nr Rouen; bur. Notre-Dame-du-Parc), Archbishop of York; also called **Geoffrey Plantagenet**; his mother is believed to be **Ykenai** or **Hikenai**.

1 — **Morgan**, provost of Beverley minster (1201) and bishop-elect of Durham (1213); son of **Nest Bloet**, the wife of **Ralph Bloet**, a knight. [2]

Saher de Quincy
(d. 1219)
Magna Charta
Surety

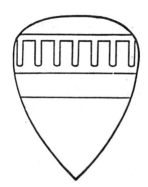

---

[1] The identity and marriages of **Ida de Longespée** are in discussion. Reference *DNB*, "Longespée or Lungespée (Longsword), William de, third Earl of Salisbury (d. 1226)"; *Ancestral* 30-26, 30-27; and *CP*, Salisbury section, pgs. 381–382, footnote (k). The note in *Ancestral* 30-26 suggests there were two **Idas** and surmises on the family ties of both. Weis in *Sureties* 50 shows an **Ida Longespée**, as daughter of **William Longespée**, who married **Walter FitzRobert**, son of **Robert FitzWalter** (d. 1235), Magna Charta baron.

[2] Given-Wilson and Curteis, pgs. 9, 99, 179, add **Morgan** to the list of identifiable bastards of **Henry II**, suggesting that the reason this illegitimate son of **Henry II** is so little known is that the king died before **Morgan** was old enough to profit from his father's assistance and influence in his career. Having been elected to the see of Durham, **Morgan** in 1213 requested and was refused papal confirmation to the see because of his illegitimacy. Given-Wilson and Curteis (pg. 99) state that **Pope Innocent** offered to confirm **Morgan** as Bishop of Durham if **Morgan** would swear that he was the son of **Nest** and her husband **Ralph Bloet**, rather than the son of **Nest** and **Henry II**. **Morgan** refused to deny his parentage.

Richard I
1189–1199
m. Berengaria of Navarre

Richard I the Lion Heart, son of **Henry II**, KING OF ENGLAND, and **Eleanor of Aquitaine,** Duke of Aquitaine, Duke of Normandy[1]; *b.* 8 Sep 1157, Beaumont Palace, Oxford; *crowned* 3 Sep 1189, Westminster; *m.* at Chapel of St. George, Limasol, Cyprus, 12 May 1191, **Berengaria of Navarre**; *d.* 6 Apr 1199, Chalus, Limousin, while beseiging the castle of Chalus; *bur.* 8 Apr 1199 Fontévrault Abbey[2]; his heart was buried at Rouen[3]; his entrails at Charroux in Poitou.[4]

Berengaria of Navarre, daughter of **Sancho VI the Wise** (d. 1194), King of Navarre, and his wife, **Beatrice/Sancha of Castile** (d. 1179) (daughter of **Alfonso VII**, King of Castile); *b.* abt 1163, Pamplona; *crowned* 12 May 1191, Limasol,

---

[1] **Richard I**, though king of England, spent less than a year there (Mitchell states six months; Seymour states "only ten months"), seeing his kingdom as only a source of revenue to support his love of fighting. He raised money "by fair means and foul" and was quoted as saying that he would sell London itself if he could find a buyer. He considered the Aquitaine his home and never learned to speak English. His crowned queen, **Berengaria**, never visited England. (Ross, *The Monarchy of Britain*, pg. 27; Mitchell, *Berengaria, Enigmatic Queen of England*, pg. 30; Seymour, *Sovereign Legacy*, pg. 64)
[2] Mitchell, *Berengaria, Enigmatic Queen of England*, pg. 91.
[3] Parsons, *Eleanor of Castile 1290–1990*, pg. 16.
[4] Hallam, *The Plantagenet Chronicles*, pg. 173.

Cyprus[1]; *d.* aft. 1230/23 Dec 1230,[2] L'Epau Abbey, near Le Mans; *bur.* L'Epau Abbey.[3]

Ancestors of Berengaria of Navarre

```
                                  ┌Garsias IV Ramires (d. 1150)
                  ┌Sancho VI the Wise (d. 1194)
                  │               └Margaret de l'Aigle (d. 1141)
    Berengaria of Navarre (d. 1230)
                  │               ┌Alfonso VII, King of Castile (d. 1157)
                  └Beatrice/Sancha of Castile (d. 1179)
                                  └Berengaria of Barcelona (d. 1149)
```

Issue

No issue.

Illegitimate Issue

1 — **Philip** (b. bef his father came to the throne; d. abt 1211)[4] by unknown mistress; known as **Philip de Cognac** as he was given by his father the castle and honor of Cognac; it is possible he was given as a wife **Amelie**, the daughter of the Lord of Cognac. **Philip** later sold his lordship to **Richard's** successor, **John**. Nothing more is known of his fate.[5]

---

[1] **Berengaria** was crowned by the Archbishop of Bordeaux and the Bishops of Evreux and Bayonne as queen of England and queen of Cyprus. Other titles included Duchess of Normandy and Countess of Anjou and of Maine. (*DNB*, "Berengaria (d. after 1230)"); Mitchell, *Berengaria, Enigmatic Queen of England*, pg. 57)

[2] Mitchell reports that historians have conflicting opinions on the actual date of **Berengaria's** death. The date of 23 Dec 1230 is "generally accepted," though some believe it occurred several years later. She adds that the anniversary of **Berengaria's** death was celebrated in the abbey of du Pré as occurring in 1230, though the date of the actual celebration was 20 Dec. (*Berengaria, Enigmatic Queen of England*, pgs. 126–127)

[3] In 1230, **Berengaria** founded the Cistercian monastery, 'Pietas Dei,' at Espau in Maine. The official date of the founding is given as 25 Mar 1229. She died "soon after" and was buried there. (DNB, "Berengaria (d. after 1230)"; Mitchell, *Berengaria, Enigmatic Queen of England*, pg. 130)

[4] Tauté.

[5] Given-Wilson and Curteis, pgs. 126, 127.

John

1199–1216

m. (1) Hadwisa/Avisa/Isabella of Gloucester
m. (2) Isabella of Angoulême

John Lackland,[1] son of **Henry II, KING OF ENGLAND,** and **Eleanor of Aquitaine;** *b.* 24 Dec 1167, Beaumont Palace, Oxford; *crowned* 27 May 1199, Westminster Abbey; *m.* (1) at Marlebridge 29 Aug 1189 (annulled 1200) **Hadwisa**[2]; *m.* (2) at Bordeaux 24 Aug 1200 **Isabella of Angoulême;** *d.* 18/19 Oct 1216, Newark Castle; *bur.* Worcester Cathedral; he left his heart to Croxton Abbey.

Hadwisa/Avisa/Isabella,[3] third daughter of **William**

---

[1] Called Lackland because by the time he was born, his older brothers' inheritances had been decided, and there was little left for him (Warren, *King John*, pgs. 28–28). Barber, *The Devil's Crown*, pg. 53, adds that "no provision was made for John, who [born nine years after the last son's birth] was too young to be considered in an age when infant mortality was very high."

[2] Also called **Avice** and **Isabella.** She was not crowned queen. Rather, John sought an end to the marriage soon after his accession, and, since he and **Hadwisa** were related in the third degree of consanguinity, an annullment was easily obtained. (Warren, *King John*, pg. 66)

[3] *CP*, Hertford section. **Hadwisa** was the granddaughter of **Robert,** Earl of Gloucester, illegitimate son of **Henry I, KING OF ENGLAND** (*KQB*, pg. 66). Her sisters (their father's coheirs) were **Mabel** (m. abt 1170 **Aumarie de Montfort** (d. 1191), Count of Evreux) and **Amice** (m. **Richard de Clare** (d. 1217), Earl of Hertford, **Magna Charta Surety**). (*CP*, Gloucester section, Hertford section)

According to the *CP*, Gloucester section, **Hadwisa** m. (2) bet.

(continued...)

FitzRobert (d. 23 Nov 1183), 2nd Earl of Gloucester, and his wife, **Hawise de Beaumont** (d. 24 Apr 1197) (daughter of **Robert de Beaumont** (d. 5 Apr 1168), 2nd Earl of Leicester, Justice of England); *d.* 14 Oct 1217; *bur.* Canterbury Cathedral. No issue.

Ancestors of Hadwisa of Gloucester

```
                        ┌Robert, Earl of Gloucester (d. 1147)¹
         ┌William FitzRobert (d. 1183)
         │              └Marguerite de Turenne (d. 1120)
Hadwisa of Gloucester (d. 1217)
         │              ┌Robert de Beaumont (d. 1168)
         └Hawise de Beaumont (d. 1197)
                        └Amice of Gael and Montfort in Brittany
```

Isabella of Angoulême, [2] daughter of **Aymer de Valence/ Aymer Taillefer** (d. 1218), Count of Angoulême, and his wife, **Alice/Alix de Courtenay** (daughter of **Peter of France/Pierre de Courtenay** (b. abt 1125; d. bef 1183[3]), youngest son of **Louis VI**, King of France); *b.* abt 1188, Angoulême; *crowned*

---

[3] (...continued)
16 Jan and 26 Jan 1213 **Geoffrey de Mandeville** (d. 23 Feb 1215/1216, killed at a tournament in London), Earl of Essex and Gloucester, a Magna Charta Surety; no issue (Browning, *The Magna Charta Barons and their American Descendants*, pg. 108; *CP*, Gloucester section); she m. (3) abt Oct 1217 as his second wife **Hubert de Burgh** (d. 12 May 1243, at his manor of Banstead in Surrey; bur. Church of the Black Friars, Holborn, London), 1st Earl of Kent, Justiciar of England under **Henry III**; no issue. The *CP* Kent, Essex, and Gloucester sections state that she and **Hubert de Burgh** were married "probably a few days before her death."

[1] **Robert**, Earl of Gloucester (d. 1147), was the illegitimate son of **Henry I**, KING OF ENGLAND, great-grandfather of **John**, KING OF ENGLAND.

[2] **Isabella of Angoulême** m. (2) **Hugh X de Lusignan** (d. 1249), Count of la Marche. See chapter, "Issue of Isabella of Angoulême and Hugh de Lusignan."

[3] *Ancestral* 117-25, 117-26; 153-26, 153-27. **Peter of France** was the son of **Louis VI**, King of France, and his second wife, **Adelaide of Savoy**. The wife of **Peter of France**, **Elizabeth de Courtenay**, was a descendant of **Hugh Capet** (d. 24 Oct 996), King of France.

8 Oct 1200, Westminster Abbey [1]; *d.* 31 May 1246,
Fontévrault Abbey; *bur.* (1) common graveyard of Fontévrault,
(2) Fontévrault Abbey. [2]

Ancestors of Isabella of Angoulême

```
                     ┌William IV de Taillefer (d. 1178)
          ┌Aymer de Taillefer (d. 1218)
          │          └Marguerite de Turenne
Isabella of Angoulême Taillefer (d. 1246)
          │          ┌Peter de Courtenay, Prince of France (d. bef 1183)
          └Alice/Alix de Courtenay
                     └Elizabeth de Courtenay (liv. 1205)
```

Issue by Isabella of Angoulême

1 — **Henry III**, KING OF ENGLAND.
1 — **Richard of Cornwall** [3] (b. 5/6 Jan 1209, Winchester

---

[1] Isabella's varying situations demonstrate the modern-day definitions
of the different kinds of queens. When she was married to the reigning
king, she was a queen consort. When John died, she became a queen
dowager, and if she had ruled for her young son, Henry III, she would
also have been a queen regent. Her descendant, Queen Elizabeth II, is a
queen regnant, who rules in her own right as successor to the throne.
Queen Mother is an informal title, being the one that Elizabeth II's
mother chose for herself when her husband, the king, died. (Packard,
The Queen & Her Court, pgs. 124–125)

[2] "As a penance for her sins, she desired to be buried humbly in a
common cemetary at Fontevrault" (Strickland, *Lives of the Queens of
England*, Vol. I, pg. 44). Her son, **Henry III** "some years later" had
her body moved into the Abbey and ordered an effigy for her tomb
(*KQB*, pg. 68).

[3] *DNB*, "Richard, Earl of Cornwall and King of the Romans
(1209–1272)," states that **Richard of Cornwall** had three illegitimate
children:

2 — **Richard de Cornwall** (d. 1272, Berkhamstead Castle; bur. Hayles
Abbey), Earl of Cornwall, "ancestor of the knightly families of the
Cornwalls called barons of Burford in Shropshire, and of those of
Berington in Herefordshire"; m. **Joan**. His mother was **Joan**, wife or
daughter of **Reginald de Vautort** or **Valletort**. (*Ancestral* 258-27,
258-28)

2 — **Walter**.

(continued...)

Castle; d. 2 Apr 1271/1272, Berkhamsted[1]; bur. Hayles
Abbey, which he founded), 1st Earl of Cornwall, elected King
of the Romans Jan 1256/1257[2]; crowned at Aachen 17/27 May
1257; Holy Roman Emperor; m. (1) at Fawley 30 Mar[3] 1231
Isabel Marshal[4] (b. 9 Oct 1200, Pembroke Castle, Wales;
d. 15/16/17 Jan 1239/1240, Berkhamsted, Hertfordshire[5];
bur. Beaulieu Abbey[6]), daughter of **William the Marshal** the
Regent (d. 14 May 1219[7]), Earl of Pembroke, and his wife
Isabel de Clare (d. 1220) (daughter of **Richard Strongbow de
Clare** (b. abt 1130; d. abt 20 Apr 1176), Earl of Pembroke,
Earl of Striguil, Justiciar of Ireland, and his wife, **Eve**,
daughter of **Dermot MacMurrough**, King of Leinster in

---

[3] (...continued)
The *DNB* article lists a third child, **Isabel** (d. 7 Jul 1276 or 1277;
bur. St. Augustine, Bristol), who m. abt 12 Jul 1247 **Maurice of
Berkeley** (b. 1218; d. 4 Apr 1281), 6th Lord Berkeley, "who may bee
called Maurice the Resolute." However, the *CP*, Berkeley section,
pg. 127, footnote (a), states that that relationship is refuted. The **Isabel**
who married **Maurice de Berkeley** was the daughter of **Richard
FitzRoy** (illegitimate son of **King John**) by **Rohese** (d. 1264/1265),
daughter of **Robert of Dover**. (*CP*, Berkeley section; *Ancestral* 26-28
and 26-27, which identifies **Rohese's** father as **Fulbert of Dover**)

[1] **Richard of Cornwall** was at Berkhampstead on 12 Dec. "The next
night he was smitten with paralysis of the right side, and almost lost his
speech and reason. He lingered on until 2 April 1272, when he died."
He was buried beside his second wife, **Sanchia**. His heart was buried in
the Franciscan church at Oxford. (*DNB*, "Richard, Earl of Cornwall and
King of the Romans (1209–1272)")

[2] Snellgrove, *The Lusignans in England 1247-1258*, pg. 12.

[3] *DNB*, "Richard, Earl of Cornwall and King of the Romans
(1209–1272)."

[4] **Isabel Marshal** was widow (m. 9 Oct 1217) of **Gilbert de Clare**
(b. abt 1180; d. 25 Oct 1230, Penros, Brittany; bur. 10 Nov 1230,
Tewkesbury), **Magna Charta Surety**, Earl of Hertford and Gloucester.
(*Ancestral* 63-28, 66-27; *CP*, Gloucester section)

[5] She died in childbed of jaundice. (*CP*, Gloucester section)

[6] Her heart was buried at Tewkesbury, the burial place of her first
husband's family. (*DNB*, "Richard, Earl of Cornwall and King of the
Romans (1209–1272)")

[7] *CP*, Pembroke section.

Ireland[1]). Issue:

   2 — **John** (b. 31 Jan 1232,[2] Marlow, Buckinghamshire; d. 22 Sep 1232/1233, Marlow, Buckinghamshire; bur. Reading Abbey).

   2 — **Isabella** (b. 9 Sep 1233, Marlow; d. 6 Oct 1234[3]; bur. Reading Abbey).

   2 — **Henry of Almayne/Henry of Cornwall** (b. 1 Nov 1235,[4] Hayles[5]/Haughley Castle, Suffolk[6]; "murdered by his cousins Simon and Guy de Montfort in the Church of San Silvestro, Viterbo, 13 Mar/13 Apr 1271"; bur. Hayles Abbey[7]) m. at Windsor 15 May 1269 **Constance** (d. abt 1299), daughter of **Gaston VII** of Béarn and his first wife, **Mathe**, and widow of **Alfonso** (son and heir of **James I**, King of Aragon). No issue.

   2 — **Richard** (d. yng).

   2 — **Nicholas** (b. 1240, Berkhamsted; d. Jan 1240, "immediately after he was christened,"[8] Berkhamsted; bur. Beaulieu Abbey).[9]

Richard of Cornwall, as above, husband of **Isabel Marshal**, m. (2) at Westminster Abbey 23 Nov 1243 **Sanchia of Provence** (b. abt 1225, Aix-en-Provence; crowned at Aachen Queen of the Romans when her husband was crowned King of

---

[1] *Ancestral* 66-26.

[2] *DNB*, "Richard, Earl of Cornwall and King of the Romans (1209–1272)"; Denholm-Young, *Richard of Cornwall*, pg. 18.

[3] Denholm-Young, *Richard of Cornwall*, pg. 18.

[4] *DNB*, "Richard, Earl of Cornwall and King of the Romans (1209–1272)."

[5] *DNB*, "Richard, Earl of Cornwall and King of the Romans (1209–1272)."

[6] Burke's *Royal Family*, pg. 195.

[7] According to *DNB*, "Henry of Cornwall (1235–1271)," "the more perishable parts of his body" were buried between two popes at Viterbo; his heart was buried in Westminster Abbey "in a golden heart shrine near the Confessor's Shrine," and his bones were buried 21 May 1271 at his birthplace. (*Westminster Abbey: Official Guide*, pg. 43)

[8] Anderson, *Royal Genealogies*, Table CCCCXCI.

[9] His mother died a few days after his birth.

the Romans[1]; d. 9 Nov 1261, Berkhamsted; bur. Hayles
Abbey), third daughter of **Raymond V Berengar** (d. 19 Aug
1245[2]), Count of Provence, and his wife, **Beatrice of Savoy**
(daughter of **Tommaso I**, Count of Savoy). **Sanchia** was sister
of **Henry III's** queen, **Eleanor**. Issue (two sons[3]):

2 — **Richard** (b. Jul 1246, Wallingford, Berkshire;
d. 15 Aug 1246, Wallingford, Berkshire; bur. Grove Mill).

2 — **Edmund of Almayne/Edmund of Cornwall**
(b. 26 Dec 1249/1250, Berkhamsted; d. 1 Oct 1300,
Ashbridge Abbey, Buckinghamshire, which he had founded;
bur. 23 Mar 1300/1301[4] Hayles/Hailes Abbey), 2nd Earl
of Cornwall[5]; m. (diss. Feb 1293/1294) at Ruislip, Middx,
6/7 Oct 1272 **Margaret de Clare** (b. 1249/1250;
d. bef 16 Sep 1312/Feb 1313; bur. Chertsey Abbey),
daughter of **Richard de Clare**[6] (b. 1222; d. 1262), 8th
Earl of Clare, 6th Earl of Hertford, 7th Earl of Gloucester,
and his second wife, **Maud de Lacy** (d. bef 10 Mar
1288/1289[7]) (daughter of **John de Lacy** (d. 22 Jul 1240),
Magna Charta Surety, Earl of Lincoln, and his second
wife, **Margaret de Quincy** (d. bef 30 Mar 1266), daughter
of **Robert de Quincy**). No issue.

2 — **Richard** (b. abt 1252; k. 1296, siege of Berwick).
Unm.[8]

---

[1] Burke's *Royal Family*, pg. 196.

[2] Denholm-Young, *Richard of Cornwall*, pg. 51.

[3] *DNB*, "Richard, Earl of Cornwall and King of the Romans
(1209-1272)." "...two, if not three, children, of whom Edmund survived
to become Earl of Cornwall." (Denholm-Young, *Richard of Cornwall*,
pg. 51)

[4] *CP*, Cornwall section.

[5] Previté-Orton, Table 17.

[6] *DNB*, "Clare, Richard de, eighth Earl of Clare, sixth Earl of
Hertford, and seventh Earl of Gloucester (1222-1262)."

[7] *CP*, Gloucester section.

[8] This third son is listed by Tauté. However, the *DNB* does not
include this son in its article on **Richard of Cornwall**, and Burke's
Royal Family (pg. 196) states that this young **Richard** may not have

(continued...)

Richard of Cornwall, as above, husband of **Sanchia of Provence**, m. (3) at Kaiserlautern in Germany 16 Jun 1269 **Beatrice of Falkenburg** (b. abt 1253; d. 17 Oct 1277; bur. Franciscan Church at Oxford), second daughter of **Dirk/ Dieter II**, Lord of Falkenburg, and his second wife, **Johanna van Loon**.[1]

1 — **Joan/Joanna** (b. 22 Jul 1210, Gloucester; d. 4 Mar 1238, nr London[2]; bur. Tarrant Crawford, Dorset[3]) m. at York 18/19 Jun 1221 as his first wife[4] **Alexander II** (b. 24 Aug 1198, Haddington; d. 8 Jul 1249, Island of Kerrera), King of Scots. No issue.

1 — **Isabella** (b. 1214, Gloucester; d. 1 Dec 1241, in childbirth,[5] Foggia; bur. Andria), second daughter; m. at

---

[8] (...continued)
existed but may have been confused with **Richard of Cornwall's** illegitimate son, **Richard**, who became the ancestor of **John Cornwall**, Baron Fanhope and Milbroke, K.G. **John Cornwall** married **Elizabeth**, daughter of **John of Gaunt** and his first wife, **Blanche of Lancaster**.

[1] **Dirk II** was the brother of **Engelbert**, Archbishop of Cologne (*Royal Family*, pg. 196) and, thus, **Beatrice** was the niece of **Engelbert** (Denholm-Young, *Richard of Cornwall*, pg. 141).

[2] *KQB*, pg. 66; Burke's *Royal Family*, pg. 316.

[3] From Green, *Lives of the Princesses of England*, Vol. I, pg. 378 and pgs. 399–400: **Joan/Joanna** was born 1203, probably in Caen or Bonneville, and died 12 Mar 1238; bur. in the nunnery of Tarente in Dorsetshire.

[4] **Alexander II** m. (2) at Roxburgh 15 May 1239 **Marie de Coucy** of the French nobility, daughter of **Enguerrand III de Coucy**. She was mother of his only son and heir, **Alexander III** (b. 1241; d. Mar 1286). **Alexander II** died on the island of Kerner/Kerrera in the Hebrides in 1249 at age of 48/50 years. His widow m. **Jean de Brienne** (d. 1296), "the son of [**Jean de Brienne** (d. 1237)] the King of Jerusalem"; no issue. (Bingham, *Kings and Queens of Scotland*, pgs. 29–30; *Ancestral* 120–30; Burke's *Royal Family*, pg. 315–316)

[5] The child did not survive her. (*DNB*, "Isabella (1214–1241), wife of the emperor Frederic II")

Worms 20 Jul 1235 as his third wife[1] **Frederick II
Hohenstaufen** (b. 26 Dec 1194, Jesi nr Ancona; d. 13 Dec
1250, Firenzuola/Fiorentino; bur. Palermo), Holy Roman
Emperor/Emperor of Germany, King of Sicily (1198) and of
Germany (1212), son of Emperor **Henry VI** and Empress
Constance of Germany.[2] Issue (two sons, two daughters):

2 — **Jordan** (b. 1236, Ravenna; d. inf.).[3]

2 — **Margaret** (b. Feb 1237), an only daughter,[4] "the first
child of the marriage"; m. as the first of his three wives
Albertus[5] (b. 1240; d. 1314, aged 74), Margrave of
Misnia, son of **Henry the Illustrious** (b. 1218; d. 1287 or

---

[1] **Frederick II Hohenstaufen**, grandson of **Frederick I Barbarossa**,
m. (1) **Constance** (d. 1222), daughter of **Alfonso II** of Aragon;
m. (2) **Yolande of Brienne** (d. 1228), heiress of Jerusalem and daughter
of **John of Brienne** (Previté-Orton, Table 16b; Riley-Smith, *The Feudal
Nobility and the Kingdom of Jerusalem, 1174–1277*, Table B). He was
"the last Emperor of the Hohenstaufen line." (*The Barnes & Noble
Encyclopedia* (1990), "Frederick II (Emperor)"; Andrewes, *Frederick II
of Hohenstaufen*, pg. 19)

[2] *The Columbia-Viking Desk Encyclopedia* (1953), "Frederick,
emperors and German kings." Seen also as **Constance of Sicily**
(d. 1198) in Andrewes, *Frederick II of Hohenstaufen*, pg. 59.

[3] Green, *Lives of the Princesses of England*, Vol. II, pg. 34. There is
"no contemporary authority" for the existence of this child. (*DNB*,
"Isabella (1214–1241), wife of the emperor Frederic II")

[4] Green, *Lives of the Princesses of England*, pg. 46, lists **Margaret**
as being the fourth child, being born in 1241, whose birth caused the
death of **Isabella**. However, *DNB*, "Isabella (1214–1241), wife of the
emperor Frederic II," lists her as the first child.

[5] Seen as **Henry**, but *DNB*, "Isabella (1214–1241), wife of the
emperor Frederic II," calls him **Albert**, landgrave of Thuringia, by
which marriage **Margaret** became "a remote ancestress of the house of
Saxe-Coburg and Gotha." Green, *Lives of the Princesses of England*,
Vol. II, pg. 46, calls the husband **Albert**, marquess of Thuringia and
Misnes; Green adds that **Isabella** and the Marquess had several children,
but that he later abandoned her for his mistress, **Cunegonde of
Elsemberg**. Anderson, *Royal Genealogies*, Table 247, calls him
Albertus the Froward, Markgrave of Misnia and Landgrave of
Thuringia.

1288), Markgrave of Meissen/Misnia and Landgrave of
Thuringia, and his first wife, **Constantia** (d. 1234 or 1262)
(daughter of **Leopold**, Duke of Austria. Issue [1]:
   3 — **Henry** (b. 1256; d. 1299) m. **Hedwig**, daughter of
   Henry, Duke of Glogan.
   3 — **Frederick** (b. 1257; d. 1324, aged 67), Margrave
   of Misnia and Landgrave of Thuringia, claimant to
   Sicily [2]; m. (1) **Agnes** (d. 1293), daughter of **Mainhard**,
   Duke of Carinthia 1282; m. (2) **Elizabeth of Arnshaug**
   (d. 1359), his step-mother's daughter. Issue [3]:
      4 — **Frideric the Grave** or **Stern** (b. 1309; d. 2 Feb
      1349; betrothed to **Jutha** or **Judith**, daughter of
      John, King of Bohemia, but they did not marry;
      m. **Mechtild** (d. 2 Jul 1349), daughter of **Lewis the**
      Bavarian, Emperor.
      4 — **Frideric the Crooked** (b. 1293; slain 1315).
   3 — **Dietricus** (d. 1270; murdered 24 Dec 1307)
   m. **Jutha**, daughter of the Count of Henneburg. [4]
   3 — **Agnes** (d. 1322) m. **Henry**, Duke of Braunschweig
   in Grubenhagen.
2 — **Henry** (b. 18 Feb 1238 [5]; murdered 1253/1254),
"titular king of Jerusalem." [6]
2 — **Agnes** (d. yng). [7]
1 — **Eleanor** (b. 1215, Gloucester; d. 13 Apr 1275, Montargis
("a cell of Fontevrault, to which she retired after the battle of

---

[1] Anderson, *Royal Genealogies*, Table CCXLVII.
[2] Runciman, *The Sicilian Vespers*, Table IV, "Imperial House of
Hohenstaufen."
[3] Anderson, *Royal Genealogies*, Table CCXLVII.
[4] The Count's name may have been **Buetbold VII**. The microfilm of
Anderson's *Royal Genealogies* was difficult to read.
[5] Green, *Lives of the Princesses of England*, pg. 34.
[6] *DNB*, "Isabella (1214-1241), wife of the emperor Frederic II."
[7] *DNB*, "Isabella (1214-1241), wife of the emperor Frederic II,"
states that **Isabella** died "at the birth of a child, which did not survive
her," but does not name the child. Green, *Lives of the Princesses of*
England, Vol. II, pg. 34, names the second daughter as **Agnes** and states
she was born Feb 1237 and died young.

Evesham"[1]) in France; bur. Montargis, France) m. (1) 23 Apr
1224 as his second wife **William Marshal** the Younger
(d. 6[2]/24 Apr 1231; bur. New Temple Church, London), 2nd
Earl of Pembroke; no issue; m. (2) at Royal Chapel at
Westminster[3] 7 Jan 1237/1238[4] **Simon de Montfort**
(b. abt 1208(?); k. 4 Aug 1265, battle of Evesham;
bur. Evesham Abbey[5]), 2nd Earl of Leicester, son of **Simon
IV de Montfort** (b. abt 1160; d. 1218) and **Alice of
Montmorency**. Issue by **Simon de Montfort** (five sons, two
daughters[6]):

   2 — **Henry of Montfort** (b. Dec 1238,[7] Kenilworth
   Castle; k. 4 Aug 1265, "by his father's side,"[8] Battle of
   Evesham), eldest son.
   2 — **Simon the Younger of Montfort** (b. summer 1240, nr
   Brindisi, Italy; d. 1271, nr Siena), second child.[9]

---

[1] *CP*, Leicester section.
[2] *CP*, Pembroke section, wherein the burial date is given as 15 Apr;
Bémont, *Simon de Montfort, Earl of Leicester 1208–1265*, pg. 30.
[3] "The King himself giving away the bride" (*DNB*, "Montfort, Simon
of, Earl of Leicester (1208?–1265)"). The marriage was celebrated
despite the fact that **Eleanor** had taken vows of chastity, witnessed by
the Archbishop of Canterbury, and wore the ring that united her to "the
mystic bridegroom, Jesus Christ." Her husband, **Simon de Montfort**,
"hastened to Rome in order to regularize his marriage" and the couple
received assurances that "there was no obstacle to the validity" of the
marriage (Bémont, *Simon de Montfort, Earl of Leicester 1208–1265*,
pgs. 54–57).
[4] *CP*, Leicester section.
[5] "The tomb and the church which contained it have perished."
(*DNB*, "Montfort, Simon of, Earl of Leicester (1208?–1265)")
[6] Bémont, *Simon de Montfort, Earl of Leicester 1208–1265*, pg. 258.
[7] Green, *Lives of the Princesses of England*, pg. 73, gives the birth
date of **Henry** as Advent Sunday, 28 Nov 1238.
[8] *DNB*, "Montfort, Henry of (1238–1265)."
[9] The *DNB*, "Montfort, Simon of, the younger (1240–1271)," states
that **Simon**, unwelcome in England, covertly visited the graves of his
father and brother and shortly afterward was at Viterbo, where he and
his brother **Guy** murdered **Henry of Cornwall** "and was only saved
from justice by his death in the same year, at a castle near Siena."

2 — **Guy** (b. probably 1243; d. 1287 or 1287, Sicilian prison[1]) m. 10 Aug 1270 **Margaret**, only child of **Count Aldobrandino Rosso**. "Said to have had two daughters, both of whom married and left descendants in Italy."[2]

2 — **Amaury/Almeric** (b. bet 1244 and 1250; d. 1292(?)/ liv. Feb 1300/1301[3]), canon and treasurer of York Minster 1265; "the last male survivor of his family."[4]

2 — A daughter (b. abt 1248, Bordeaux; d. inf).[5]

2 — **Richard** (b. 1249; d. aft 1265, France).[6]

2 — **Eleanor** (b. Oct 1252, Kenilworth Castle[7]; d. 19 Jun 1282, in childbed; bur. Friars Minors, Llanvaes, Isle of Anglesea), only daughter[8]; m. by proxy 1275, in person 13 Oct 1278 **Llywelyn the Last ap Gruffydd** (k. 1282).[9] Issue:

---

[1] **Guy** and his brother, **Simon**, on 13 Apr 1271 murdered their cousin, **Henry of Cornwall**, in a church at Viterbo to avenge their father's death. (*DNB*, "Montfort, Guy of (1243?-1288?)")

[2] *DNB*, "Montfort, Guy (1243?-1288?)"; Bémont, *Simon de Montfort, Earl of Leicester 1208-1265*, pg. 263. The *DNB* articles states that he and his brother Simon murdered their cousin, "Guy taking the most prominent and brutal part in the crime...."

[3] *CP*, Leicester section.

[4] *DNB*, "Montfort, Almeric of (d. 1292?)."

[5] Gies and Gies, *Women in the Middle Ages*, pg. 134.

[6] According to Bateman, pg. 281, **Richard's** fate was "unknown after 1265." The *CP*, Leicester section, states, "Of the son Richard nothing is known."

[7] Gies and Gies, *Women in the Middle Ages*, pg. 135.

[8] *DNB*, "Eleanor of Montfort (1252-1282)." Such terminology as "only daughter" or "only son" can sometimes be read as only *surviving* daughter or son.

[9] **Eleanor de Montfort** was married to **Llywelyn** by proxy in 1275. Later that year, she left for Wales, but her ship was captured "on behalf of the English king" in the Bristol Channel. She was imprisoned till 1278, when her husband finally submitted to **Edward I**. She was then married to her husband in the presence of the king on 13 Oct at Worcester. (*DNB*, "Montfort, Eleanor of (1252-1282)")

3 — **Gwenciliana/Gwenllian** (b. 1282; d. 7 Jun 1337), a nun at Sempringham..[1]

Illegitimate Issue

Given-Wilson and Curteis, pgs. 127 and 178–179, state that **John** had "at least seven bastards" who were identifiable. They name the seven shown in the listing below. Notes are from Given-Wilson and Curteis. Warren in *King John*, pg. 189, names the king's mistress as **Suzanne** and lists five of the king's known bastards: **Joan**, daughter of **Clementia** and wife of **Llewelyn of Wales**; **Geoffrey**, "who helped his father as a commander of troops"; **Oliver**; **Richard**, who served his father as a captain during the revolt of the barons; and **Osbert**. The *DNB*[2] mentions **Richard** ("who slew Eustace the Monk after the sea-fight of 1217"), **Oliver** ("who joined the crusade against Damietta, 1218"), and **Joan** (d. 1237). Given-Wilson and Curteis list as possible illegitimate issue a second **Richard**, who was in 1216 constable of Wallingford Castle, and **Eudo/Ivo**. Where particular issue of further generations proves historically interesting, information has been included but should not be considered inclusive.

1 — **Joan** (b. 1191/bef 1200; d. 30 Mar 1236/2 Feb 1237, Aber; bur. Llanvaes in Anglesey[3]), Princess of Wales, **John's** "only known illegitimate daughter," "said to have been" the daughter of Queen Clementia[4]; m. 1205/1207 **Llywelyn the**

---

[1] Bateman, pg. 281; *DNB*, "Eleanor of Montfort (1252–1282)." After her father's death, **Gwenllian** was taken to England where she "passed her whole life as a nun at Sempringham...." (*DNB*, Montfort, Eleanor of (1252–1282)")

[2] *DNB*, John (1167?–1216), king of England."

[3] *DNB*, "Joan, Joanna, Anna, or Janet (d. 1237), princess of North Wales." Her grave was destroyed at **Henry VIII's** dissolution of the monasteries and her coffin used as a horse trough. It, along with its covering slab, was later rescued. On it was sculptured **Joan's** effigy.

[4] *Ancestral* 27-27; Given-Wilson and Curteis, pg. 128.

Great/Llewellyn ap Iorworth[1] (b. 1173; d. 11 Apr 1240, Aberconway), Prince of Gwynedd/Prince of North Wales. They were parents of:

2 — **David/Dafydd ap Llywelyn**[2] (d. 1246), Prince of North Wales; m. **Isabella**, daughter of **William de Braose**.

2 — **Ellen/Helen** (d. bef 24 Oct 1253) m. (1) 1222 **John Scot** (d. bef 6 Jun 1237; bur. Werburg's, Chester[3]), Earl of Chester, youngest son of **David** (d. 1219), Earl of Huntingdon, and **Maud** (d. 1219) (daughter of **Hugh de Kevelioc** (d. 1181), 6th Earl of Chester,[4] and **Bertrade d'Evreux** (d. 1227)[5]); no issue; m. (2) bef 5 Dec 1237 **Robert de Quinci** (d. Aug 1257), youngest son of **Saher de Quinci/Quency**, Earl of Winchester.[6]

1 — **Richard FitzRoy** (d. 1264/1265), a captain in his father's army during the revolt of the barons; also called **Richard de Dover** or **Richard de Chilham**; his mother was the sister of **William**, Earl of Warenne; m. abt 1214 **Rohese**,[7] an heiress, daughter of "the Lord of Dover and baron of Chilham." His daughter:

---

[1] *Ancestral* 176-7.

[2] **David's** half-brother, **Gruffydd** (k. 1244), was father of **Llywelyn the Last ap Gruffydd** (k. 1282), who m. **Eleanor** (d. 1282), daughter of **Simon de Montfort** (k. 1265) and his wife, **Eleanor** (d. 1275) (daughter of **John**, KING OF ENGLAND).

[3] According to the *CP*, Chester section, it is suspected that **John Scot** "by [his wife] is suspected to have been poisoned." There are many instances of suspected poisonings throughout the time period covered in this book. St. Aubyn, *The Year of Three Kings*, pg. 201, remarks, "It was customary in the Middle Ages to attribute sudden deaths to the agency of poison."

[4] Tauté.

[5] *CP*, Vol. IV, Chart IV; *CP*, Chester section.

[6] *CP*, Winchester section.

[7] According to *Ancestral* 26-27 and Anderson, *Royal Genealogies*, Table CCCXCI, **Rohese** (d. 1264/1265) was the daughter of **Fulbert of Dover**.

2 — **Isabel** (d. 7 Jul 1276) m. abt 12 Jul 1247 **Maurice de Berkeley** (b. 1218; d. 4 Apr 1281), 6th Lord Berkeley, "who may bee called Maurice the Resolute." [1]

1 — **Oliver** (d. 1219, Damietta; bur. Westminster Abbey [2]) went on the Fifth Crusade in 1218.

1 — **Geoffrey** (d. 1205), held the honor of Perche. [3]

1 — **Osbert Giffard**. [4]

1 — **John**, "perhaps a clerk at Lincoln."

1 — **Henry**.

Robert de Ufford
(d. 1369)
Earl of Suffolk

---

[1] *CP*, Berkeley section. The *CP* notes that this is the correct parentage for **Isabel**.

[2] "...the antiquarian William Camden (1521–1623) recorded its burial place in Westminster Abbey." (Given-Wilson and Curteis, pg. 130)

[3] Given-Wilson and Curteis, pg. 130.

[4] "...is easily confused with a contemporary of the same name." (Given-Wilson and Curteis, pg. 130)

Henry III
1216–1272
m. Eleanor of Provence

Henry III, Henry of Winchester, elder son of **John**, KING OF ENGLAND, and **Isabella of Angoulême**; *b*. 1 Oct 1207, Winchester Castle; *crowned* 28 Oct 1216, Gloucester Cathedral, and 17 May 1220, Westminster Abbey; *m*. at Canterbury Cathedral 14 Jan 1236[1] **Eleanor of Provence**; *d*. 16 Nov 1272, Palace of Westminster; *bur*. Westminster Abbey; his heart was buried at Fontévrault.[2]

Eleanor of Provence, second daughter[3] and co-heiress of **Raymond V Berengar** (d. 1245), Count of Provence, and **Beatrice of Savoy** (d. 1266); *b*. abt 1217[4]/abt 1223,[5] Aix-en-Provence; *crowned* 20 Jan 1236, Westminster Abbey; *d*. 24 Jun

---

[1] *Ancestral* 1-27, 111-30; Burke's *Royal Family*, pg. 196; Burke's *Peerage*, 103rd ed., pg. lix.

[2] Parsons, *Eleanor of Castile 1290–1990*, pgs. 13, 16.

[3] **Eleanor** was one of four daughters of **Raymond V Berengar**. Her sister, **Margaret** (d. 1295), m. **Louis IX** (d. 1270), King of France (they were parents of **Philip III**, King of France); her sister, **Sanchia** (d. 1261), was the second wife of **Richard of Cornwall** (d. 1271), King of the Romans and brother of **Edward III**, KING OF ENGLAND; and her sister, **Beatrice** (d. 1267), m. **Charles of Anjou** (d. 1285), King of Sicily and brother of **Louis IX** (they were parents of **Charles of Salerno**). (Bateman, *Simon de Montfort: His Life and Work*, pg. 282; *KQB*, pg. 70; Previté-Orton, Table 17; Bisson, *The Medieval Crown of Aragon*, Table III)

[4] Burke's *Royal Family*, pg. 196; *Ancestral* 1-27, 17-27.

[5] *KQB*, pg. 70.

1291, Amesbury, Wiltshire; *bur.* Convent Church, Amesbury; her heart was buried in the Church of Friars Minors (Minories), London.[1]

Ancestors of Eleanor of Provence

```
                              ┌Alfonso II, King of Provence (d. 1209)
              ┌Raymond V Beringerus (d. 1245)
              |               └Gersenda II of Saban (d. aft 1222)
Eleanor of Provence (d. 1291)
              |               ┌Thomas I of Savoy (d. 1232/1233)
              └Beatrice of Savoy (d. 1266)
                              └Marguerite of Foucigny (b. abt 1180)
```

Issue

1 — **Edward I**, KING OF ENGLAND.

1 — **Margaret** (b. 29 Sep 1240, Windsor Castle; d. 26 Feb 1275, Cupar Castle, Fife; bur. Dunfermline) m. at York 26 Dec 1251 as his first wife **Alexander III** (b. 4 Sep 1241, Roxburgh; enthroned 13 Jul 1249, Scone; d. 19 Mar 1286, nr Kinghorn; bur. Dunfermline), King of Scots 1249–1286. Issue (one daughter, two sons[2]):

    2 — **Margaret** (b. 28 Feb 1261, Windsor Castle; d. 9 Apr 1283, Tönsberg; bur. Bergen) m. at Bergen abt 31 Aug 1281 as his first wife **Eric II Magnusson**, King of Norway. Issue (an only daughter):

        3 — **Margaret** (b. bef 9 Apr 1283, Norway; d. abt 26 Sep 1290, Orkney; bur. Bergen), the Maid of Norway, Queen of Scots.

    2 — **Alexander** (b. 21 Jan 1264, Jedburgh; d. 28 Jan 1284, Lindores Abbey, Fife; bur. Dunfermline Abbey), Prince of Scotland; m. at Roxburgh 15 Nov 1282 **Marguerite**, daughter of **Guy de Dampierre**, Count of Flanders. No issue.[3]

    2 — **David** (b. 20 Mar 1273; d. Jun 1281, Stirling Castle; bur. Dunfermline).

1 — **Beatrice** (b. 25 Jun 1242, Bordeaux; d. 24 Mar 1274/

---

[1] *KQB*, pg. 70.

[2] Tauté.

[3] Burke's *Royal Family*, pg. 316.

1275,[1] London; bur. Grey Friars Church, Newgate, London; heart buried in Fontévrault Abbey in Anjou) m. at Abbey of St. Denis, Paris, 22 Jan 1260 **John of Dreux/John II of Brittany** (b. 3 Jan 1238/1239; d. 16 or 17/18 Nov 1305, Lyons[2]; bur. Carmelite Church, Ploernel, Brittany), Earl of Richmond, 1st Duke of Brittany, son of **John I Rufus (Le Roux)** of Brittany (b. 1217; d. 8 Oct 1286) and **Blanca** (d. 1283) (daughter of **Theobald IV**, Count of Champagne and King of Navarre[3]). Issue (3 sons, 3 daughters[4]):

2 — **John of Brittany** (b. 1266[5]; d. 17 Jan 1333/1334; bur. Church of the Franciscans at Nantes), second son, Earl of Richmond, Count of Richmond, 2nd Duke of Brittany. No issue.[6] Unm.

2 — **Mary of Brittany** (b. 1268; d. 3 May 1339) m. 1292 **Guy de Châtillon**, Count of St. Pol/Paul (d. 1371). Issue:

3 — **Marie of St. Pol** (d. 1377) m. 3 or 5 Jul 1321 as his second wife[7] **Aymer de Valence** (b. abt 1270; d. 23 Jun 1324, perhaps from a broken blood vessel; bur. 1 Aug 1324, Westminster Abbey), Earl of

---

[1] *Royal Family*, pg. 197; Tauté; *CP*, Richmond section.

[2] Anderson, *Royal Genealogies*, Table CCCLXXVIII, and *CP*, Richmond section. The latter reports from medieval sources that **John**, Duke of Brittany, was in a procession with **Charles of Valois** (brother of the French king) and the Pope when a wall collapsed from the weight of spectators. "The Pope was knocked down, Charles was badly and John mortally injured."

[3] Anderson, *Royal Genealogies*, Table CCCLXXVII.

[4] *CP*, Richmond section, states that he left three sons and three daughters. Majority of following issue listed from *CP*, Richmond; additional dates taken from Anderson, *Royal Genealogies*, Tables CCCLXXVII and CCCLXXVIII.

[5] *CP*, Richmond section.

[6] *CP*, Brittany section.

[7] **Aymer de Valence** m. (1) **Beatrice de Clermont** (d. 14 Sep 1320), daughter of **Ralph de Clermont**, Lord of Neelle and Brios, Constable of France; no issue. (*CP*, Pembroke section)

Pembroke, third son of **William of Valence**[1]
(d. bef 18 May 1296), Earl of Pembroke, and **Joan de
Munchensy** (d. bef 20 Sep 1307). No issue.[2]

2 — **Arthur II** or **I** (b. 25 Jul 1262; d. 27 Aug 1312[3]),
Duke of Brittany/Bretaigne; m. (1) 1275 **Mary** (d. 1290/
1291), only daughter and heir of **Guy VI**, Vicomte de
Limoges.[4] Issue (three sons[5]):

3 — **John III** (b. 7 Mar 1285/1286, Champtoceaux;
d. 30 Apr 1341, Caen; bur. church of the Carmelites at
Ploermel) m. (1) 1296/1298 **Isabel** (d. 1309), daughter
of **Charles** (d. 9 Oct 1325), Count of Valois, and
Margaret (daughter of **Charles II**, King of Jerusalem
and Sicily), and the sister of **Philip VI**, King of France;
no issue; m. (2) at Burgos 1310 **Isabel** (d. 24 Jul 1328),
daughter of **Sancho IV** (d. 1295), King of Castile and
Leon, and **Mary** (daughter of **Alfonso de Molina**); no
issue; m. (3) at Chartres 21 Mar 1328/1329 **Joan/
Johanna** (d. 29 Jun 1344), only daughter of **Edward**,
Count of Savoy, and **Blanche** (d. 1348) (daughter of
Robert II (d. 1305), Duke of Burgundy); no issue.[6]

3 — **Guy** (b. 1287; d. 27 Mar 1330), Viscount of
Limoges, Count of Penthievre; m. 1318 **Johanna**
(d. 1384), daughter of **Henry IV**, Lord of Avagour.
Issue[7]:

---

[1] **William of Valence** (d. 1296) was son of **Isabella of Angoulême**,
QUEEN OF ENGLAND, and her second husband (m. 1217), **Hugh X
de Lusignan** (d. 1246), Count of la Marche. See chapter, "Issue of
Isabelle of Angoulême and Hugh de Lusignan."

[2] *CP*, Pembroke section.

[3] Vale, *The Angevin Legacy and the Hundred Years War 1250–1340*,
pgs. 272–273, Table 2; Prestwich, *Edward I*, pg. 573; *CP*, Richmond
section.

[4] *CP*, Richmond section.

[5] *CP*, Richmond section; Anderson, *Royal Genealogies*,
Table CCCLXXVIII.

[6] *CP*, Richmond section, indicates that he had an illegitimate son,
John the Bastard.

[7] Anderson, *Royal Genealogies*, Table CCCLXXVIII.

4 — **Joanna** (b. 1319; d. Oct 1384), Countess of
Penthievre; m. **Charles of Blois**, Lord of Guise and
Mayenne, nephew of **Philip VI**, King of France.
3 — **Piers/Peter** (b. 1290). No issue. Unm.
Arthur II, as above, Duke of Brittany, m. (2) 1294
Yolande de Dreux (d. 1322), daughter of **Robert IV**
(d. 14 Nov 1282), Count of Dreux, Braine, Montfort, and
l'Amaury, and widow (no issue) of **Alexander III**, King of
Scots. Issue (one son, five daughters[1]):
  3 — **John de Montfort** (b. 1293; d. 26 Sep 1345,
Hennebont; bur. (1) church of Ste. Croix, Quimperlé,
(2) convent of the Jacobins), Duke of Brittany, Count of
Montfort, Lord of Richmond; m. **Joan**, daughter of
Louis of Flandre, Count of Nevers. Issue:
    4 — **John V de Montfort** (d. 1 Nov 1399, Nantes;
bur. in the cathedral at Nantes), Count of Richmond
and Montfort, Duke of Brittany; m. (1) at Woodstock
1361 **Mary** (b. 9 or 10 Oct 1344, Walton, nr
Winchester; d. 1362[2]; bur. Abingdon Abbey),
daughter of **Edward III**, KING OF ENGLAND; no
issue; m. (2) 1366 **Joan/Johanna** (b. abt 1256;
d. Nov 1384, Nantes; bur. abbey of Notre Dame de
Prieres, Nantes), first daughter of **Thomas de Holand**
(d. 1360), 1st Earl of Kent; no issue; m. (3) at Saillé
11 Sep 1386 **Joan**[3] (d. 1437[4]), daughter of
Charles II (d. 1387[5]), King of Navarre, and **Joan**

---

[1] Anderson, *Royal Genealogies*, Table CCCLXXVIII.
[2] The *CP*, Richmond section, adds that **Mary** died "30 weeks after
the marriage." Green, *Lives of the Princesses of England*, Vol. III,
pgs. 286 and 299, states that **Mary** was "attacked by a lethargic disease,
from which it was impossible to rouse her; and under its influence she
gradually sank away and died...." Her sister, **Margaret** died about the
same time, and the "remains of the royal sisters were conveyed together
to the abbey of Abingdon..." where they shared the tomb erected for
them by their mother, **Philippa**, the queen.
[3] **Joan** m. as his second wife **Henry IV**, KING OF ENGLAND.
[4] *KQE*, pg. 185.
[5] *KQE*, pg. 185.

(daughter of **John II**, King of France); by his third wife he had four sons and four daughters.[1] For historical interest, the issue is listed[2]:

  5 — **John VI de Montfort** (b. 24 Dec 1389; d. 28 Aug 1442), Duke of Bretaign; m. 1404 **Johanna** (d. 2 Dec 1432), daughter of **Charles VI**, King of France.

  5 — **Joanna de Montfort** (b. 1387; d. 1388), twin with **Mary**.

  5 — **Mary de Montfort** (b. 1387; d. 16 Dec 1446), twin with **Joanna**; m. **John I**, Duke of Alencon 1396.

  5 — **Blanca de Montfort** m. 27 Jun 1407 **John IV**, Count of Armagnac.

  5 — **Margaret de Montfort** (b. 1390; d. 13 Apr 1428) m. 26 Jun 1407 **Alan IX**, Count of Rohan.

  5 — **Joanna de Montfort** (b. 1391) m. an earl of Scotland.

  5 — **Arthur II** (b. 24 Aug 1393; d. 26 Dec 1458), Count of Richmond, Duke of Bretaign; m. (1) **Johanna**, daughter of **Charles II**, Duke of Albret; m. (2) 1442 **Margaret**, daughter of **John**, Duke of Burgundy; m. (3) 1446 **Catharin of Luxemburg**, daughter of **Peter**, Count of St. Paul.

  5 — **Aegidius de Montfort** (b. 1394; d. 18 Jul 1412), Lord of Chantocè.

  5 — **Richard de Montfort** (b. 1395; d. 1438), Count of Estampes; m. **Margaret** (d. 22 Apr 1466), Countess of Vertus, daughter of **Lewis**, Duke of Orleans.

  4 — **Joan**[3] (d. 8 Nov 1402; bur. Abbey of Lavendon, nr Olney, Buckinghamshire) m. as his

---

[1] *CP*, Richmond section, pg. 824, note e.
[2] Anderson, *Royal Genealogies*, Table CCCLXXVIII
[3] Anderson, *Royal Genealogies*, Table CCCLXXVIII, states that **Joan/Joanna** was to have married **John of Blois**, Count of Penthievre, but that she never married.

second wife **Ralph Basset** (d. 10 May 1390;
bur. Lichfield Cathedral[1]), 3rd Lord Basset of
Brayton.

3 — **Johanna** (b. 1294) m. **Robert of Flanders**, Lord of
Cassel.

3 — **Beatrix** (b. 1295; d. 1384) m. 1315 **Guy X**, Baron
of Laval.

3 — **Alice** (b. 1297; d. 1377) m. 1320 **Burchard VI**,
Count of Vendosme.

3 — **Blanca** (d. yng).

3 — **Mary** (b. 1302; d. 1371), a nun.

2 — **Piers**, Count of Léon. No issue.[2]

2 — **Blanche/Blanca** (d. 19 Mar 1327) m. 1280 **Philip of
Artois** (k. 11 Sep 1298, Battle of Furna in Flanders), Count
of Artois, Lord of Conches, son of **Robert II** (d. 1300),
Count of Artois (**Robert II** was the grandson of
Louis VIII, King of France). Issue[3]:

3 — **Robert III** of Artois (d. 1343, from wounds
received at the Siege of Vannes), Count of Beaumont le
Roger (in Normandy); m. 1318 **Joanna** (d. 9 Jul 1363),
daughter of **Charles**, Count of Valois, and his second
wife, **Catharin**, daughter of **Philip of Courtenay**.
Issue[4]:

4 — **John** of Artois (d. 6 Apr 1386) m. 1362 **Isabel
of Melun**, daughter of **John**, Count of Tankerville,
and widow of **Peter**, Count of Dreux.

4 — **Catharin** m. **John** of Ponthieu, Count of
Aumale.

4 — **Charles** of Artois (d. 1402), Count of Pexenas;
m. **Joanna**, daughter of **Hugh**, Lord of Baucay, and
widow of **Godfrey** of Beaumont.

3 — **Margaret of Artois** (d. 23 Apr 1311) m. 1300
Lewis of France (d. 1319), Count of Evreux, son of

---

[1] *CP*, Basset section.

[2] Anderson, *Royal Genealogies*, Table CCCLXXVIII.

[3] Anderson, *Royal Genealogies*, Table CCCLIV.

[4] Anderson, *Royal Genealogies*, Table CCCLIV.

Philip III Audax, King of France.[1] Issue[2]:

    4 — **Philip III the Good**[3] (d. 26 Sep 1343, Granada), Count of Evreux, crowned March 1329 King of Navarre in right of his wife; m. 1316 **Joan II** (d. 1349), Queen of Navarre.

    4 — **Charles of France** (d. 24 Aug 1336), Count of Estampes; m. 1335 **Mary** (d. 19 Nov 1369), Countess of Biscay, daughter of **Ferdinand de la Cerda**,[4] Prince of Spain (son of **Ferdinand the Infant de la Cerda** (d. Aug 1275)).

    4 — **Joan of France** m. **Charles IV**, King of France.

    4 — **Mary of France** (d. 13 Oct 1325) m. 1313 **John III** (b. 1300; d. 5 Dec 1355), Duke of Brabant.

    4 — **Margaret of France** m. 1325 **William X**, Count of Auvergne.

  3 — **Joanna of Artois** (d. 1343) m. 1301 **Gasto(?) I**, Count of Foix.

  3 — **Mary of Artois** m. 1313 **John of Flanders** (d. 1330), Count of Namure, son of **Guido of Dampierre** (d. 1304/1305), Count of Flanders and Namure.

 2 — **Eleanor** (b. 1275; d. 16 May 1346), a nun at Amesbury, Abbess of Fontévrault.

1 — **Edmund Crouchback**[5] (b. 16 Jan 1245, London; d. 5 Jun 1296, Bayonne; bur. Westminster Abbey), Earl of Leicester, Derby, and Lancaster, King of Sicily; m. (1) at Westminster Abbey 6/8/9 Apr 1269 **Aveline de Forz/Fortibus** (b. 20 Jan 1259; d. 10 Nov 1274, Stockwell; bur. Westminster Abbey), only surviving daughter[6] of **William de**

---

[1] Previté-Orton, Table 20.

[2] Anderson, *Royal Genealogies*, Table CCCCLVI and CCCLXXVI.

[3] Duby, *France in the Middle Ages*, Table 3.

[4] Anderson, *Royal Genealogies*, Table CCCCLIX.

[5] It is believed he was called **Crouchback** because of the Crusader's cross on the back of his clothing.

[6] **William de Fors/Fortibus** had four sons, who "died early." (*DNB*, "William de Fors or de Fortibus, Earl of Albemarle (d. 1260)"

Forz/Fortibus (d. 1260), Lord of Aumâle and Holderness, Earl of Albemarle, Count of Albemarle; no issue; m. (2) in Paris bef 3 Feb 1276 **Blanche of Artois** (b. abt 1245–1250; d. 2 May 1302), Queen of Navarre, Countess of Champagne and Brie, Lady of Beaufort and Nogent, only daughter of **Robert I** (b. 1216; d. 1250), Count of Artois (son of **Louis VIII the Lion**, King of France), and widow of **Henry I**, King of Navarre (d. 1274). [1] Issue (three sons, one daughter[2]):

  2 — **Thomas** (b. abt 1276 or 1278[3]; ex. 22 Mar 1322, Pontefract; bur. Priory of St. John at Pontefract Abbey, before the high altar[4]), Earl of Lancaster, Derby, Leicester, Lincoln, and Salisbury, Seneschel of England; m. on or bef 28 Oct 1294[5]/1310 (diss. abt 1318) **Alice de Lacy**[6] (b. 25 Dec 1281, "probably" Denbigh; d. 2 Oct 1348; bur. Barlings Abbey/Birling, Kent), Countess of Lincoln, only daughter and heiress of **Henry de Lacy** (b. 6 or 13 Jan 1250/1251; d. 5 Feb 1310/1311; bur. 28 Feb 1310/1311, St. Paul's), Earl of Lincoln and Salisbury, by his first wife, **Margaret Lungespee/ Longespee** (liv. Sep 1306) (first daughter and heir of **William Lungespee/Longespee**[7]). No issue. [8]

  2 — **John of Lancaster** (b. bef May 1286; d. 1327, France), Lord of Beaufort and Nogent/Nogent Lartauld. No

---

[1] By **Henry I**, King of Navarre, **Blanche of Artois** was mother of **Jeanne of Navarre** (b. 1272; d. 1305), wife of **Philip IV**, King of France. **Philip IV** and **Jeanne of Navarre** were parents of **Isabella of France**, wife of **Edward II**, KING OF ENGLAND. (*Ancestral* 45-30, 45-31, and 101-31)

[2] Tauté.

[3] *CP*, Lancaster section.

[4] Hutchinson, *Edward II*, pg. 114.

[5] *CP*, Lancaster section.

[6] **Alice de Lacy** m. (2) bef 10 Nov 1324 **Ebles Lestraunge/Strange** (d. 8 Sep 1335; bur. Barlings Abbey); no issue; m. (3) bef 23 Mar 1335/ 1336 **Hugh de Frene** (d. Dec 1336 or Jan 1336/1337, Perth). (*CP*, Lancaster section, Salisbury section, Lincoln section)

[7] *CP*, Lancaster section, Lincoln section.

[8] Armitage-Smith, *John of Gaunt*, pg. 21; *CP*, Salisbury section.

issue.[1] Unm.

2 — **Mary** (d. yng).

2 — **Henry Plantagenet** (b. abt 1281, Grosment Castle,
Monmouth; d. 22 Sep 1345, Leicester; bur. Newark Abbey,
Leicester), Earl of Lancaster and Leicester, Seneschal of
England, the blind Earl; m. (1) bef 2 Mar 1296/1297 **Maud
de Chaworth** (b. 1282; liv. 19 Feb 1317; d. bef 3 Dec
1322[2]; bur. Mottisfont Priory), only daughter and heiress
of **Patrick Chaworth** (d. abt 7 Jul 1282/1283), Kt., Lord
of Kidwelly, and his wife, **Isabel de Beauchamp**
(d. abt 30 May 1306) (daughter of **William de Beauchamp**
(d. 1298), 1st Earl of Warwick). **Henry Plantagenet**
m. (2) as her second husband **Alix de Joinville**, daughter of
John de Joinville, Seneschal of Champagne and "historian
of St. Louis."[3] Issue by first marriage (a son, six
daughters[4])[5]:

   3 — **Henry of Grosment** (b. abt 1314, Grosment Castle;
   d. 24 Mar 1361 of the plague, Leicester; bur. Leicester
   Abbey), the Good Duke,[6] Duke of Lancaster, Earl of
   Derby, Lincoln and Leicester, Seneschal of England,
   First Founder Knight of the Garter[7]; m. abt 1334/
   1337[8] **Isabel de Beaumont** (liv. 24 Mar 1356; d. 1361;
   bur. Leicester Abbey), daughter of **Henry de Beaumont**
   (d. 10 Mar 1339/1340[9]), Lord Beaumont, Earl of
   Buchan, and his wife, **Alice Comyn** (d. bef 10 Aug
   1349) (daughter of **Alexander Comyn**, Sheriff of

---

  [1] Armitage-Smith, *John of Gaunt*, pg. 21.

  [2] *CP*, Lancaster section.

  [3] *CP*, Lancaster section. **Alix de Joinville** was widow of **Jean, Sleur
d'Arcies sur Aube et de Chacenay**. Her mother, **Alix de Risnel**, was
Joinville's second wife.

  [4] *CP*, Lancaster section.

  [5] Tauté.

  [6] Burke's *Royal Family*, pg. 196.

  [7] *CP*, Lancaster section.

  [8] *CP*, Lancaster section.

  [9] *CP*, Beaumont section.

Aberdeen[1]). Issue (two daughters[2]):

4 — **Maud** (b. 4 Apr 1335/1339; d. 10 Apr 1362,
aged 23[3]) m. (1) 1 Nov 1344 **Ralph de Stafford**
(dead in 1347), son of **Ralph de Stafford** (d. 31 Aug
1372; bur. Tonbridge), 1st Earl of Stafford, and his
second wife, **Margaret de Audeley** (d. aft 28 Jan
1347/1348) (daughter of **Hugh de Audeley**
(d. 10 Nov 1347), Earl of Gloucester)[4]; no issue;
m. (2) in the King's Chapel, Westminster,
1352 **William I** (d. Apr 1389; bur. Valenciennes),
Duke of Bavaria, son of **Lewis/Ludwig IV** of
Bavaria, Emperor, and his wife, **Margarete** (daughter
of **William I**, Count of Hainault, and sister of **Queen
Philippa**). No issue.[5]

4 — **Blanche** (b. 25 Mar 1341/1345; d. 12 Sep 1369,
Bolingbroke Castle; bur. St. Paul's Cathedral) m. at
Reading 13 May 1359 **John of Gaunt** (d. 3 Feb 1399,
Leicester Castle), son of **Edward III**, KING OF
ENGLAND. See chapter, "The Marriages of John of
Gaunt."

3 — **Blanche** (b. abt 1305; d. 10 Jul 1380) m. bef
24 Nov 1320/bef Jun 1317 **Thomas Wake**[6] (b. Mar
1297; d. 30/31 May 1349), 2nd Lord Wake of Lydell,
son of **John Wake** (d. 1300) and his wife, **Joan**
(d. 1310) (daughter of **John FitzBarnard** of Kingsdown,
Kent). No issue.[7]

3 — **Maud** (b. abt 1310; d. bef 5 May 1377, Campsey

---

[1] *CP*, Beaumont section.

[2] *DNB*, "Henry of Lancaster, first Duke of Lancaster (1299?-1345)";
CP, Lancaster section. There may have been a son who died young
(Tauté).

[3] *CP*, Stafford section.

[4] *CP*, Stafford section.

[5] Armitage-Smith, *John of Gaunt*, pg. 21.

[6] **Margaret Wake** (d. 27 Sep 1349), sister of **Thomas Wake**,
married **Edmund**, Earl of Kent, brother of **Edward II**, KING OF
ENGLAND. (*DNB*, "Wake, Thomas (1297-1349)")

[7] *DNB*, "Wake, Thomas (1297-1349)."

Abbey, Suffolk; bur. Campsey) m. (1) abt 1330 **William de Burgh** (b. 17 Sep 1312; murdered 6 Jun 1333, Le Ford, "now Belfast"), 3rd Earl of Ulster, son of **John de Burgh** (d. 1313) and his wife, **Elizabeth de Clare** (daughter of **Gilbert de Clare** (d. 1295)). Issue (an only daughter[1]):

 4 — **Elizabeth de Burgh** (b. 6 Jul 1332, "probably" at Carrickfergus Castle; d. 10(?) Dec 1363, Dublin; bur. Clare Priory, Suffolk) m. in the Tower of London 9 Sep 1342 when the bride was about ten years old and the groom, three, **Lionel of Antwerp** (d. 7 Jun 1368/10 Oct 1368, Alba in Piedmont; bur. (1) Pavia, (2) Clare Priory, Suffolk), Duke of Clarence and son of **Edward III**, KING OF ENGLAND.

Maud, as above, wife of **William de Burgh**, m. (2) by 8 Aug 1343[2] as his second wife **Ralph de Ufford**[3] (d. 9 Apr 1346, Kilmainham in Ireland; bur. Campsey Priory, Suffolk[4]), Chief Justice of Ireland.[5] Issue ("an only daughter"[6]):

 4 — **Maud de Ufford** (d. 25 Jan 1412/1413; bur. Bruisyard, Suffolk) m. bef 10 Jun 1350 **Thomas de Vere** (d. 12–18 Sep 1371, Great Bentley, Essex; bur. (1) Earls Colne, (2) 1935 St. Stephen's Chapel, Bures[7]), Earl of Oxford, Hereditary Chamberlain of England.

 3 — **Joan Plantagenet** (b. abt 1312; d. aft 6 Feb 1345/ 7 Jul 1349[8]; "said to have been" bur. before the high

---

[1] *CP*, Ulster section.

[2] *Ancestral* 94A-33; *CP*, Ulster section.

[3] **Ralph de Ufford** was brother of **Robert de Ufford**, 1st Earl of Suffolk. (*CP*, Ulster section)

[4] *CP*, Ulster section.

[5] *CP*, Oxford section.

[6] *CP*, Ulster section.

[7] *CP*, Oxford section.

[8] *CP*, Mowbray section.

alter at Byland[1]/Bella Landa[2]), youngest daughter;
m. as his first wife[3] **John II de Mowbray** (b. 29 Nov
1310, Hovingham, Yorkshire; d. 4 Oct 1361, York, of
the plague; bur. Franciscan church at Bedford[4]/Grey
Friars Church, York[5]), 3rd Baron Mowbray, son of
John I de Mowbray, Kt. (ex. 23 Mar 1322, York).
Issue (one son, two daughters[6]):

    4 – **John III de Mowbray** (b. "probably" 1328;
d. 1368[7]), 10th Baron Mowbray; m. "before her
father's death" **Elizabeth Segrave** (b. 25 Oct 1338;
"she predeceased her husband"), only child and heir
of **John Segrave** (d. 1 Apr 1353), 6th Lord Segrave,
and his wife, **Margaret**[8] (d. 24 Mar 1398/1399;
bur. Grey Friars, London) (daughter and heir of
Thomas of Brotherton, Earl of Norfolk and Marshal
of England, by his first wife, **Alice Hales**).[9]

    4 – **Eleanor/Alinore de Mowbray** (d. bef 18 Jun

---

[1] *CP*, Mowbray section.

[2] Burke's *Royal Family*.

[3] **John II de Mowbray** m. (2) **Elizabeth de Vere**, daughter of **John de Vere** (d. 23 or 24 Jan 1359/1360, seige of Rheims), Earl of Oxford, and his wife, **Maud Badlesmere** (d. 1366) (second daughter of **Bartholomew de Badlesmere** (ex. 14 Apr 1322) and sister of **Giles Badlesmere**). **Elizabeth** was widow of **Hugh de Courtenay** (dead in 1349), son and heir of **Hugh de Courtenay** (d. 2 May 1377), 2nd Earl of Devon. (*CP*, Mowbray section)

[4] *DNB*, "Mowbray, John (II) de, ninth Baron (d. 1361)."

[5] Burke's *Royal Family*.

[6] Burke's *Royal Family*, pg. 197.

[7] **John III Mowbray** "met with an untimely death at the hands of the Turks near Constantinople, on his way to the Holy Land, in 1368." His "elder" son, **John IV de Mowbray** was created Earl of Nottingham on the same day **Richard II** was crowned; his "second son," **Thomas (I) de Mowbray**, became the 1st Duke of Norfolk. (*DNB*, "Mowbray, John (II) de, ninth baron (d. 1361)")

[8] **Margaret**, as widow of **John de Segrave**, m. (2) **Walter de Manny** (d. 1371/1372). (*CP*, Segrave section)

[9] *CP*, Segrave section.

1387) m. (1) bef 23 Jul 1358 as his third wife[1]
Roger la Warre, Baron de la Warre (b. 30 Nov
1326; d. 27 Aug 1370, Gascony), son of **John la
Warre** (d. bef 24 Jun 1331) and **Margaret de Holand**
(d. 20 or 22 Aug 1349) (daughter of **Robert de
Holand** (ex. 7 Oct 1328), 1st Lord Holand, and his
wife, **Maud la Zouche** (d. 31 May 1349))[2];
m. (2) bef 12 Feb 1372/1373 **Lewis de Clifford**
(d. 1404).[3]

4 — **Blanche de Mowbray** (d. 21 Jul 1409)
m. (1) abt 1349 (as a child) **John de Segrave**
(d. yng), son and heir of **John de Segrave**, Lord
Segrave; m. (2) as his second wife by 1356 or 1357
Robert Bertram (d. Nov 1363), Baron of Bothal,
Northumberland; m. (3) bef 5 Jun 1372 **Thomas de
Poynings** (b. Slaugham, Sussex; bap. 19 Apr 1349;
d. bef 25 Jun 1375; will directed burial in
St. Radigund's Abbey, Kent, but he was bur. at
Poynings), son of **Michael de Poynings** (d. 7 Mar
1368/1369) and his wife, **Joan** (d. 16 May 1369; will
requests burial at Poynings), widow of **John de
Moleyns**; m. (4) bet. 28 Jun 1377 and 21 Mar 1377/
1378 **John de Worth** (d. 1391); m. (5) by Nov 1394
John Wiltshire (liv. Aug 1405).[4]

---

[1] **Roger de la Warre** m. (1) bef 14 Oct 1338 **Elizabeth de Welle**
(liv. 24 Feb 1344/1345), daughter of **Adam de Welle** (d. 24–28 Feb
1344/1345; bur. Lady Chapel, Greenfield Priory) of Well, co. Lincoln,
and his wife, **Margaret**; m. (2) bef 2 Feb 1353/1354 **Elizabeth**. (*CP*,
De La Warr section)

[2] *Ancestral* 18-31; 47B-30 through 47B-32.

[3] *CP*, De La Warr section. According to Beltz, pg. 264, **Lewis
Clifford** is "said to have married Eleanor, the daughter of John lord la
Warre; and, according to another authority, Juliana the daughter and heir
of John Egglesfield." Beltz adds that "it is clear" that **Clifford** had a
daughter, **Elizabeth**, "who, at the time of his decease, was the wife of
Sir Philip de la Vache," K.G. Both articles identify **Clifford** as being
involved with the Lollards and dying in 1404.

[4] *CP*, Poynings section.

3 — **Isabel** (b. abt 1317; d. aft 1 Feb 1347), Prioress of Amesbury, became a nun bef 6 Apr 1337[1]; m. **Henry de la Dale**.

3 — **Eleanor Plantagenet/Eleanor of Lancaster** (b. abt 1318; d. 11 Jan 1372, Arundel Castle; bur. Lewes Priory) m. (1) bef 23 Aug 1337/bef Jun 1337[2] **John de Beaumont**[3] (b. 1318; d. bet 24 Feb 1342 and 25 May 1342), 2nd Baron Beaumont, son of **Henry Beaumont** (d. bef 10 Mar 1339/40), Kt., Earl of Buchan, and (m. abt 1310[4]) **Alice Comyn** (d. bef 10 Aug 1349[5]) of Buchan. Issue (one son, one daughter[6]):

4 — **Henry Beaumont**, Lord Beaumont (b. 1340, Brabant; d. 17 Jun 1369[7]; bur. Sempringham, co. Lincoln), K.G.; m. as her first husband[8] bef 1361 **Margaret de Vere** (d. 15 Jun 1398; bur. Grey Friars, Newgate), daughter of **John de Vere** (d. 23 or 24 Jan 1359/1360), 7th Earl of Oxford, and his wife, **Maud de Badlesmere** (b. 1308–1310; d. "probably" 24 May 1366, Earls Colne; bur. Colne Priory[9]) (widow of **Robert FitzPayn** (d. without issue bef 10 Dec 1322[10]) and second daughter of **Bartholomew de**

---

[1] Burke's *Royal Family*, pg. 197.

[2] *CP*, Beaumont section.

[3] *Ancestral* 114-31.

[4] *CP*, Buchan section.

[5] *CP*, Beaumont section.

[6] Burke's *Royal Family*, pg. 197.

[7] *Ancestral* 17-31, 17-30.

[8] The *CP*, Beaumont section, states that **Margaret de Vere** was the widow of **Nicholas Lovain**. The order of marriages has been stated differently: **Margaret de Vere** m. (2) abt 1370 **Nicholas Louvain** (b. abt 1325; d. 1376) of Penhurst; m. (3) **John Devereux** (d. 22 Feb 1392/1393; bur. Grey Friars, Newgate), Lord Devereux. (*Ancestral* 79-32, referencing various *CP* articles)

[9] *CP*, Oxford section.

[10] *CP*, FitzPayn section, surmises **Robert FitzPayn** was killed in the Scottish wars, "perhaps in the rout at Byland Abbey, 14 Oct. 1322."

Badlesmere (ex. 14 Apr 1322, Canterbury), 1st Lord Badlesmere, by his wife, **Margaret de Clare** [1] (d. 1333)).

4 — A daughter.

Eleanor Plantagenet, as above, wife of **John de Beaumont**, m. (2) at Ditton 5 Feb 1344/1345 as his second wife [2] **Richard II Copped Hat FitzAlan** (b. abt 1313; d. 24 Jan 1375/1376, Arundel Castle; bur. Lewes Priory), "with whom she had intrigued in her husband's lifetime," [3] 9th Earl of Arundel and Warenne, K.G., son of **Edmund FitzAlan** (b. 1 May 1285, Castle of Marlborough; ex. 17 Nov 1326), Earl of Arundel, and **Alice de Warenne** (d. bef 23 May 1338). Issue ("three sons" and "four daughters" [4]):

4 — **Richard III FitzAlan** (b. 1346; ex. 21 Sep 1397; bur. church of the Augustin Friars, Bread Street, London), 10th Earl of Arundel and Surrey; m. abt 28 Sep 1359 **Elizabeth de Bohun** (d. 3 Apr 1385; bur. Lewes), daughter of **William de Bohun** (b. 1310/1312; d. 16 Sep 1360), Earl of Northampton, and his wife, **Elizabeth de Badlesmere** (b. abt 1313;

---

[1] **Margaret de Clare** was the widow of **Gilbert de Umfreville** (d. bef 23 May 1303) and the elder daughter of **Thomas de Clare**, Lord of Inchiquin and Youghal, and **Julian FitzMaurice. Thomas**, 2nd Lord Clare, was her nephew. **Margaret de Clare** was known for having refused **Edward II's** queen, **Isabella of Angoulême**, admittance to the royal castle of Leeds in the summer of 1321. For this insult, **Edward II** besieged Leeds, captured the castle and **Margaret de Clare** 11 Nov, and imprisoned her in the Tower of London until the following 2 Nov. (*CP*, Badlesmere section)

[2] **Richard II Copped Hat FitzAlan** m. (1) 9 Feb 1320/1321 **Isabel Despenser**, daughter of **Hugh the younger le Despenser** (ex. 24 Nov 1326, Hereford). "In 1345 he repudiated his wife, **Isabella**, on the ground that he had never consented to the marriage"; he received "papal recognition of the nullity of the union." (*DNB*, "FitzAlan, Richard II, Earl of Arundel and Warenne (1307?-1376)")

[3] *CP*, Beaumont section.

[4] *DNB*, "FitzAlan, Richard II, Earl of Arundel and Warenne (1307?-1376)."

d. 8 Jun 1355/1356) (daughter of **Bartholomew de
Badlesmere** (ex. 14 Apr 1322) and **Margaret de
Clare** (d. 1333)); issue of three sons, four daughters;
m. (2) 15 Aug 1390 **Philippa de Mortimer**[1]
(b. 21 Nov 1375, Ludlow; d. 24 Sep 1401, Halnaker,
Sussex; bur. Boxgrove Priory nr Lewes), daughter of
Edmund II de Mortimer (d. 1381), 3rd Earl of
March, and widow of **John Hastings** (d. 30/31 Dec
1389, killed while practicing for a jousting
tournament; bur. (1) church of the Friars Preachers,
Hereford, (2) "in or after Mar. 1391/2" church of the
Friars Minors (Grey Friars), London), Earl of
Pembroke.[2] No issue of this second marriage.

4 — **John FitzAlan** (d. 1379, perished at sea[3]),
Marshal of England; m. 17 Feb 1358/1359 **Eleanor
Maltravers** (b. 1345; d. 10 Jan 1404/1405), daughter
of **John Maltravers** (d. 22 Jan 1348/1349) and
Gwenthlin/Welthiana (d. bef Oct 1375).

4 — **Thomas FitzAlan/Thomas Arundel** (b. 1353;
d. 19 Feb 1414; bur Canterbury Cathedral[4]),
Archbishop of Canterbury, third and youngest son.

4 — **Joan FitzAlan** (d. 7 Apr 1419; bur. Walden
Abbey) m. aft 9 Sep 1359 **Humphrey IX Bohun**
(b. 25 Mar 1342; d. 16 Jan 1372; bur. Walden Abbey
"at the feet of his father"), Earl of Hereford, Essex,

---

[1] **Philippa Mortimer** m. (3) as his second wife aft Apr 1398/
bef 24 Nov 1399 **Thomas de Poynings** (d. 7 Mar 1428/1429), Lord
St. John of Basing. (*CP*, Pembroke section, Arundel section, Poynings
section)

[2] *DNB*, "FitzAlan, Richard III, Earl of Arundel and Surrey
(1346–1397)"; *CP*, Pembroke section.

[3] *DNB*, "FitzAlan, Richard II, Earl of Arundel and Warenne
(1307?–1376)."

[4] Also called **Thomas Arundel**. He died "following of a sudden
attack of some complaint in the throat." "He was buried in his own
cathedral, where he had caused a tomb to be erected in his own lifetime,
but it has been since destroyed." (*DNB*, "Arundel, Thomas
(1353–1414)")

and Northampton.[1]

4 — **Alice FitzAlan** (d. 17 Mar 1415/1416) m. **Thomas Holand** (b. abt 1350; d. 25 Apr 1397; bur. Abbey of Bourne, co. Lincoln), K.G., 2nd Earl of Kent.

4 — **Mary FitzAlan** (d. in the lifetime of her father).

4 — **Eleanor FitzAlan** (d. in the lifetime of her father).

3 — **Mary Plantagenet** (b. abt 1321; d. 1 Sep 1362; bur. Alnwick), youngest daughter[2]; m. at Tutbury Castle in or bef 1334[3] as his first wife **Henry de Percy** (b. 1320; d. 17 Jun[4]/abt 18 May[5] 1368; bur. Alnwick), 3rd Baron Percy of Alnwick, eldest son of **Henry de Percy** (d. 26 Feb 1351/1352; bur. Alnwick) (2nd Baron Percy of Alnwick, and his wife **Idoine Clifford**[6] (d. 24 Aug 1365; bur. Beverley Minster)). Issue (two sons[7]):

4 — **Henry de Percy** (b. 10 Nov 1341/1342; d. 19 Feb 1407/1408, Bramham Moor), 1st Earl of Northumberland, K.G., Marshal of England;

---

[1] Their daughter, **Mary de Bohun**, m. **Henry**, Earl of Derby, but died before he became **Henry IV**, KING OF ENGLAND.

[2] *DNB*, "Percy, Thomas, Earl of Worcester (d. 1403)."

[3] *CP*, Percy section; *Ancestral* 19-30.

[4] *DNB*, "Percy, Henry, second Baron Percy of Alnwick (1299?–1352)."

[5] *Ancestral* 19-30, referencing the *CP*, states that **Henry de Percy** died 18 May. *CP*, Percy section, also gives the death date as 18 May.

[6] *DNB*, "Percy, Henry, second Baron Percy of Alnwich (1299?–1352)" states that "in his will she is called Imania." She was the daughter of **Robert de Clifford** (d. 1365), 1st Lord Clifford (*CP*, Percy section).

[7] *DNB*, "Percy, Henry, second Baron Percy of Alnwick (1299?–1352)" and Burke's *Royal Family*, pg. 197. The *DNB* article states that **Henry Percy's** second wife was **Joan de Orby** (d. 1369), daughter of **John de Orby**, by whom he had a daughter **Mary** (b. 1367; d. 1395, "aged two at her mother's death"), who married **John**, Lord Ros of Hamlake. The *CP*, Percy section, spells **Orby** as **Orreby** and substitutes Helmsley for Hamlake.

m. (1) 12 Jul 1358/1359 **Margaret de Neville**[1]
(d. May 1372), widow of **William de Ros**[2]
(d. by 3 Dec 1352) of Helmsley or Hamlake and
daughter of **Ralph Neville** (d. 5 Aug 1367), 2nd Lord
Neville of Raby, and his wife **Alice de Audley**
(d. 12 Jan 1373/1374) (daughter of **Hugh de Audley**
"senior").[3] Issue (three sons and a daughter[4])
included:

> 5 — **Henry Hotspur Percy** (b. 20 May 1364;
> k. 21 Jul 1403, Battle of Shrewsbury)
> m. bef 10 Dec 1379 **Elizabeth Mortimer**
> (liv. 8 Oct 1407/d. 20 Apr 1417[5]), daughter of
> **Edmund Mortimer** (d. 27 Dec 1381), 3rd Earl of
> March, and **Philippa Plantagenet** (b. 16 Aug
> 1355) (daughter of **Lionel of Antwerp** (d. 1368)
> and **Elizabeth de Burgh** (d. 1363)).

Henry de Percy (d. 1407/1408), as above, 1st Earl of
Northumberland, m. (2) 1384/bef 3 Oct 1383[6] **Maud
de Lucy**[7] (d. 18 Dec[8]/24 Dec 1398), only daughter
of **Thomas de Lucy** of Cockermouth, widow of
Gilbert de Umfraville (d. 6 Jan 1380/1381), Earl of
Angus, and sister of **Anthony de Lucy**, last Baron
Lucy. No issue.

---

[1] *Ancestral* 186-6.

[2] **William de Ros** (d. 1352), 3rd Lord Ros, was son of **William de Ros** (d. 1342/1343) and his wife **Margery de Badlesmere** (d. by 22 Oct 1363). (*CP*, Ros section)

[3] *DNB*, "Percy, Sir Henry, called Hotspur (1364–1403)"; *CP*, Westmorland section, Northumberland section, Ros section.

[4] *DNB*, "Percy, Henry, first Earl of Northumberland (1342–1408)."

[5] *CP*, Camoys section.

[6] *CP*, Angus section.

[7] *DNB*, "Percy, Henry, first Earl of Northumberland (1342–1408)."

[8] *CP*, Angus section.

> 4 — **Thomas de Percy** (b. abt 1344; ex. 23 Jul 1403, two days after the Battle of Shrewsbury), Earl of Worcester, K.G.[1] Unm.

1 — **Richard** (b. abt 1247; d. bef 1256; bur. Westminster Abbey).

1 — **John** (b. 1256; d. 1256; bur. Westminster Abbey).

1 — **William** (b. 1256; d. 1256).

1 — **Katherine** (b. 25 Nov 1253, Westminster Palace; d. 3 May 1257, Windsor Castle; bur. Westminster Abbey).

1 — **Henry** (d. young; bur. Westminster Abbey).

Illegitimate Issue

It is "extremely unlikely" that **Henry III** had any mistresses, and no illegitimate issue for him is recorded.[2] "Through thirty-six years of married life, until Henry's death [at age sixty-five], he and his Queen remained devoted to one another."[3]

Edmund
Crouchback
(d. 1296)

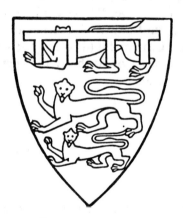

---

[1] **Thomas de Percy** died unmarried "as far as is known" but "appears" to have had an illegitimate son, **Thomas.** (*CP*, Worcester section)

[2] Given-Wilson and Curteis, pg. 135.

[3] Harvey, *The Plantagenets*, pg. 96.

Edward I
1274–1307
m. (1) Eleanor of Castile
m. (2) Margaret of France

Edward I Longshanks, called the Hammer of the Scots, son of **Henry III** and **Eleanor of Provence**; *b.* 17 Jun 1239, Palace of Westminster; *crowned* 19 Aug 1274, Westminster Abbey; *m.* (1) at Las Huelgas Oct 1254 **Eleanor of Castile**; *m.* (2) at Canterbury Cathedral 10 Sep 1299 **Margaret of France**; *d.* 7 Jul 1307, Burgh-on-the-Sands; *bur.* 27 Oct 1307,[1] Westminster Abbey.

Eleanor of Castile, daughter of **Ferdinand III** (b. 1191; d. 30 May 1252), King of Castile and Leon, and his second wife, **Joanna de Dammartin** (d. 1278/1279), Countess of Ponthieu
b. abt 1244, Castile; *crowned* 19 Aug 1274, Westminster Abbey; *d.* 28 or 29 Nov 1290,[2] Herdeby, Lincolnshire; *bur.* Westminster Abbey; her heart was buried in the Dominican Blackfriars Church, London; her entrails in Lincoln Cathedral.[3]

---

[1] *DNB*, "Edward I (1239–1307)"; Hutchinson, *Edward II*, pg. 54, wherein is stated that the body of **Edward I** rested at Waltham Abbey "by Harold's grave for nearly four months."

[2] According to Burke's *Royal Family*, pg. 197, **Eleanor of Castile** d. 28 or 29 Nov 1290. According to *Ancestral* 110-30, she d. 28 Nov 1290. According to *KQB*, she d. 24 Nov 1290.

[3] Parsons, *Eleanor of Castile 1290–1990*, pg. 16. The grief-stricken **Edward I** ordered the erection of a memorial cross in each of the twelve

(continued...)

Ancestors of Eleanor of Castile

```
                              ┌Alfonso IX, King of Leon (d. 1229/1230)
                  ┌Ferdinand III, King of Castile and Leon (d. 1252)
                  │           └Berengaria of Castile (d. 1244)¹
Eleanor of Castile (d. 1290)
                  │           ┌Simon de Dammartin, Count of Aumale (d. 1239)
                  └Joanna Dammartin (d. 1278/1279)
                              └Countess Marie (d. 1250/1251)
```

* * *

Margaret of France (second wife of **Edward I**), daughter
of **Philip III** (d. 1285), King of France, and **Marie of Brabant**
(b. abt 1260, Liege; d. 12 Jan 1322, Murel); *b.* 1279;
d. 14 Feb 1317, Marlborough Castle; *bur.* Grey Friars Church,
London; she was not crowned.[2]

Ancestors of Margaret of France

```
                              ┌Louis IX, King of France (d. 1270)
                  ┌Philip III, King of France (d. 1285)
                  │           └Margaret Beringerus (d. 1295)
Margaret of France (d. 1317/1318)
                  │           ┌Henry III, Duke of Brabant (d. 1260/1261)
                  └Marie of Brabant (d. 1322)
                              └Alice of Burgundy (d. 1273)
```

* * *

Issue by Eleanor of Castile

1 — **Joan** (b. 1260; d. 1260).
1 — **Eleanor** (b. abt 17 Jun 1264/1269, Windsor Castle;
d. 12 Oct 1297/1298, Ghent; bur. Chapter-House of
Westminster Abbey) m. (1) by proxy (marriage never
consummated[3]) **Alfonso III** (d. 1291/1292/1293), King of
Aragon; m. (2) at Bristol 20 Sep 1293 **Henry III** (d. 1302;

---

[3] (...continued)
towns where her body rested on its return to London. See chapter, "The
Eleanor Crosses."
    [1] **Berengaria of Castile** (d. 1244) was the granddaughter of **Eleanor
of Aquitaine** and **Henry II**, KING OF ENGLAND.
    [2] Burke's *Royal Family*, pg. 197, remarks that **Margaret of France**
"appears to have been the first Queen Consort since the conquest not to
have been crowned."
    [3] Fuller, *The Worthies of England*, 1952, pg. 26.

bur. Naples Cathedral), Count of Bar. Issue (one son, one "or possibly two" daughters[1]):

2 — **Edward I** (b. abt 1294; while on Crusade, "died abroad of the plague, at Famagosta, in the Island of Cyprus"[2]), Count of Bar; m. **Mary**,[3] daughter of **Robert II** (d. 1305), Duke of Burgundy, and his wife, **Agnes** (d. 1327[4]) (daughter of **Louis IX the Saint**, King of France).

2 — **Joan** (d. 31 Aug 1361; bur. "abroad"[5]), "only daughter," "demoiselle de Bar"; m. at the Franciscan church at Newgate 25 May 1306[6] **John de Warenne** (b. 30 Jun 1286; d. 29 or 30 Jun 1347,[7] Conisborough; bur. Lewes priory "under an arch on the left side of the high altar"[8]), Earl of Surrey, son of **William de Warenne** (d. 15 Dec 1286[9]) and his wife, **Joanna/Joan** (d. on or

---

[1] Burke's *Royal Family*, pg. 197; in *DNB*, "Warenne, John de, Earl of Surrey and Sussex, or Earl Warenne (1286–1347)," **Joan** is described as the "only daughter" of **Henry III**, Count of Bar.

[2] Green, *Lives of the Princesses of England*, Vol. II, pgs. 310, 317.

[3] **Mary** was the sister of **Joan/Joanna** (d. 1348) wife (m. 1313) of **Philip VI**, King of France, and of **Margaret**, who in 1313 "was [with her own shroud] strangled for adultery by order of her husband, Louis X." (Anderson, *Royal Genealogies*, Table CCCLVIII; Bush, *Memoirs of the Queens of France*, pgs. 200, 191)

[4] Anderson, *Royal Genealogies*, Table CCCLXXVI.

[5] *CP*, Surrey section.

[6] Green, *Lives of the Princesses of England*, Vol. II, pg. 316, gives the marriage date as 20 May 1306, "when she could not be more than eleven years old." Green states concerning the wedding, "it was celebrated the same day on which her cousin, **Eleanora de Clare** (d. 30 Jun 1337), was married to **Hugh le Despenser**." The *CP*, Despenser section, states that **Hugh le Despenser** (ex. 24 Nov 1326), favorite of **Edward II**, married **Eleanor de Clare** after 14 Jun 1306.

[7] *CP*, Surrey section.

[8] *DNB*, "Warenne, John de, Earl of Surrey and Sussex, or Earl Warenne (1286–1347)."

[9] "…having attended a tournament at Croydon, where he is said to have been ambushed and cruelly slain by his rivals." (*CP*, Surrey section)

before 23 Nov 1293; bur. Lewes) (daughter of **Robert de Vere** (d. bef 7 Sep 1296), 5th Earl of Oxford). No issue. [1]

1 — **Katherine** (d. 1264). [2]

1 — **Joan** (b. and d. abt Sep 1265; bur. Westminster Abbey).

1 — **John** (b. 10 Jun or Jul 1266, Winchester or Windsor Castle; d. 1 or 3 Aug 1271, Westminster Palace; bur. Westminster Abbey).

1 — **Henry** (b. 13 Jul 1267, Windsor Castle; d. 14 Oct 1274, Merton, Surrey; bur. Westminster Abbey).

1 — **Alphonso** (b. 24 Nov 1273, Bordeaux/Maine; d. 19 Aug 1284, Windsor Castle; bur. Westminster Abbey; his heart was buried at Blackfriars, London), Earl of Chester. [3]

1 — **Edward II**, KING OF ENGLAND.

1 — **Julian/Katherine** (b. 1271, Holy Land; d. possibly 5 Sep 1271, Holy Land).

1 — **Joan of Acre** (b. Spring 1272, Acre, Palestine; d. 23 Apr 1307, Clare, Suffolk; bur. Clare Priory) was betrothed to **Hartmann** (drowned 1281/Dec 1282[4]), son of **Emperor Rudolf**[5]; m. (1) 30 Apr or "the beginning of May" 1290 at Westminster Abbey as his second wife[6] **Gilbert de Clare**

---

[1] *CP*, Surrey section, indicates that he died without male issue; *DNB*, "Warenne, John de, Earl of Surrey and Sussex, or Earl Warenne (1286–1347)," wherein is stated that he was born 24 Jun 1287, married to **Joan** 20 May 1306, and died 30 Jun 1347 and that there was "no issue of the marriage." The marriage was reportedly an unhappy one; **Warenne** left "numerous" illegitimate issue, some by **Matilda de Nerford**; toward the end of his life he lived with **Isabella de Holand**, the daughter of **Robert de Holand** (d. 16 Mar 1372/1373, Halse or Hawes, Brackley; bur. St. James' Chapel, Brackley), brother of the 1st Earl of Kent (*CP*, Holand section).

[2] Prestwich, *Edward I*, pg. 573.

[3] *CP*, Chester section.

[4] *DNB*, "Joan or Joanna of Acre, Countess of Gloucester and Hertford (1272–1307)."

[5] *DNB*, "Edward I."

[6] **Gilbert de Clare** m. (1) (div. 18 Jul 1271) 1253 **Alice de Lusignan**, daughter of **Hugh le Brun de Lusignan**, Count of La Marche and Angoulême, and **Yolande**, daughter of **Pierre Mauclerk**, Duke of Brittany. There was issue of two daughters. (*CP*, Gloucester section)

(b. 2 Sep 1243, Christchurch, Hampshire[1]; d. 7 Dec 1295, Monmouth Castle; bur. 22 Dec 1295, Tewkesbury Abbey), Earl of Clare, 7th Earl of Hertford, 3rd Earl of Gloucester. Issue (one son, three daughters[2]):

  2 — **Gilbert de Clare** (b. 11 or 10 May 1291, Winchcombe(?) nr Tewkesbury[3]; k. 24 Jun 1314, Battle of Bannockburn; bur. Tewkesbury Abbey), Earl of Gloucester, Earl of Hertford, Earl of Clare; m. at Waltham Abbey "in the presence of his uncle the King" 29 Sep 1308 **Maud de Burgh** (d. 1320; bur. Tewkesbury Abbey), daughter of **Richard de Bùrgh** (b. abt 1259; d. 29 Jul 1326), 2nd Earl of Ulster, and **Margaret de Burgh** (d. 1304) ("said to have been" daughter of **John de Burgh** of Lanvalley[4]). "...left no children" [there was no surviving issue].[5]

    3 — **John de Clare** (b. 3 Apr 1312, Cardiff; d. 1312; bur. St. Mary's Chapel, Tewkesbury), only son and heir.[6]

  2 — **Eleanor de Clare** (b. Oct or Nov 1292, Caerphilly Castle, co. Glamorgan in Wales[7]; d. 30 Jun 1337) m. (1) at Westminster aft 14 Jun 1306 **Hugh the younger le Despenser** (ex. 24 Nov 1326, Hereford; bur. "some years afterwards"[8] in Tewkesbury Abbey), son of **Hugh the**

---

[1] *DNB*, "Clare, Gilbert de, called the Red, ninth Earl of Clare, seventh Earl of Hertford, and eighth Earl of Gloucester (1243-1295)"; *CP*, Gloucester section, wherein he is called the Red Earl.

[2] Burke's *Royal Family*, pg. 197; Sorley, *King's Daughters*, Pedigrees I, II.

[3] Green, *Lives of the Princesses of England*, Vol. II, pg. 336.

[4] *CP*, Ulster section.

[5] *DNB*, "Clare, Gilbert de, tenth Earl of Clare, eighth Earl of Hereford, and ninth Earl of Gloucester (1291-1314)."

[6] *CP*, Gloucester section.

[7] Green, *Lives of the Princesses of England*, Vol. II, pg. 337.

[8] **Hugh the younger le Despenser** was "hanged on a gallows 50 feet high, 24 Nov 1326. His head was set up on London Bridge, 4 Dec., and his quarters in four different places [towns]. Some years afterwards his bones were collected, and bur. in Tewkesbury Abbey." "The permit for

(continued...)

elder le Despenser (ex. 27 Oct 1326, Hereford; bur. Tewkesburg Abbey). Both father and son were favorites of **Edward II**, KING OF ENGLAND. Issue included[1]:

3 — **Hugh le Despenser** (aged about 18 in 1326; d. 8 Feb 1348/1349; bur. Tewkesbury Abbey), Lord Despenser; m. bef 27 Apr 1341 as her second husband[2] **Elizabeth Montagu** (d. 30 or 31 May 1359, Ashley, Hampshire; bur. Tewkesbury Abbey), daughter of **William de Montagu** (d. 1343), 1st Earl of Salisbury, and his wife, **Katherine Grandison** (d. 1349) (daughter of **William de Grandison** (d. 1335[3]), Lord Grandison). No issue.[4]

3 — **Edward le Despenser** (d. 30 Sep 1342, Siege of Vannes), second son; m. at Groby 20 Apr 1335 **Anne de Ferrers** (d. 8 Aug 1367), daughter of **William de Ferrers**, Lord Ferrers of Groby, co. Leicester.[5] Issue:

4 — **Edward, Lord Despenser** (b. 24 Mar 1335/1336, Essendine; d. 11 Nov 1375, Cardiff Castle/ Llanblethian, co. Glamorgan;

---

[8] (...continued)
his bones to be collected and buried was given on 15 Dec 1330." (*CP*, Despenser section)

[1] *CP*, Gloucester section, "Chart Pedigree of the Earls & Dukes of Gloucester"; *DNB*, "Despenser, Hugh le, the younger (d. 1326)."

[2] **Elizabeth Montagu** m. (1) **Giles de Badlesmere** (b. 18 Oct 1314, Hambleton, Rutland; d. 7 Jun 1338), Lord Badlesmere; m. (3) bef 10 Jul 1350 as his second wife **Guy de Briene/Bryan** (d. 17 Aug 1390; bur. Tewkesbury Abbey), Lord Briene, of Laugharne, co. Carmarthen, and Walwyn's Castle, co. Pembroke (*CP*, Despenser section). Jenner, *Journeys into Medieval England*, pg. 117, states that **Hugh Despenser** and his wife, **Elizabeth Montagu** were buried side by side. **Guy de Brien**, her third husband, ordered his own tomb and effigy and "had them made during his own lifetime and followed the progress of the work with great interest."

[3] *CP*, Grandison section.

[4] *DNB*, "Despenser, Hugh le, the younger (d. 1326)"; *CP*, Despenser section.

[5] *CP*, Despenser section.

bur. Tewkesbury Abbey/church of St. Mary at
Tewkesbury), K.G.; m. bef Dec 1364[1]/2 Aug
1354[2] **Elizabeth Burghersh** (aged 27 or more in
May 1369[3]; d. Aug 1409[4]/26 Jul 1409[5];
bur. Tewkesbury Abbey), only daughter of
Bartholomew the younger Burghersh (aged 26 and
more in 1355[6]; d. 5 Apr 1369; will directed burial at
Walsingham), Lord Burghersh,[7] and his first wife
(m. bef 10 May 1335), **Cecily Weyland** (daughter of
Richard de Weyland).[8]
4 — **Henry le Despenser** (b. 1341 or 1342;
d. 23 Aug 1406; bur. before the high alter in Norwich
Cathedral), fourth son, canon of Salisbury, Bishop of
Norwich (1370–1406).[9]
3 — **Isabel le Despenser** m. 9 Feb 1320/1321 (annulled
1345[10]) as his first wife **Richard II Copped Hat**

---

[1] *CP*, Burghersh section.
[2] *CP*, Despenser section.
[3] *CP*, Despenser section.
[4] *CP*, Burghersh section.
[5] *CP*, Despenser section.
[6] *CP*, Burghersh section. This **Bartholomew Burghersh** was one of
the twenty-five First Founder Knights of the Order of the Garter.
[7] *CP*, "Chart Pedigree of the Earls & Dukes of Gloucester"; *DNB*,
"Burghersh, Bartholomew, Lord, the younger (d. 1369)."
[8] Their son, **Thomas le Despenser** (d. 1400), was on 29 Sep 1397
created Earl of Gloucester. His daughter, **Isabelle le Despenser**
(d. 1439), m. **Richard Beauchamp** (d. 1422), Earl of Worcester, and
Richard Beauchamp (d. 1439), Earl of Warwick. (*DNB*, "Despenser,
Thomas le, Earl of Gloucester (1373–1400)")
[9] The *DNB*, "Despenser or Spencer, Henry le (d. 1406)," remarks
that his career was more "that of a soldier rather than of a
churchmen...."
[10] According to the *CP*, Arundel section, **Richard** and **Isabel** were
respectively 7 and 8 years of age when they were espoused. "In 1345 he
repudiated his wife, **Isabella le Despenser**, on the ground that he had
never consented to the marriage"; he received "papal recognition of the
nullity of the union" (*DNB*, "FitzAlan, Richard II, Earl of Arundel and
(continued...)

FitzAlan (b. abt 1313; d. 24 Jan 1375/1376,
bur. Lewes), Earl of Arundel and Warenne. Issue[1]:
    4 — **Edmund de Arundel** (liv. 1377) m. bef Jul 1349
    Sibyl, daughter of **William de Montagu**
    (d. 1343/1344), 1st Earl of Salisbury, and **Katherine**
    Grandison (d. 1349) (daughter of **William de**
    Grandison (d. 1335)); bastardised when the Pope
    annulled his parents' marriage.[2]
    4 — **Mary** or **Isabel**[3] (d. 29 Aug 1396) m. **John**

---

[10] (...continued)
Warenne (1307?–1376)"). The *CP* adds that the truth more likely was
that **Richard** no longer consider his marriage with **Isabella le Despenser**
to be of any political importance since her father's attainder and
execution. He preferred, instead, to marry the woman with whom he was
living, and the Pope annulled the marriage and "bastardised the issue: a
very unfair proceeding as far as Edmund d'Arundel was concerned."

[1] The *CP*, Arundel section, lists three children as issue of **Richard II**
Copped Hat FitzAlan and **Isabel le Despenser**: the bastardised
Edmund de Arundel (as shown above); **Philippe** (m. **Richard**
Sergeaux (d. 1393)); and **Isabel** (m. **John**, 4th Lord Strange of
Blackmere). However, note that *CP*, Oxford section, pg. 236, states that
Philippe (who m. **Richard Sergeaux**) was in the *CP*, Arundel section,
pg. 244, "wrongly described as **Edmund's** sister." Rather, she was the
daughter of the bastardised **Edmund de Arundel**, who m. **Sibyl**
Montagu.

The *DNB*, "FitzAlan, Richard II, Earl of Arundel and Warenne
(1307?–1376)," states that **Copped Hat** had only issue of a daughter by
his first marriage.

[2] Daniel Williams, ed., *England in the Fifteenth Century: Proceeding*
of the 1986 Harlaxton Symposium, pg. 197, Table "The Salisbury Roll."
Alice FitzAlan, the daughter of **Edmund de Arundel** and **Sibyl**
Montagu, married **Leonard Carew** (b. 1342; d. 1370). **Leonard Carew**
was the son of **John de Carew** (d. 1362) and **Margaret de Mohun**
(daughter of **John, Lord Mohun**) (MacLean, *The Life and Times of Sir*
Peter Carew, Kt., Table in Appendix I).

[3] According to *CP*, Strange or Lestrange (of Blackmere) section,
John Lestrange (b. abt Easter 1332, Whitchurch; d. 12 May 1361)
m. **Mary** (d. 29 Aug 1396) [not **Isabel**], daughter of **Richard FitzAlan**,
Earl of Arundel, by his first wife, **Isabel**, daughter of **Hugh Despenser**,
Lord le Despenser.

Lestrange (b. abt Easter 1332, Whitchurch;
d. 12 May 1361), son of **John Lestrange** (d. 21 Jul
1349), Lord Strange of Blackmere, and his wife
Ankaret Boteler (d. 8 Oct 1361) of Wem, daughter
of **William Boteler** of Wem, Salop.

Eleanor de Clare, as above, wife of **Hugh the younger le
Despenser**, m. (2) abt Jan 1328/1329[1] as his second wife[2]
William la Zouche formerly **de Mortimer** (d. 28 Feb
1336/1337; bur. Tewkesbury Abbey), Lord Zouche, son of
Robert de Mortimer (d. 7 Apr 1287) of Richard's Castle,
co. Hereford, and his wife, **Joyce la Zouche** (daughter of
William la Zouche (d. bef 3 Feb 1271/1272) of King's
Nympton, Devon, and Norton, Northamptonshire[3]).

2 — **Elizabeth de Clare** (b. 16 Sep 1295, Tewkesbury;
d. 4 Nov 1360; will directed burial in the Convent of the
Minoresses without Aldgate, London[4]), third and youngest
daughter; m. (1) at Waltham Abbey, Essex, 30 Sep 1308
John de Burgh (b. abt 1290; d. 18 Jun 1313, Galway),
second but first surviving son of **Richard de Burgh**, Earl
of Ulster.[5] Issue:

3 — **William de Burgh** (b. 13 or 17 Sep 1312; murdered
6 Jun 1333, Le Ford (now Belfast)), 3rd Earl of Ulster;

---

[1] Her first husband was executed in 1326. Even though she may have
been contracted to another man, **Eleanor** was abducted (bef 26 Jan
1328/1329) from Hanley Castle by **William la Zouche de Mortimer**,
who subsequently married her. (*CP*, Zouche or la Zouche section)

[2] **William la Zouche de Mortimer** m. (1) bef 25 Feb 1316/1317
Alice de Toeni (d. bet. 7 Nov 1324 and 8 Jan 1324/1325), widow of
Guy de Beauchamp (d. 10 Aug 1315), Earl of Warwick, and daughter
of **Ralph de Toeni VII**. She was also the widow of **Thomas de
Leyburn** (d. bef 30 May 1307), son of **William Leyburn**, 1st Lord
Leyburn. (*CP*, Zouche or la Zouche section)

[3] *CP*, Zouche section.

[4] *CP*, Ulster section.

[5] *DNB*, "Burgh, Richard de, second Earl of Ulster and fourth Earl of
Connaught (1259?-1326)."

m. abt 1330 as her first husband[1] **Maud** (b. abt 1310;
d. bef 5 May 1377, Campsey Abbey, Suffolk), daughter
of **Henry Plantagenet** (b. 1281; d. 1345), Earl of
Lancaster, and **Maud de Chaworth** (b. 1282; d. bef
3 Dec 1322) (only daughter and heiress of **Patrick
Chaworth** (d. 1283)). Issue (an only daughter and
heir[2]):

> 4 — **Elizabeth de Burgh** (b. 6 Jul 1332, "probably"
> at Carrickfergus Castle; d. 10(?) Dec 1363, Dublin;
> bur. Clare Priory, Suffolk) m. in the Tower of
> London 9 Sep 1342 **Lionel of Antwerp** (b. 29 Nov
> 1338, Antwerp; d. 17 Oct 1368, Alba/Piedmont;
> bur. (1) Pavia, (2) Clare Priory, Suffolk), Duke of
> Clarence, third son of **Edward III, KING OF
> ENGLAND.**

Elizabeth de Clare, as above, wife of **John de Burgh,**
m. (2) nr Bristol "against the King's will and without his
lic."[3] 4 Feb 1315/1316 as his second wife[4] **Theobald de**

---

[1] **Maud** m. (2) bef 8 Aug 1343 **Ralph de Ufford** (d. 9 Apr 1346,
Kilmainham in Ireland; bur. Campsey Priory, Suffolk), brother of
Robert de Ufford (d. 4 Nov 1369), Earl of Suffolk. Their only
daughter, **Maud** (d. 25 Jan 1412), m. **Thomas de Vere** (d. Sep 1371),
8th Earl of Oxford. (*CP*, Ulster section; *CP*, Suffolk section)

[2] *DNB*, "Burgh, William de, sixth Lord of Connaught and third Earl
of Ulster (1312–1332)."

[3] *CP*, Verdun section.

[4] **Theobald de Verdun** m. (1) 29 Jul 1302, Wigmore, co. Hereford,
Maud de Mortimer (d. 17 or 18 Sep 1312, after childbirth; bur. 9 Oct
1312, Croxden Abbey), daughter of **Edmund de Mortimer**
(m. abt 1285; d. 1304) and **Margaret de Fenles/Fiennes** (d. 7 Feb
1333/1334) (daughter of **William de Fenles/Fiennes** (d. 11 Jul 1302,
battle of Courtrai)), and sister of **Roger Mortimer**, 1st Earl of March).
They had issue of three daughters: **Joan de Verdun** (b. 9 or 11 Aug
1303, Wootton, Stanton Lacy, Salop; d. 2 Oct 1334, Alton; bur. 7 or
8 Jan 1334/1335, Croxden Abbey) m. (1) at King's Chapel, Windsor
Park 28 Apr 1317 **John de Montagu** (d. 1317; bur. 14 Aug 1317,
Lincoln Cathedral); no issue; m. (2) 24 Feb 1317/1318 **Thomas de
Furnivalle** (d. Oct 1339); **Elizabeth de Verdun** (b. abt 1306; d. 1 May

(continued...)

Verdun (b. 8 Sep 1278; d. 27 Jul 1316, Alton Castle;
bur. 19 Sep 1316, Croxden Abbey, Staffs). Issue (an only
child/daughter[1]):

   3 — **Isabel de Verdun** (b. born posthumously, 21 Mar
1316/1317, Amesbury, Wiltshire; d. 25 Jul 1349 during
the pestilence) m. bef 20 Feb 1330/1331 **Henry de
Ferrers** (aged 22 and more in March 1324; d. 15 Sep
1343, Groby; bur. Priory of Ulvescroft), Lord Ferrers,
Lord of Groby, son of **William de Ferrers** of Groby
(b. 30 Jan 1271/1272, Yoxall, co. Stafford; d. 20 Mar
1324/1325) and his wife, **Ellen** (liv. 9 Feb 1316/1317)
("said to have been da. of Sir John de Segrave, of
Chacombe, Northamptonshire [Lord Segrave] by his
wife, Christine de Plessy"[2]). Issue[3]:

   4 — **William de Ferrers** (b. 28 Feb 1332/1333,
Newbold Verdon, co. Leicester; d. 8 Jan 1370/1371,
Stebbing) m. (1) bef 25 Apr 1344 **Margaret de
Ufford**,[4] third daughter of **Robert de Ufford**
(b. 9 Aug 1298; d. 4 Nov 1369; bur. Campsey
Priory), Earl of Suffolk, K.G., and his wife,
Margaret de Norwich (d. 2 Apr 1368), and the sister
of **William de Ufford** (d. 15 Feb 1381/1382[5]), Earl
of Suffolk; m. (2) bef 25 May 1368 **Margaret de
Percy** (d. 2 Sep 1375, Gyng (now Buttsbury), Essex;
bur. it is believed in the Church of the Friars

---

   [4] (...continued)
1360) m. bef Jun 1320 **Bartholomew Burghersh** (d. 3 Aug 1355);
Margaret/Margery de Verdun (b. 10 Aug 1310, Alton; d. abt 1377)
m. (1) bef 20 Feb 1326/1327 **William le Blount** (d. bef 3 Oct 1337);
m. (2) **Mark Husee** (d. bef 10 Feb 1345/1346); m. (3) bef 10 Sep 1355
John de Crophull (d. 3 Jul 1383). (*CP*, Verdun section; *DNB*, "Verdon,
Theobald de (1248?–1309)"; *CP*, Mortimer section)
   [1] *CP*, Warwick section; *DNB*, "Verdon, Theobald de (1248?–1309)."
   [2] *CP*, Ferrers section.
   [3] Their son, **William de Ferrers** (d. 1370/1371), mentions his two
sisters in his will. (*CP*, Ferrers section)
   [4] Seen also as **d'Ufford**.
   [5] *CP*, Suffolk section.

Preachers at Chelmsford), daughter of **Henry de Percy** (d. Feb 135.1/1352; bur. Alnwick) of Alnwick, Northumberland, and his wife, **Idoine/Imaine Clifford** (d. 24 Aug 1365; bur. Beverley Minster) (daughter of **Robert de Clifford** and **Maud de Clare**), and widow (no issue) of **Robert d'Umfraville** of Pallethorp and Hessle, co. York, and Stallingborough, co. Lincoln. [1]

4 — **Philippa de Ferrers** (d. "shortly before" 10 Aug 1384) m. bef 1353 **Guy de Beauchamp** (d. 28 Apr 1360 in the lifetime of his father, France; bur. Vendôme, France) of Warwick. [2]

4 — **Elizabeth de Ferrers** (d. 22 or 23 Oct 1375, Ashford, Kent; bur. Ashford, Kent) m. (1) bet 24 Sep 1342 and 1361 **David Dassals** (aged 3 in 1335; d. 10 Oct 1369), Earl of Atholl, "only son and heir" [3]; m. (2) **John Malewayn**.

Elizabeth de Clare, as above, wife of **Theobald de Verdun**, m. (3) bef 3 May 1317 **Roger d'Amory** or **Damory** or **D'Amorie** (d. 13 or 14 Mar 1321/1322, Tutbury Castle; bur. St. Mary's, Warwick [4]). Issue ("only daughter and heir" [5]):

3 — **Elizabeth d'Amory** (b. bef 23 May 1318; liv. 1360, d. bef her husband) m. bef 25 Dec 1327 **John Bardolf** (b. 13 Jan 1311/1312; d. 29 Jul 1363, Assisi, Italy), Lord Bardolf, of Wormegay, Norfolk, [6] son of **Thomas Bardolf** (d. 15 Dec 1328), Lord Bardolf, and

---

[1] *CP*, Ferrers section; Percy section.

[2] Their two daughters died without issue. After her husband's death, **Philippe de Beauchamp** made "a solemn vow of chastity in St. Mary's, Warwick, before the Bishop of Worcester." (*CP*, Warwick section)

[3] *CP*, Atholl section.

[4] *CP*, Damory section, in which is stated that his wife, **Elizabeth**, was buried with him in St. Mary's.

[5] *CP*, Bardolf section.

[6] *CP*, Bardolf section.

Agnes[1] (d. 11 Dec 1357). Issue:

    4 — **William Bardolf** (b. 21 Oct 1349; d. 29 Jan 1385/1386; will directed burial at the Friar Carmelites at Lynn in Norfolk), Lord Bardolf; m. **Agnes Poynings**[2] (d. 12 Jun 1403; bur. Trinity Priory, Aldgate, London), daughter of **Michael Poynings** (d. 7 Mar 1368/1369), Lord Poynings, and his wife, **Joan Rokesley** (d. 16 May 1369[3]) (daughter of **Richard Rokesley**).[4]

2 — **Margaret de Clare** (d. 9 Apr 1342; bur. Queenhithe) m. (betrothed 29 Oct 1307) 1309 **Piers Gaveston**[5] (b. abt 1284; ex. 19 Jun 1312, Blacklow Hill, Warwick; bur. 2 Jan 1314/1315,[6] church of the Friars Preachers (newly founded by **Edward II, KING OF ENGLAND**), King's Langley, Hertfordshire), Earl of Cornwall. Issue (an only child):

    3 — **Joan** (d. 14 Jan 1324/1325, aged 15, Amesbury Priory) was to have married **John de Multon** (b. Oct 1308; d. bef 23 Nov 1334), son of **Thomas de Multon, Lord of Egremont**.[7]

Margaret de Clare, as above, wife of **Piers Gaveston**, m. (2) at Windsor 28 Apr 1317 **Hugh de Audeley** (or **d'Audley**) the younger (d. 10 Nov 1347; bur. Tonbridge

---

[1] The *CP*, Bardolf section, states **Agnes** was probably the daughter of **William de Grandson** of Switzerland.

[2] *DNB*, "Bardolf or Bardolph, Thomas, fifth baron Bardolf (1368–1408)." As his widow, **Agnes Poynings** m. aft 10 Apr 1386 **Thomas Mortimer** (d. bef 9 Jan 1402/1403) (*CP*, Bardolf section).

[3] *CP*, Poynings section.

[4] *CP*, Bardolf section.

[5] **Piers Gaveston** was considered a "favorite" of **Edward II**. He was captured by a group of barons and beheaded.

[6] Chaplais, *Piers Gaveston: Edward II's Adoptive Brother*, pgs. 110–111. According to Hutchinson, *Edward II*, pg. 90, the black friars at Oxford cared for Gaveston's remains until the burial at Langley.

[7] *CP*, Multon of Egremont or Egremond section.

Priory with his wife), [1] Earl of Gloucester; died without
male issue. Issue ("only daughter and heir" [2]):
  3 — **Margaret de Audeley** (d. aft 28 Jan 1347/1348)
  m. bef 6 Jul 1336 [3] as his second wife [4] **Ralph de
  Stafford** (b. 24 Sep 1301; d. 31 Aug 1372;
  bur. Tonbridge, "at the feet of Margaret's parents"),
  Earl of Stafford, a First Founder Knight of the Order of
  the Garter. [5] Issue (two sons and four daughters [6]):
    4 — Four daughters.
    4 — **Ralph de Stafford** (dead in 1347), first son;
    m. 1 Nov 1344 **Maud** [7] (d. 10 Apr 1362), daughter
    of **Henry of Grosment** (d. 24 Mar 1360/1361), Duke
    of Lancaster, and his wife **Isabel de Beaumont** (d.
    1361) (daughter of **Henry de Beaumont** (d. 10 Mar
    1339/1340)). No issue.

---

[1] *DNB*, "Gaveston, Piers, Earl of Cornwall (d. 1312)"; *CP*,
Gloucester section and "Chart Pedigree of the Earls & Dukes of
Gloucester"; *CP*, Stafford section.

[2] *CP*, Gloucester section.

[3] It was on this date a commission was appointed to look into **Hugh
de Audley's** complaint that **Ralph de Stafford** (and probably some of
his relatives) had broken into his home, abducted his daughter, and
married her against his will (*CP*, Stafford section). Harris, *Edward
Stafford: Third Duke of Buckingham, 1478–1521*, pg. 9, states, "In 1336
he abducted and married Margaret, daughter and heiress of Hugh de
Audley, earl of Gloucester." **Margaret** was a "valuable prize" with a
"potential income [which] was worth at least twenty times his own"
(Rawcliffe, *The Staffords, Earls of Stafford and Dukes of Buckingham
1394–1521*, pg. 8).

[4] **Ralph de Stafford** m. (1) abt 1326 or 1327 **Katherine Hastang**,
daughter of **John Hastang** of Chebsey, co. Stafford. (*CP*, Stafford
section)

[5] *CP*, Stafford section.

[6] *DNB*, "Stafford, Ralph de, first Earl of Stafford (1299–1372)";
Rawcliffe, *The Staffords, Earls of Stafford and Dukes of Buckingham
1394–1521*, pg. 9, Table 1.

[7] As widow of **Ralph de Stafford, Maud** m. (2) in the King's
Chapel in Westminster 1352 **William V**, Duke of Bavaria; no issue.
(*CP*, Stafford section)

4 — **Hugh de Stafford** (b. in or bef 1342; d. 16 Oct 1386, Rhodes; bur. Stone), Earl of Stafford, Lord Stafford, Lord Audley, second son; m. bef 1 Mar 1350/1351 **Philippe de Beauchamp** (d. bef 6 Apr 1386; bur. Stone), second daughter of **Thomas de Beauchamp** (d. 13 Nov 1369), Earl of Warwick, K.G., and his wife **Katherine de Mortimer** (d. bet. 4 Aug and 6 Sep 1369) (daughter of **Roger de Mortimer**, 1st Earl of March). Issue is listed for historical interest[1]:

    5 — **Ralph de Stafford** (murdered May 1385; bur. Langley, Hertfordshire). Unm.

    5 — **Thomas de Stafford** (b. in or bef 1368; d. 4 Jul 1392, Westminster; bur. Stone), 3rd Earl of Stafford, Earl of Kent; m. **Anne** (d. 1438), daughter of **Thomas of Woodstock**, Duke of Gloucester.

    5 — **William de Stafford** (b. 21 Sep 1375; d. 6 Apr 1395, Pleshy, Essex; bur. Tonbridge), 4th Earl of Stafford.

    5 — **Edmund de Stafford** (b. 2 Mar 1377/1378; k. 21 Jul 1403, Battle of Shrewsbury; bur. Church of the Austin Friars, Stafford), 5th Earl of Stafford[2]; m. his brother's widow, **Anne** (d. bet. 16 and 24 Oct 1438), daughter of **Thomas of Woodstock**, Duke of Gloucester.

    5 — **Margaret de Stafford** (d. 9 Jun 1396) m. bef 1370 as his first wife **Ralph de Neville** (d. 1425), 1st Earl of Westmorland.

    5 — **Catherine de Stafford** (d. 1419) m. **Michael de la Pole** (d. 8 Apr 1415, Siege of Harfleur; bur. Wingfield), 3rd Earl of Suffolk.

    5 — **Joan de Stafford** (d. 30 Sep or 1 Oct 1442)

---

[1] *DNB*, "Stafford, Ralph de, first Earl of Staffrod (1299–1372)"; *CP*, Stafford section, Suffolk section, Kent section.

[2] **Edmund de Stafford** (d. 1403) was father of **Humphrey de Stafford**, 1st Duke of Buckingham.

m. bef 20 Oct 1392 **Thomas de Holand** (ex. 7 or
8 Jan 1399/1400), Duke of Surrey, Earl of Kent,
son of **Thomas de Holand** (d. 1397), Earl of Kent.
Joan of Acre, as above, wife of **Gilbert de Clare**,
m. (2) "against the will of her father"[1] Jan 1297 as his first
wife[2] **Ralph de Monthermer** (d. bet 6 Feb 1325 and 18 Feb
1326[3]; bur. Grey Friars' church, Salisbury), 1st Baron
Monthermer, Earl of Gloucester. Issue (two sons and a
daughter[4]):

    2 — **Thomas de Monthermer** (b. 4 Oct 1301; k. 24 Jun
1340, Battle of Sluys, in a sea-fight between the English
and French) m. **Margaret** (d. May 1349), "probably the
widow of Henry Teyes"[5] (ex. 1321), Lord Teyes. Issue
(no male issue):

      3 — **Margaret de Monthermer** (b. 14 Oct 1329,
Stokenham; d. 24 Mar 1394/1395[6]), daughter and heir,

---

[1] DNB, "Edward I (1239–1307)." The *CP*, Gloucester section,
reports that **Joan**, when confronted by her father concerning the
marriage, remarked, "It was no disgraceful thing for a great and mighty
earl to marry a poor woman in a lawful union, and so it was neither
blameworthy nor impossible for a countess to advance a capable young
man." On **Joan's** death, **Ralph de Monthermer** "ceased to be an Earl."
Joan's son by her first marriage succeeded to the Earldom.

[2] **Ralph de Monthermer** m. (2) as her second husband **Isabel le
Despenser** (d. 4 or 5 Dec 1334), daughter of **Hugh the elder le
Despenser** (ex. 27 Oct 1326), Earl of Winchester, and **Isabel de
Beauchamp** (d. "shortly before" 30 May 1306) (daughter of **William de
Beauchamp** (d. 1298), Earl of Warwick). **Isabel le Despenser** was the
widow of **John de Hastings** (d. 10 Feb 1313). Her mother, **Isabel de
Beauchamp**, was the widow of **Patrick de Chaworth** of Kidwelly. (*CP*,
Monthermer section, Hasting section; Green, *Lives of the Princesses of
England*, Vol. II, pg. 358)

[3] *CP*, Monthermer section, gives a death date of 5 Apr 1325.

[4] *DNB*, "Monthermer, Ralph de, Earl of Gloucester and Hertford
(d. 1325?)"; *DNB*, "Joan or Joanna of Acre, Countess of Gloucester and
Hertford (1272–1307)." Burke's *Royal Family*, pg. 197, states **Joan** had
two sons and two daughters by **Ralph de Monthermer**.

[5] *CP*, Monthermer section.

[6] *CP*, Monthermer section.

Baroness Monthermer; m. bef end of 1343 **John de Montagu** (b. London; d. 25 Feb or 4 Mar 1389/1390; bur. Salisbury Cathedral), younger son of **William de Montagu** (d. 30 Jan 1343/1344), 1st Earl of Salisbury, and **Katherine Grandison** (d. 1349). Issue (three sons, four daughters[1]):

    4 — **John de Montagu** (ex. 5 Jan 1399/1400, Cirencester; bur. Cirencester[2]), Lord Montagu and Lord Monthermer, 3rd Earl of Salisbury, a First Founder Knight of the Order of the Garter; m. bef 4 May 1383 **Maud Francis** (d. bef 5 Aug 1424; will directed burial at Bisham), daughter of **Adam Francis**, Mayor of London (1339–1340 and 1351), and widow (m. 1373 or 1374) of **John Aubrey** (d. 1380 or 1381) and of **Alan Buxhall** (d. 2 Nov 1381) of Sussex, Dorset and Staffs."[3]

    4 — **Richard de Montagu** (d. Jun 1429). No issue.

    4 — **Thomas de Montagu** (may have been buried in the Cathedral near his father), Dean of Salisbury 1382–1404.

    4 — **Eleanor de Montagu**.

    4 — **Sibyl de Montagu**, a nun; Prioress of Amesbury.

    4 — **Katherine de Montagu**.

    4 — **Margaret de Montagu**, a nun.

2 — **Edward de Monthermer** (d. by 3 Feb 1339/1340; bur. by his mother at Stoke Clare/Austin Friars' church at Clare, Suffolk), his mother's youngest son,[4] "does not seem to have left any heirs."[5] Unm.

2 — **Mary de Monthermer** (liv. 30 Mar 1371) m. (papal

---

[1] *CP*, Montagu section.

[2] "His head, it is said, being sent to London." He was perhaps buried (2) Bisham in 1420 when his widow had license to "remove his bones." (*CP*, Salisbury section)

[3] *CP*, Salisbury section. **John Aubrey** was the son of **Andrew Aubrey**.

[4] Green, *Lives of the Princesses of England*, Vol. II, pg. 359.

[5] *DNB*, "Monthermer, Ralph de, Earl of Gloucester and Hertford (d. 1325?)."

disp. Nov 1307 when she was nine years old) **Duncan** (aged 3 at his father's death; d. 1353, Scotland), Earl of Fife, only son of **Duncan** (murdered 25 Sep 1288, Petpolloch[1]), Earl of Fife, and his wife, **Joan de Clare**, daughter of **Gilbert de Clare**, Earl of Gloucester, by his first wife; no male issue. Issue ("only daughter and heir"[2]):

   3 — **Isabel** or **Elizabeth** (liv. 12 Aug 1389 but died soon afterward without issue), Countess of Fife;
   m. (1) **William Ramsay** (liv. Mar 1359/1360) of Colluthie; m. (2) **Walter Stewart** (liv. 14 Aug 1362), second son of **Robert II**; no issue;
   m. (3) aft 10 Jan 1362/1363 **Thomas Byset** (d. bef 17 Apr 1365) of Upsetlington; no issue;
   m. (4) **John de Dunbar** (d. bef 1371); no issue.[3]

1 — **Margaret** (b. 11 Sep 1275, Windsor Castle; d. 1318,[4] Brussels; bur. Collegiate Church of St. Gudule, Brussels) m. at Westminster Abbey 8 Jul 1290 **John II**, Duke of Brabant ("scarcely three years old" in 1278[5]; d. 27 Oct 1312, castle of Vueren[6]; bur. St. Gudule, Brussels), son of **John I** the Victorious, Duke of Brabant.[7] Issue:

   2 — **John III** the Triumphant (b. 1300; d. 5 Dec 1355), Duke of Brabant; m. 1313 or 1314 **Mary of France** (d. 13 Oct 1325), daughter of **Louis/Lewis**, Count of Evreux. Issue[8]:

---

[1] Murdered by a group which included **Patrick Abernethy**. **Duncan** "was cruel and greedy beyond all that we commonly have seen...." (*CP*, Fife section)

[2] *CP*, Fife section.

[3] *CP*, Fife section.

[4] Green, *Lives of the Princesses of England*, Vol. II, pgs. 363, 400.

[5] Green, *Lives of the Princesses of England*, Vol. II, pg. 366.

[6] DNB, "Edward I (1239–1307)"; Burke's *Royal Family*, pg. 197, gives the death date as 27 Oct 1312; Green, *Lives of the Princesses of England*, Vol. II, pg. 396, gives only the year, 1312, but on pgs. 399–400 gives the further details of the death as stated above.

[7] Green, *Lives of the Princesses of England*, Vol. II, pg. 366.

[8] Anderson, *Royal Genealogies*, Table 355.

3 — **Johanna** (d. 1406) m. (1) **William IV**[1] (d. 1345),
Count of Holland, son of **William III Bonus**[2]
(d. 1337), Count of Holland, Zeeland, and Hainault, and
his wife **Jeanne of Valois/Johanna of France** (d. 1342)
(sister of **Philip VI**, King of France); no issue;
m. (2) 1347 **Wenceslaus** (d. 8 Dec 1384), Duke of
Luxemburg, son of **John**[3] (k. 27 Aug 1346, Battle of
Crecy), King of Bohemia, and his wife, **Elizabeth of
Bohemia** (d. 28 Sep 1330). Issue[4]:

    4 — **John** (d. 1373), Bishop of Strasburg 1366–1371,
    Archbishop of Mentz.

3 — **Mary** (d. 1398) m 1347 **Reinald III** (d. 1371),
Duke of Gelders, son of **Reynald/Reginald II**[5]
(d. 12 Oct 1343, Arnhem[6]), Duke of Gueldres and
Zutphen/Count of Guelderland, and his wife **Eleanor of
Woodstock** (d. 22 Apr 1355) (daughter of **Edward II**,
KING OF ENGLAND).

3 — **Margaret** (d. 1368) m. 1347 **Louis III** (b. 1330;

---

[1] **William IV** (d. 1345) was brother of **Philippa of Hainault**, wife of
Edward III, KING OF ENGLAND.

[2] **William III Bonus's** siblings included **Margaret** (d. 1300), one of
the wives (m. 1298) of **Robert II**, Count of Artois, son of **Robert I**
(d. 1247), Count of Artois (son of **Louis VIII**, King of France).
(Anderson, *Royal Genealogies*, Tables CCCLII and CCCLIV)

[3] **John**, King of Bohemia, was slain in the famous Battle of Crecy,
while fighting against the English. It is **John's** armorial bearings of
ostrich feathers and motto (Ich Dien or I Serve) that the 16-year-old
Prince of Wales took from that battlefield in honor of a valiant fighter.
He adopted them as his own and they remain today as symbols of each
Prince of Wales. (Joelson, *England's Princes of Wales*, pgs. 49–50)

[4] Anderson, *Royal Genealogies*, Table CCCIV.

[5] **Raynald II** m. (1) **Sophia of Malines** (d. 4 May 1329). He was
already the father of four daughters: **Margaret** (d. yng); **Matilda**
m. (1) **Geoffrey**, Count of Henneberg in Upper Saxony, (2) **John**, Earl
of Cleves, (3) **John**, Earl of Blois; **Mary** m. the Earl of Juliers; and
Isabel, Abbess of Graventhal. (Green, *Lives of the Princesses of
England*, Vol. III, pgs. 73, 81)

[6] Green, *Lives of the Princesses of England*, Vol. III, pg. 92.

d. 1383), Count of Flanders. Issue (only child)[1]:
4 — **Margaret** (b. 1350; d. 1405), heiress of
Flanders, was to have married **Philip of Burgundy**
(b. 1345; d. 1361, aged 16, before they were
married); m. 1369 **Philip Audax** (d. 1405), Duke of
Burgundy, son of **John**, King of France.[2]

1 — **Berengaria** (b. 1276, Kennington; d. abt 1279; bur. chapel
of St. Edward, Westminster[3]).

1 — **Mary** (b. 11 Mar 1278, Windsor Castle; d. bef 8 Jul 1332,
Amesbury; bur. Amesbury), a nun at Amesbury.

1 — **Alice** (b. 12 Mar 1279, Woodstock; d. 1291).

1 — **Isabella** (b. 1279; d. 1279).

1 — **Elizabeth Plantagenet** (b. Aug 1282, Rhuddlan Castle,
co. Carnarvon; d. abt 5 May 1316; bur. 23 May 1316,
St. Mary's Chapel, Walden Priory,[4] Essex), eighth daughter,[5]
"the Welshwoman"[6]; m. (1) at Priory Church, Ipswich, 8/
18 Jan 1297[7] **John I**[8] (d. 10 Nov 1299, Haarlem, of
dysentery; bur. Dort), Count of Holland, a descendant of
David I, King of Scots[9]; no issue; m. (2) at Westminster
14 Nov 1302 or perhaps "at Caversham, in Oxfordshire, on the
25th of December"[10] **Humphrey VIII de Bohun**[11]

---

[1] Anderson, *Royal Genealogies*, Table CCCLIV.

[2] Anderson, *Royal Genealogies*, Tables CCCLIV and CCCLVIII.
Margaret and **Philip Audax** were ancestors of the Valesian Dukes of
Burgundy.

[3] Green, *Lives of the Princesses of England*, Vol. II, pg. 402.

[4] "...where the dust of [her second husband's] parents and of many
of the proud line of the De Bohuns lay already interred." (Green, *Lives
of the Princesses of England*, Vol. III, pg. 56)

[5] Green, *Lives of the Princesses of England*, Vol. III, pg. 1

[6] DNB, "Edward I (1239–1307)"; *Ancestral* 6-29.

[7] Green, *Lives of the Princesses of England*, pg. 13, gives the date as
8 Jan. Such ten-day date discrepancies can be caused by the change in
calendars, which was mentioned in the Preface to this book.

[8] Called **John II** of Avesnes, Count of Hainault, by Previté-Orton,
Table 17.

[9] Prestwich, *Edward I*, pg. 575.

[10] Green, *Lives of the Princesses of England*, Vol. III, pg. 37.

(b. abt 1276; k. 16 Mar 1321, **Battle of Boroughbridge**, in Yorkshire; bur. **Church of the Friars Preachers of York**[1]), 4th Earl of Hereford and Essex. Issue (six sons, four daughters[2]):

2 — **Margaret de Bohun** (d. yng 1303; bur. Walden Priory).[3]

2 — **Humphrey** (d. yng 1307(?); bur. Walden Priory).[4]

2 — **John de Bohun** (b. 23 Nov 1306, St. Clements; d. 20 Jan 1335, Kirkby-Thore, co. Westmorland; bur. Abbey of Stratford Langthorne nr London), second son and successor, 5th Earl of Hereford, 4th Earl of Essex; m. (1) 1325 **Alice FitzAlan**, daughter of **Edmund FitzAlan** (ex. without trial 17 Nov 1326, Hereford), Earl of Arundel, and **Alice de Warenne** (d. bef 23 May 1338) (only daughter of **William de Warenne**); no issue[5]; m. (2) **Margaret Basset**, daughter of **Ralph Basset** (d. 25 Feb 1342/1343), Lord Basset of Drayton, and **Joan Grey** (d. 1353) (daughter of **John de Grey**, Lord Grey of Wilton and Ruthin, and **Anne de Ferrers** of Groby); no issue.[6]

2 — **Humphrey de Bohun** (b. abt 1309; d. 15 Oct 1361, Pleshy; bur. church of the Friars Augustine, London[7]), 6th Earl of Hereford and 5th Earl of Essex. No issue. Unm.

2 — **Edward de Bohun** (d. 1334(?), "said to have drowned about Martinmas 1334 in Scotland when trying to rescue

---

[11] (...continued)

[11] *Ancestral* 97-31; Green, *Lives of the Princesses of England*, Vol. III, pg. 37.

[1] "By his will...he desired burial at Walden near the body of his wife Elizabeth...." *CP*, Hereford section.

[2] *DNB*, "Bohun, Humphrey VIII de, fourth Earl of Hereford, and third Earl of Essex (1276–1322)"; Green, *Lives of the Princesses of England*, pgs. 1–59 *passim*.

[3] Green, *Lives of the Princesses of England*, Vol. III, pg. 47.

[4] Green, *Lives of the Princesses of England*, Vol. III, pgs. 49–50.

[5] Addison, *Essex Worthies*, pg. 26, states that both **John** and his brother, **Humphrey**, died without issue.

[6] *CP*, Hereford section; Basset (of Drayton) section.

[7] *CP*, Hereford section.

one of his followers" [1]; bur. Walden Priory), twin with
William; m. **Margaret de Ros**, daughter of **William de
Ros**. No issue.

2 — **William de Bohun** [2] (b. abt 1310 or 1312; d. 16 Sep
1360; bur. Walden Abbey, Essex [3]), fifth son, "twin with
Edward," [4] Earl of Northampton, K.G.; m. (lic. 1335)
Elizabeth de Badlesmere (b. abt 1313; d. 8 Jun 1356; will
directed burial in Black Friars, London [5]), daughter of
Bartholomew de Badlesmere (ex. 14 Apr 1322), sister of
Giles de Badlesmere, and widow of **Edmund de Mortimer**
(d. 1331/1332). Issue:

   3 — **Humphrey IX de Bohun** (b. 25 Mar 1342;
   d. 16 Jan 1372/1373; bur. Walden Abbey), as heir of his
   father and uncle, he became Earl of Hereford, Essex,
   and Northampton; m. aft 9 Sep 1359 **Joan FitzAlan**
   (d. 7 Apr 1419; bur. Walden Abbey), daughter of
   Richard Copped Hat FitzAlan (d. 1375), Earl of
   Arundel, and his wife, **Eleanor Plantagenet** (d. 11 Jan
   1372; bur. Lewes) (daughter of **Henry**, Earl of
   Lancaster, and widow of **John de Beaumont** (d. 25 May
   1342 [6])). No male issue. [7]

      4 — **Eleanor de Bohun** (d. 1399) m. **Thomas of
      Woodstock** (d. 1397), Earl of Buckingham, Duke of
      Gloucester. [8]

---

   [1] *CP*, Hereford section.

   [2] "...the only one of the numerous sons of the Princess Elizabeth
who had any male issue." (Green, *Lives of the Princesses of England*,
pg. 59)

   [3] *DNB*, "Bohun, William de, Earl of Northampton (d. 1360)."

   [4] *CP*, Hereford section.

   [5] *CP*, Northampton section.

   [6] *CP*, Beaumont section.

   [7] *CP*, Northampton section.

   [8] "Of their daughters, the only one to leave issue was Anne, who
m. 1stly, Edmund (Stafford), Earl of Stafford." **Isabel** was a nun in the
House of Minoresses without Aldgate before 9 Aug 1399. **Joan** d. 1399/
1400. (*CP*, Hereford section)

4 — **Mary de Bohun** (d. 1394) m. **Henry IV,** [1]
KING OF ENGLAND.
3 — **Elizabeth de Bohun** (d. 3 Apr 1385; bur. Lewes)
m. abt 28 Sep 1359 [2] as his first wife [3] **Richard
FitzAlan** (ex. 21 Sep 1397, Cheapside; bur. church of
the Augustin Friars, Bread Street, London), Earl of
Arundel, son of **Richard Copped Hat FitzAlan**
(d. 1375). Issue (three sons, four daughters [4]):
     4 — **Thomas FitzAlan** (b. 13 Oct 1381; d. 13 Oct
1415, Arundel, of dysentery contracted at the siege of
Harfleur, "on his birthday, aged 34"; bur. chapel at
Arundel), second son, only surviving son, [5] K.G.;
m. at Lambeth 26 Nov 1405 **Beatrice**, illegitimate
daughter of **John I**, King of Portugal, and his mistress
Inez Perez. No issue. [6]
     4 — **Elizabeth FitzAlan** (aged 40 or more in 1415 [7];
d. 8 Jul 1425) m. (1) bef Dec 1378 **William de
Montagu** (k. 6 Aug 1382 "it is said by his father" at
a tilting match at Windsor [8]), son of **William de
Montagu** (d. 1397), Earl of Salisbury; m. (2) Jul
1384 m. **Thomas Mowbray**, Earl of Nottingham,
Duke of Norfolk (d. 22 Sep 1399, of the plague,
Venice; bur. Abbey of St. George, Venice);
m. (3) bef 19 Aug 1401 **Robert Goushill** of
Hoveringham, Notts; m. (4) bef Jul 1414 **Gerard
Usflete.** [9]

---

[1] He did not become KING OF ENGLAND until after her death. He
m. (2) **Joan of Navarre**.
[2] *CP*, Arundel section.
[3] **Richard III FitzAlan** (d. 1397) m. (2) (no issue) **Philippa de
Mortimer**.
[4] *DNB*, "FitzAlan, Richard III, Earl of Arundel and Surrey
(1346–1397)."
[5] *CP*, Arundel section.
[6] *CP*, Arundel section.
[7] *CP*, Arundel section.
[8] *CP*, Salisbury section.
[9] *CP*, Norfolk section.

4 — **Joan FitzAlan** (b. 1375; aged 40 in 1415;
d. 14 Nov 1435; bur. Black Friars, Hereford)
m. **William de Beauchamp** (d. 8 May 1411;
bur. Black Friars, Hereford), Lord Abergavenny,
fourth son of **Thomas Beauchamp** (d. 13 Nov 1369),
Earl of Warwick, and his wife, **Katherine de
Mortimer** (d. 1369). [1]

4 — **Margaret FitzAlan** (aged 33 in 1415)
m. **Rowland Lenthall.**

4 — **Alice FitzAlan** m. bef Mar 1392 **John Charlton**
(b. 25 Apr 1362; d. 19 Oct 1401), Lord Charlton of
Powys, son of **John Cherleton** (d. 13 Jul 1374), Lord
Cherleton, and his wife **Joan de Stafford** [2]
(d. bef 1397) (daughter of **Ralph de Stafford**
(d. 1372), Earl of Stafford, and **Margaret de Audeley**
(d. 1347)).

2 — **Eneas de Bohun** (bur. Walden Priory).

2 — **Margaret de Bohun** (d. 16 Dec 1391; bur. Exeter
Cathedral), first surviving daughter; m. 11 Aug 1325 **Hugh
de Courtenay** (b. 12 Jul 1303; d. 2 May 1377; bur. Exeter
Cathedral), Earl of Devon. Issue (eight sons, nine
daughters [3]):

3 — **Hugh de Courtenay** (b. 22 Mar 1326/1327;
d. bef 2 Sep 1349; bur. Ford Abbey), first son, a First
Founder Knight of the Order of the Garter; m. bef Sep
1341 **Elizabeth** (d. 23 Sep 1375), said to have been but
probably *not* the daughter of **Guy de Bryan** (d. 1390) of
Tor Bryan, Devon. [4] According to the *CP*, Mowbray

---

[1] *CP*, Warwick section.

[2] **Joan de Stafford** (d. bef 1397) m. (2) bef 16 Nov 1379 **Gilbert
Talbot** (d. 24 Apr 1387). (*CP*, Cherleton section)

[3] *CP*, Devon section, wherein is stated that only three of his
children—**Hugh, Edward,** and **Philip**—had issue; *Peerage and
Baronetage*, Devon section.

[4] *CP*, Devon section. For reference, the *Peerage and Baronetage*
(1907) states that in 1341, **Hugh de Courtenay** m. "Elizabeth, dau. of
Guy Brian, Lord of Tor-Brian, in Devonshire, and sister of the famous

(continued...)

section, he m. **Elizabeth de Vere** (d. Aug or Sep 1375),
daughter of **John de Vere** (d. 23 or 24 Jan 1359/1360),
Earl of Oxford, by his wife, **Maud Badlesmere**
(d. 1366) (daughter of **Bartholomew Badlesmere**
(d. 1322) and sister of **Giles Badlesmere**). Issue ("an
only son"[1]):

4 — **Hugh de Courtenay** (d. 20 Feb 1373/1374)
m. (1) **Margaret de Bryan** (d. "shortly after 1361"),
daughter of **Guy de Bryan**, Lord Bryan of Tor Bryan,
Devon, K.G., "probably by his 1st wife, but certainly
by one antecedent to **Elizabeth [Montagu]**"[2]; no
issue; m. (2) **Maud de Holand**[3] (d. bef 13 Apr
1392), daughter of **Thomas de Holand** (d. 1360), 1st
Earl of Kent, and **Joan the Fair Maid of Kent**
(d. 1385) (daughter of **Edmund of Woodstock**
(d. 1330), Earl of Kent); no issue.

3 — **Thomas de Courtenay** (d. in the lifetime of his
father), Knight of the Shire for Devon.[4]

3 — **Edward de Courtenay** (b. abt 1331/1332;
d. bet 2 Feb 1368 and 1 Apr 1371), third son, of
Goodrington/Godlington; m. in or bef 1346 **Emmeline
Dawnay** (d. 28 Feb/20 Mar 1371), daughter of **John
Dauney** or **Dawnay**, Kt., and **Sybil Treverbin**. Issue:

4 — **Edward de Courtenay** (b. abt 1357; d. 5 Dec

---

[4] (...continued)
Guy, Lord Brian, K.G., standard-bearer to the king at Crecy..." His
only son, **Hugh de Courtenay** (d. 1373/1374) is shown in the same
source as marrying an only wife, **Matilda (Maud)**, daughter of **Thomas
de Holand** and **Joan Plantagenet**. However, note that the *CP*, Devon
section, remarks this **Elizabeth** was confused with her son's first wife,
Margaret de Bryan.

[1] Burke's Peerage, Devon section; Beltz, pg. 54.
[2] *CP*, Devon section.
[3] **Maud de Holand**, as widow of **Hugh de Courtenay**, m. at
Windsor 1380 as his first wife **Waleran de Luxemburg** (d. 19 Apr
1415, Castle of Ivoi, Luxemburg), Count of Ligny and St. Pol. (*CP*,
Devon section)
[4] *Peerage and Baronetage*, Devon section.

1419; bur. "probably" Ford Abbey), Earl of Devon, Earl Marshal, the blind Earl; m. **Maud**, "said to be da. of Thomas (Camoys), Lord Camoys, K.G." [1]

4 — **Hugh de Courtenay** (d. 5 or 6/15 Mar 1424/ 1425) of Haccomb m. (1) (lic. 11 Feb 1392/1393) **Elizabeth Cogan** (aged 8 or more in 1382; d. 29 Oct 1397), [2] only daughter of **William Cogan** (d. 1382) and his second wife, **Isabel Loring** [3]; no issue; m. (2) **Philippa l'Arcedekene**, daughter of **Warin l'Arcedekene** (d. 10 Dec 1400 [4]) and his wife, **Elizabeth Talbot** (aged 24 in 1388; d. 3 Aug 1407) (daughter of **John Talbot** (d. 18 Feb 1374/1375 [5]) of Richard's Castle, co. Hereford). Issue ("an only daughter" [6]):

    5 — **Joan de Courtenay** m. **Nicholas Carew** (d. 1446), Baron Carew and Molesford, son of **Thomas Carew** and his wife, **Elizabeth Bonville** (daughter of **William Bonville** (d. 1407/1408) and **Margaret d'Aumary**); m. (2) **Robert de Vere**. [7]

Hugh de Courtenay, as above, husband of **Philippa l'Arcedekene**, m. (3) **Maud Beaumont**, daughter of **John Beaumont** of Sherwell in Dorset. [8]

3 — **William de Courtenay** (b. abt 1342, St. Martin's parish, Exeter; d. 31 Jul 1396, Maidstone, Kent; bur. Canterbury Cathedral at the feet of the Black Prince and near the shrine of **Thomas Becket** [9]), fourth son,

---

[1] *CP*, Devon section.

[2] **Elizabeth Cogan** was the sister of **John Cogan**, who died without issue in 1382, and the widow of **Fulk FitzWarin** (d. 8 Aug 1391, aged 29). (*CP*, FitzWarin section)

[3] *CP*, FitzWarin section.

[4] *CP*, Talbot section.

[5] *CP*, Talbot section.

[6] *Ancestral* 6-32.

[7] *Ancestral* 28-37, 6-33; *Peerage and Baronetage* (1907), Devon section.

[8] *Peerage and Baronetage*, Devon section.

[9] *DNB*, "Courtenay, William (1342?–1396)."

Bishop of Hereford and London, Archbishop of
Canterbury 1381–1396. No issue.
3 — **John de Courtenay**, Knight of the Shire for Devon.
No issue.
3 — **Philip de Courtenay** (d. 1406) of Powderham
Castle, Devonshire, Lord Lieutenant of Ireland
1383–1393; m. **Anne Wake**, daughter of **Thomas
Wake**. Issue (two sons "with other issue"[1]):
    4 — **Richard de Courtenay** (b. "it is said" at
    Powderham Castle; d. 15 Sep 1415, Harfleur,
    probably of dysentery; bur. Confessor's Chapel,
    Westminster Abbey[2]), Bishop of Norwich.[3]
    4 — **John de Courtenay**.[4]
3 — **Piers/Peter Courtenay** (d. 1409), seventh son,
K.G., "a highly distinguished soldier"[5]; "standard-
bearer to Edward III, constable of Windsor Castle,
governor of Calais, and chamberlain to Richard II."[6]
No issue. Unm.
3 — **Humphrey de Courtenay** (d. yng).
2 — **Eleanor de Bohun** (b. Oct 1304, Knaresborough[7];
d. 7 Oct 1363) m. 1327 **James Butler/Boteler** (b. abt 1305;
d. Jan or Feb 1337/1338; bur. Gowran), 1st Earl of
Ormond, son of **Edmund Butler** (d. 13 Sep 1321) and his
wife, **Joan FitzGerald** (d. bef 2 May 1320) (daughter of
John FitzThomas FitzGerald of Kildare).[8] Issue:
3 — **Pernel Butler** (liv. 28 May 1365; "said to have

---

[1] *Peerage and Baronetage*, Devon section.
[2] *DNB*, "Courtenay, Richard (d. 1415)."
[3] His uncle, **William de Courtenay** (d. 1396), Archbishop of
Canterbury, left him in his will "a number of books in case he should
become a clerk, and his best mitre if he should become a bishop."
(*DNB*, "Courtenay, Richard (d. 1415)")
[4] **John de Courtenay's** son, **Philip de Courtenay** of Powderham,
m. **Elizabeth Hungerford**, daughter of **Walter Hungerford**, K.G.
[5] *CP*, Devon section.
[6] *Peerage and Baronetage* (1907), Devon section.
[7] Green, *Lives of the Princesses of England*, pg. 42.
[8] *Ancestral* 73-31.

d. in 1368") m. (1) bef 8 Sep 1352 as his first wife[1]
Gilbert Talbot (b. abt 1332; d. 24 Apr 1387, perhaps
"of the pestilence at Roales, in Spain"), son of **Richard
Talbot** (b. 1305; d. 23 Oct 1356) and **Elizabeth Comyn**
(b. 1 Nov 1299; d. 20 Nov 1372) (daughter of **John
Comyn**, Lord of Badenoch, and **Joan de Valence**[2]).
Issue:

> 4 — **Richard Talbot** (b. abt 1366; d. 8 or 9 Sep
> 1396, London), Lord Talbot; m. bef 23 Aug 1383
> **Ankaret Strange**[3] (aged 22 in 1383; d. 1 Jun 1413)
> of Blackmere, only daughter of **John Lestrange**, 4th
> Lord Strange of Blackmere, and **Isabel** or **Mary
> FitzAlan** (daughter of **Richard FitzAlan**, 10th Earl of
> Arundel[4]).

3 — **John Butler** (d. inf.).

3 — **James Butler** (b. 4 Oct 1331, Kilkenny; d. 18 Oct
or 6 Nov 1382, Knocktopher castle; bur. church of
Gowran), the Noble Earl, the Chaste Earl, Earl of
Ormond; m. **Elizabeth Darcy** or **d'Arcy**[5] (d. 24 Mar
1389/1390), daughter of **John Darcy** of Knaith. Issue
(three sons and a daughter mentioned in will[6]):

> 4 — **James Butler** (b. aft 1361; d. 6 or 7 Sep 1405,
> Gowran; bur. Gowran), Earl of Ormond;
> m. bef 17 Jun 1386 **Anne de Welles** (liv. 1396),

---

[1] **Gilbert Talbot** m. (2) bef 16 Nov 1379 **Joan de Stafford**
(d. bef 1397), widow of **John Cherleton** (d. 13 Jul 1374), Lord of
Powis, and daughter of **Ralph de Stafford** (d. 1372), 1st Earl of
Stafford, and his second wife, **Margaret de Audeley** (d. aft 28 Jan
1347/1348) (only daughter and heir of **Hugh de Audley** (d. 1347), Earl
of Gloucester). (*CP*, Cherleton section, Gloucester section)

[2] **Joan de Valence** was sister of **Aymer de Valence**, Earl of
Pembroke. (*CP*, Talbot section)

[3] **Ankaret Strange**, as widow of **Richard Talbot**, m. bet 8 Mar and
4 Jul 1401 **Thomas Neville** (d. 14 Mar 1406/1407), Lord Furnivalle.

[4] *CP*, Strange section.

[5] **Elizabeth Darcy** m. (2) bet. 28 Dec 1383 and 30 Mar 1384 **Robert
de Hereford**. (*CP*, Ormond section)

[6] *CP*, Ormond section.

daughter of **John de Welles** (b. 23 Aug 1334,
Bonthorpe, Lincolnshire; d. 11 Oct 1361[1]) and his
wife, **Maud de Ros** (d. 9 Dec 1388) ("probably"
daughter of **William de Ros** (d. 3 Feb 1342/1343[2]),
2nd Lord Ros).
    4 — **Thomas Butler**.
    4 — **Maurice Butler**.
    4 — **Joan Butler** m. **Taig O'Carroll**.
Eleanor de Bohun, as above, wife of **James Butler**
m. (2) bef 20 Apr 1344 **Thomas de Dagworth** (k. 1350,
Brittany). Issue (a "daughter and heir"):
    3 — **Eleanor de Dagworth** (liv. 29 Nov 1375;
    bur. Dunmow Priory) m. (lic. 23 Jun 1362 "to marry in
    the chapel of the manor of Vachery, in Cranley,
    Surrey"[3]) as his first wife[4] **Walter FitzWalter**
    (b. 31 May 1345, Henham; d. 26 Sep 1386, nr Oronse
    in Galicia, Spain), son of **John FitzWalter** (d. 18 Oct
    1361), Lord FitzWalter, and his wife, **Eleanor de Percy**
    (d. bef 18 Oct 1361) (daughter of **Henry de Percy**
    (d. 1351/1352), 2nd Baron Percy of Alnwick, and
    Idoine/Idonea or **Imaine Clifford** (d. 1365)). Issue[5]:
        4 — **Walter FitzWalter** (b. 5 Sep 1368, Henham;

---

[1] *CP*, Welles section. **Anne de Welles** was the sister of **John de Welles** (b. 20 Apr 1352; d. 26 Aug 1421), Lord Welles, and **Margery de Welles**. **Margery** m. (1) **John de Huntingfield** and (2) **Stephen le Scrope**, 2nd Lord Scrope of Masham.

[2] *CP*, Ros section.

[3] *CP*, FitzWalter section.

[4] **Walter FitzWalter** m. (2) bef 27 Jun 1385 **Philippa** (d. 17 Jul 1431; bur. Chapel of St. Nicholas, Westminster Abbey), daughter of **John de Mohun** (d. 15 Sep 1375) of Dunster, Somerset, and his wife, **Joan Burghersh** (d. 4 Oct 1404, bur. Canterbury Cathedral) (daughter of **Bartholomew Burghersh**); no issue; **Philippe** m. (2) bef 13 Nov 1389 **John Golafre** (d. 18 Nov 1396; bur. Royal Chapel, Westminster Abbey); no issue; she m. (3) **Edward**, Duke of York (d. 25 Oct 1415, Battle of Agincourt; will directed burial in the Collegiate Church of Fotheringhay); no issue. (*CP*, Mohun section)

[5] *CP*, FitzWalter section.

d. 16 May 1406, Venice), Lord FitzWalter, second
but first surviving son; m. **Joan Devereux** (d. 10 or
11 May 1409; bur. Dunmow Priory), only daughter of
John Devereux (d. 22 Feb 1392/1393; bur. Church of
the Grey Friars, London[1]) of Dinton,
Buckinghamshire, and his wife, **Margaret de Vere**
(d. 15 Jun 1398; bur. church of the Grey Friars,
London, with her husband) (daughter of **John de Vere**
(d. 23 or 24 Jan 1359/1360), Earl of Oxford, by
Maud de Badlesmere (d. "probably" 24 May 1366),
second daughter of **Bartholomew de Badlesmere**
(ex. 14 Apr 1322[2])).[3]

2 — **Isabella** (b. 5 May 1316, Quenden, Essex; d. May
1316; bur. "in the south wall" of St. Mary's Chapel,
Walden Priory, Essex).[4]

1 — **Beatrice** (b. abt 1286, Aquitaine; d. young).

1 — **Blanche** (b. 1290; d. 1290).

Hubert de Burgh
(d. 1243)
Earl of Kent

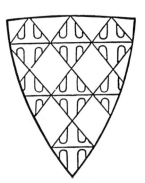

---

[1] *CP*, Devereux section.

[2] He was captured after the battle of Boroughbridge, attainted, and
hung as a traitor. (*CP*, Badlesmere section)

[3] Their son and heir, **Humphrey FitzWalter** (b. 18 Oct 1398;
d. 1 Sep 1415, aged 16), was unmarried. (*CP*. FitzWalter section)

[4] The event "was fatal alike to mother and infant." (Green, *Lives of
the Princesses of England*, Vol. III, pg. 55.

* * *
Issue by Margaret of France

1 — **Thomas of Brotherton** (b. 1 Jun 1300, Brotherton, Yorkshire; d. Aug 1338; bur. Bury St. Edmunds), Earl of Norfolk; m. (1) abt 1316 **Alice Hayles**[1] (d. aft 8 May 1326/in or bef 1330[2]), daughter of **Roger Hayles**, Kt., of Harwich, coroner of Norfolk till 1313. Issue (a son, two daughters):

   2 — **Edward** (b. abt 1319; d. abt 1332/d. bef 13 Sep 1337[3]), his father's only son[4]; m. May or Jun 1328 **Beatrice de Mortimer**[5] (d. 16 Oct 1383/1384), daughter of **Roger de Mortimer** (ex. 29 Nov 1330), 1st Earl of March, and his wife, **Joan de Joinville** (b. 2 Feb 1285/ 1286; d. 19 Oct 1356) (daughter of **Piers de Joinville** of Ludlow, Salop). No issue.

   2 — **Margaret** (b. abt 1320; d. 24 Mar 1399/1400; bur. Carthusian Church/Charterhouse/Grey Friars, London, beside her second husband), on 29 Sep 1397 created Duchess of Norfolk for life, and therefore, as Marshal of England, she was sometimes called **Margaret Marshal**, **Countess Marshal**, or **Countess of Norfolk and Marshal of England**[6]; m. (1) **John de Segrave** (aged 10 at his father's death; d. 20 Mar or 1 Apr 1353; bur. Chacombe

---

[1] Spelled as **Harley** in Packe's *King Edward III*, Table 2. Spelled as **Hales** by Tauté and in *DNB* article, "Thomas of Brotherton, Earl of Norfolk and Marshal of England (1300–1338)."

[2] *CP*, Norfolk section.

[3] *CP*, Norfolk section.

[4] *DNB*, "Thomas of Brotherton, Earl of Norfolk and Marshal of England (1300–1338)."

[5] **Beatrice** m. (2) abt 1334 **Thomas de Braose** (d. 9 or 16 Jun 1361) (or **Brewose** or **Breouse** or **Brewes**), 1st Baron Braose, "brother of her late husband's stepmother," and had issue, including **John de Braose** (d. 3 Feb 1366/1367). (Burke's *Royal Family*, pg. 198; *DNB*, "Thomas of Brotherton, Earl of Norfolk and Marshal of England (1300–1338)"; *CP*, Brewes section, Norfolk section)

[6] The use of these titles "points to *Marshal* being, not the mere designation of an office, but a title of dignity…" (*CP*, Norfolk)

Priory, Northamptonshire), 4th Baron Segrave, Earl of
Norfolk, Marshal of England, son of **Stephen de Segrave**
(d. bef 12 Dec 1325; bur. Chaucombe priory). Issue (no
male issue[1]; only child and heiress[2]):

   3 — **Elizabeth Segrave** (b. 25 Oct 1338, Croxton
Abbey; "she predeceased her husband"[3]), Baroness
Segrave; m. abt 1349[4]/bef 1353[5] **John III de
Mowbray** (b. 25 Jun 1340, Epworth; k. 9 Oct 1368,
"being slain by the Saracens" near Constantinople as he
traveled to the Holy Land[6]) of Axholme, Lincolnshire.
Issue:

     4 — **John IV de Mowbray** (b. 1 Aug 1365, Epworth
in the Isle of Axholme; d. 10 Feb 1383; bur. White
Friars' Church, Fleet Street, London), elder son,
11th Baron Mowbray, Lord Segrave, Earl of
Nottingham.[7] Unm.

     4 — **Thomas I de Mowbray** (b. 22 Mar 1365/1366;
d. 22 Sep 1399 of plague, Venice), 12th Baron
Mowbray, Earl of Nottingham, 1st Duke of Norfolk,
Earl of Norfolk; Earl Marshal of England;
m. (1) **Elizabeth Strange** (d. 23 Aug 1383 "in her
10th year"), Baroness Strange of Blackmere, daughter
of **Roger le Strange** of Blackmere; no issue;
m. (2) Jul 1384 **Elizabeth FitzAlan**[8] (d. 8 Jul
1425[9]), daughter of **Richard FitzAlan** (d. 1397),
Earl of Arundel, and his wife, **Elizabeth de Bohun**

---

[1] *CP*, Segrave section.

[2] *DNB*, "Mowbray, John (II) de, ninth Baron (d. 1361)."

[3] *CP*, Segrave section.

[4] Burke, *Peerage and Baronetage*, 1907, pg. 1214.

[5] *DNB*, "Mowbray, John (II) de, ninth Baron (d. 1361)."

[6] *CP*, Mowbray section.

[7] *CP*, Nottingham section.

  [8] **Elizabeth FitzAlan** m. (3) bef 19 Aug 1401 **Robert Goushill** of
Hoveringham, Notts; m. (4) bef 3 Jul 1414 **Gerard Usflete**. (*CP*,
Norfolk section)

  [9] *DNB*, "Mowbray, Thomas (I), twelfth Baron Mowbray and first
Duke of Norfolk (1366?–1399)."

(daughter of **William de Bohun**, Earl of
Northampton, and widow of **William de Montagu** [1]
(k. "it is said by his father" 1382 at a tilting
tournament at Windsor [2])).
4 — **Eleanor de Mowbray** (b. "shortly before"
25 Mar 1364; perhaps liv. 1399), "eldest daughter";
m. **John de Welles** (b. 20 Apr 1352, Conisholme,
Lincolnshire; d. 26 Aug 1421). [3]
Margaret, as above, wife of **John de Segrave**,
m. (2) bef 30 May 1354 [4]/bef Dec 1355 [5] **Walter Manny/
Mauny** (b. abt 1310; d. 8 or 15 Jan 1371/1372, Great
Chesterford, Essex; bur. Carthusian Church/Charterhouse, [6]
London), 1st Baron Manny, K.G. Issue [7]:
3 — **Thomas de Manny** (d. in the lifetime of his father,
"being drowned in a well at Deptford" [8]).
3 — **Anne de Manny** (b. 1355; d. Apr 1384), only
surviving legitimate child and heir, Baroness Mauny;
m. abt Jul 1368 as his second wife [9] **John Hastings**
(b. 29 Aug 1347, Sutton Valence; d. 16 Apr 1375, bet
Paris and Calais, in Picardy; bur. aft 28 Apr, church of
the Friars Preachers, Hereford), Earl of Pembroke,
K.G., only son of **Laurence Hastings** (d. 1348), 1st Earl
of Pembroke, and his wife, **Agnes de Mortimer**
(daughter of **Roger de Mortimer** (d. 1330), 1st Earl of
March). Issue:

[1] Packe, *King Edward III*, Table 1.
[2] *CP*, Salisbury section.
[3] *CP*, Mowbray section; *CP*, Welles section, wherein (pg. 436,
footnote *a*) is stated that the usual spelling of the name was **Welle**, but
that the 5th Lord, **John** (d. 1421), changed the name to **Welles**.
[4] "...which he had founded." (Burke's *Royal Family*, pg. 198)
[5] *CP*, Mauny section.
[6] "...which he had founded." (Burke's *Royal Family*, pg. 198)
[7] *CP*, Mauny section.
[8] *CP*, Mauny section.
[9] **John Hastings** m. (1) **Margaret** (d. aft 1361), daughter of
Edward III, KING OF ENGLAND. (*DNB*, "Hastings, John, second
Earl of Pembroke (1347–1375)")

4 — **John Hastings** (b. 11 Nov 1372; k. 30 or 31 Dec 1389 while tilting at Woodstock; bur. (1) church of the Friars Preachers, Hereford, (2) in or aft Mar 1391/1392 church of the Friars Minors (Grey Friars), London), 3rd Earl of Pembroke; m. (1) (diss. aft 24 Sep 1383) at Kenilworth 24 Jun 1380 **Elizabeth of Lancaster** (d. 24 Nov 1425; bur. Burford Church, Salop), second daughter of **John of Gaunt** and his first wife, **Blanche**; m. (2) **Philippe de Mortimer**[1] (b. 21 Nov 1375, Ludlow; d. 24 Sep 1401, Halnaker, Sussex; bur. Boxgrove nr Lewes), daughter of **Edmund II de Mortimer** (d. 1381), 3rd Earl of March, and his wife, **Philippe** (daughter of **Lionel of Antwerp**, Duke of Clarence); no issue.[2]

2 — **Alice** (d. bef 16 Nov 1351) m. bef 16 Jan 1339 as his first "and only known"[3] wife, **Edward de Montagu**[4] (b. abt 1304; d. 14 Jul 1361), 1st Baron Montagu. Issue:

3 — **Joan de Montagu** (b. 2 Feb 1348/1349, Bungay, Suffolk; d. bef 12 Jun 1376) m. bef 2 Feb 1362/1363 as his first wife **William de Ufford** (d. 15 Feb 1381/1382, "suddenly, while ascending the steps to the House of Lords"[5]), "the last Earl of Suffolk of his house,"[6] son of **Robert de Ufford** (b. 9 Aug 1298; d. 4 Nov 1369; bur. Campsey Priory) and his wife, **Margaret de Norwich** (d. 2 Apr 1368) (daughter of **Walter de Norwich** (d. 1329) and sister of **John de Norwich**

---

[1] **Philippa de Mortimer** m. (2) as his second wife **Richard FitzAlan** (ex. 21 Sep 1397), Earl of Arundel; m. (3) **Thomas de Poynings** (d. 1428), Lord St. John of Basing. (*CP*, Pembroke section)

[2] Packe, *King Edward III*, Table 1.

[3] *CP*, Brewes section.

[4] **Edward de Montagu** was brother of **William de Montagu** (d. 1343), 1st Earl of Salisbury. (*DNB*, "Thomas of Brotherton, Earl of Norfolk and Marshal of England (1300–1338)")

[5] *CP*, Suffolk section.

[6] *DNB*, "Thomas of Brotherton, Earl of Norfolk and Marshal of England (1300–1338)."

(d. 1362)[1]). Issue (four sons, each of whom died
without issue in his father's lifetime)[2]:

4 — **Robert de Ufford** (d. abt 1 Aug 1375[3]), first
son; m. abt 28 Oct 1371 **Eleanor FitzAlan**
(d. abt 1 Aug 1375), daughter of **Richard III
FitzAlan** (d. 1397), Earl of Arundel, and his first
wife **Elizabeth de Bohun**.[4]

4 — **Thomas de Ufford** (d. yng).

4 — **William de Ufford** (d. yng).

4 — **Edward de Ufford** (d. yng).

4 — **Margaret de Ufford** (d. yng).

3 — **Elizabeth de Montagu** m. **Walter de Ufford**, son
of **Robert de Ufford** (b. 9 Aug 1298; d. 4 Nov 1369;
bur. Campsey Priory) and his wife, **Margaret de
Norwich** (d. 2 Apr 1368) (daughter of **Walter de
Norwich** (d. 1329) and sister of **John de Norwich**), and
brother of **William de Ufford** (d. 1381), Earl of
Suffolk.[5]

3 — **Margaret de Montagu** (d. without issue in the
lifetime of her father).

3 — **Maud de Montagu**, a nun.[6]

Thomas of Brotherton, as above, m. (2) abt 1328 **Mary de
Brewes** (d. bet. 17 Apr 1361 and 15 Jun 1362), daughter of
Piers de Brewes or **Brewose** of Tetbury, widow of **Ralph de
Cobham**, Lord Cobham (d. Feb 1325/1326), and sister of

---

[1] *CP*, Suffolk section; *CP*, Norwich section.

[2] *DNB*, "Thomas of Brotherton, Earl of Norfolk and Marshal of
England (1300–1338)"; *CP*, Suffolk section, Ufford section.

[3] The *CP*, Ufford section, surmises that "some terrible tragedy" such
as the plague befell the family at this time and took the lives of his wife,
his three young sons, his daughter, his brother, and his uncle.

[4] *CP*, Suffolk section.

[5] *CP*, Suffolk section. *CP*, Brewes section, mentions a **John de
Brewose** or **Breouse** (d. 3 Feb 1366/1367) who contracted
marriage 15 Jan 1360/1361 with **Elizabeth**, daughter of **Edward
Montagu**, Lord Montagu, and his second wife, "whose name is
unknown." This **Elizabeth** d. bef 29 Nov 1361 "when yet a child."

[6] *CP*, Brewes section, footnote to John de Brewose or Breouse.

Thomas de Brewes, Lord Brewes[1]; no surviving issue.

1 — **Edmund of Woodstock** (b. 5 Aug 1301, Woodstock; ex. 19 Mar 1329/1330, Winchester; bur. (1) Church of the Friars Minors, Winchester, (2) Westminster Abbey[2]), Earl of Kent, youngest son of **Edward I**; m. Dec 1325 **Margaret Wake** (b. abt 1299; d. 29 Sep 1349), Baroness Wake,[3] only daughter of **John Wake** (b. prob. 1268; d. "shortly before" 10 Apr 1300[4]), 1st Baron Wake of Lyddel, widow (no issue) of **John Comyn** (k. 24 Jun 1314, Battle of Bannockburn), Lord of Badenoch, and sister and heir of **Thomas Wake** (b. abt 20 Mar 1297/1298; d. without issue 31 May 1349), 2nd Baron Wake. Issue (two sons, two daughters[5]):

  2 — **Edmund** (b. abt 1326/1327; d. 5 Jan 1333/bef 5 Oct 1331,[6] aged about 5), 2nd Earl of Kent.

  2 — **Margaret** m. **Amanco**, Seigneur d'Albret, eldest son of the Lord d'Albret in Gascony.[7] No issue.

  2 — **John** (b. 7 Apr 1330, Arundel Castle, Sussex; d. 26 or 27 Dec 1352; bur. Church of the Grey Friars at Winchester), Earl of Kent; m. abt 1352 as her first husband[8] **Elizabeth** (d. 6 Jun 1411; bur. Grey Friars, Winchester[9]), daughter of **Wilhelm V**, Margrave of Juliers/Duke of Jülich, and his wife, **Jeanne** (daughter of **Guillaume I** or **III**, Count of Hainault and Holland, and

---

[1] *CP*, Norfolk section.

[2] *CP*, Kent section.

[3] *DNB*, "Edmund of Woodstock, Earl of Kent (1301–1330)"; *CP*, Wake section.

[4] *CP*, Wake section.

[5] *DNB*, "Edmund of Woodstock, Earl of Kent (1301–1330)."

[6] *CP*, Kent section.

[7] Tauté; *DNB*, "Edmund of Woodstock, Earl of Kent (1301–1330)."

[8] **Elizabeth** m. (2) at Wingham in Kent 29 Sep 1360 **Eustace d'Aubrécicourt** (d. 1 Dec 1372, Evreux), who was, "almost certainly, brother of **Sanchet** (a First Founder of the Order of the Garter) and **Nicholas d'Aubrécicourt**." (*CP*, Kent section; Beltz, *Memorials of the Most Noble Order of the Garter*, pg. 90)

[9] Her will directed burial with her husband, **John**, Earl of Kent. (*CP*, Kent section)

sister of **Edward I's Queen Philippa**). No issue.
2 — **Joan the Fair Maid of Kent** (b. 29 Sep 1328;
d. 8 Aug 1385, Wallingford Castle, Berkshire; bur. Church
of the Grey Friars, Stamford, Lincolnshire), Countess of
Kent, Baroness Woodstock, Baroness Wake;
m. (1) bef 1347[1] **Thomas de Holand** (d. 26 or 28 Dec
1360, Normandy; bur. Church of the Grey Friars,
Stamford), 1st Earl of Kent, Baron Wake, a First Founder
Knight of the Order of the Garter,[2] son of **Robert de
Holand** (d. 7 Oct 1328; believed bur. Grey Friars' Church
at Preston, Lancashire[3]) of Upholland, co. Lancashire. and
his wife, **Maud la Zouche** (d. 31 May 1349; bur. Brackley)
(second daughter of **Alan la Zouche**, Lord Zouche of
Ashby, co. Leicester); m. (2) bef 15 Oct 1348 (annulled
13 Nov 1349[4]) as his first wife **William de Montagu**, 2nd
Earl of Salisbury (d. 3 Jun 1397), K.G.; m. (3) **Thomas de
Holand**, her first husband. Issue[5] by **Thomas de Holand**
(three sons, two daughters):
3 — **Thomas de Holand** (b. 1350; d. 25 Apr 1397;
bur. Brune Abbey/Abbey of Bourne, co. Lincoln), 2nd
Earl of Kent, Lord Holland, Lord Wake, Lord

---

[1] According to the *CP*, Wake section, **Joan** and **Thomas de Holand**
were married before 1339.

[2] "No less than seven members of this family were Knights of the
Garter." **Thomas de Holand's** younger brother, **Otes Holand** (d. 1359),
was also a First Founder Knight of the Order of the Garter. Others were
Thomas de Holand, 2nd Earl of Kent; **John de Holand** (ex. 9 or 10 Jan
1399/1400), son of the 1st Earl of Kent, Earl of Huntingdon and Duke
of Exeter; **Thomas de Holand**, 3rd Earl of Kent and Duke of Surrey;
Edmund de Holand, 4th Earl of Kent; and **John de Holand** (d. 5 Aug
1447), Duke of Exeter. (*CP*, Kent section)

[3] *CP*, Holand section.

[4] **Thomas de Holand** fought at the Battle of Crécy 26 Aug 1346.
"About 1346, during his absence abroad, Joan his wife went through a
form of marriage (possibly under compulsion) with William (Montagu),
Earl of Salisbury." On 17 Nov 1349, the Pope ordered that **Joan** should
be restored to her lawful husband. (*CP*, Kent section)

[5] *DNB*, Holland articles.

Woodstock; m. aft 10 Apr 1364/1366 **Alice FitzAlan**
(b. abt 1350; d. 17 Mar 1415/1416), daughter of
Richard II Copped Hat FitzAlan (d. 1375/1376), Earl
of Arundel, and his second wife, **Eleanor Plantagenet**
(d. 1372) (daughter of **Henry**, Earl of Lancaster, and
Maud de Chaworth). Issue (two sons, five daughters[1]):

4 — **Thomas de Holand** (b. 1374; ex. 7 or 8 Jan
1400; bur. (1) Abbey of Cirencester, (2) aft 11 Jul
1412 Mountgrace Abbey, which he had founded),
eldest son, 3rd Earl of Kent, Duke of Surrey, K.G.;
m. **Joan Stafford** (d. 30 Sep or 1 Oct 1442), daughter
of **Hugh de Stafford** (d. 16 Oct 1386), Earl of
Stafford, and his wife **Philippa de Beauchamp**
(d. bef 6 Apr 1386). No issue.

4 — **John Holand** (d. yng).

4 — **Thomas Holand** (d. yng).

4 — **Elizabeth Holand** (d. 4 Jan 1422/1423;
bur. Greyfriars, London) m. **John Neville** (b. in or
bef 1387; d. bef 20 May 1420), son of **Ralph Neville**
(d. 1425), 1st Earl of Westmorland.

4 — **Margaret de Holand**[2] (d. 30 Dec 1429)
m. (1) bef 28 Sep 1397 **John Beaufort** (d. 16 Mar
1410), 1st Earl of Somerset, son of **John of Gaunt**;
m. (2) **Thomas Plantagenet** (b. 1388 Kenilworth;
k. 22 Mar 1421, Battle of Baugé), Duke of Clarence,
K.G.[3]; no issue by second marriage.

4 — **Eleanor de Holand** (d. 6 or 18 Oct 1405/23 Oct
1405[4]) m. (1) abt 1388 **Roger VI de Mortimer**
(d. 15 Aug/20 Jul[5] 1398), Earl of March and

---

[1] Ramsay, *Lancaster and York*, Vol. I, Table IV, lists more than the
seven, including the children who died young.

[2] **Margaret de Holand** and **John Beaufort** were parents of **Joan
Beaufort**, Queen of Scots.

[3] *Ancestral* 47-33.

[4] *CP*, March section, states she died 6 or 18 Oct 1405; *CP*,
Cherleton section states that she died in childbed 23 Oct 1405.

[5] *CP*, March section.

Ulster.[1] Issue is listed in chapter, "Edward III."
Eleanor de Holand, as above, wife of **Roger VI
Mortimer**, m. (2) Jun 1399 as his first wife **Edward
Cherleton** (aged 30 in 1401; d. 14 Mar 1420/1421),
Lord Cherleton, of Powis,[2] son of **John Cherleton**
(d. 13 Jul 1374), Lord of Powis, and **Joan de
Stafford**[3] (d. bef 1397) (daughter of **Ralph de
Stafford** and **Margaret d'Audley**). Issue listed for
historical interest (two daughters[4]):

    5 — **Joan Cherleton** (b. abt 1400) m. **John Grey,
K. G.**, Earl of Tankerville in Normandy.

    5 — **Joyce Cherleton** (b. abt 1403; d. 22 Sep
1446) m. as his second wife **John Tiptoft**
(d. 27 Jan 1442/1443), 1st Lord Tiptoft.

4 — **Eleanor de Holand**, "2nd dau. of the name, 5th
child"[5]/"3rd da."[6]; m. on or bef 23 May 1399 as
his first wife[7] **Thomas de Montagu** (b. 1388;
d. 3 Nov 1428), Earl of Salisbury.

4 — **Joan de Holand** (d. 12 Apr 1434) m. (1) 1395
Edmund (d. 1 Aug 1402, Langley; bur. church of the
Dominicans, Langley), Duke of York; m. (2)
bef Aug 9 1404 as his second wife **William
Willoughby d'Eresby** (d. 4 Dec 1409); m. (3) license

---

[1] They were parents of **Edmund IV de Mortimer** (b. 6 Nov 1391,
New Forest; d. 1425), 5th Earl of March, 3rd Earl of Ulster; m. **Anne
Stafford** (d. 20 or 24 Sep 1432, Church of St. Katherine by the Tower),
daughter of **Edmund de Stafford** (d. 1403), Earl of Stafford. **Anne
Stafford** m. bef 1427 **John Holand** (d. 1447), Duke of Exeter, Earl of
Huntingdon. (*CP*, March section; *CP*, Stafford section; *CP*, Exeter
section)

[2] Also seen as **Powys** and **Charleton**.

[3] **Joan de Stafford** m. (2) bef 16 Nov 1379 **Gilbert Talbot**
(d. 24 Apr 1387). (*CP*, Cherleton section)

[4] *CP*, Cherleton section.

[5] *Ancestral* 78-34.

[6] *CP*, Salisbury section.

[7] **Thomas de Montacute** m. (2) **Alice Chaucer**, only child of
Thomas Chaucer and **Maud Burghersh**.

6 Sep 1410 "to marry in the chapel of Faxflete, co.
York" as his second wife **Henry le Scrope** (ex. 5 Aug
1415, Southampton), 3rd Baron Scrope of Masham;
no issue; m. (4) bet. Michaelmas 1415 and 27 Apr
1416 as his first wife **Henry Bromflete**, 1st Baron
Vesci/Vessy (d. 16 Jan 1468/1469); no issue.[1]

4 — **Edmund de Holand** (b. 6 Jan 1382/1383;
d. 18 Sep 1408 from wounds received at siege Briant
castle in Brittany), second son, 4th Earl of Kent, Lord
Wake, Lord Woodstock; m. 24 Jan 1406/1407 at
St. Mary Overy, Southwark, **Lucia Visconti**
(d. 14 Apr 1424; bur. Church of the Austin Friars,
London), tenth and youngest daughter of **Barnabo
Visconti**, Lord of Milan, and the sister of **Barnabo
Visconti**, Duke of Milan.[2] No legitimate issue.[3]

4 — **Bridget Holand**, a nun.

3 – **Joan de Holand** (d. Nov 1384, Nantes; bur. Abbey
of Notre Dame de Priéres, Nantes), first daughter;
m. 1366 as his second wife[4] **John the Valiant de
Montfort** (b. "probably in Nov or Dec 1339"[5];
d. 1 Nov 1399, Nantes; bur. Nantes Cathedral), Duke of
Brittany, K.G., only son and heir of **John I de Montfort**
(d. 1345) and his wife, **Jeanne/Joan of Flanders**
(d. abt 1373).[6] No issue.

---

[1] *CP*, York section.

[2] *DNB*, "Holland, Thomas, second Earl of Kent of the Holland
family (1350–1397)."

[3] CP, Kent section.

[4] **John de Montfort** m. (3) at Saillé 11 Sep 1386 **Joan of Navarre**
(d. 2, 9, or 10 Jul 1437, Havering-atte-Bower, Essex; bur. Canterbury
Cathedral), daughter of **Charles II the Bad**, King of Navarre; issue of
nine children. Their great-granddaughter, **Anne of Brittany** (b. 1477;
d. 1514), in 1499 became the second wife of **Louis XII**, King of France.
Joan of Navarre, as widow of **John de Montfort**, married **Henry IV**,
KING OF ENGLAND. (*KQB*, pg. 87; *CP*, Richmond section; Galliou
and Jones, *The Bretons*, Table II)

[5] *CP*, Richmond section.

[6] Galliou and Jones, *The Bretons*, Table II.

3 — **Edmund de Holand**.

3 — **John de Holand**[1] (b. 1352; ex. 9 or 10 Jan 1399/1400, Pleshy Castle, and his head set upon London Bridge; bur. College Church of Pleshey[2]), third son, Earl of Huntingdon, Duke of Exeter; m. at or nr Plymouth 24 Jun 1386 **Elizabeth of Lancaster**[3] (d. 24 Nov 1425; bur. Burford Church, Salop), second daughter of **John of Gaunt** by his first wife, **Blanche**. For issue, see chapter, "The Marriages of John of Gaunt."

3 — **Maud/Matilda de Holand** (d. bef 13 Apr 1392) m. abt 1365 as his second wife[4] **Hugh de Courtenay** (d. 20 Feb 1373/1374), son of **Hugh de Courtenay** (b. 22 Mar 1326/1327; d. bef 2 Sep 1349; bur. Ford

---

[1] About May 1384, **John de Holand** murdered "with circumstances of peculiar atrocity, a Carmelite Friar, who had charged John of Gaunt with high treason." Later, in July 1385, "he slew the Earl of Stafford's eldest son **[Ralph de Stafford]** in the quarrel which ensued between them" and then took sanctuary. The *CP*, Stafford section, states that he killed **Ralph de Stafford** "in revenge for the death of his favorite esquire, who was killed in a quarrel by one of Stafford's archers." Though the king, **Richard II**, promised **Stafford's** father, **Hugh de Stafford** (d. 16 Oct 1386), that he would not pardon the murderer, in February 1385/1386, he did pardon **Holand** (his own half-brother) and returned his possessions to him. **Stafford's** father (who in 1378 had killed **Robert Hawksley** "in the quire of Westminster Abbey") in March 1386 received license to voyage overseas on a pilgrimage to Jerusalem. He died at Rhodes 16 Oct 1386. (*CP*, Exeter section, Stafford section)

[2] *CP*, Exeter section.

[3] **Elizabeth of Lancaster** had been affianced to **John de Hastings**. She m. (3) bef 12 Dec 1400 **John Cornwall** (d. 11 Dec 1443, Ampthill; bur. chapel in the cemetery of the Black Friars by Ludgate), created 17 Jul 1432 Baron of Fownhope, co. Hereford, and 30 Jan 1441/1442 Baron of Millbrook, co. Bedfordshire. He had no surviving legitimate issue; his only son was **John Cornwall** (d. unm. Dec 1421, siege of Meaux, aged 17). (*CP*, Exeter section)

[4] **Hugh de Courtenay** (d. 20 Feb 1373/1374) m. (1) bef May 1361 **Margaret de Bryan** (d. aft 1361), daughter of **Guy de Bryan** (d. 1390) of Tor Bryan, Devon. (*CP*, Devon section)

Abbey) and his wife, **Elizabeth**, and grandson of **Hugh de Courtenay** (d. 2 May 1377), 2nd Earl of Devon; no issue; m. (2) at Windsor 1380 as his first wife **Waleran de Luxemburg** (d. 19 Apr 1415, Castle of Ivoi, Luxemburg), Count of Ligny and St. Pol.[1] There was issue.

Joan the Fair Maid of Kent, as above, m. (3) at Windsor 10 Oct 1361 **Edward the Black Prince** (d. 8 Jun 1376, Westminster Palace; bur. Canterbury Cathedral), Prince of Wales, "her first cousin once removed"[2] and eldest son of **Edward III**, KING OF ENGLAND. For issue, see under **Edward III.**

1 — **Eleanor** (b. 4 May 1306, Winchester; d. 1311, Amesbury, Wiltshire[3]), youngest daughter.

Illegitimate Issue

John de Botetourte (d. 25 Nov 1324), 1st Lord Botetourte, is listed by Tauté and Weis (*Ancestral* 122A-31, 216-29) as an illegitimate son of **Edward I**; Given-Wilson and Curteis (pg. 179) list him as a "doubtful" bastard of the king. He m. **Maud,** daughter of **Thomas Fitz Otes** (b. abt 1231; d. by 28 Mar 1274) and **Beatrice de Beauchamp** (d. abt 1280/1281). **Beatrice de Beauchamp** was a great-granddaughter of **William Longespée,** an illegitimate son of **Henry II** of England.

---

[1] *CP*, Devon section.

[2] Burke's *Royal Family*, pg. 198.

[3] According to Burke's *Royal Family*, **Eleanor** was buried in Beaulieu Abbey, Hampshire, or Westminster Abbey. Fuller's *Worthies*, Vol. II, pg. 40, 1965 reprint, gives her burial in St. Peter's, Westminster. Green, *Lives of the Princesses of England*, Vol. III, pg. 63, states, "her remains were conveyed for interment to the monastery of Beaulieu, in Hampshire."

Edward II
1307–1327
m. Isabella of France

Edward II of Caernarvon the first Prince of Wales,[1] fourth surviving son of **Edward I** and **Eleanor of Castile**; *b.* 25 Apr 1284,[2] Caernarvon Castle; *crowned* 23[3]/24[4]/25[5] Feb 1308, Westminster Abbey; *deposed* 20 Jan 1327; *m.* at Boulogne 25 Jan 1308 **Isabella of France**[6]; *murdered* 21 Sep(?) 1327, Berkeley Castle, Gloucestershire; *bur.* Gloucester Cathedral.

Isabella of France,[7] eldest daughter of **Philip IV**, King of

---

[1] In 1301, royal charters conferred on **Edward II** territory in Wales and in the charter of May 10 referred to him as the Prince of Wales. (Joelson, *England's Princes of Wales*, pg. 35; Palmer, *Princes of Wales*, pg. 9)

[2] Hutchinson, *Edward II*, pg. 5.

[3] Pitkin's *Britain's Kings & Queens*, pg. 10; Burke's *Peerage* (1963), pg. lx.

[4] Burke's *Royal Family*, pg. 198.

[5] *KQB*, pg. 76; Chaplais, *Piers Gaveston*, pg. 42; and King, *Medieval England 1066–1485*, pg. 162. Chaplais adds that the 25th was Sunday.

[6] Hutchinson, *Edward II*, pg. 55, states that **Isabella** was sixteen years old when she was married. *KQB*, pg. 77, and Burke's *Royal Family*, pg. 198, state that **Isabella** was born 1295, making her about thirteen when she was married.

[7] **Isabella of France** was a descendant of **Harold II** (d. 1066), KING OF ENGLAND. See chapter. "Some Genealogy of Harold II."

France,[1] and **Jeanne I**, Queen of Navarre; *b.* 1295, Paris[2]; *crowned* with her husband in Westminster Abbey; *d.* 22 Aug 1358, probably at Castle Rising, Norfolk; *bur.* Grey Friars Church, London.

Ancestors of Isabella of France

```
                           ┌Philip III, King of France (d. 1285)
               ┌Philip IV, King of France (d. 1314)
               │           └Isabella of Aragon (d. 1270/1271)
Isabella of France (d. 1358)
               │           ┌Henry I, King of Navarre (d. 1274)
               └Jeanne of Navarre (d. 1304/1305)
                           └Blanche of Artois (d. 1302)
```

Issue

1 — **Edward III**, KING OF ENGLAND.
1 — **John of Eltham** (b. abt 15/25 Aug 1316, Eltham Palace, Kent; d. 13/14 Sep 1336, Perth in Scotland, killed by his brother the king[3]; bur. Westminster Abbey), Earl of Cornwall; m. Oct 1334 **Mary**, daughter of **Fernando IV**, King of Castile and Leon, and his wife, **Costanza** (daughter of **Diniz**, King of Portugal). No issue.
1 — **Eleanor of Woodstock/Isabella**[4] (b. 8/18[5] Jun 1318, Woodstock; d. 22 Apr 1355, Deventer; bur. "probably" Convent of Deventer, Gueldres[6]) m. at Nimeguen May 1332

---

[1] When **Isabella's** brother died, leaving no heir to the throne of France, her son, **Edward III**, claimed the French throne through his mother and thus began the Hundred Years War.

[2] *KQB*, pg. 77.

[3] *CP*, Cornwall section.

[4] *DNB*, "Edward II of Carnarvon (1284–1327)"; Hutchinson, *Edward II*, pg. 127.

[5] *DNB*, "Edward II of Carnarvon (1284–1327)" states that **Eleanor** was born 8 Jun; *KQB*, 18 Jun; Burke's *Royal Family*, gives the date as 18 Jun.

[6] "Her tomb-stone, which, in the last century was still in existence in the church of Deventer, bore but a single word, as inscription, eulogy, and epitaph, ELEANORA." (Green, *Lives of the Princesses of England*, Vol. III, pg. 96. Note that this source was published in 1851.)

Reynald/Reginald II[1] (d. 12 Oct 1343, Arnhem, from injuries received in a fall; bur. Monastery of Munchausen nr Arnheim or beside his parents in Graventhal, the burial place of the ducal house of Gueldres[2]), Duke of Gueldres and Zutphen/Count of Guelderland. Issue (two sons):

  2 — **Reynald/Reginald III** (b. 13 May 1334; d. 1371), Duke of Gueldres; m. 1347 **Mary** (d. 1398), daughter of **John III** (b. 1300; d. 5 Dec 1355), Duke of Brabant.[3] No issue.[4]

  2 — **Edward** (b. 1336; k. 1371 in battle), Duke of Gueldres; m. 1362 **Catherine** (d. 1400), daughter of **Albert** (d. 1403 or 1404), Count of Holland.[5] No issue.[6]

1 — **Joan of the Tower/Joan Make-Peace**[7] (b. 5 Jul 1321, Tower of London; crowned and anointed with her husband 24 Nov 1331[8]; d. 7 Sep 1362[9]; bur. near her mother in Grey Friars Church (now Christ Church), London) m. at Berwick-on-Tweed 17 Jul 1328 **David II**[10] (d. 22 Feb 1370/1371,

---

[1] **Raynald II** m. (1) **Sophia of Malines** (d. 4 May 1329). He was already the father of four daughters: **Margaret** (d. yng); **Matilda** m. (1) **Geoffrey**, Count of Henneberg in Upper Saxony, (2) **John**, Earl of Cleves, (3) **John**, Earl of Blois; **Mary** m. the Earl of Juliers; and **Isabel**, Abbess of Graventhal. (Green, *Lives of the Princesses of England*, Vol. III, pgs. 73, 81)

[2] Green, *Lives of the Princesses of England*, Vol. III, pg. 92.

[3] Anderson, *Royal Genealogies*, Tables CCCXLIX, CCCLV.

[4] Green, *Lives of the Princesses of England*, Vol. III, pgs. 80, 95.

[5] Anderson, *Royal Genealogies*, Tables CCCXLIX, CCCLII.

[6] Green, *Lives of the Princesses of England*, Vol. III, pgs. 83, 95.

[7] The marriage between **Joan** and **David of Scotland** was designed to bring a cessation to the hostilities between the two countries. (Green, *Lives of the Princesses of England*, Vol. III, pg. 106)

[8] Green, *Lives of the Princesses of England*, Vol. III, pg. 111.

[9] Two death dates have been given for **Joan**, 14 Aug 1362 and 7 Sep 1362, but the more accepted date seems to be the latter. (*DNB*, "Joan (1321-1362), queen of Scotland")

[10] **David** m. (2) "a woman of inferior birth." They were later divorced (Green *Lives of the Princesses of England*, Vol. III, pg. 161). Donaldson, *Scottish Kings*, pg. 35, states that **David's** second wife was **Margaret Logie**.

Edinburgh Castle; bur. Holyrood Abbey[1]), son of **Robert Bruce** (d. 7 Jun 1329, Cardross) and King of Scots. No issue.

Illegitimate Issue of Edward II

1 — **Adam** (b. 1310),[2] about whom almost nothing is known except that he accompanied his father on the 1322 Scottish campaign.

---

[1] **David** was "the last relict of the honoured race of Bruce." His nephew, **Robert**, "the first of the royal race of Stuarts," succeeded. (Green, *Lives of the Princesses of England*, Vol. III, pgs. 161–162)

[2] Given-Wilson and Curteis, pgs. 8, 136.

Edward III
1327–1377
m. Philippa of Hainault

Edward III, son of **Edward II** and **Isabella of France**; *b.* 13 Nov 1312, Windsor Castle; *crowned* 2 Feb 1327, Westminster Abbey; *m.* 24 Jan 1328, York Minster, **Philippa of Hainault**; *d.* 21 Jun 1377, Sheen Palace; *bur.* Westminster Abbey.[1]

Philippa of Hainault, third daughter of **William III Bonus** (d. 7 Jun 1337), Count of Hainault and Holland, and **Jeanne of Valois** (d. 1352), daughter of **Charles** (d. 1325), Count of Valois, and sister of **Philip VI**, King of France[2]; *b.* 24 Jun 1311, Valenciennes; *crowned* 18 Feb 1330,[3] Westminster Abbey; *d.* 14 Aug 1369, Windsor Castle; *bur.* Westminster Abbey.

---

[1] **Charles IV**, King of France, died in 1328, leaving no sons or brothers to succeed him. He had one sister, **Isabella of France**, mother of **Edward III**. Because France's Salic law did not allow a woman to succeed to the throne, **Philip VI**, **Charles'** cousin, succeeded. However, England did not recognize the Salic law, and **Edward III** claimed the throne of France through his mother, thus beginning the Hundred Years' War. (Mowry, *First Steps in the History of England*, pgs. 107–108)

[2] *Ancestral* 1-30, 103-33, 168-62.

[3] *Corrections and Additions to the Dictionary of National Biography*, G. K. Hall & Co., Boston, Mass., 1966. *KQE*, pg. 81, gives March 1330 as the coronation date for **Philippa of Hainault**.

Ancestors of Philippa of Hainault

```
                            ┌John II d'Avesnes (d. 1304)
           ┌William III d'Avesnes (d. 1337)
           │                └Philippa of Luxembourg
Philippa of Hainault (d. 1369)
           │                ┌Charles, Count of Valois (d. 1325)
           └Jeanne of Valois (d. 1352)
                            └Margaret of Naples (d. 1299)
```

Issue

1 — **Edward of Woodstock**, the Black Prince[1] (b. 15 Jun 1330, Woodstock; d. 8 Jun 1376, Palace of Westminster; bur. Canterbury Cathedral),[2] Prince of Wales; m. at Windsor 10 Oct 1361 **Joan** (b. 29 Sep 1328; d. 8 Aug 1385, Wallingford Castle, Berkshire; bur. Stamford, Lincolnshire), the Fair Maid of Kent, Countess of Kent, younger daughter of **Edmund of Woodstock** (ex. 19 Mar 1330), Earl of Kent, son of **Edward I**, and widow of **Thomas de Holand** (d. 1360), 1st Earl of Kent, K.G. Issue[3]:

---

[1] Called the Black Prince because of the black armor he wore or because of his temper (Delderfield, *Kings and Queens of England*, pg. 54). Sedgwick (*The Black Prince*, pg. 27) indicates that the name came about because of his "dreadful deeds in war" but adds that "the name does not appear in recorded history until two hundred years after his death," so a certain explanation may not be forthcoming. Costain, *The Three Edwards*, pg. 252, reminds us that **Edward** wore black armor ("sable mail"— a gift from his father) at the battle of Crécy and that he used black in his heraldic devices. *Edward the Black Prince: His Tomb and Funeral Achievements in Canterbury Cathedral*, a booklet published by Canterbury Cathedral, 1987, states that the name "was probably contemporary and alluded to the colour of the livery worn by his retainers."

[2] Fuller's *Worthies*, Vol. II, 1965, London reprint, pg. 181.

[3] **Edward of Woodstock**, the Black Prince, had an illegitimate son, **John Sounder**, believed to be the child of **Edith de Willesford**. He was "honorably mentioned by [the chronicler] Froissart." A second illegitimate son was **Roger de Clarendon**, who was executed by his cousin, **Henry IV** (Sedgwick, *The Black Prince*, pg. 169). Costain, *The Three Edwards*, pg. 356, states that there was also a daughter ("Historians have ignored her existence") and that records show her to

(continued...)

2 — **Edward of Angoulême** (b. 27 Jan 1365, Angoulême; d. 1372, Bordeaux; bur. Austin Friars, London).

2 — **Richard II** (b. 6 Jan 1367; deposed 29 Sep 1377; d. Feb 1400, probably murdered), KING OF ENGLAND; m. (1) **Anne of Bohemia**; no issue; m. (2) **Isabella of France**; no issue.

1 — **Isabel** (b. 16 Jun 1332, Woodstock; d. bef 7 Oct 1382, London; bur. Grey Friars (Christ Church), London, "at the head of the tomb of [Edward I's] Queen Margaret,"[1] Newgate, London), eldest daughter; m. at Windsor 27 Jul 1365 as his first wife[2] **Enguerrand**[3] **VII le Brun de Coucy** (b. 1340; he was taken prisoner at Nicopolis when the Christian army was defeated by the Turks 28 Sep 1396; d. 18 Feb 1397 of the plague, Bursa, Anatolia; bur. Abbey of Villeneuve nr Soissons[4]), Earl of Bedford, Lord of Coucy, K.G., only son of **Enguerrand VI de Coucy** (d. 1347[5]), Lord of Coucy, and his

---

[3] (...continued)
have been married to "one" **Waleran de Luxemburg**, Count of Ligny and St. Pol; however, little else is known of her.

[1] Green, *Lives of the Princesses of England*, Vol. III, pg. 221.

[2] *DNB*, "Isabella (1332–1379)"; *CP*, Bedford section.
Enguerrand VII le Brun de Coucy m. (2) 1380 **Isabel**, daughter of **Jean I**, Duke of Lorraine, and his first wife **Sophie** (daughter of **Eberhard III**, Count of Wurtemberg). By this second marriage, he had a daughter, **Isabel**, who m. 1409 **Philip of Bungundy** (d. 1415), Count of Nevers.

Green, *Lives of the Princesses of England*, Vol. III, pg. 228, lists four **Ladies de Coucy** living in 1397: **Isabella of Lorraine**, widow (second wife) of **Ingelram VII/Enguerrand VII**; **Mary de Coucy**, eldest daughter of **Ingelram** and **Isabel of England**, and widow of **Henry of Bar**; **Philippa de Coucy**, younger daughter of **Ingelram VII**, Countess of Oxford, Duchess of Ireland; and **Isabella de Coucy**, daughter of **Ingelram VII** by his second wife.

[3] Other versions of this name include **Enguerraud** and **Ingelram**.

[4] Green, in *Lives of the Princesses of England*, Vol. III, pg. 225, states that his heart "was brought back to France and placed in the church of the Celestines, which he had found [in 1390] at Soissons."

[5] *DNB*, "Isabella (1332–1379)."

wife, **Catherine of Austria/Hapsburg** (d. 1349 of the plague[1]) (daughter of **Leopold II** (d. 1327), Duke of Austria, and granddaughter of the Emperor **Albert I**, King of the Romans[2]). Issue (two daughters):

2 — **Mary de Coucy** (b. Apr 1366, Château de Coucy; d. 1404) m. 1393 **Henry** (d. 1397, of the plague[3]), Duke of Bar, son of **Robert**, Duke of Bar. Issue (an "only daughter"[4]):

3 — **Joanna** m. "the heir of Luxembourg."

2 — **Philippa de Coucy** (b. 1367, Eltham; d. Oct 1411; bur. Church of the Grey Friars, London[5]), second daughter; m. on or bef 5 Oct 1376 (div. 1387[6]) as his first wife[7] **Robert de Vere** (d. 1392, Louvain, "from an injury received in a boar hunt"[8]; bur. (1) Louvain; (2) 1395 Earls Colne in England[9]), Earl of Oxford. No issue.

1 — **Joan/Joanna** (b. abt Feb 1335, Woodstock[10]; d. 2 Sep 1348, Bayonne, of the plague[11]; bur. Bayonne Cathedral), second daughter. Unm.

1 — **William of Hatfield** (b. bef 16 Feb 1337, Hatfield,

---

[1] Green, *Lives of the Princesses of England*, Vol. III, pg. 199.

[2] Green, *Lives of the Princesses of England*, Vol. III, pg. 199; *CP*, Bedford section.

[3] Green, *Lives of the Princesses of England*, Vol. III, pg. 225.

[4] Green, *Lives of the Princesses of England*, Vol. III, pg. 226.

[5] *DNB*, "Isabella (1332–1379)."

[6] On 17 Oct 1389, Papal bulls declared the divorce null and void. (*CP*, Oxford section)

[7] **Robert de Vere** m. (2) **Agnes Lancecrone/Landskron/ Lanchecron/Launcecrona**, one of the maidens of the queen's bedchamber, "whom he caused to be abducted and took to live with him in Chester." (*CP*, Oxford section)

[8] *CP*, Oxford section.

[9] **Richard II**, KING OF ENGLAND, and the Archbishop of Canterbury attended the second burial, "but few of the nobility, owing to their hatred of Vere." "The tomb has perished." (*CP*, Oxford section)

[10] *KQB*, pg. 79; Burke's *Royal Family*. Green, *Lives of the Princesses of England*, Vol. III, pg. 229, states that **Joan** was born at the Tower of London toward the end of 1333.

[11] Green, *Lives of the Princesses of England*, Vol. III, pg. 257.

Hertfordshire; d. bef 8 Jul 1337; bur. King's Langley, Hertfordshire).

1 — **Lionel of Antwerp** (b. 29 Nov 1338, Antwerp; d. 17 Oct 1368, Alba/Piedmont; bur. (1) Pavia, (2) Clare Priory, Suffolk), third son, Duke of Clarence; m. (1) in the Tower of London 9 Sep 1342 [1] **Elizabeth de Burgh** (b. 6 Jul 1332, "probably" at Carrickfergus Castle; d. 10(?) Dec 1363, Dublin; bur. Clare Priory, Suffolk), only daughter of **William de Burgh** (d. 1313), 3rd Earl of Ulster. Issue (an "only child" [2]):

   2 — **Philippa** (b. 16 Aug 1355, Eltham Palace, Kent; d. on or bef 7 Jan 1378 or 5 Jan 1381/1382; bur. Wigmore "with almost regal pomp" [3]), only daughter; m. in Queen's Chapel, Reading, abt May 1368 [4] **Edmund II de Mortimer** (b. 1 Feb 1351/1352, Langonith/Llangynwyd/Llangynog/ Llangoed in Llyswen, co. Brecon; d. 27 Dec 1381, Dominican Friary, Cork, "caught cold in crossing a river in winter time"; bur. (1) Dominican Friary, Cork, (2) Wigmore Abbey, [5] Herefordshire), 3rd Earl of March, eldest son of **Roger V de Mortimer** (d. 26 Feb 1359/1360), 2nd Earl of March, and his wife, **Philippa de Montagu** (d. 5 Jan 1381/1382) (daughter of **William de Montagu** (d. 1397), Earl of Salisbury). Issue ("two daughters and two

---

   [1] "In 1352 the actual marriage took place." The title of Clarence was derived from Clare in Suffolk. **Elizabeth** inherited the lordship of Clare from her grandmother, **Elizabeth of Clare**, sister and coheiress of Gilbert of Clare (1291–1314). (*DNB*, "Lionel of Antwerp, Earl of Ulster and Duke of Clarence (1338–1368)")

   [2] *Sureties* 161-18.

   [3] *DNB*, "Mortimer, Edmund (II) de, third Earl of March (1351–1381)."

   [4] Burke's *Royal Family*, pg. 199, gives the marriage date as "*post* 15 Feb 1359.*"

   [5] "According to an Irish chronicle, **Edmund II de Mortimer** was buried in the church of the Holy Trinity at Cork; however, it is believed this refers to only the "more perishable parts of his body." (*DNB*, "Mortimer, Edmund (II) de, third Earl of March (1351–1381)")

sons"[1]):

3 — **Elizabeth de Mortimer** (b. 12 Feb 1370/1371,
Usk; d. 20 Apr 1417[2]), eldest; m. (1) bef 10 Dec
1379[3] **Henry Hotspur Percy** (b. 20 May 1364;
k. 21 Jul 1403, Battle of Shrewsbury; bur. (1) family
chapel at Whitchurch, (2) (?)[4]), eldest son and heir of
Henry de Percy (b. 10 Nov 1341/1342; d. 20 Feb 1407/
1408), 1st Earl of Northumberland. Issue (one son, "a
daughter"):

4 — **Henry de Percy** (b. 3 Feb 1392/1393;
k. 22 May 1455, Battle of St. Albans), 2nd Earl of
Northumberland; m. at Berwick "soon after"
Oct 1414 as her second husband **Eleanor Neville**

---

[1] *CP*, March section. **John Mortimer** (ex. 1423), "sometimes
described as a son of Mortimer's, must, if a son at all, have been
illegitimate. He is not mentioned in March's will." (*DNB*, "Mortimer,
Edmund (II) de, third Earl of March (1351-1381)")

[2] *DNB*, "Percy, Sir Henry, called Hotspur (1364-1403)," suggests
that **Elizabeth** "may be the Isabel Camoyse, wife of Thomas Camoyse
[d. 28 Mar 1421, bur. Trotton], knt., who died in 1444, and was buried
in Friars Minors." However, note that *CP*, Camoys section, specifically
refutes that suggestion, stating, "the Isabel Camoys who was bur. at the
Grey Friars in 1444, was not the widow of Henry Percy (Hotspur), and
of Thomas, Lord Camoys" and adds that "an inquisition taken in 1417
states explicitly that Elizabeth the wife of Thomas Camoys died on
20 Apr. in that year...." According to Burke's *Royal Family*, pg. 199,
Elizabeth Mortimer died abt 1417/1418 and was buried at Trotton,
Sussex. According to the *CP*, Camoys section, **Elizabeth**, widow of
Henry Hotspur Percy, died 20 Apr 1417.

[3] According to Burke's *Royal Family*, pg. 199, they were married
before 1 May 1380.

[4] To prevent insurrections on his behalf, resulting from rumors that
he was still alive, **Hotspur's** body was taken from his place of burial,
"brought back to Shrewsbury, rubbed in salt, and placed erect between
two millstones by the side of the pillory in the open street. After a few
days' exposure, the head was cut off, and sent to be fixed on one of the
gates of York; the quarters were hung above the gates of London,
Bristol, Newcastle, and Chester." (*DNB*, "Percy, Sir Henry, called
Hotspur (1364-1403)")

(d. 1463), widow (no issue) of **Richard le Despenser** (d. 7 Oct 1414) and daughter of **Ralph Neville** (d. 1425), 1st Earl of Westmorland, and his second wife, **Joan Beaufort**.

4 — **Elizabeth Percy** (d. 25 Oct 1437) m. (1) bet. Aug 1403 and Nov 1412 **John de Clifford** (d. 13 Mar 1421/1422, siege of Meaux in France), Lord Clifford, only son and heir of **Thomas de Clifford** (d. 18 Aug 1391 in Germany) and **Elizabeth de Ros** (d. Mar 1424); m. (2) 1426 as his first wife **Ralph Neville** (b. 1408; d. 3 Nov 1484), 2nd Earl of Westmorland. [1]

Elizabeth, as above, wife of **Henry Hotspur Percy**, m. (2) as his second wife[2] **Thomas de Camoys** (d. 28 Mar 1421; bur. Trotton), Lord Camoys, 1st Baron Camoys, K.G.,[3] son and heir of **John de Camoys**.

3 — **Roger VI de Mortimer** (b. 11 Apr 1374,[4] Usk, Monnouthshire; k. 20 Jul 1398,[5] Ireland; bur. Wigmore, Herefordshire), eldest son, second child,

---

[1] *DNB*, "Percy, Sir Henry, called Hotspur (1364-1403)"; *CP*, Clifford section; Westmorland section.

[2] According to *CP*, Camoys section, by his first wife, **Elizabeth**, daughter of **William Louches** of Milton, co. Oxford, **Thomas de Camoys** had **Richard de Camoys** (d. 18 Jun 1426 in the lifetime of his father), who married **Joan Poynings**, daughter of **Richard Poynings**; they were parents of an only surviving son, **Hugh**, who died a minor, and two daughters, **Margaret de Camoys** (m. **Ralph Radmylde**) and **Eleanor de Camoys** (m. **Roger Lewknor**). (*CP*, Camoys section)

[3] Burke's *Royal Family*, pg. 199; *CP*, Camoys section.

[4] *DNB*, "Mortimer, Roger (VI) de, fourth Earl of March and Ulster (1374-1398)." According to Burke's *Royal Family*, pg. 199, **Roger VI de Mortimer** was born 1 Sep 1373 and married to **Eleanor de Holand** abt 7 Oct 1388.

[5] *DNB*, "Mortimer, Sir Edmund III de (1376-1409?)," gives a death date of 15 Aug." According to Burke's *Royal Family*, pg. 199, **Roger VI Mortimer** was "killed in a skirmish with the Irish at Kenis 20 Jul 1398" and was buried at Wigmore. *CP*, March section, also gives the death date as 20 Jul 1398.

4th Earl of March, 7th Earl of Ulster, in Oct 1385[1]
"declared heir to the throne by Richard II,"[2] KING OF
ENGLAND; m. not later than early 1388 as her first
husband[3] **Eleanor de Holand** (b. abt 1373; d. 23 Oct
1405, in childbed), eldest daughter of **Thomas de
Holand** (b. abt 1355; d. 25 Apr 1397), 2nd Earl of Kent,
K.G., (half-brother of **Richard II**, KING OF
ENGLAND), and his wife, **Alice FitzAlan** (d. 17 Mar
1415/1416). Issue ("four children"[4]):

   4 — **Edmund IV de Mortimer** (b. 4/6 Nov 1391, the
New Forest; d. 18/19 Jan 1424/1425, of the plague,
Trim Castle, co. Meath; bur. Austin Friars' Church,
Clare, Suffolk), 5th Earl of March, Earl of Ulster;
m. abt 1415 **Anne Stafford**[5] (d. 20 or 24 Sep 1432;
bur. Church of St. Katherine by the Tower), eldest
daughter of **Edmund Stafford** (d. 1403), 5th Earl of
Stafford, by his wife, **Anne** (d. 1438) (eldest daughter
of **Thomas of Woodstock**, Duke of Gloucester). No
issue.[6]

   4 — **Roger de Mortimer** (b. 24 Mar/23 Apr 1393,

---

[1] *CP*, March section.

[2] *DNB*, "Mortimer, Roger (VI) de, fourth Earl of March and Ulster
(1374-1398)."

[3] **Eleanor de Holand** m. (2) aft 19 Jun 1399 **Edward Charlton/de
Cherleton** (d. 14 Mar 1420/1421), 5th Lord Charlton of Powys/4th
Baron Cherleton of Powys (or Powis), K.G., by whom she had issue.
(*DNB*, "Mortimer, Roger (VI) de, fourth Earl of March and Ulster
(1374-1398)"; Burke's *Royal Family*, pg. 199)

[4] *CP*, March section.

[5] **Anne Stafford** m. (2) **John de Holand** (d. 1447), Earl of
Huntingdon, Duke of Exeter, by whom she had issue. (Burke's *Royal
Family*, pg. 199)

[6] **Edmund IV de Mortimer** succeeded his father as heir to the
throne; however, rather than claim the throne for himself, he was a
staunch supporter of the king. He had no descendants. His sister, **Anne
de Mortimer**, was the grandmother of **Edward IV** and **Richard III**.
According to the Wigmore chronicler, **Edmund IV de Mortimer** was
"devout in the service of God, discreet in worldly affairs, pleasant in
speech, and liberal in giving." (*CP*, March section)

Netherwood; d. abt 1409). No issue. Unm.

4 — **Eleanor de Mortimer** (b. abt 1395; d. 1418)
m. bet 13 May 1406 and 20 Nov 1409 **Edward
Courtenay** (b. abt 1388; d. 1 May 1418/"in or
shortly after Aug. 1418"[1]), K.B., son of **Edward de
Courtenay** (d. 5 Dec 1419), 3rd Earl of Devon, the
blind Earl, and **Maud**, "said to be" the daughter of
Thomas Camoys, Lord Camoys. No issue.

4 — **Anne de Mortimer**[2] (b. 27 Dec 1388/1390;
d. Sep 1411; bur. King's Langley, Hertfordshire.)
m. abt May 1406 as his first wife **Richard of
Cambridge** (b. abt Sep 1376, Conisborough Castle,
Yorkshire; ex. 5/6 Aug 1415,[3] Southampton,
Hampshire; bur. Chapel of God's House,
Southampton), Earl of Cambridge, son of **Edmund of
Langley** (b. 5 Jun 1341, King's Langley,
Hertfordshire; d. 1 Aug 1402, King's Langley,
Hertfordshire), K.G., Earl of Cambridge, Duke of
York.[4]

3 — **Philippa de Mortimer** (b. 21 Nov 1375, Ludlow;
d. 25[5] Sep 1400/24 Sep 1401,[6] Halnaker, Sussex;
bur. Boxgrove priory nr Lewes, Sussex), second

---

[1] *CP*, Devon section.

[2] **Anne de Mortimer** was descended from **Roger IV de Mortimer**
(ex. 1330), who suffered the traitor's death for, among other things, his
complicity in the deposition and murder of **Edward II**, KING OF
ENGLAND. She was the "only child that left issue of Roger, 4th Earl of
March and Earl of Ulster." She was grandmother of **Edward IV** and
Richard III, KINGS OF ENGLAND. (*CP*, York section)

[3] According to the *DNB*, "Richard, Earl of Cambridge (d. 1415),"
Richard was involved in a plot to place his wife's brother, **Edmund IV
de Mortimer**, Earl of March, on the throne.

[4] They had issue of **Richard Plantagenet** and **Isabel of Cambridge**,
who are listed elsewhere in this chapter.

[5] *CP*, Saint John section.

[6] *CP*, Pembroke section, Arundel section.

daughter; m. (1) abt 1385 as his second wife[1] **John Hastings** (b. 11 Nov 1372; d. 30 or 31 Dec 1389, "killed in a tournament at Woodstock"; bur. (1) Friars Preachers at Hereford, (2) church of the Friars Minors (Grey Friars), London[2]), 3rd Earl of Pembroke; no issue; m. (2) bef 15 Aug 1390 as his second wife, **Richard III FitzAlan**,[3] Earl of Arundel (b. 1346; ex. 21 Sep 1397, Cheapside; bur. church of the Austin Friars, London), K.G. Issue:

  4 — One son (d. yng).

Philippa de Mortimer, as above, wife of **Richard III FitzAlan**, m. (3) bef 24 Nov 1399 as his second wife[4] **Thomas Poynings** (d. 7 Mar 1428/1429; will requested burial at Boxwood priory near his wife, **Philippa**), 5th Baron St. John of Basing. No surviving issue.

3 — **Edmund III de Mortimer** (b. 9 Nov 1376,[5] Ludlow; d. 1409, Harlech Castle), "youngest child"; m. abt 1402 **Katherine** (d. bef 1 Dec 1413;

---

[1] **John Hastings** (d. 1389) m. (1) (diss. abt 1383/aft 24 Sep 1383) 24 Jun 1380 **Elizabeth of Lancaster** (d. 1425), daughter of **John of Gaunt** and his first wife, **Blanche of Lancaster**. (*CP*, Pembroke section)

[2] *CP*, March section, Pembroke section.

[3] **Richard III FitzAlan** was a "gallant, hot tempered, popular man" and "one of the best sea-captains of the time." (*CP*, Arundel)

[4] **Thomas Poynings**, Lord St. John of Basing, m. (1) **Joan** (d. 1398(?)), believed to be the daughter of **Roger Strange**, Lord Strange of Knockin. He m. (3) bef Jan 1419/1420 **Maud Mawley** (d. 14 Jun 1453), widow of **John Halsam** (d. 16 Apr 1415) of Coombe, Sussex. *CP*, Saint John section, mentions his issue, but does not identify the wife to which each child belongs.

[5] "Strange portents were said to have occurred at his birth" (*CP*, March section). "At the very moment he came into the world it was believed that the horses in his father's stables were found standing up to their knees in blood." In 1409, he was besieged in Harlech Castle and "perished miserably." His wife and daughters were in the custody of **Henry V**, and by the end of 1413 all were dead. They were buried in the Church of St. Swithin's, London, "at the expense of one pound." (*DNB*, "Mortimer, Sir Edmund (III) de (1376–1409?)")

bur. St. Swithin's Church, London), daughter of **Owen Glendower**, Prince of Wales, by his wife, **Margaret** (daughter of **David Hanmer** of Hanmer, Flint). Issue:

    4 — A son, **Lionel**.
    4 — Three daughters (d. yng).

Lionel of Antwerp, as above, son of **Edward III** and **Philippa of Hainault**, m. (2) at Milan 28 May 1368 **Violante Visconti** [1] (b. abt 1353; d. Nov 1386), daughter of **Galeazzo II**, Duke of Milan, Lord of Milan, and his wife, **Bianca Maria** (daughter of **Aimone**, Count of Savoy). No issue.

1 — **John of Gaunt**. See chapter, "The Marriages of John of Gaunt," for the three generations of his issue.

1 — **Edmund of Langley** (b. 5 Jun 1341, King's Langley, Hertfordshire; d. 1 Aug 1402, King's Langley; bur. (1) by the side of his first wife, Church of the Mendicant Friars, Langley; (2) 1574 King's Langley Church), fifth son, Earl of Cambridge,[2] Duke of York, K.G.; m. (1) at Hertford abt 1 Mar 1372[3] **Isabel of Castile**[4] (d. 3 Nov 1393; bur. Langley[5]), second daughter and co-heiress[6] of **Peter I/Pedro I the Cruel** (b. 30 Aug 1334; k. 23 Mar 1369), King of Castile and Leon 1350–1369, and his mistress (whom

---

[1] **Violante Visconti** m. (2) at Pavia 2 Aug 1377 **Ottone Paleologo** (k. Dec 1378, Langhirano), Marquis of Montferrat; she m. (3) 18 Apr 1381 **Lodovoco Visconti** (d. 1404), Lord of Lodi (Burke's *Royal Family*, pg. 199). **Violante** died without issue (Burke's *Royal Family*, pg. 199; *Sureties* 161-17).

[2] Fuller's *Worthies*, Vol. II, pg. 40, 1965 reprint. *DNB*, "Langley, Edmund de, first Duke of York (1341-1402)," describes **Edmund of Langley** as an "easy-going man of pleasure, who had no care to be a 'lord of great worldly riches.'"

[3] Burke's *Royal Family*, pg. 200. According to *CP*, York section, **Edmund of Langley** and **Isabel** were married between 1 Jan and 30 Apr 1372, "it is said at Hereford Castle."

[4] **Isabel's** sister, **Constance/Constanza**, Queen of Castile, was the second wife of **John of Gaunt**.

[5] According to *CP*, York section, **Isabel** died 23 Dec 1392 and was buried 14 Jan 1392/1393 in the Church of the Dominicans at Langley.

[6] Burke's *Royal Family*, pg. 200, states that **Isabel of Castile** was the third and youngest daughter of **Pedro I**.

he claimed to have secretly wed), **Maria de Padilla**. Issue (two sons, a daughter[1]):

2 — **Edward** (b. 1373, Norwich?; k. 25 Oct 1415, Battle of Agincourt; bur. church at Fotheringhay), Earl of Cambridge, Earl of Rutland, Earl of Cork, Duke of Aumale, 2nd Duke of York; m. (1) at Lisbon "shortly after" Jul 1381 (child-marriage which was annulled) **Beatrice**, daughter of **Ferdinand I**, King of Portugal; m. (2) abt 1398[2] **Philippa de Mohun**[3] (d. 17 Jul 1431; bur. Chapel of St. Nicholas, Westminster Abbey), daughter of **John de Mohun**[4] (b. 1320; d. 15 Sep 1375), 2nd Baron Mohun of Dunster, and his wife, **Joan** (daughter of **Bartholomew Burghersh the elder** (d. 1355), 1st Lord Burghersh). No issue.

2 — **Constance Plantagenet**[5] (b. abt 1374; d. 28 Nov

[1] *DNB*, "Langley, Edmund de, first Duke of York (1341-1402)."

[2] According to the *CP*, York section, **Edward of York** and **Philippa** were married between 27 Feb 1396/1397 and "apparently" 7 Oct 1398.

[3] **Philippa de Mohun** was widow of (1) **Walter FitzWalter** (m. bef 27 Jun 1385 as his second wife; d. 26 Sep 1386, nr Oronse in Galicia), 4th Baron FitzWalter, Lord FitzWalter and (2) **John Golafre/ Golofre** (m. bef 13 Nov 1389; d. 18 Nov 1396; Royal Chapel, Westminster Abbey) of Langley, Oxfordshire, knight of the king's chamber and constable of Wallingford Castle (*CP*, FitzWalter section). She "is said to have" m. (4) **John Vesey** (Burke's *Royal Family*, pg. 201). **Philippa de Mohun's** sister, **Elizabeth de Mohun** (d. 1415), m. **William de Montagu** (d. 1397), 1st Earl of Salisbury. Her other sister, **Matilda de Mohun** (d. bef 1376/20 /Sep 1400), m. **John** (d. 28 Jul 1397), Lord Strange, of Knockin in Shropshire (*DNB*, "Mohun, John de (1320-1375)"; *CP*, Strange section).

[4] **John de Mohun** (d. 1375) was a First Founding Knight of the Order of the Garter. (*CP*, Vol. 2, Appendix B)

[5] **Constance Plantagenet** is described as "a woman of evil reputation" (*DNB*, "Langley, Edmund de, first Duke of York (1341-1402)"). After her husband's death, **Constance** "lived with [**Edmund de Langley**] the Earl of Kent as his wife, and in 1405 accused her brother [**Edward**], the Duke of York, of treason" (*DNB*, "Despenser, Thomas le, Earl of Gloucester (1374-1400)").

1416; bur. 1420 Reading Abbey) m. bef 7 Nov 1379[1]
Thomas le Despenser[2] (b. 22 Sep 1373; ex. 13/16 Jan
1400, Bristol; bur. Tewkesbury Abbey[3]), Lord Despenser,
6th Baron le Despenser, Lord of Glamorgan and
Morgannoc, 1st Earl of Gloucester, K.G., third but first
surviving son of **Edward le Despenser** (b. 24 Mar
1335/1336, Essendine; d. 11 Nov 1375, Llanblethian, co.
Glamorgan; bur. Tewkesbury Abbey[4]) and his wife
(m. bef 2 Aug 1354), **Elizabeth Burghersh** (d. 26 Jul
1409; bur. Tewkesbury Abbey[5]) ("an only daughter" of
Bartholomew Burghersh the younger (d. 1369), Lord
Burghersh[6]). Issue (a son, a daughter[7]):

3 — **Richard le Despenser** (b. 30 Nov 1396; d. 7 Oct
1414, Merton, Surrey, "aged nearly eighteen";
bur. Tewkesbury Abbey), Lord le Despenser;
m. aft. 23 May 1412 as her first husband[8] **Eleanor
Neville** (d. 1463), daughter of **Ralph Neville** (d. 1425),
1st Earl of Westmorland, and his second wife, **Joan de
Beaufort**. No issue.[9]

3 — **Elizabeth** (d. yng; bur. Cardiff).[10]

---

[1] **Thomas le Despenser** and **Constance** were married between
16 Apr 1378 (when "his marriage was granted to the Earl, in order that
he might marry the Earl's daughter") and 14 Jan 1383/1384. (*CP*,
Despenser section)

[2] **Thomas le Despenser** was a descendant of **Edward II's** favorites,
Hugh the elder le Despenser and his son, **Hugh the younger le
Despenser**.

[3] And not, as previously supposed, in the Priory Church at
Abergavenny. (*CP*, Abergavenny section)

[4] *CP*, Despenser section.

[5] She was "aged 27 and more in May 1369." (*CP*, Despenser
section)

[6] *DNB*, "Burghersh, Bartholomew, Lord, the younger (d. 1369)."

[7] *DNB*, "Despenser, Thomas le, Earl of Gloucester (1373–1400)."

[8] **Eleanor Neville** m. (2) **Henry de Percy** (d. 22 May 1455, Battle of
St. Alban's), Earl of Northumberland.

[9] *CP*, Despenser section.

[10] "…according to the Chronicle of Tewkesbury." (*CP*, Despenser
section)

3 — **Isabel le Despenser** (b. 26 Jul 1400, Cardiff;
d. 27 Dec 1439, Friars Minoresses, London; bur. 13 Jan
1439/1440, Tewkesbury[1]), heiress; m. (1) at
Tewkesbury 27 Jul 1411 **Richard de Beauchamp** (b. in
or bef 1397; d. 18 Mar 1421/1422, "mortally wounded"
at the siege of Meaux in France; bur. 25 Apr 1422,
Tewkesbury[2]), Lord Bergavenny, Earl of Worcester and
Lord Abergavenny, son of **William de Beauchamp**
(d. 1411) and his wife, **Joan FitzAlan** (d. 1435)
(daughter of **Richard FitzAlan** (d. 1397) and **Elizabeth
de Bohun** (d. 1385)). Issue (a daughter and heir[3]):
    4 — **Elizabeth de Beauchamp** (b. 16 Sep 1415,
    Hanley Castle, co. Worchester; d. 18 Jun 1448; bur.
    at the Carmelites, Coventry[4]), only daughter,
    Baroness Bergavenny; m. bef 18 Oct 1424 as his first
    wife[5] **Edward Neville** (d. 18 Oct 1476[6]), 1st Baron

---

[1] *CP*, Warwick section, wherein is mentioned an unusual request in
Isabel's will that she be buried in the Abbey of Tewkesbury with a tomb
effigy she describes as "...my Image to be made all naked, and no thyng
on my hede but myn here cast bakwardys." *CP* adds, "It is not known
whether this interesting monument was set up...." Naked, and with her
hair cast backwards, as if over her pillow—naturally this request left
your compiler wondering for many months, until in Hampton's
Memorials of the Wars of the Roses, pg. 69, I read that in 1874–75,
during restoration of the abbey choir, **Isabel's** grave was found. Her
body was wrapped in linen, and her hair, perfectly preserved, was found
to be red-gold.

[2] *CP*, Abergavenny section; Worcester section.

[3] *CP*, Despenser section, Abergavenny section.

[4] *CP*, Abergavenny section.

[5] **Edward Neville** (d. 1476) m. (2) **Catherine Howard** (liv. 29 Jun
1478), "with whom he had cohabited in the lifetime of his 1st wife." She
was daughter of **Robert Howard** (d. 1436) and **Margaret de Mowbray**
(daughter of **Thomas de Mowbray** (d. 1399), Duke of Norfolk). (*CP*,
Abergavenny section; *DNB*, "Neville, Edward (d. 1476), first Baron of
Bergavenny or Abergavenny")

[6] *CP*, Abergavenny section, adds that a monument in the Priory
Church, Abergavenny, once thought to be his, is now thought to be of
an earlier date.

of Bergavenny/Abergavenny, K.G., Lord
Abergavenny, youngest son of **Ralph Neville**
(d. 1425), 1st Earl of Westmorland, and his second
wife, **Joan Beaufort** (daughter of **John of Gaunt** and
Katherine de Roet Swynford).
Isabel le Despenser, as above, wife of **Richard de
Beauchamp** (d. 1422), Earl of Worcester, m. (2) at
Hanley Castle, co. Worcester, 26 Nov 1423 as his
second wife[1] **Richard de Beauchamp**, Earl of Warwick
(b. 25/28 Jan 1381/1382, Salwarpe, co. Worchester;
d. 30 Apr 1439, Rouen; bur. 4 Oct 1439, "in
St. Mary's, Warwick, being afterwards removed to the
Lady Chapel"), cousin of her first husband and son of

---

[6] (...continued)
[6] *CP*, Abergavenny section, adds that a monument in the Priory
Church, Abergavenny, once thought to be his, is now thought to be of
an earlier date.
[1] **Richard de Beauchamp** (b. 28 Jan 1382, Salwarp in
Worcestershire; d. 30 Apr 1439, Rouen; bur. Warwick), 13th Earl of
Warwick; m. (1) **Elizabeth Berkeley** (b. abt 1386; d. 28 Dec 1422;
bur. Kingswood Abbey, co. Gloucester), daughter of **Thomas**, Lord
Berkeley. Issue (three daughters):
1 — **Margaret de Beauchamp** (b. 1404; d. 14 Jun 1467; bur. the Jesus
Chapel of St. Paul's) m. (1) at Warwick Castle 6 Sep 1425 as his second
wife **John Talbot** (b. abt 1384; k. 17 Jul 1453, in France;
bur. St. Alkmund's, Whitchurch, Salop), Earl of Shrewsbury, Earl of
Salop, Earl of Waterford, Hereditary Steward of Ireland, son of **Richard
Talbot** and **Ankaret Strange**. (*CP*, Shrewsbury section)
1 – **Eleanor de Beauchamp** (b. 1407/1408, Wedgenock, co. Warwick;
d. 4–6 Mar 1467/1468) m. (1) **Thomas de Ros** (d. 18 Aug 1430),
9th Baron de Ros; m. (2) bef 1436 **Edmund Beaufort** (b. abt 1406;
k. 22 May 1455, First Battle of St. Albans), Duke of
Somerset; (3) **Walter Rokesley**, Esq. (bur. Croyland, co. Lincoln).
(*Ancestral* 87-34, 1-33; *CP*, Somerset section, Ros section)
1 — **Elizabeth de Beauchamp** (aged 22 in 1439; d. bef 2 Oct 1480))
m. (1) bef Feb 1435/1437 **George Neville** (d. 30 or 31 Dec 1469;
bur. Well, co. York), Lord Latimer, youngest son of **Ralph Neville**
(d. 1425), 1st Earl of Westmorland by his second wife, **Joan Beaufort**;
m. (2) **Thomas Wake** (d. 20 May 1476) of Blisworth, Esq. (*CP*,
Latimer section)

Thomas de Beauchamp (b. abt 1339; d. 1401), 12th Earl of Warwick.[1] Issue ("only son and heir of his mother, by her second husband"[2]):

    4 — **Henry de Beauchamp** (b. 22 Mar 1424/1425, Hanley Castle, co. Worcester; d. 11 Jun 1446, Hanley Castle; bur. Tewkesbury Abbey), Duke of Warwick; m. 1434 **Cecily Neville** (d. 28 Jul 1450; bur. 31 Jul 1450),[3] second daughter of **Richard Neville**, Earl of Salisbury, and his wife, **Alice Montagu** (d. bet. 3 Apr and 9 Dec 1462) (daughter of **Thomas de Montagu** (d. 1428), Earl of Salisbury). No male issue.[4]

    4 — **Anne de Beauchamp** (b. abt Sep 1426, Caversham; d. abt 1490[5]/"shortly before" 20 Sep 1492[6]), Countess of Warwick; m. 1434 **Richard Neville the Kingmaker** (b. 22 Nov 1428; d. 14 Apr 1471, Battle of Barnet; bur. Bisham Abbey, Berkshire), 16th Earl of Warwick, son of **Richard Neville** (ex. 30 Dec 1460, Battle of Wakefield), Earl of Salisbury, and his wife, **Alice de Montagu** (d. bet. 3 Apr and 9 Dec 1462).[7]

  2 — **Richard of Cambridge/Richard of Conisburgh**

---

[1] **Thomas Beauchamp** (d. 1401) and **William Beauchamp** (d. 1411), father of **Isabel's** first husband, were sons of **Thomas Beauchamp** (d. 1369), Earl of Warwick. (Storey, *The End of the House of Lancaster*, pgs. 232–233; *CP*, Warwick section)

[2] *CP*, Despenser section.

[3] **Cecily Neville** (d. 1450) next married (lic. 3 Apr 1449) as his first wife **John Tiptoft** (ex. 18 Oct 1470, Tower Hill), 1st Earl of Worcester. She served as Sheriff of Worcestershire. (*CP*, Worcester section)

[4] **Henry de Beauchamp's** "only child" was **Anne** (b. 13 or 14 Feb 1443/1444, Cardiff; d. 3 Jan 1448/1449, Ewelme, Oxfordshire; bur. Reading Abbey). (*CP*, Despenser section; *DNB*, "Beauchamp, Henry de, Duke of Warwick (1425–1445)")

[5] **Anne de Beauchamp**, wife of the Kingmaker, "is supposed to have died about 1490." (*DNB*, "Neville, Richard, Earl of Warwick and Salisbury 1428–1471), the Kingmaker")

[6] *CP*, Warwick section.

[7] *CP*, Warwick section, Salisbury section.

(b. abt Sep 1375, Conisborough Castle, co. York;
ex. 5 Aug 1415[1]), second son, Earl of Cambridge, eldest
surviving son of **Isabel of Castile** and **Edmund of
Langley**; m. (1) abt May 1406 **Anne de Mortimer**
(b. 27 Dec 1390; d. Sep 1411; bur. King's Langley), elder
daughter of **Roger VI de Mortimer** (d. 20 Jul 1398), 4th
Earl of March, and granddaughter of **Lionel**, Duke of
Clarence, Earl of March.[2] Issue:

> 3 — **Isabel of Cambridge** (b. 1409; d. 2 Oct 1484;
> bur. (1) Beeleigh Abbey, Maldon, Essex, (2) Little
> Easton Church, Essex), only daughter; m. (1) (diss. bef
> 1430) **Thomas Grey** (d. bef 26 Jul 1443) of Heton/of
> Werke; m. (2) bef 25 Apr 1426/abt 1430 **Henry
> Bourchier** (b. 1406[3]; d. 4 Apr 1483, "aged about 79";
> bur. (1) Abbey of Beeleigh/Bylegh by Maldon, (2) Little
> Easton, Essex), Viscount Bourchier, 1st Earl of Essex,
> K.G., son of **William Bourchier** (d. 28 May 1420),
> Count of Eu, and **Anne Plantagenet** (d. 1438) (daughter
> of **Thomas of Woodstock**). Issue (seven sons, one
> daughter[4]):

> > 4 — **William Bourchier** (d. bet. 12 Feb 1482/1483
> > and 4 Apr 1483[5]), eldest son, Viscount Bourchier;

---

[1] **Richard of Cambridge** (also called **Richard of York** or **Richard of Conisborough**) was executed for being involved in a plot to place his wife's brother, **Edmund IV de Mortimer** (d. 1424/1425), Earl of March, on the throne. (*DNB*, "Richard, Earl of Cambridge (d. 1415)"; *DNB*, "Richard, Duke of York (1411–1460)")

[2] **Anne de Mortimer's** grandmother, **Philippa**, Countess of March, was the only daughter and heir of **Lionel**, Duke of Clarence, second surviving son (after **Edward** the Black Prince) of **Edward III**. **Anne de Mortimer** "transmitted to her grandson Edward IV (who, through her, was heir gen. of Edward III), the right to the Crown...."

[3] Ramsay, *Lancaster and York*, Vol. I, Table V.

[4] *CP*, Essex section; *DNB*, "Bourchier, Henry, Earl of Essex (d. 1483)"; Ramsay, *Lancaster and York*, Vol. I, Table V.

[5] *DNB*, "Bourchier, Henry, Earl of Essex (d. 1483)."

m. bef 15 Aug 1467 as her first husband[1] **Anne Woodville** (d. 30 Jul 1489), third daughter of **Richard Woodville** (ex. 12 Aug 1469), Earl Rivers, and **Jacquetta of Luxembourg** (b. 1415; d. 30 May 1472) (daughter of **Peter of Luxembourg**, Count of St. Pol and Conversano), and sister of **Elizabeth Woodville**, queen consort of **Edward IV**, KING OF ENGLAND.

4 — **Henry Bourchier** (d. Aug(?) 1458/bef Dec 1462[2]), second son; m. as her first husband[3] **Elizabeth Scales** (d. 2 Sep 1473), Baroness Scales, daughter and heiress of **Thomas de Scales** (murdered 25 Jul 1460, London), Lord Scales. No issue.

4 — **Humphrey Bourchier** (d. 14 Apr 1471, Battle of Barnet; bur. Westminster Abbey), third son, Lord Cromwell; m. bef 14 Feb 1455/1456 as her first husband[4] **Joan Stanhope** (d. 10 Mar 1490), daughter of **Richard Stanhope** (d. 1436) of Rampston and his second wife, **Maud Cromwell** (only sister of **Ralph Cromwell** (d. 4 Jan 1454/1455; bur. Tattershall),

---

[1] According to the *CP*, Essex section, **Anne Woodville** m. (2) as his first wife **George Grey** (d. 21 Dec 1503), Earl of Kent. According to the *CP*, Bourchier section, **Anne Woodville** m. (2) **Edward Wingfield**; m. (3) **George Grey**.

[2] Ramsay, *Lancaster and York*, Vol. I, Table V.

[3] Hicks, *False, Fleeting, Perjur'd Clarence: George, Duke of Clarence 1449-78*, pgs. 13, 28; *CP*, Rivers section. **Elizabeth Scales** (d. 1473) m. (2) bef 22 Dec 1462 **Anthony Woodville** (d. 25 Jun 1483), 2nd Earl Rivers, brother of **Edward IV's** queen consort, **Elizabeth Woodville**. No issue.

[4] **Joan Stanhope** m. (2) **Robert Radcliffe** of Hunstanton, co. Norfolk. **Joan's** sister, **Maud Stanhope** (d. 30 Aug 1497), m. as his second wife **Robert Willoughby** (d. 25 Jul 1452; bur. Mettingham, Suffolk), Baron Willoughby de Eresby (*DNB*, "Cromwell, Ralph, fourth Baron Cromwell (1394?-1456)"). According to Ramsay, *Lancaster and York*, Vol. I, Table V, and the *CP*, Willoughby de Eresby section, **Joan Stanhope** and her sister were nieces of **Ralph**, 3rd Lord Cromwell, the Treasurer.

Lord Cromwell).[1] No issue.

4 — **John Bourchier** (d. 1495/1485[2]), fourth son;
m. bef 2 May 1462 as her second husband **Elizabeth
Ferrers** (d. abt 23 Jan 1482/1483), widow of **Edward
Grey** (d. 18 Dec 1457), Lord Ferrers of Groby, and
only daughter of **Henry Ferrers** (b. abt 1394, Raglan,
co. Monmouth; d. bef 5 Dec 1463, Berkeley Castle;
bur. Berkeley Church) and **Isabel de Mowbray**
(m. bef time 13 Jul 1416) (d. 23 Sep 1452, Gloucester
Castle, "being then a prisoner there"[3]; bur. Church
of the Grey Friars, Gloucester) (daughter of **Thomas
de Mowbray** (d. 22 Sep 1399, Venice, of the plague),
Duke of Norfolk). No issue.

4 — **Thomas Bourchier** (d. 26 Oct 1491; bur. Ware,
Hertfordshire) m. (1) in or bef 1472 **Isabel Barre**
(d. 1 Mar 1488/1489), daughter of **John Barre** of
Knebworth, Hertfordshire, and widow of **Humphrey
Stafford** (b. 1439; ex. 17 Aug 1469, Bridgwater;
bur. Glastonbury Abbey), Earl of Devon.[4]

---

[1] *CP*, Cromwell section. **Maud's** brother, **Ralph de Cromwell**
(d. 4 Jan 1454/1455), Lord Cromwell, rebuilt the castle of Tattershall in
1440.

[2] Ramsay, *Lancaster and York*, Vol. I, Table V.

[3] *CP*, Ferrers section. **Isabel de Mowbray** m. (2) 1423 or 1424
James de Berkeley (d. Nov 1463), Lord Berkeley, who, as the *CP*
quotes, "may bee called *James the Just.*" Their son, **William de
Berkeley** (d. 14 Feb 1491/1492 in the Sanctuary at Westminster) "may
bee called *William the Wast all.*" (*CP*, Norfolk section, Nottingham
section, Berkeley section)

It seems the descent of the barony of Berkeley was in dispute and
that the granddaughter of the last Lord Berkeley, believing her mother to
be the correct heir, had **Isabel** imprisoned at Gloucester, where she died.
(*CP*, Berkeley section)

[4] Ramsay, *Lancaster and York*, Vol. I, Table V; *CP*, Devon section.
Humphrey Stafford, Earl of Devon and Baron Stafford of Southwick,
was son of **William Stafford** (k. 18 Jun 1450 by the Kentish rebels at
Sevenoaks) of Hook, Dorset, and his wife, **Katherine Chidiock**
(daughter of **John Chidiock**). **Humphrey Stafford** died without
surviving issue.

4 — **Edward Bourchier** (k. 30 Dec 1460, Wakefield).

4 — **Fulke Bourchier** (d. yng).

4 — **Isabel Bourchier** (d. yng).

3 — **Richard Plantagenet/Richard of York** (b. 20/21 Sep 1411/1412; ex. 31 Dec 1460, Battle of Wakefield[1]; bur. (1) Pontefract, (2) 30 Jul 1476 Fotheringhay), Duke of York, Earl of March, Earl of Ulster, Lord Mortimer (of Wigmore,) only son; he assumed the surname Plantagenet[2]; m. abt 1437/1438 or bef 18 Oct 1424 **Cecily Sweet Cis Neville** (b. 3 May 1415, Raby Castle; d. 31 May 1495, Berkhamsted Castle; bur. Fotheringhay), youngest daughter of **Ralph Neville** (d. 1425), 1st Earl of Westmorland, K.G., by his second wife, **Joan Beaufort** (daughter of **John of Gaunt**). Issue[3]:

4 — **Anne Plantagenet** (b. 10/11 Aug 1439, Fotheringhay; d. 14 Jan 1475/1476; bur. St. George's Chapel, Windsor), eldest daughter[4]; m. (1) (div. 12 Nov 1472) bef 30 Jul 1447 **Henry de Holand**[5] (b. 27 Jun 1430, Tower of London; d. Sep 1475, found dead in the English Channel), 2nd Duke of Exeter; no issue; m. (2) 1472/1473 **Thomas**

---

[1] "His head, bearing a crown of paper and straw, being set up on Micklegate Bar, York, but afterwards interred with his body, the whole being exhumed, 24 Jul, and buried with great pomp, 30 Jul 1476, at Fotheringhay." (*CP*, York section)

[2] *DNB*, "Richard, Duke of York (1411–1460)."

[3] Markham, *Richard III: His Life Character*, pg. 6; Johnson, *Duke Richard of York 1411–1460*; Weightman, *Margaret of York, Duchess of Burgundy 1446–1503*, Table 1. Note that these are the siblings of **Edward IV** and **Richard III**, KINGS OF ENGLAND.

[4] **Anne's** dowry of 4,500 marks was one of the largest of that period. (Jones and Underwood, *The King's Mother*, pg. 26)

[5] According to the *CP*, Exeter section, **Henry de Holand** was seriously hurt in the Battle of Barnet (14 Apr 1471) and was "lefte nakede for dede in the felde" until he was discovered and taken to sanctuary at Westminster.

St. Leger, Kt., (ex. 8 Nov 1483, Exeter;
bur. St. George's Chapel, Windsor). Issue (one
daughter):
    5 — **Anne St. Leger**.
4 — **Henry** (b. 10 Feb 1441, Hatfield, Hertfordshire;
d. yng), first son.
4 — **Edward IV** (b. 28 Apr 1442; d. 9 Apr 1483,
Palace of Westminster; bur. St. George's Chapel,
Windsor), KING OF ENGLAND; m. at Grafton
Regis, Northamptonshire, 1 May 1464 as her second
husband[1] **Elizabeth Woodville/Wydeville**
(b. abt 1437, Grafton Regis, Northamptonshire;
d. 8 Jun 1492, Bermondsey Abbey; bur. St. George's
Chapel, Windsor), daughter of **Richard Woodville**
(ex. 12 Aug 1469), 1st Earl Rivers, and **Jacquetta of
Luxembourg** (b. 1415; d. 30 May 1472) and widow
of **John Grey** (k. 1461, Second Battle of
St. Albans).[2]
4 — **Edmund** (b. 17 May 1443, Rouen; ex. 29/
31 Dec 1460 with his father, Battle of Wakefield[3];
bur. (1) Pontefract; (2) 22–29 Jul 1466,
Fotheringhay), Earl of Rutland. Unm.
4 — **Elizabeth** (b. 22 Apr 1444, Rouen; d. aft Jan
1503/1504 or bet. 7 Jan 1502/1503 and May 1504[4];
bur. Wingfield), second daughter; m. 1458/bef Oct
1460[5]/in or bef Aug 1461[6] as his second wife[7]

---

[1] **Elizabeth Woodville** m. (1) **John Grey** (d. 17 Feb 1461, Second
Battle of St. Albans), Baron Grey of Groby, and had issue of two sons.
(*KQB*, pg. 97)

[2] The issue of **Edward IV** and **Elizabeth Woodville** included
Edward V, uncrowned KING OF ENGLAND, and **Richard of York**,
the two princes in the Tower who were believed murdered after the
usurpation of the throne by their uncle, **Richard III**.

[3] "...flying from the field across the bridge at Wakefield, he was
killed by Lord Clifford, and his head, cut from his dead body, was
exposed at York." (*CP*, Rutland section)

[4] *CP*, Suffolk section.

[5] *CP*, Suffolk section.

John de la Pole (b. 27 Sep 1442; d. "between
29 Oct. 1491 and 27 Oct. 1492"[1]; bur. Wingfield),
2nd Duke of Suffolk, son of **William de la Pole**
(b. 16 Oct 1396, Cotton, co. Suffolk; beheaded at sea
2 May 1450), 1st Duke of Suffolk, and his wife **Alice
Chaucer** (d. 20 May 1475, Ewelme) (daughter of
Thomas Chaucer and his wife, **Maud Burghersh**,
and granddaughter of poet **Geoffrey Chaucer**[2]).
Some further generations have been included here for
their historical interest; however, the listing should not
be considered complete. Issue[3]:

    5 — **John de la Pole** (b. abt 1462; k. 16 Jun 1487,
Battle of Stoke), eldest son, Earl of Lincoln, K.B.;
m. (1) **Margaret FitzAlan** (liv. 1493), daughter of
Thomas FitzAlan (d. 25 Oct 1524, Downly Park,
Singleton, Sussex; bur. Arundel), 12th Earl of
Arundel, and **Margaret Woodville** (daughter of
Richard Woodville, 1st Earl Rivers (d. 1469)); no
issue; m. (2) daughter and heiress of **John
Golafre**.[4] No issue.

    5 — **Edward de la Pole** (d. bef 8 Oct 1485), "said
to have been Archdeacon of Richmond, co.
York"[5]; Archbishop of Richmond.[6]

---

[6] (...continued)

[6] *CP*, Lincoln section.

[7] **John de la Pole's** first wife was **Margaret Beaufort**, but this was a
child marriage which was dissolved bef 24 Mar 1452/1453 (*CP*, Suffolk
section). See chapter, "The Beaufort Women."

[1] *CP*, Suffolk section.

[2] See chapter, "Some Royal Connections of Poet Geoffrey Chaucer."

[3] *DNB*, "Pole, John de la, second Duke of Suffolk (1442-1491)."
See also chapter, "Some Royal Connections of Poet Geoffrey Chaucer."

[4] *CP*, Lincoln section. The second marriage is mentioned in a source
referenced by the *CP*, but the *CP* states that there are no authorities
given or found for this second marriage.

[5] *CP*, Vol. 12, Pt. 1, Appendix I, "The Sons of John (de la Pole),
2nd Duke of Suffolk, by Elizabeth (of York), Sister of Edward IV and
Richard III."

[6] *DNB*, "Pole, Richard de la (d. 1525)."

5 — **Edmund de la Pole** (b. abt 1472; ex. 1513,
the Tower; bur. Church of the Minoress (Minories)
without Aldgate[1]), eldest surviving son, 3rd Earl
of Suffolk, K.B.; m. bef 10 Oct 1496 **Margaret
Scrope** (d. Feb 1514/1515; will requested her
burial be with her husband), a daughter of **Richard
Scrope**, Lord Scrope, and his wife, **Eleanor
Washbourne** (daughter of **Norman
Washbourne**).[2] Issue (no male issue, an only
daughter):

   6 — **Anne**, a nun at the Minories without
   Aldgate.[3]

5 — **Humphrey de la Pole** (b. 1 Aug 1474;
d. shortly bef 15 Feb 1513), a priest.[4]

5 — **William de la Pole** (b. abt 1478; d. "probably
before" 20 Nov 1539, the Tower[5]) m. "probably
in 1497" and bef 8 Jun 1501 **Catherine Stourton**
(d. 25 Nov 1521, London),[6] daughter of **William**

---

[1] *DNB*, "Pole, Edmund de la, Earl of Suffolk (1472?–1513)." He
was imprisoned in the Tower for seven years and, "without any further
proceedings against him, was beheaded on Tower Hill...." (*CP*, Suffolk
section)

[2] *CP*, Suffolk section.

[3] "May have been one of the 27 nuns of that house who d. of the
plague in 1515." (*CP*, Suffolk section)

[4] *CP*, Vol. 12, Pt. 1, Appendix I, "The Sons of John (de la Pole),
2nd Duke of Suffolk, by Elizabeth (of York), Sister of Edward IV and
Richard III."

[5] On his death, "...the male line of his race became extinct." After
he was attainted, he was referred to as "William Pole, late of Wyngfeld
in the County of Suff' Knight." (*CP*, Vol. 12, Part 1, Appendix I, "The
Sons of John (de la Pole), 2nd Duke of Suffolk, by Elizabeth (of York),
sister of Edward IV and Richard III")

[6] **Catherine Stourton** was a "woman of fifty with a fortune...." She
was the widow of (1) **William Berkeley** of Beverston, co. Gloucester;
(2) **Henry Grey** (d. 8 Apr 1496), 7th Lord Grey of Codnor (no legit.
issue). (*CP*, Vol. 12, Pt. 1, Appendix I, "The Sons of John (de la Pole),
2nd Duke of Suffolk, by Elizabeth (of York), Sister of Edward IV and
Richard III")

Stourton (b. abt 1430; d. 18 Feb 1477/1478;
bur. Mere, Wiltshire), 2nd Baron Stourton, and
Margaret Chidiock[1] (d. 12 Mar 1502/1503)
(daughter of **John Chidiock**). No issue.
5 — **Geoffrey de la Pole**(?).[2]
5 — **Richard de la Pole,**[3] White Rose,
(k. 24 Feb 1525, Battle of Pavia, while fighting for
the French king; bur. monastic church of
St. Augustine, Pavia), "pretender to the crown."[4]
Unm.
5 — **Catherine**, eldest, "is said to have"
m. **William Stourton** (b. abt 1457; d. 17 Feb
1523/1524; will requesting burial in the new Lady
Chapel at St. Peter's, Stourton[5]), Lord Stourton,
son of **William Stourton** (d. 1477) and **Margaret
Chidiock** (d. 1502).[6] No issue.
5 — **Elizabeth** (bur. Hallingbury, Essex), youngest

---

[1] As widow of **William Stourton**, **Margaret Chidiock** m. **John
Cheyne** (d. 30 May 1499), Lord Cheyne. **Margaret Chidiock's** issue by
her first marriage was "one surv. child," a daughter, **Warburga**, who
m. (1) **Francis Cheyne** and (2) **William Compton**.
[2] "...unless confused with Humphrey above-named; perhaps the son
of **John**, Duke of Suffolk." *CP*, Vol. 12, Pt. 1, Appendix I, "The Sons
of John (de la Pole), 2nd Duke of Suffolk, by Elizabeth (of York), Sister
of Edward IV and Richard III."
[3] *DNB*, "Pole, Richard de la (d. 1525)." After being attainted,
Richard de la Pole was referred to as "Richard Pole, late of Wingfield
in the County of Suffolk, Squire." His brother, **William**, was referred to
as "William Pole of Wingfield, Knight."
[4] As grandson of **Richard**, Duke of York (father of **Edward IV** and
Richard III), **Richard de la Pole** White Rose claimed the throne of
England. He had the support of France and was planning an invasion of
England to claim the crown. "Wolsey was arranging for his abduction or
assassination...." He was referred to as "the King's dreaded enemy."
(*CP*, Vol. 12, Part 1, Appendix I, "The Sons of John (de la Pole), 2nd
Duke of Suffolk, by Elizabeth (of York), Sister of Edward IV and
Richard III")
[5] *CP*, Stourton section.
[6] *CP*, Stourton section.

daughter; m. at Wingfield, Suffolk, **Henry Lovel**
("aged 10 in 1476"; d. 13 Jun 1489, slain "with a
gun" at Dixmude in Flanders; bur. Calais), 2nd
and last Lord Morley of that surname. No issue.[1]
5 — Two other daughters.
4 — **Margaret of York** (b. 3 May 1446,
Fotheringhay; d. 28 Nov 1503, Malines; bur. Church
of the Cordeliers, Malines), youngest daughter,
Duchess of Burgundy; m. at Dame 3 Jul 1468 as his
third wife **Charles the Bold** (k. 5 Jan 1477, Battle of
Nancy; bur. St. George's Church, Nancy), Count of
Charolais, Duke of Burgundy, K.G. No issue.
4 — **William** (b. 7 Jul 1447, Fotheringhay; d. yng).
4 — **John** (b. 7 Nov 1448, Neyte, nr Worcester;
d. yng).
4 — **George** (b. 2/21 Oct 1449, Dublin, Ireland; put
to death in the Tower 17 or 18 Feb 1478[2];
bur. Tewkesbury Abbey with his wife), sixth son,
Duke of Clarence, Earl of Warwick and Salisbury,
K.B., K.G.; m. in Calais, Church of Notre Dame,
11 Jul 1469 **Isabel Neville** (b. 5 Sep 1451, Warwick
Castle; d. 12 Dec 1476, Warwick Castle;
bur. Tewkesbury Abbey), daughter of **Richard
Neville the Kingmaker** (d. 1471), Earl of Warwick,
and **Anne de Beauchamp** (d. 1492).[3] Issue:
5 — Child (b. and d. at sea, 1470; bur. Calais).
5 — **Edward**[4] (b. 21/25 Feb 1474/1475, Warwick

---

[1] *CP*, Morley section.
[2] **George**, Duke of Clarence, is well known for supposedly having
been "drowned in a butt of malmsey wine...." His "judicial death" was
a result of his "record of weakness and treachery." (*DNB*, "Plantagenet,
George, Duke of Clarence (1449-1478)"; Crawford, *Letters of the
Queens of England 1100-1547*, pg. 141)
[3] **Isabel's** sister, **Anne**, married **George's** brother, **Richard III**,
KING OF ENGLAND.
[4] **Edward** had a pitiable life. His mother died after giving birth to a
little brother, who died soon afterwards. He was barely three when his

(continued...)

Castle; ex. 28 Nov 1499, Tower Hill; bur. Bisham Abbey, Berkshire), eldest son, Earl of Warwick. Unm.

5 — **Richard Plantagenet** (b. Dec 1476; d. 1 Jan 1477).

5 — **Margaret Plantagenet** (b. 14 Aug 1473, Castle Farley nr Bath, Somerset; ex. 27 May 1541, Tower Hill[1]; bur. Chapel of St. Peter ad Vincula

---

[4] (...continued)

father was executed for treason. His remaining family was basically his sister **Margaret** and his aunt, **Anne**, Duchess of Gloucester, afterwards QUEEN OF ENGLAND. When he was eight, he was knighted by **Richard III** along with the king's son. He may have been considered as heir by **Richard** after his own son died. However, for whatever reason, **Richard** later ordered **Edward** confined to Sheriff Hutton Castle and then nominated **John de la Pole** (d. 1487), Earl of Lincoln, his sister's son, as his heir. After **Richard's III** defeat at Bosworth (22 Aug 1485), **Henry VII** sent **Robert Willoughby** to Sheriff Hutton Castle to bring **Edward** to London and imprison him in the Tower "for no other crime than being the son of [**George**, Duke of] Clarence," and nephew of two kings. Two years later, amid rumors of **Edward's** death, **Lambert Simnel**, impersonating **Edward**, was, with Yorkist support, crowned in Ireland in 1487 as Edward VI, King of England. **Henry VII** had no choice but to prove the falseness of the impersonation and so had the real **Edward** taken from the Tower and paraded to St. Paul's for mass. He was then returned to the Tower where he spent the next twelve years, until another captured impostor, **Perkin Warbeck** (who had impersonated **Richard**, Duke of York, the second of the two princes who disappeared from the Tower), drew the unsuspecting **Edward** into an escape plan which failed. **Warbeck** was executed 23 Nov 1499. **Edward** was tried for conspiring to depose the king ("a clearly trumped-up charge"), pleaded guilty ("in mere simplicity from his total ignorance of the world"), and was beheaded ("judicially murdered") 28 Nov 1499.

Burke's *Royal Family*, pg. 201, notes that on **Edward's** death, "the legitimate male line of Henry II, King of England, became *extinct*."

[1] **Margaret**, Countess of Salisbury, was the devoted governess of the young **Princess Mary**, daughter of **Henry VIII**, KING OF ENGLAND, and was considered by the Princess as a second mother. **Margaret** was mother of **Reginald Pole**, Cardinal and Archbishop of Canterbury, who

(continued...)

in the Tower), Countess of Salisbury;
m. abt 1491–1494 **Richard Pole** (d. bef 15 Nov

---

[1] (...continued)
refused to support **Henry VIII** in his break with Rome. **Henry VIII** had
her imprisoned in the Tower where she would remain about two years,
suffering "by the severity of the weather and the insufficiency of her
clothing." Early on the morning of 27 May 1541, she was beheaded,
despite the fact she was nearing the age of seventy. "The executioner
was a clumsy novice, who hideously hacked her neck and shoulders
before the decapitation was accomplished." (*DNB*, "Edward, Earl of
Warwick (1475–1499)"; *DNB*, "Pole, Margaret, Countess of Salisbury
(1473–1541)"; *CP*, Warwick section) When **Pole** heard of his mother's
execution ("without trial or formal charge"), he is reported to have said,
"I am now the son of a martyr." It is believed that **Henry VIII**, despite
the fact that he had once called her the most saintly woman in England,
was executing **Margaret** because he could not get at the son.

There are varying accounts of her execution. Some sources describe
the Countess as refusing to place her head on the block. Stating that she
had done nothing traitorous, she fled from the executioner, who chased
her around the courtyard, hacking her with the axe. Fuller, *The Worthies
of England*, 1952, pg. 612, states, "On the scaffold, as she stood, she
would not gratify the executioner with a prostrate posture of her body."
Since the Countess refused to put her head on the block, "Here happened
an unequal contest betwixt weakness and strength, age and youth,
nakedness and weapons, nobility and baseness, a princess and an
executioner, who at last dragging her by the hair, grey with age, may
truly be said to have took off her head, seeing she would neither give it
to him, nor forgive him the doing thereof." However, the *DNB* reports
that the Countess died with dignity, requesting prayers for those near to
her and for the king and queen and his children. She then submitted to
the clumsy executioner, an "inexperienced youth," "who hacked her
neck and shoulders before the decapitation was accomplished."
(According to Hampton (pg. 72), the experienced executioners were
either out of town or had been executed themselves.)

Before her death, **Margaret** saw her father executed in the Tower,
her brother **Edward** executed, her eldest son "judicially murdered,"
another son bear witness (perhaps unwittingly) against his brother, and
another son marked for assassination by the king. (Scarisbrick,
Henry VIII, pg. 365; Hampton, *Memorials of the Wars of the Roses*,
pg. 72; *DNB*, "Pole, Margaret, Countess of Salisbury (1473–1541)")
See also chapter, "The Poles and the de la Poles."

1504), son of **Geoffrey Pole** (will proved 21 Mar 1474/1475) and his wife **Edith St. John**[1] (daughter of **Oliver St. John** (d. 1437) and **Margaret de Beauchamp** (liv. 28 May 1468 and d. bef 3 Jun 1482[2])). Issue listed for interest[3]:

    6 — **Henry Pole** (b. abt 1492; ex. 9 Dec 1539, Tower Hill), Lord Montagu, eldest son; m. abt 1513 **Jane Neville**, daughter of **George Neville** (b. abt 1471; d. Jun 1535[4]), Lord Bergavenny.

        7 — A son (d. yng).[5]

        7 — **Catherine** m. **Francis Hastings**, Lord Hastings, Earl of Huntingdon.

        7 — **Winifred** m. "a brother of her sister's husband."[6]

    6 — **Arthur Pole**.

    6 — **Reginald Pole** (b. Mar 1500, Stourton Castle, Staffordshire; d. 17 Nov 1558; bur. 15 Dec 1558, St. Thomas Chapel, Canterbury Cathedral), Archbishop of Canterbury; Cardinal.[7]

    6 — **Geoffrey Pole** (b. bet 1501 and 1505; d. 1558; bur. Stoughton Church), "youngest

---

[1] **Edith St. John**, daughter of **Oliver St. John** (d. 1437) and **Margaret Beauchamp**, was half-sister of **Henry VII's** mother, **Margaret Beaufort**. (*CP*, Salisbury section)

[2] *CP*, Somerset section.

[3] Harris, *Edward Stafford: Third Duke of Buckingham, 1478–1521*, pgs. 234–235. See also chapter, "The Poles and the de la Poles."

[4] *DNB*, "Neville, George, third Baron of Bergavenny (1471?–1535)."

[5] Though the son was not mentioned by peerage historians, "he was included with his father in the bill of attainder of 1539, and probably died not many years after in prison" (*DNB*, "Pole, Sir Henry, Baron Montague or Montacute (1492?–1539)"). According to Scarisbrick, *Henry VIII*, pg. 364, "Henry Pole's small son and heir disappeared in the Tower...."

[6] *DNB*, "Pole, Sir Henry, Baron Montague or Montacute (1492?–1539)."

[7] *DNB*, "Pole, Reginald (1500–1558)."

son"[1]; m. **Constance Pakenham**, elder
daughter of **John Pakenham**. Issue:
    7 — **Arthur Pole** (b. 1531; d. 1570(?), the
    Tower), eldest son, "conspirator."[2]
    7 — **Thomas Pole**.
    7 — **Edmund Pole** (b. 1541; d. 1570(?), the
    Tower).
    7 — Two other sons.
    7 — Six daughters (two daughters married;
    "one was a nun of Sion"[3]).
6 — **Ursula Pole** (d. 12 Aug 1570[4])
m. "apparently on 16 Feb 1518–19" **Henry
Stafford** (b. 18 Sep 1501, Penhurst, Kent;
d. 30 Apr 1563, Caus Castle, Salop;
bur. 6 May, Worthen, Salop[5]), Lord Stafford,
son of **Edward Stafford** (b. 3 Feb 1478;
ex. 17 May 1521), 3rd Duke of Buckingham.
Issue[6]:
    7 — Thirteen children.
4 — **Thomas** (b. 1450, Fotheringhay; d. yng).[7]

---

[1] *DNB*, "Pole, Sir Geoffrey (1502?–1558)."

[2] **Arthur Pole** and his brother, **Edmund**, being persuaded that **Arthur** had a good claim to the English throne, applied to various quarters for support of the claim. They were arrested October 1562 and on 26 Feb 1562/1563 found guilty of treason but were not executed "in consideration of their youth and the futility of the plot." They were imprisoned in the Tower where they died, "probably in 1570." Their inscriptions, carved into the walls, are said to be still visible. *DNB*, "Pole, Arthur (1531–1570?)."

[3] *DNB*, "Pole, Sir Geoffrey (1502?–1558)."

[4] *DNB*, "Stafford, Henry, first Baron Stafford (1501–1563)."

[5] *CP*, Stafford section.

[6] Harris, *Edward Stafford, Third Duke of Buckingham, 1478–1521*, pgs. 234–235. According to the *CP*, Stafford section, by 1534, **Henry Stafford** had ten children, "of whom Henry, Henry and Thomas were the only sons" (the first son, Henry, died as an infant), and by March 1537, he had twelve children living, "though one d. about 1537, at least one more was b. after that date."

[7] Markham, *Richard III: His Life & Character*, pg. 6.

4 — **Richard III** (b. 2 Oct 1452, Fotheringhay;
k. 22 Aug 1485, Battle of Bosworth; bur. (1) Grey
Friars Abbey, Leicester, (2) at the Reformation, his
bones were thrown into the River Soar), KING OF
ENGLAND; m. **Anne Neville** (b. 1456; d. 1485),
daughter of **Richard Neville the Kingmaker**
(d. 1471), Earl of Warwick, and **Anne de
Beauchamp** (d. abt 1492).
4 — **Ursula** (b. 20 Jul 1455/abt 1453/1455; d. yng).
Richard of Cambridge, as above, husband of **Anne de
Mortimer**, m. (2) abt 1414 **Maud de Clifford** (d. 26 Aug
1446; bur. Abbey of Roche, co. York), [1] daughter of
Thomas de Clifford (d. 18 Aug 1391), 4th Baron Clifford,
and his wife, **Elizabeth de Ros** (d. Mar 1424) (daughter of
Thomas de Ros, Lord Ros). No issue.
Edmund of Langley, as above, son of **Edward III** and
Philippa of Hainault, m. (2) bef 4 Nov 1393 **Joan de
Holand** [2] (b. abt 1380; d. 12 Apr 1434), second daughter of
Thomas de Holand (d. 1397), 2nd Earl of Kent, K.G., half-
brother of **Richard II**. No issue.

---

[1] According to Burke's *Royal Family*, pg. 201, **Maud de Clifford**
m. (2) **John Neville** (d. 1430), 5th Baron Latimer of Danby. According
to *CP*, Cambridge and Latimer sections, **Maud Clifford** was the
divorced wife of **John Neville** when she married (bef 24 Jul 1406)
Richard of Cambridge. There was no issue of her marriage with **John
Neville**.

[2] **Joan de Holand** (d. 1434) survived **Edmund of Langley** and
married three times more (*DNB*, "Langley, Edmund de, first Duke of
York (1341-1402)"). She m. (2) as his second wife **William
Willoughby** (d. 1409), 5th Baron Willoughhy de Eresby, K.G.;
m. (3) bef 9 Dec 1410 as his second wife **Henry Scrope** (ex. 5 Aug
1415, Southampton), 3rd Baron Scrope of Masham, K.G.; no issue;
m. (4) bef 14 Aug 1416 as his first wife **Henry Bromflete** (d. 6 Jan
1468/1469), 1st Baron Vesey. **Joan** died without issue. Burke's *Royal
Family*, pg. 202, gives the death date of **William Willoughby** as 30 Nov
1410; *CP*, Willoughby section, gives a death date of 4 Dec 1409 at
Edgefield, with burial at Spilsby, where a "remarkable fine brass"
represents him and his first wife, **Lucy Strange/Lestrange** (liv. 28 Apr
1398; bur. "probably" Spilsby).

1 — **Blanche** (b. Mar 1342; d. Mar 1342, Tower of London; bur. Chapel of St. Peter, Westminster Abbey, in a tomb she would share with her infant brother, **William of Windsor**[1]), third daughter.

1 — **Mary** (b. 9/10 Oct 1344, Waltham/Walton nr Winchester; d. autumn 1361/1362[2]; bur. Abbington Abbey, Berkshire), fourth daughter[3]; m. at Woodstock summer 1361 as his first wife[4] **John V the Valiant de Montfort** (b. "probably in Nov or Dec 1339"[5]; d. 1 Nov 1399, Nantes; bur. Nantes Cathedral), Duke of Brittany, K.G., only son and heir of **John I de Montfort** (d. 26 Sep 1345, Hennebont; bur. (1) Quimperlé, (2) convent of the Jacobins) and **Joan of Flanders** (liv. 14 Feb 1373/1374) (daughter of **Louis of Flanders**, Count of Nevers). No issue.

1 — **Margaret** (b. 20 Jul 1346, Windsor Castle; d. aft 1 Oct 1361; bur. Abingdon Abbey, Berkshire), fifth daughter; m.[6] at

---

[1] Green, *Lives of the Princesses of England*, Vol. III, pgs. 261–262.

[2] "Within thirty weeks after her marriage, [**Mary**] was attacked by a lethargic disease, from which it was impossible to rouse her; and under its influence she gradually sank away and died...." Her sister, **Margaret**, died about the same time. "The remains of the royal sisters were conveyed together to the abbey of Abington...." (Green, *Lives of the Princesses of England*, Vol. III, pg. 287)

[3] Green, *Lives of the Princesses of England*, Vol. III, pg. 264.

[4] **John V de Montfort** m. (2) 1366 **Joan de Holand** (d. Nov 1384; bur. Abbey of Notre Dame de Priéres, Nantes), daughter of **Thomas de Holand** (d. 1360), 1st Earl of Kent, and his wife, **Joan of Kent** (who later married **Edward** the Black Prince); no issue; **John V de Montfort** m. (3) at Saillé 11 Sep 1386 **Joan** (d. 2, 9 or 10 Jul 1437, Havering-atte-Bower, Essex; bur. Canterbury Cathedral), daughter of **Charles II the Bad**, King of Navarre; issue of nine children (*KQB*, pg. 87). **Joan**, as his widow, married **Henry IV**, KING OF ENGLAND.

[5] *CP*, Richmond section.

[6] According to Green, *Lives of the Princesses of England*, Vol. III, pg. 298, "...the court was gay with preparations for twofold nuptials, which were celebrated on the same day. The Princess Margaret became the bride of the Earl of Hastings, and her brother Lionel was married to Elizabeth de Burgh...." According to the *DNB*, "Edward III (1312–1377)," she was betrothed to **John Hastings** and died unmarried.

Reading 19 May 1359 as his first wife[1] **John Hastings**
(b. 29 Aug 1347, Sutton Valence; d. 16 Apr 1375, bet Paris
and Calais/at Arras, in Picardy[2]; bur. aft 28 Apr, church of
the Friars Preachers, Hereford), 2nd Earl of Pembroke, K.G.,
son of **Laurence Hastings** (d. 1348), Earl of Pembroke, and his
wife, **Agnes de Mortimer** (d. 1368) (third daughter of **Roger
de Mortimer**, 1st Earl of March[3]). No issue.
1 — **William of Windsor** (b. bef 24 Jun 1348,[4] Windsor
Castle; d. Sep 1348; bur. 5 Sep 1348, St. Edmund's Chapel,
Westminster Abbey).
1 — **Thomas of Woodstock** (b. 7 Jan 1355, Woodstock;
murdered 8 or 15 Sep 1397, Calais; bur. Westminster Abbey),
fifth son, youngest son, Duke of Gloucester, Earl of
Buckingham, K.G.; m. 1374 **Eleanor de Bohun**[5] (b. 1366;
d. 3 Oct 1399, a nun at Barking Abbey, Essex; bur. Chapel of
St. Edmund, Westminster Abbey[6]), eldest daughter and
co-heiress of **Humphrey IX de Bohun** (b. 25 Mar 1342;

---

[1] **John Hastings** m. (2) abt Jul 1368 **Anne** (b. 1355; d. 1384),
daughter of **Walter de Manny** (d. 1371/1372) and his wife, **Margaret**,
Duchess of Norfolk (daughter of **Thomas of Brotherton**, Earl of
Norfolk). (*CP*, Pembroke section; Green, *Lives of the Princesses of
England*, Vol. III, pg. 299)

[2] **John Hastings**, Earl of Pembroke, was on his way home after his
release from a two-year captivity by Spaniards, in which he was "treated
with inhuman severity." He left an only child, **John**, who was two and a
half years old, "the last male heir of his race," who was "accidentally
killed at a tournament in 1390." Green, *Lives of the Princesses of
England*, Vol. III, pg. 300.

[3] *CP*, Pembroke section. **Joan de Mortimer** (d. 1337–1351), sister
of **Agnes**, m. **James de Audley** (d. 1 Apr 1386, Heleigh; bur. Hulton
Abbey), son of **Nicholas de Audley** (d. bef 6 Dec 1316) (*CP*, March
section).

[4] Green, *Lives of the Princesses of England*, Vol. III, pg. 164, gives
1334–1335 as the birth date for **William of Windsor**.

[5] **Eleanor's** sister, **Mary de Bohun** (aged 3 or 4 in 1372; d. 1394),
married **Henry of Bolingbroke** (**Henry IV**, KING OF ENGLAND), son
of **John of Gaunt** and **Blanche of Lancaster**. (*CP*, Hereford section)

[6] The alter tomb of **Eleanor de Bohun** possesses "the finest brass in
the Abbey...." (*Westminster Abbey: Official Guide*, pg. 83.)

d. 16 Jan 1372; bur. Walden Abbey "at the feet of his father"),
Earl of Hereford, Essex and Northampton, and his wife, **Joan
FitzAlan** (d. 7 Apr 1419) (daughter of **Richard II Copped Hat
FitzAlan** (d. 1375), Earl of Arundel). Issue (an only son and
three daughters[1]):

   2 — **Humphrey** (b. abt Apr 1382; d. 2 Sep 1399, Chester;
bur. Walden Priory, Essex[2]), 2nd Duke of Gloucester,
Earl of Buckingham. Unm.

   2 — **Anne**[3] (b. Apr 1383; d. 16 Oct 1438; bur. with her
third husband in Llanthony Priory, Monmouthshire)
m. (1) abt 1390/1392 **Thomas Stafford** (d. 4 Jul 1392), 3rd
Earl of Stafford; no issue; m. (2) abt 28 Jun 1398 **Edmund
de Stafford** (k. 21 Jul 1403, Battle of Shrewsbury;
bur. Stafford), 5th Earl of Stafford, 5th Earl of
Buckingham, K.G., brother of her first husband. Issue[4]:

      3 — **Anne Stafford** (d. 20 or 24 Sep 1432;
bur. St. Katherine by the Tower) m. (1) **Edmund IV de
Mortimer** (b. 4/6 Nov 1391, the New Forest; d. 18/
19 Jan 1424/1425 of the plague, Trim Castle,
co. Meath[5]; bur. Austin Friars' Church, Clare,
Suffolk), 5th Earl of March; no issue; m. (2) as his first
wife **John de Holand**[6] (b. 1395; d. 5 Aug 1447;

---

[1] Ramsay, *Lancaster and York*, Vol. I, Table I, lists one son and four
daughters, one who died young.

[2] *CP*, Essex section. After his father's murder (**Richard II** "desired
his death"), **Humphrey** was kept in custody by the king and finally
released by **Henry IV**, who deposed **Richard II**. However, he died
unmarried, aged about 17. It is not known with certainty how or where
he died. (*CP*, Gloucester section)

[3] Of the children of **Eleanor de Bohun** and **Thomas of Woodstock**,
Anne was the "only one to leave issue." (*CP*, Hereford section)

[4] Harris, *Edward Stafford: Third Duke of Buckingham, 1478–1521*,
pgs. 234–235; Ramsay, *Lancaster and York*, Vol. I, Table V.

[5] CP, Exeter section.

[6] It is believed that this **John Holand** (d. 1447), Duke of Exeter,
introduced the rack into the Tower of London. (Hibbert, *Tower of
London*, pg. 87; Wilson, *The Tower of London*, pgs. 67–68)

bur. Church of St. Katherine[1]), Duke of Exeter, Earl of
Huntingdon, Constable of the Tower, K.G. Issue:

4 — **Henry de Holand** (b. 27 Jun 1430, the Tower of
London; d. Sep 1475, found dead in the English
Channel between Calais and Dover[2]), Duke of
Exeter, Earl of Huntingdon, Constable of the Tower;
m. (div. 1472) bef 30 Jul 1447 **Anne Plantagenet**
(b. 10 Aug 1439, Fotheringhay Castle; d. 14 Jan
1475/1476; bur. at George's Chapel, Windsor),
daughter of **Richard** (ex. 1460), Duke of York, the
Protector, and **Cecily Neville**.

4 — **Anne Holand**, his only sister; m. (1) **John
Neville** (d. 7 Mar 1449/1450); no issue; m. (2) **John
Neville** (d. 29 Mar 1461, Battle of Towton), her first
husband's uncle; m. (3) **James** (d. 26 Dec 1486), Earl
of Douglas.

3 — **Philippa Stafford** (d. yng).

3 — **Humphrey Stafford** (b. 1402; k. 10 Jul 1460,
Battle of Northampton[3]; bur. Church of the Greyfriars
at Northampton), Earl of Stafford, 1st Duke of
Buckingham; m. **Anne Neville**[4] (d. 20 Sep 1480),

---

[1] **John de Holand** (d. 1447), **Anne de Mortimer** (his first wife), and
Anne Montagu (his third wife) were buried together in the Church of
St. Katherine by the Tower. According to Wilson, *The Tower of London*,
pgs. 69–70, St. Katherine's Hospital was demolished in 1825 when
building was begun on St. Katherine's Docks. The "remains and
benignly smiling effigies" of Holand and the two wives were moved to
Regent's Park, then moved again in 1951 to the Tower.

[2] It was recorded that **Henry de Holand** was found dead in the
English Channel, but how he was drowned was not known. He was
possibly the captain of *The Nicholas of the Tower*, which twenty-five
years earlier had intercepted, captured, and executed **William de la Pole**
in the English Channel as he was sent into exile from England. (Burke's
Royal Family, pg. 201; *CP*, Exeter section)

[3] *DNB*, "Stafford, Humphrey, first Duke of Buckingham
(1402–1460)."

[4] **Anne Neville** m. (2) **Walter Blount** (d. 1474), Lord Mountjoy.
(*DNB*, "Stafford, Humphrey, first Duke of Buckingham (1402–1460)")

daughter of **Ralph Neville** (d. 1425), 1st Earl of
Westmorland, and his wife, **Joan Beaufort** (daughter of
John of Gaunt). Issue (twelve children) included[1]:
    4 — **Humphrey Stafford** (d. aft 22 May 1455/1458,
in the lifetime of his father[2]), 7th Earl of Stafford;
m. **Margaret Beaufort**[3] (d. spring 1474), daughter
of **Edmund Beaufort** (b. abt 1406; k. 22 May 1455,
First Battle of St. Albans; bur. chapel of the Blessed
Virgin in the Abbey Church), 2nd Duke of Somerset,
and his wife, **Eleanor de Beauchamp** (b. 1407/1408
Edgenoch, co. Warwick; d. 6 Mar 1466/1467,
Baynard's Castle, London), second daughter of
Richard de Beauchamp (d. 1439), Earl of Warwick,
by his first wife, **Elizabeth Berkeley** (b. abt 1386;
d. 28 Dec 1422). Some issue listed briefly for
historical interest:
    5 — **Henry Stafford** (b. 4 Sep 1455; ex. 2 Nov
1483, Salisbury[4]; bur. Grey Friars), 2nd Duke of

---

[1] Griffiths, *The Reign of Henry VI*, Table 4; Harris, *Edward Stafford: Third Duke of Buckingham, 1478-1521*, pgs. 234–235, indicates that there were twelve children of this marriage; *DNB*, "Stafford, Humphrey, first Duke of Buckingham (1402–1460)."

[2] **Humphrey Stafford** was "gretly hurt" in the First Battle of St. Albans, 22 May 1455, and died "soon afterward" (*DNB*, "Stafford, Humphrey, first Duke of Buckingham (1402–1460)." Harris, *Edward Stafford: Third Duke of Buckingham, 1478-1521*, pgs. 234–235, 19, states that he died of the plague in 1458.

[3] **Margaret Beaufort** was cousin of **Margaret Beaufort** (d. 1509), Countess of Richmond and mother of **Henry VII**, KING OF ENGLAND. See chapter, "The Beaufort Women."

[4] *CP*, Buckingham section. He was instrumental in assisting **Richard of Gloucester** in his usurpation of the throne; but suddenly, and for reasons that can be only surmised, he turned against **Richard III** and was captured and, "without any legal trial," beheaded. Griffiths and Thomas (*The Making of the Tudor Dynasty*, pg. 101) describe him as a "self-conscious descendant of Edward III." Some historians believe that he had aspirations to the throne and that **Richard** saw him as a rival claimant.

Buckingham, K.G.; m. **Katherine Woodville**[1]
(d. 1497), daughter of **Richard Woodville**
(ex. 12 Aug 1469) and **Jacquetta of Luxembourg**
(d. 30 May 1472) and the sister of **Edward IV's**
queen consort, **Elizabeth Woodville** (d. 1492).
Issue:

   6 — **Edward Stafford** (b. 3 Feb 1477/1478,
Brecknock Castle; ex. 17 May 1521, Tower
Hill; bur. Church of the Austin Friars, London),
3rd and 4th Duke of Buckingham[2]; m. 1500
Eleanor Percy (d. 1530), daughter of **Henry de
Percy** (murdered 28 Apr 1489, "by the rabble at
his manor house"; bur. Beverley Minster), Earl
of Northumberland, and his wife, **Maud
Herbert** (d. bef 27 Jul 1485; bur. Beverley
Minster). Issue[3]:

      7 — **Henry Stafford** (b. 1501; d. 1563), 1st
Baron Stafford, Lord Stafford, "an only
son"; m. "apparently on 16 Feb
1518–19" **Ursula Pole** (d. 12 Aug 1570[4]),
daughter of **Richard Pole** (d. 1504) and

---

[1] **Katherine Woodville** m. (2) bef Nov 1485 **Jasper Tudor**
(d. 21 Dec 1495), Duke of Bedford, who died without legitimate issue;
m. (3) as his first wife **Richard Wingfield** (d. 22 Jul 1525), K.G.

[2] **Edward Stafford** was six years old when **Richard III** offered
rewards for the capture of **Edward's** father and family. His father was
betrayed by **Ralph Bannaster**, one of his old servants, who received
from the appreciative king a manor and lordship in Kent which had
belonged to **Stafford**. **Edward**, dressed as a young girl, escaped
Richard III's grasp, and was taken safely to Hereford in the company of
protectors which included a nurse (**Elizabeth Mores**), **Richard de la
Bere**, and **William Knyvett**. On the accession of **Henry VII**, **Edward**
was made a Knight of the Bath. (On a romantic note: Sometime after the
adventure, **Elizabeth Mores** and her employer, **Richard de la Bere**,
were married.) (Griffiths and Thomas, *The Making of the Tudor
Dynasty*, pgs. 99–101; St. Aubyn, *The Year of Three Kings 1483*,
pg. 191)

[3] *DNB*, "Stafford, Edward, third Duke of Buckingham (1478–1521)."

[4] *DNB*, "Stafford, Henry, first Baron Stafford (1501–1563)."

of Salisbury. Issue:

8 — Thirteen children.

7 — **Elizabeth Stafford** (d. 1558)
m. **Thomas Howard** (d. 1554), 3rd Duke of
Norfolk. Issue:

8 — Five children.

7 — **Catherine Stafford** m. **Ralph Neville**
(d. 1549), 4th Earl of Westmorland. Issue:

8 — Sixteen children.

7 — **Mary Stafford** m. as his third wife
George Neville (b. abt 1471; d. Jun 1535),
3rd Baron Bergavenny, Lord Bergavenny,[1]
son of **George Neville** (b. abt 1420, "said to
have been born at Raby"; d. 20 Sep 1492),
Lord Bergavenny (Abergavenny), and
Margaret Fenne (d. 28 Sep 1485) (daughter
of **Hugh Fenne**, Treasurer of the Household
to Henry VI). Issue:

8 — Six children.

6 — **Henry Stafford** (d. 1523), Earl of
Wiltshire; m. **Cecily Bonville** (aged 13 in 1474;
d. 12 Apr/bef 2 Jun 1530; bur. Astley, co.
Warwick), Baroness Bonville and Harington,
daughter of **William Bonville** (d. 1461), Baron
Harington, and widow of **Thomas Grey**
(d. 1501), 1st Marquess of Dorset.

6 — **Elizabeth Stafford** m. **Robert Radcliffe**,
Lord FitzWalter, Earl of Sussex.

6 — **Anne Stafford** m. (1) **Walter Herbert**
(d. 1507); m. (2) **George Hastings** (d. 1544),
Lord Hastings, Earl of Huntingdon.

4 — **Joan Stafford** (liv. 1480/at the time of
Richard III) m. (1) bef 4 Mar 1461 (marriage "set

---

[1] *CP*, Abergavenny section; *DNB*. "Neville, George, third Baron of
Bergavenny (1471?–1535)."

aside" bef 1477) as his first wife[1] **William Beaumont** (bap. 23 Apr 1438, Edenham, co. Lincoln; d. 19 Dec 1507, aged 69), Viscount Beaumont, Lord Bardolf and Lord Beaumont, son of **John Beaumont** (d. 10 Jul 1460), Viscount Beaumont, and his first wife, **Elizabeth Phelip** (d. bef 30 Oct 1441) (daughter and heir of **William Phelip**, K.G., Lord Bardolf); no issue; m. (2) abt 1477 "as the second of his three wives" **William Knyvett/Knevet** (b. 1440; liv. 1491, age 51; d. 1515[2]) of Buckingham in Norfolk.

4 — **Isabel Stafford**, a nun.

4 — **Henry Stafford** (d. 1481[3]) m. as her second husband **Margaret Beaufort** (b. 31 May 1443[4]/ 1441, Bletsoe in Bedfordshire[5]; d. 29 Jun 1509; bur. Westminster Abbey), Countess of Richmond and mother of **Henry VII**, KING OF ENGLAND; she was daughter of **John Beaufort** (d. 1444), 1st Duke of Somerset. No issue.

4 — **Katherine Stafford** (d. 26 Dec 1476), fifth

---

[1] **William Beaumont** m. (2) 24 Apr 1486 **Elizabeth Scrope**, daughter of **Richard Scrope** and his wife, **Eleanor Washbourne** (daughter of **Norman Washbourne** of co. Worcester). *CP*, Beaumont section

[2] *CP*, Beaumont section; Harris, *Edward Stafford: Third Duke of Buckingham, 1478–1521*, pg. 235.

[3] *DNB*, "Stafford, Humphrey, first Duke of Buckingham (1402–1460)." The year of death has been seen as 1471 (*CP*, Suffolk section, under John de la Pole (d. 1492), and Richmond section; Rawcliffe, *The Staffords, Earls of Stafford and Dukes of Buckingham 1394–1521*, pg. 22). However, Hogrefe, *Women of Action in Tudor England*, pg. 139, gives 1481 as the year of death, and Cooper, *Memoir of Margaret Beaufort, Countess of Richmond and Derby*, pg. 17, states that Henry Stafford "appears to have died in 1482, as his will was proved on the 4th May in that year" and that the will "is dated 2 Oct 1481."

[4] *CP*, Suffolk section, footnote to John de la Pole (d. 1492); *CP*, Richmond section.

[5] Cooper, *Memoir of Margaret Beaufort, Countess of Richmond and Derby*, pgs. 1–2.

daughter; m. abt 1467 **John Talbot** (b. 12 Dec 1448 [1]; d. 28 Jun 1473, Coventry; bur. Worksop Priory, Nottinghamshire), Earl of Shrewsbury, son of **John Talbot** (k. 10 Jul 1460, Battle of Northampton), Earl of Shrewsbury, and his wife, **Elizabeth Butler** (daughter of **James Butler**, 4th Earl of Ormond [2]).

4 — **John Stafford** (d. 8 May 1473) m. **Constance Green**.

4 — **Anne Stafford** (d. 1472) m. (1) **Aubrey de Vere** (ex. with his father 1462 [3]); no issue; (2) **Thomas Cobham** (d. 1471) of Sterborough.

4 — **Edward Stafford** (d. yng).

4 — **George Stafford** (d. yng), twin with **William**.

4 — **William Stafford** (d. yng), twin with **George**.

Anne (d. 1438), as above, daughter of **Thomas of Woodstock** and wife of **Edmund de Stafford** (d. 1403), m. (3) 20 Nov 1405 [4]/abt 1408 [5] **William Bourchier**, Kt. (d. 28 May 1420, Troyes; bur. Priory of Llanthony by Gloucester), Count of Eu, Earl of Ewe, son of **William Bourchier** (d. 1375) and **Eleanor de Lovayne** (b. 27 Mar 1345, Little Easton; d. 5 Oct 1397 [6]) (daughter of **John de Lovayne** (d. 30 or 31 Jan 1346/1347) of Little Easton by his second wife, **Margaret de Weston** [7]). Issue [8]:

3 — **Henry Bourchier** (b. 1406 [9]; d. 4 Apr 1483; bur. Bylegh), Viscount Bourchier, Earl of Essex; m. bef 25 Apr 1426 **Isabel of Cambridge** (d. 2 Oct

---

[1] *DNB*, "Talbot, George, fourth Earl of Shrewsbury and Earl of Waterford (1468-1538)."

[2] *DNB*, "Talbot, John, second Earl of Shrewsbury (1413(?)-1460)."

[3] Griffiths, *The Reign of Henry VI*, Table 4.

[4] *CP*, Eu section. A "pardon for marrying without royal licence" was granted on 20 Nov 1405.

[5] Burke's *Royal Family*, pg. 202.

[6] *CP*, Eu section, Lovaine section.

[7] *CP*, Lovaine section.

[8] *CP*, Essex section, Berners section; *DNB*, "Bourchier"; Ross, *Edward IV*.

[9] Ramsay, *Lancaster and York*, Vol. I, Table V.

1484), widow of **Thomas Grey** (d. bef 26 Jul 1443) of Heton and only daughter of **Richard of Cambridge** (ex. 1415), Earl of Cambridge, and his wife **Anne de Mortimer** (d. bef 1415). For issue, see under **Isabel of Cambridge** elsewhere in this chapter.

3 — **John Bourchier** (d. 16 or 21 May 1474, Troyes[1]; bur. Chertsey Abbey, Surrey), 1st Baron Berners, Lord Berners, Count of Eu/Earl of Ewe, K.G.; m. **Margery/ Margaret Berners** (d. 18 Dec 1475), widow of **John Ferreby** (d. without issue, will pr. 12 Nov 1441) and daughter of **Richard Berners** of West Horsley, Surrey, and **Philippa Dalyngridge** (daughter of **Edward Dalyngridge**). Issue[2]:

4 — **Humphrey Bourchier**[3] (d. 14 Apr 1471, Battle of Barnet) m. as her first husband[4] **Elizabeth Tylney** (d. 4 April 1497; bur. in Chapel of St. Edmund, Westminster Abbey) of Boston, co. Lincoln, daughter of **Frederick Tylney** of Ashwellthorpe, co. Norfolk. Some issue listed briefly for historical interest:

5 — **Margaret Bourchier** (d. 1551/1552), **Lady Bryan**, governess of the young princesses, **Elizabeth** and **Mary**, daughters of **Henry VIII** and both later QUEENS OF ENGLAND; m. **Thomas Bryan**.

5 — **John Bourchier** (b. 1467; d. 16 Mar 1532/ 1533), 2nd Lord Berners, the translator of, among

---

[1] *CP*, Berners section.

[2] *CP*, Latimer section.

[3] Not to be confused with his cousin, **Humphrey Bourchier**, Lord Cromwell, who also died 14 Apr 1471 at the Battle of Barnet. Lord Cromwell was son of **Henry Bourchier**, Viscount Bourchier, Earl of Essex (d. 4 Apr 1483) and **Isabel of Cambridge** (d. 1484), daughter of **Richard of Cambridge** (ex. 1415), Earl of Cambridge.

[4] **Elizabeth Tylney** m. (2) 30 Apr 1472 **Thomas Howard** (b. 1443; d. 21 May 1524), Earl of Surrey, Duke of Norfolk. By this second marriage, she was mother of **Elizabeth Howard** who would become the second wife of **Thomas Boleyn**, the father of **Anne Boleyn**, QUEEN OF ENGLAND.

other things, Froissart's *Chronicles*.

4 — **Joan/Jane Bourchier** (d. 7 Oct 1470) m. **Henry
Neville** (k. 26 Jul 1469, Battle of Edgecot nr Banbury;
bur. Beauchamp Chapel, Warwick), son of **George
Neville** (d. 1469), Lord Latimer, and his wife,
Elizabeth Beauchamp (d. 1480).

4 — **Thomas Bourchier**.

4 — **Elizabeth Bourchier** (d. bet. 2 and 8 Oct 1470;
bur. Church of the White Friars), Lady Welles;
m. **Robert de Welles** (d. 19 Mar 1469/1470;
bur. Church of the White Friars, Doncaster), Lord
Wells and Willoughby. No issue.[1]

4 — "Other issue."[2]

3 — **William Bourchier** (d. bef 12 Dec 1469/abt 1471[3];
bur. Church of the Austin Friars, London), Lord
FitzWarin/FitzWarren,[4] third son; m. (1) bef 3 Aug
1437 **Thomasine Hankeford**[5] (b. 23 Feb 1422/1423,
Tawstock, Devon; d. 3 Jul 1453; bur. Bampton Church),
daughter of **Richard Hankeford** (b. abt 21 Jul 1397;
d. 8 Feb 1430/1431) and **Elizabeth FitzWarin**
(d. bet. 10 Feb 1425/1426 and 16 Jan 1427/1428). Issue
(eight children[6]):

4 — **Fulk Bourchier** (b. 25 Oct 1445; d. 18 Sep
1479; bur. Bampton Church), Lord FitzWarin;
m. **Elizabeth Dinham** (d. 19 Oct 1516; bur. Church
of the Grey Friars, London),[7] daughter of **John**

---

[1] *CP*, Welles section.

[2] Ramsay, *Lancaster and York*, Vol. I, Table V.

[3] Ramsay, *Lancaster and York*, Vol. I, Table V.

[4] From whom descend the Earls of Bath.

[5] **Thomasine Hankeford** had two sisters, **Elizabeth** (aged 6 or more
in 1431; d. unm. 13 Oct 1433) and **Joan**, who died in the lifetime of her
father.

[6] *CP*, FitzWarin section. Issue are not listed.

[7] **Elizabeth Dinham** m. (2) bef 7 Dec 1480 **John Sapcotes** (d. 5 Jan
1500/1501) of Elton, Hunts; m. (3) bef 10 Jan 1506/1506 as his second
wife **Thomas Brandon** (d. 27 Jan 1509/1510; bur. 29 Jan 1509/1510,

(continued...)

Dinham (d. 25 Jan 1457/1458, Nutwell, Devon; bur. Church of the Black Friars, Exeter), Lord Dinham of Hartland, Devon, and **Joan Arches** (d. 1497; will requested burial with her husband) (daughter of **Richard Arches** of Eythorpe, Buckinghamshire).

4 — Seven other children.

William Bourchier (d. bef 12 Dec 1469), as above, husband of **Thomasine Hankeford**, m. (2) bef 9 Jan 1458/1459, **Katherine Affeton** (d. 26 Mar 1467, widow of **Hugh Stucley** of Trent, Somerset, Sheriff of Devon, and daughter and heir of **John Affeton** of Afton, [1] Devon. [2]

3 — **Thomas Bourchier** (b. 1404(?); d. 30 Mar 1486, Knowle; bur. Canterbury Cathedral), Bishop of Worchester, Bishop of Ely, Archbishop of Canterbury (appointed 1454), Cardinal (1473). [3]

3 — **Eleanor Bourchier** (d. Nov 1474; bur. Thetford Priory) m. "as early as 1424" [4]/bef Jul 1437 **John VI de Mowbray** (b. 12 Sep 1415; d. 6 Nov 1461; bur. Thetford Priory), 3rd Duke of Norfolk, K.G., only son of **John V de Mowbray** (d. 19 Oct 1432), 2nd Duke of Norfolk, and his wife, **Catherine Neville**

---

[7] (...continued)
Church of the Black Friars by Ludgate), K.G., of Duddington, Northamptonshire. **Brandon's** will requested burial near "**John Wyngfeld** knyght" and under "a playne stone wtout towmbe." (*CP*, FitzWarin section, Dinham section)

[1] In *DNB*, "Stuckley or Stukely, Thomas (1525?–1578)," the place name Afton is written, "Affeton, near Ilfracombe, Devonshire."

[2] *CP*, FitzWarin section, mentions in a footnote, "Legacies to Elizabeth her da., Isabel Bourgchier, and Thomasine Bourgchier."

[3] **Thomas Bourchier**, as Archbishop of Canterbury, crowned **Edward IV**, **Richard III**, and **Henry VII**. He was among those who took **Richard**, Duke of York, from sanctuary to join his brother, **Edward V**, in the Tower of London. (St. Aubyn, *The Year of Three Kings 1483*, pg. 22)

[4] *CP*, Norfolk section.

(d. aft 1478). "She bore him one son" [1]:

    4 — **John VII de Mowbray** (b. 18 Oct 1444;
d. 17 Jan 1476, Framlingham Castle, Suffolk;
bur. Thetford), 4th Duke of Norfolk; m. by 27 Nov
1448 **Elizabeth Talbot** [2] (d. bet. 6 Nov 1506 and
10 May 1507), daughter of **John Talbot** (d. 17 Jul
1453; bur. St. Alkmund's, Whitchurch, Salop), Earl
of Shrewsbury, and his second wife, **Margaret de
Beauchamp** (b. 1404; d. 14 Jun 1467; bur. Jesus
Chapel of St. Paul's) (daughter of **Richard de
Beauchamp** (d. 30 Apr 1439)). Issue ("he left only a
daughter"):

        5 — **Anne de Mowbray** (b. 10 Dec 1472;
d. 19 Nov 1481, Greenwich; bur. chapel of
St. Erasmus, Westminster Abbey) m. at
St. Stephen's Chapel, Westminster, 15 Jan 1478
Richard (b. 17 Aug 1472/1473, Shrewsbury;
d. abt 1483), Duke of York, brother of **Edward V**,
uncrowned KING OF ENGLAND. [3] No issue of
this child marriage.

2 — **Joan** (b. 1384; d. 16 Aug 1400; bur. Walden Priory).
Unm.

2 — **Isabel** (b. 12 Mar 1386; d. abt Apr 1402), a nun of the
Order of St. Clare at the Minoresses, Aldgate. Unm.

2 — **Philippa** (b. abt 1389; d. bef 3 Oct 1399).

---

[1] *DNB*, "Mowbray, John (VI), third Duke of Norfolk, hereditary
Earl Marshal of England, and fifth Earl of Nottingham (1415–1461)."

[2] Her sister, **Eleanor Talbot**, was said to have been betrothed to
Edward IV, King of England.

[3] **Richard**, Duke of York, and **Edward V**, were the two young
princes who were last seen the summer of 1483 in the Tower of London.
The traditional belief is that they were murdered at the command of
Richard III, KING OF ENGLAND, the brother of their father,
Edward IV.

Illegitimate Issue

1 — **Nicholas Litlyngton**, Abbot of Westminster 1362–1386. [1]
1 — **John de Southeray** (prob. b. abt 1364 or 1365; liv. "early in 1383"), son of **Alice Perrers**; knighted April 1377;
m. Jan 1377 **Maud**, sister of **Henry de Percy** (d. 19 Feb 1407/ 1408), 1st Earl of Northumberland. [2]
1 — **Joan**, daughter of **Alice Perrers**; m. **Robert Skerne** (d. Apr 1437; bur. with his wife in the church of All Saints at Kingston). [3]
1 — **Jane**, daughter of **Alice Perrers**; m. **Richard Northland**. [4]

Henry of Grosment
(d. 1361/1362)
Duke of Lancaster

---

[1] *DNB*, "Edward III (1312–1377)," in which is stated that **Edward III** is "said to have had a bastard son." Given-Wilson and Curteis (pg. 179) indicate that it is doubtful **Nicholas Litlyngton** is a bastard of the king.
[2] Given-Wilson and Curteis, pgs. 138–141.
[3] Given-Wilson and Curteis, pg. 179.
[4] Given-Wilson and Curteis, pg. 179.

Other Genealogies

Other Relations
of William the Conqueror

It is said that Robert I, Duke of Normandy, saw Arlette (also called Herleve), daughter of Fulbert the Tanner, washing clothes in the stream beside the castle of Falaise. He summoned her to the castle and they eventually became parents of William the Conqueror. Both Robert and Arlette were probably in their teens, and her involvement with Robert would benefit her father ("who was given a subordinate position at the ducal court"[1]) and her brothers, Osbert and Walter.

Arlette was later married to Herluin, Count of Conteville. They were parents of Odo, Bishop of Bayeux and Earl of Kent,[2] and Robert, Count of Mortain, both distinguished individuals of the time. Douglas adds, "The whole subsequent history of north-western Europe was thus to be influenced by the offspring of this obscure but remarkable girl...."

Robert I (d. 22 Jul 1035[3]), sometimes called the Devil or the Magnificent, Duke of Normandy 1027–1035, and **Arlette/ Herleve** (d. abt 1050[4]) had issue:

---

[1] Douglas, *William the Conqueror*, pg. 15.

[2] It is now believed it was Odo who commissioned the Bayeaux Tapestry "to publicize and celebrate the herioc Norman victory" (Cannon & Griffiths, *The Oxford Illustrated History of the British Monarchy*, pgs. 164–165). The tapestry is fully described in Bruce's *The Bayeux Tapestry: The Battle of Hastings and the Norman Conquest*, first printed in 1856, reprinted 1987.

[3] *Ancestral* 121-23, 130-23.

[4] Douglas, *William the Conqueror*, pg. 15.

1 — **William the Conqueror**, KING OF ENGLAND.
1 — **Adelaide** (b. abt 1030; d. bef 1090), Countess of Aumale;
m. (1) **Enguerand II** (k. 1053, siege of Arques[1]), Count of
Ponthieu; m. (2) **Lambert of Boulogne** (k. 1054, Battle of
Lille), Count of Lens. Possible issue by her first husband[2]:
> 2 — **Judith of Lens** (b. 1054) m. 1070 **Waltheof**
> (ex. 31 May 1076), Earl of Huntingdon, Northampton, and
> Northumberland. They were parents of:
>> 3 — **Maud of Huntingdon** (b. 1072; d. 1131)
>> m. (1) 1090 **Simon St. Liz** (d. abt 1111), Earl of
>> Huntingdon and Northampton; m. (2) **David I the Saint**
>> (d. 1153), Earl of Huntingdon and Northampton, King of
>> Scots.
>> 3 — **Alice of Northumberland** (liv. 1126) m. **Ralph de
>> Toeni** (d. abt 1126).

Adelaide, as above, wife of **Enguerrand II**, m. (3) 1054/1060
Odo or **Eudes**, Count of Champagne and Aumale.[3]

Arlette, mother of **William the Conqueror**, later m. **Herluin
de Centeville/Conteville**. Issue:
1 — **Odo** (b. prob abt 1030; d. Feb 1097, Palermo;
bur. cathedral in Palermo), Bishop of Bayeux, Earl of Kent.[4]
Unm.
1 — **Robert** (b. abt 1031; d. 8 Dec 1090; bur. with his first

---

[1] *Ancestral* 130-24.

[2] *Ancestral* 148-22 states that not only is there the possibility that
Judith's father was **Enguerand II**, but that **Adelaide** "may not even
have been Lambert's wife."

[3] *Ancestral* 130-24, 136-23; Tauté; Douglas, *William the Conqueror*,
Table 2. Douglas, pgs. 380–381, states that it is "probable, though not
certain" that Herleve was the mother by Robert of this Adelaide who
married as listed above. It is known that William had a sister by that
name and it is known that she was not the daughter of Herleve's
husband; there is the possibility she may have been the daughter of
Robert by another woman. However, Douglas states that "it is more
probably that she was the Conqueror's sister of the whole blood."

[4] "His illegitimate son, John, was held in great esteem at the court of
Henry I for his eloquence and probity." (*CP*, Kent section)

wife), second son, Count of Mortain, called Earl of Cornwall; m. (1) bef 1066 **Matilda/Maud** (bur. Abbey of Grestain), daughter of **Roger Montgomery** (d. 27 Jul 1094, Shrewsbury), Earl of Shrewsbury, and his first wife, **Mabel Talvas** (murdered 2 Dec 1079).[1] They were parents of:

2 — **Emma de Mortain** m. 1080 **William IV** (d. 1093), Count of Toulouse.[2]

2 — **William de Mortain** (b. prob bef 1084; d. 1140 or after, Bermondsey Abbey), Earl of Cornwall, Count of Mortain; m. **Aldilidis**.

2 — **Nigel** (?).[3]

2 — **Agnes** m. **Andrew of Vitré**.

2 — A daughter m. **Guy de la Val**.

Robert, as above, husband of **Matilda/Maud Montgomery**, m. (2) **Almodis**.

Some Relations of William the Conqueror

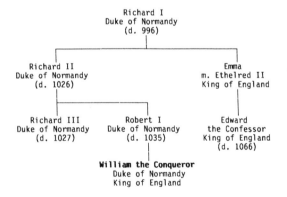

---

[1] *CP*, Cornwall section; *CP*, Shrewsbury section.

[2] *Ancestral* 185-2.

[3] According to the *DNB*, "Mortain, Robert of, Count of Mortain," he had "...possibly a son Nigel...." The same article mentions a daughter **Agnes** and two other daughters, unnamed.

Sources:

Bruce, John Collingwood, *The Bayeux Tapestry: The Battle of Hastings and the Norman Conquest*, Dorset Press, New York, 1987.

Cannon, John & Griffiths, Ralph, *The Oxford Illustrated History of the British Monarchy*, Oxford University Press, Oxford and NY, 1988.

Cokayne, G. E., *The Complete Peerage*, St Catherine Press, London.

Douglas, David C., *William the Conqueror*, University of California Press, Berkeley & L.A., 1964.

Stephen, Sir Leslie, and Lee, Sir Sidney, eds., *Dictionary of National Biography*, Oxford University Press, London, 1964.

Weis, Frederick Lewis, *Ancestral Roots of Sixty Colonists*, 6th ed., Genealogical Publishing Co., Inc., 1990.

The Marriages of Louis VII of France

Louis VII (b. abt 1120; d. 18 Sep 1180, Paris; bur. Abbey of Barbeaux, Melun), king of France, was the second son of Louis VI the Fat of France (d. 1 Aug 1137, Paris) and Adelaide of Savoy (b. abt 1092; m. at Paris 3 Aug 1115; d. 18 Nov 1154), daughter of Humbert II, Count of Maurienne and Savoy, and Gisela of Burgundy. Louis was born abt 1120, Fontainebleau; crowned at Rheims 25 Oct 1131 and again at Bourges 25 Dec 1137; d. 18 Sep 1180, Paris; bur. Abbey of Barbeaux, which he had founded[1] in Melun; reigned 1137–1180.

Eleanor of Aquitaine was the daughter of William X (b. 1099; d. 9 Apr Good Friday 1137), Duke of Aquitaine, Count of Poitou and Aenor/Eleanor de Châstellerault[2] (d. aft Mar 1130), daughter of Aimery I/Almeric, Viscount of Châstellerault. Eleanor was b. abt 1122, Bordeaux or Belin; married to Louis VII at Bordeaux 22/25 Jul 1137[3]; she was crowned queen of France at Bourges 25 Dec 1137; in 1152, her marriage to Louis VII was annulled on grounds of consanguinity; she m. (2) at Poitiers 18 May 1152 Henry of Anjou, who would become Henry II, king of England; she was crowned queen of England on 17/19 Dec 1154 Westminster Abbey; d. 31 Mar 1204, Poitiers; bur. Fontévrault Abbey, Saumur in Maine-et-Loire, France.

Eleanor of Aquitaine, as the heiress of her father, succeeded

---

[1] Parsons, *Eleanor of Castile 1290–1990*, pg. 13.

[2] *Ancestral* 183-4.

[3] According to *DNB*, "Eleanor, Alienor, or Aenor, Duchess of Aquitaine, Queen of France and Queen of England (1122?-1204)," they were married "probably on Sunday, 4 July...."

to the duchy of Aquitaine in 1137 at age fifteen and the same
year entered into the marriage her father had arranged for her
with Louis, Dauphin of France, who, about the time they
married, became Louis VII, king of France.

A second son, Louis had been brought up to have a career
in the church. However, after his older brother died in a riding
accident, Louis became heir to the throne of France.

It is traditionally believed that the marriage of Eleanor and
Louis was a marriage of opposites: Louis was pious, quiet, and
not very intelligent; Eleanor was fun-loving, intelligent, and
sensual. She soon found Louis a monkish bore. In 1147, Louis
became caught up in the enthusiam of the Second Crusade, and
Eleanor and her ladies of the court, seeking adventure, went
along with Louis to Syria. However, her "scandalous" behavior
sent Louis packing her back to France and seeking an
annulment. [1] Whether there actually was such behavior has not
been proved. Insight on Louis's displeasure might be found by
referring to the descriptions of Eleanor and Louis just given.

Henry of Anjou, son of Matilda FitzEmpress (daughter of
Henry I, king of England) went with his father, Geoffrey, in
1151 to the French court in Paris so that Henry could be
recognized as the new Duke of Normandy. Again, tradition has
it that Henry and Eleanor, queen of France, fell in love at that
time. But then, love may have had nothing to do with it.
Eleanor at twenty-eight (eleven years older than Henry) was
reportedly very beautiful and still had her inheritance of the vast
landholding of Aquitaine (an attractive asset in itself), which
bordered on Henry's lands. Chances are that the impending
annullment of Louis's marriage was public knowledge as was
the fact that Henry planned to invade England and claim the
crown in right of his mother. For her part, Eleanor was aware

---

[1] Of this "scandalous behavior" nothing is known as fact. She was
accused of "too great familiarity" with the Prince of Antioch, who was
her uncle. Some writers continue the myth of an affair between Eleanor
and Saladin, forgetting that Saladin (1138–1193) was perhaps ten or
twelve years of age at the time. (Hallam, *Plantagenet Encyclopedia*,
pg. 180; Kelly, *Eleanor of Aquitaine and the Four Kings*, pg. 62)

that there was a possible crown in the offering. Too, she knew that an unmarried heiress, even an ex-queen of France, could be abducted and forcibly wed for her inheritance. Both Henry and Eleanor were intelligent; indications were they liked each other; and, politically, the union made sense.

On 21 Mar 1152, after fourteen years and two daughters, the marriage of Eleanor and Louis VII was annulled on the grounds that they were too closely related for marriage. Eleanor went home to her duchy of Aquitaine, escaping abduction attempts along the way. On Whit Sunday 1152, Eleanor, and Henry, Duke of Normandy, Count of Anjou and Maine, were married at Poitiers, and on 19 Dec 1154, they were crowned in Westminster Abbey as king and queen of England. For their issue, see "Henry II and Eleanor of Aquitaine."

Some of Louis' descendants by his other wives married descendants of Eleanor and her second husband: his daughter, Margaret, married Eleanor's son, Henry the Young King; Louis VIII, grandson of Louis VII, married Blanche, granddaughter of Eleanor; Margaret (d. 1318), a great-great-great-granddaughter, married Edward I, king of England; and Blanche of Artois, Louis VII's great-great-granddaughter, married Edmund Crouchback, son of Henry III, king of England.

Issue of Louis VII and his wives is listed here, along with some further interesting generations. The listing of these further generations should not be considered inclusive.

Issue of Louis VII and Eleanor of Aquitaine

Louis VII m. (1) at Bordeaux 22 Jul 1137 **Eleanor of Aquitaine**. Issue (two daughters):
1 — **Marie of France** (b. 1145; d. 11 Mar 1198) m. 1164 **Henry I** (d. soon after 1181 in the Holy Land) Count of Champagne,[1] son of **Theobald IV** (d. 1152), Count of Blois and Champagne and the brother of **Stephen**, KING OF

---

[1] *Ancestral* 102-26.

ENGLAND. Issue[1]:
2 — **Henry II of Champagne** (d. 1196, Acre), Palatine of Champagne and Brie, king of Jerusalem; m. 1191 as her third husband **Isabella of Jerusalem**, widow of **Conrad**, margrave of Montserrat, and daughter of **Amalric I**[2] (d. 1174) and his second wife, **Maria Comnena**.
2 — **Marie of Champagne** m. **Baldwin VI**, Count of Hainault and Flanders, Emperor of Constantinople.
2 — **Theobald** (d. 1201), Palatine of Champaign; m. **Blanca**, sister and heiress of **Santius VI**, king of Navarre.
1 — **Alix/Alice** (b. 1150; d. 1197) m. **Theobald V** (d. 1191), Count of Blois,[3] son of **Theobald IV** (d. 1152), Count of Blois and Champagne (the brother of **Stephen**, KING OF ENGLAND).[4] Issue[5]:
2 — A daughter, Countess of Blois; m. **John of Chastillon** (d. Apr 1201), Lord of Avesnes, Count of Blois. No issue.
2 — **Lewis/Louis** ("slain in Battel at Adrianaple 1205"), Count of Charters and Blois. No issue.
2 — **Theobald** (d. 1219), Count of Charters and Blois. No

---

[1] Warren, *Henry II*, Table 7, pg. 107; Anderson, *Royal Genealogies*, Table CCCXCII, pg. 637.

[2] **Amalric I** (1136–1174), brother of **Baldwin III** (1130–1162), was the son of **Fulk V of Anjou** (d. 1143) and **Melisende**, daughter of **Baldwin II** (d. 1131), King of Jerusalem. By his first wife, **Agnes of Courtenay**, **Amalric I** was the father of **Baldwin IV** (1161–1185) and **Sibyl**, who married as her second husband **Guy of Lusignan** (d. 1192). By his first wife, **Ermentrude**, **Fulk V of Anjou** was the father of **Sibyl**, **Matilda** (who married **William Audelin**, heir of **Henry I**, KING OF ENGLAND), and **Geoffrey** (d. 1151), Count of Anjou (who married **Matilda FitzEmpress**, daughter of **Henry I**, KING OF ENGLAND). (Barber, *The Devil's Crown*, Table 3)

[3] Previté-Orton, Table 13; Meade, pg. 10.

[4] Warren, *Henry II*, Table 2, pg. 15. **Theobald IV** (d. 1152), Count of Blois and Champagne, was also father of **Stephen**, Count of Sancerre; **William**, Bishop of Sens and Archbishop of Rheims; and **Adela**, who in 1160 married **Louis VII**. See also chapter, "William I the Conqueror."

[5] Anderson, *Royal Genealogies*, Table CCCXCII, pg. 637; Meade, *Eleanor of Aquitaine*, pg. viii, lists a daughter, **Isabel**, and a son, **Louis**.

issue.

2 — **Margaret** m. **Otto I**, Palatine of Burgundy, youngest son of **Frederick Barbarossa**.

2 — Another daughter, Countess of Blois; m. **Gauthier**, Lord of Avesnes in Hainault, Count of Blois.

Issue of Louis VII and Constance of Castile

Louis VII m. (2) at Orleans 1153/1154 **Constance of Castile** (b. abt 1134; d. 4 Oct 1160; bur. St. Denis), daughter of **Alfonso VII**, king of Castile and Leon, and **Berengaria of Barcelona**. Issue (two daughters):

1 — **Margaret/Margarite** (b. 1158; d. 1197, Acre) m. 1160 **Henry the Young King** (d. 1183), son of **Henry II**, KING OF ENGLAND, and **Eleanor of Aquitaine**. Issue:

    2 — **William** (b. 19 Jun 1177, Paris; d. 22 Jun 1177). **Margaret/Margarite**, as above, wife of **Henry the Young King**, m. (2) 1186 **Béla III** (d. 1196) of Hungary.[1]

1 — **Alice/Alais of France**[2]; betrothed to **Richard the Lion-**

---

[1] Warren, *Henry II*, pg. 107.

[2] The mother of **Louis VII's** daughter, **Alice of France**, who was betrothed to **Richard I the Lion-Heart**, King of England, appears to be uncertain. Concerning **Louis's** second marriage, *KQE*, pg. 73, states that **Constance of Castile** gave **Louis** "two more daughters" and names (pg. 188, Table 10) **Margaret** (who married **Henry the Young King**) and **Adelaide** but gives no further information on the latter. *KQE* adds that **Constance** "died at the birth of the younger in [Oct] 1160." Warren in *Henry II*, Table 7, states **Constance's** daughters were **Margaret** and **Alice**, who was betrothed to **Richard the Lion-Heart** but later (1195) married the Count of Ponthieu, **William III** (b. 1179; d. 1221). Seward in *Eleanor of Aquitaine: The Mother Queen*, pg. 62, indicates that **Alice** who married **William III**, Count of Ponthieu, was one of two daughters of **Constance**. Both Kelly, *Eleanor of Aquitaine and the Four Kings*, pgs. 136 and 159, and Meade, *Eleanor of Aquitaine*, indicate that **Alais** was the daughter of **Constance**; Meade also says of **Alais** that she was "orphaned at birth" (pg. 243) and that in 1169 she was a "nine-year-old orphaned daughter" (pg. 307).

Concerning **Louis's** third marriage, *KQE*, pg. 66, states **Adele/Alix/**

(continued...)

Heart, son of **Henry II**, KING OF ENGLAND, and **Eleanor of Aquitaine**, but they did not marry. In 1195 she married **William** (b. 1179; d. 1221), Count of Ponthieu.[1] Issue:

2 — **Marie**[2] (d. 1250), Countess of Ponthieu; m. (1) 1208/1211 **Simon de Dammartin** (d. 1239), Count of Aumale, son of **Alberic II** (d. 1200), Count of Dammartin. Issue:

3 — **Joanna de Dammartin**[3] (d. 1278/1279) m. (2) 1237 **Ferdinand III the Saint**[4] (b. 1191; d. 1252), king of Castile 1217–1252 and of Leon 1230–1252, son of **Alfonso IX** (b. 1166; d. 1229), king of Leon, and his wife, **Berengaria of Castile**[5] (d. 1244) (daughter of **Eleanor of England** and granddaughter of **Henry II**, KING OF ENGLAND, and **Eleanor of Aquitaine**).

Issue of Louis VII and Alix of Champagne

Louis VII m. (3) 13 Nov 1160 **Adela/Adele/Alix of Champagne and Blois** (b. abt 1140; d. 4/24 Jun 1206, Paris; bur. abbey of Pontigny in Burgundy[6]), daughter of

---

[2](...continued)
Adela of Champagne and **Louis** had one son and two daughters. On pg. 73 it is stated that **Adele of Champagne** became mother of **Philip II Augustus** and that **Philip's** birth was followed by the birth of two daughters. The names of the daughters and their spouses are given (pg. 188, Table 10) as **Alice**, who married **William**, Count of Ponthieu, and **Agnes**, who married the three husbands listed herein. Warren in *Henry II*, Table 7, shows **Adela of Champagne** as mother of **Philip II Augustus** and a daughter, **Agnes**.

[1] Warren, *Henry II*, pgs. 107, 222; *Ancestral* 109-28.
[2] *Ancestral* 109-29.
[3] *Ancestral* 109-30.
[4] *Ancestral* 109-30, which adds that **Ferninand III** was canonized in 1671.
[5] *Ancestral* 110-26, 110-27, 110-28, 110-29.
[6] Bush, *Memoirs of the Queens of France*, pg. 138.

Theobald IV,[1] Count of Champagne and Blois, and **Matilda of Carinthia**. Issue:

1 — **Philip II Augustus** (b. 21/22 August 1165, Gonesse nr Paris; crowned 1 Nov 1179, Rheims; d. 14 Jul 1223, Mantes; bur. St. Denis), king of France 1180–1223; m. (1) at Bapaume 28 Apr 1180 **Isabella of Hainault** (b. Apr 1170, Valenciennes; d. 15 Mar 1190, Paris; bur. Notre Dame, Paris), daughter of **Baldwin VIII** (d. 1195),[2] Count of Hainault and Namur, and his second wife, **Margaret of Flanders** (d. 1194). Issue:

   2 — Twin sons (d. at birth).

   2 — **Louis VIII the Lion** (b. 5/3 Sep 1187, Paris; crowned 6 Aug 1223, Rheims; d. 8 Nov 1226, Montpensier; bur. St. Denis), king of France 1223–1226; m. 23 May 1200 **Blanche** (b. bef 4 Mar 1188; d. 27 Nov 1252, Paris; bur. Abbey of Maubuisson), queen regent of France, daughter of **Alfonso VIII** (b. 11 Nov 1155; d. 6 Oct 1214, Galcear Meynos; bur. in monastery of Las Huelgas), king of Castile, and **Eleanor of England**; **Blanche** was the granddaughter of **Henry II** and **Eleanor of Aquitaine**.[3] Issue (eleven sons, three daughters[4]) included:

     3 — **Louis IX St. Louis,** king of France 1226–1270 (b. 25 Apr 1214, Poissy; crowned 29 Nov 1226; d. 25 Aug 1270, Carthage; bur. St. Denis), fourth but eldest surviving son; m. 27 May 1234[5] **Margaret** (b. 1221, St. Maime; d. 21 Dec 1295, Paris; bur. St. Denis), daughter of **Raymond IV Berengar**

---

[1] **Theobald IV** was the son of **Adela**, daughter of **William the Conqueror**.

[2] Previté-Orton, Table 13, indicates **Baldwin V** of Hainault. On Table 18, he is identified as **Baldwin V** of Hainault and **Baldwin VIII** of Flanders.

[3] **Eleanor of Aquitaine** was almost eighty years old when she journeyed to Castile to arrange for the marriage of her granddaughter, **Blanche**, with **Louis VIII**.

[4] *KQE*, pgs. 67, 188; Richard, *St. Louis, Crusader King of France*, pg. xxiv.

[5] Socarras, *Alfonso X of Castile: A Study on Imperialistic Frustration*, Appendix IV.

(d. 1245),[1] Count of Provence, and **Beatrice of Savoy**
(d. 1266). Issue (six sons, five daughters[2]):
    4 — **Louis** (d. 1260, aged 16).
    4 — **Philip III the Bold/Philip le Hardi** (b. 1 May
    1245, Poissy; crowned 15 Aug 1271, Rheims;
    d. 5 Oct 1285, Perpignan; bur. St. Denis), king of
    France 1270-1285; m. (1) at Clermont-en-Auvergne
    28 May 1262 **Isabella** (b. 1243; d. 28 Jan 1271,
    Cosenza; bur. Cosenza), daughter of **James I**, king of
    Aragon, and his second wife, **Yolande of Hungary**
    (d. 1255). Issue (four sons[3]) included:
        5 — **Philip IV** (d. 1314), king of France
        1285-1314; m. **Jeanne I** (d. 1305), queen of
        Navarre, daughter of **Henry I** (d. 1274), king of
        Navarre.
Philip III the Bold, as above, husband of **Isabella**,
m. (2) at Vincennes 21 Aug 1274 **Marie of Brabant**
(b. abt 1260, Liege; d. 12 Jan 1322, Murel), daughter
of **Henry III**, Duke of Brabant (d. 1260/1261), and
his wife, **Alice of Burgundy** (d. 1273). Issue (one
son, two daughters[4]) included:
    5 — **Margaret** (d. 1318) m. as his second wife
    Edward I, KING OF ENGLAND.
    4 — **John** (d. 1248).
    4 — **John Tristan** (b. Damietta), Count of Valois;
    m. **Yolande of Burgundy**.
    4 — **Peter I** (d. 1283), Count of Alençon, Count of
    Chartres.
    4 — **Robert** (d. 1317), Count of Clermont
    m. **Beatrice of Burgundy**.
    4 — **Isabella** (b. 2 Mar 1242; d. 27 Apr 1271)

---

[1] Previté-Orton names him as **Raymond Berengar V** of Provence.
[2] *KQE*, pg. 67; Bush, *Memoirs of the Queens of France*, pg. 174;
Richard, *St. Louis, Crusader King of France*, pg. xxiv.
[3] *KQE*, pg. 67.
[4] *KQE*, pg. 67.

m. **Theobald II**[1] (d. 1270), king of Navarre, son of
Theobald IV (d. 1253) of Champagne, king of
Navarre.
4 — **Blanche** (b. 1253; d. 1320[2]/13 Nov 1269[3])
m. 1269 **Ferdinand IX de la Cerda** (d. Aug 1275) of
Castile, son of **Alfonso X of Castile** (b. 23 Nov 1221;
d. 4 Apr 1284) (half-brother of **Edward I's** queen,
Eleanor of Castile) and **Violante of Aragon**
(d. 1300).
4 — **Margaret**, Duchess of Brabant; m. **John** of
Brabant.
4 — **Agnes** (d. 1327) m. **Robert II** (d. 1305), Duke
of Burgundy.
4 — **Blanche** m. **Henry III** of Champagne.
4 — **Robert II**, Count of Artois.
3 — **Robert I** (b. 1216; d. 1250), Count of Artois;
m. 1237 **Matilda of Brabant** (d. 29 Sep 1288), daughter
of **Henry II** (d. 1 Feb 1247/1248), Duke of Brabant.
Issue:
4 — **Robert**.
4 — **Blanche of Artois** (d. 1302) m. (1) 1269
Henry I (d. 1274), king of Navarre; m. (2) 29 Oct
1276 **Edmund Crouchback** (b. 16 Jan 1244/1245;
d. 5 Jun 1296, Bayonne), Earl of Lancaster, Earl of
Leicester, son of **Henry III**, KING OF ENGLAND.[4]
3 — **Alphonso** (d. 1271), Count of Toulouse, Count of
Poitou; m. **Joanna** (d. 1271), daughter and heiress of
Raymond VII of Toulouse. No issue.
3 — **Charles I** (b. 1226; d. 1285), Count of Anjou, king
of Sicily 1266 m. (1) 31 Jan 1246 **Beatrice of Provence**

---

[1] **Theobald's** brother, **Henry of Navarre** (d. 1274), was father of
Joanna/Jeanne who married **Philip IV**, King of France. (Previté-Orton,
Table 20)
[2] Anderson, *Royal Genealogies*, Table CCCCLIX.
[3] Socarras, *Alfonso X of Castile: A Study on Imperialistic Frustration*,
Appendix IV.
[4] *Ancestral* 45-30.

(d. 1267),[1] daughter of Count **Raymond Berengar V** of
Provence; m. (2) **Margaret of Burgundy** (d. 1308),
daughter of **Odo** of Burgundy. Issue of his first marriage
included[2]:
> 4 — **Charles II** (d. 1309), king of Sicily; m. **Mary of
> Hungary** (d. 1323), daughter of **Stephen IV** of
> Hungary.
> 4 — **Philip** (d. 1227), Prince of Achaia; m. **Isabella
> de Villehardouin** (d. 1312), Princess of Morea.
> 4 — **Beatrice** (d. 1275) m. **Philip of Courtenay**
> (d. 1283), titular Emperor of Constantinople.
> 4 — **Elizabeth** m. **Ladislas IV** (d. 1290) of Hungary.

3 — **Isabella.**
3 — **John.**
3 — **Philip-Dagobert.**
3 — **Stephen.**
3 — Three children (d. yng).

Philip II Augustus, as above, husband of **Isabella of Hainault,**
m. (2) (repudiated 5 Nov 1193) at Amiens 14 Aug 1193
Ingeborg of Denmark (b. 1175; d. 29 Jul 1236, Corbeil),
daughter of **Waldemar I**, king of Denmark, and **Sophie of
Polotsk**. No issue.

Philip II Augustus, as above, husband of **Ingeborg of
Denmark,** m. (3) (repudiated 1200) 1 Jun 1196 **Agnes of
Meran** (d. 29 Jul 1201, Poissy), daughter of **Berthold VI**,
Duke of Meran, and his wife, **Agnes of Wettin-Rochlitz**. Issue:
> 2 — **Marie** (d. 1224) m. (1) **Philip I** (d. 1212) of Namur/
> Count of Flanders; m. (2) **Henry I** (d. 5 Sep 1235[3]), Duke
> of Brabant.

---

[1] Pernoud, *Blanche of Castile*, pg. 244.
[2] Richard, *St. Louis, Crusader King of France*, pg. xxiv; Previté-
Orton, Table 19.
[3] *Ancestral* 155-26, 165-27.

2 — **Philip Hurepel** (d. 1234),[1] Count of Clermont/Count of Mortain; m. **Mahaut** of Dammartin, Countess of Boulogne.[2]

1 — **Agnes** m. (1) **Alexius II Comnenus** (d. 1183), Byzantine Emperor, son of **Manuel I** and his wife, **Mary** (daughter of **Raymond of Antioch**[3]); m. (2) as his fourth wife[4] **Andronicus I Comnenus** (d. 1185), Byzantine Emperor; m. (3) **Theodore Branas**.

Sources:

Anderson, James, *Royal Genealogies: or, the Genealogical Tables of Emperors, Kings and Princes, from Adam to these Times*, Bettenham, London, 1732.

Barber, Richard, *The Devil's Crown: Henry II, Richard I, John*, British Broadcasting Corporation, London, 1978.

Bush, Mrs. Annie Forbes, *Memoirs of the Queens of France with Notices of the Royal Favorites*, Vol. I, Henry Colburn, Publisher, London, 1843.

Hallam, Elizabeth, ed., *The Plantagenet Encyclopedia*, Grove Weidenfeld, NY, 1990.

Kelly, Amy, *Eleanor of Aquitaine and the Four Kings*, Harvard University Press, Cambridge, Mass., 1950.

Meade, Marion, *Eleanor of Aquitaine*, Hawthorn Books Publishers, Inc., NY, 1977.

Parsons, David, ed., *Eleanor of Castile 1290-1990*, Paul Watkins, Lincolnshire, 1991.

Previte-Orton, C. W., *The Shorter Cambridge Medieval History*, The University Press, Cambridge, 1962.

Seward, Desmond, *Eleanor of Aquitaine: The Mother Queen*, Dorset Press, NY, 1978.

Socarras, Cayetano J., *Alfonso X of Castile: A Study on Imperialistic Frustration*, Ediciones Hispam, Coleccion Blanquerna, Barcelona.

Stephen, Sir Leslie, and Lee, Sir Sidney, eds., *Dictionary of National Biography*, Oxford University Press, London, 1964.

---

[1] *KQE*, Table 10, pg. 188.
[2] Richard, *St. Louis, Crusader King of France*, pg. xxiv.
[3] Previté-Orton, Table 15.
[4] Previté-Orton, Table 13.

Warren, W. L., *Henry II*, University of California Press, Berkeley and
    Los Angeles, 1973.

Weis, Frederick Lewis, *Ancestral Roots of Sixty Colonists*—6th ed.,
    Genealogical Publishing Co., Inc., 1990.

Williamson, David, *Debrett's Kings and Queens of Britain*, Dorset
    Press, New York, 1992.

Williamson, David, *DeBrett's Kings and Queens of Europe*, Salem
    House Publishers, Mass., 1988.

The Marriages of John of Gaunt

John of Gaunt (b. Mar 1340, Abbey of St. Bavon, Ghent; d. 3 Feb 1399, Leicester Castle; bur. St Paul's Cathedral), fourth son of **Edward III** and **Philippa of Hainault**, 2nd Duke of Lancaster,[1] 5th Earl of Lancaster, Derby, Lincoln, and Leicester, Duke of Aquitaine, Duke of Richmond, titular King of Castile and Leon, K.G.; m. (1) at the Queen's Chapel, Reading, 19 May 1359[2] **Blanche of Lancaster** (b. 25 Mar 1341/1345[3]; d. 12/31 Sep 1368,[4] Bolingbroke Castle; bur. St.

---

[1] The title of Lancaster began in 1267, when **Edmund Crouchback** (d. 1296), son of **Henry III**, KING OF ENGLAND, was given this title by his father. The title passed to **Edmund's** son, **Thomas** (ex. 1322). His brother, **Henry Plantagenet/Henry of Lancaster** (d. 1345), inherited the title as 3rd Earl of Lancaster. He was "chief advisor to Edward III" in his seizure of power from his mother and her lover, **Roger IV Mortimer** (ex. 1330). **Henry's** son, **Henry of Grosment** (d. 1361), 4th Earl of Lancaster and 1st Duke of Lancaster, left no male issue, and the title went to his elder daughter's husband, **John of Gaunt**. (*Columbia-Viking Desk Encyclopedia*, 1968, "Lancaster, house of")

[2] Armitage-Smith, *John of Gaunt*, pg. 14. **Blanche of Lancaster** was **John of Gaunt's** cousin (Hallam, *The Plantagenet Encyclopedia*, pg. 109). Both were great-great-grandchildren of **Henry III**.

[3] According to Armitage-Smith, *John of Gaunt*, pg. 94, **Blanche of Lancaster** was born in 1341; Burke's *Royal Family*, pg. 199, gives a birth year of 1345.

[4] Silva-Vigier, *This Moste Highe Prince...John of Gaunt*, pg. 120, states that 1369 was long accepted at the year of **Blanche's** death; however, Silva-Vigier asserts that the year of **Blanche's** death is now believed to have been 1368. On pg. 123, Silva-Vigier states that the annual services for her death were performed from 1370 till 1399.

Paul's Cathedral[1]), daughter of **Henry of Grosment**
(b. 1299?; d. 1361; bur. at Leicester in the collegiate church
which he founded), 4th Earl and 1st Duke of Lancaster, Earl of
Derby, Lincoln and Leicester, K.G., and his wife, **Isabel
Beaumont** (liv. 24 Mar 1356/d. 1361) (daughter of **Henry
Beaumont** (d. 10 Mar 1339/1340), 1st Lord Beaumont, and his
wife, **Alice Comyn**).[2] Both **John of Gaunt** and **Blanche of
Lancaster** were great-great-grandchildren of **Henry III**, KING
OF ENGLAND.

Three generations of John of Gaunt are shown. In some
cases, further generations are listed, but that listing should not
be considered complete.

---

[1] Silva-Vigier's book, *This Moste Highe Prince...John of Gaunt*,
contains a sketch of the tomb of **John of Gaunt** and **Blanche** in Old
St. Paul's Cathedral. The tomb was designed by **Henry Yevele**, and the
engraving of the tomb was taken from Hollar's Old St. Paul's, London.
According to Silva-Vigier, the effigies on the tomb were destroyed in the
wars of the Roses but replaced by **Henry VII**. The Great Fire of London
destroyed the tomb. Silva Vigier describes **John of Gaunt** as "the
greatest feudal Baron of his age" and states that he owned almost a third
of England. (Silva-Vigier, pgs. x, xix, 76)

[2] **Henry of Grosment** and **Isabel Beaumont** had two daughters:
1 — **Maud** (d. 10 Apr 1362, aged 23) m. (1) 1 Nov 1344 **Ralph de
Stafford** (d. 1348 in the lifetime of his father), Lord Stafford;
m. (2) 1352 **William V** (d. 1389), Count of Holland and Hainault, Duke
of Bavaria. No issue. (*CP*, Stafford section)
1 — **Blanche** m. **John of Gaunt**. Fuller's *Worthies* (1965, AMS Press,
Vol. II, pg. 439) states that **Blanche** was the only one of his daughters
who had issue.

Henry of Grosment was the son of **Henry of Lancaster**, also called
Henry Plantagenet (b. 1281; d. 22 Sep 1345), Earl of Lancaster, and
his wife, **Maud de Chaworth** (b. 1282; d. bef 3 Dec 1322), daughter of
Patrick Chaworth (d. abt 7 Jul 1283), Lord of Kidwelley, Wales, son
of **Patrick de Chaworth**.

Ancestors of Blanche of Lancaster

```
                          ┌Henry of Lancaster (d. 1345)
            ┌Henry of Grosment (d. 1361)
            │             └Maud de Chaworth (d. 1322))
Blanche of Lancaster (d. 1368/1369)
            │             ┌Henry de Beaumont (d. 1339/1340)
            └Isabel de Beaumont (d. 1361)
                          └Alice Comyn (d. 1349)¹
```

Issue by Blanche of Lancaster

1 ² — **Philippa of Lancaster** (b. 31 Mar 1360, Leicester; d. 19 Jul 1415, Odivelas, nr Lisbon; bur. Batalha), from whom descended the Kings of Portugal; m. at Oporto 2³/11 Feb 1387 **John I** (b. 11 Apr 1358; d. 14 Aug 1433, Lisbon; bur. Batalha), King of Portugal 1385–1433, K.G. Issue ("six sons, two daughters"⁴):

  2 — **Branca** (b. 1388; d. 1389).

  2 — **Alfonso** (b. 1390; d. 1400).

  2 — **Duarte I/Edward I** (b. 31 Oct 1391; d. 18 Sep 1438; bur. Alcobaça), King of Portugal 1433–1438; m. 22 Sep 1428 **Leonor of Aragon** (d. 19 Feb 1445, Toledo), daughter of **Ferdinand I**, King of Aragon. Issue (three sons, three daughters⁵):

    3 — **Alfonso V** (b. 15 Jan 1432, Cintra; d. 24 or 28 Aug 1481, Cintra; bur. Batalha), King of Portugal 1438–1481; m. 6 May 1477 **Isabel** (b. 1432; d. 2 Dec 1455, Evora; bur. Batalha), daughter of **Pedro**, Duke of Coimbra (b. 1392; d. 1449) (brother of **Duarte I**) and

---

¹ *CP*, Lancaster section, Beaumont section.

² Note that the numbering employed in this chapter will indicate that this individual is one generation removed from **John of Gaunt**, thus two generations removed from the king and queen. Some great-great-grandchildren of **John of Gaunt** are included here for their historical interest; however, the emphasis has been to carry his descendants through the great-grandchildren, which would be the great-great-grandchildren of **John of Gaunt's** parents, **Edward III** and **Philippa**.

³ Silva-Vigier, *This Moste Highe Prince...John of Gaunt*, pg. 274.

⁴ Armitage-Smith, *John of Gaunt*, pg. 308; *KQE*, Table 2 and pg. 14; Anderson, *Royal Genealogies*, Table CCCCLXIX.

⁵ *KQE*, pg. 15; Anderson, *Royal Genealogies*, Table CCCCLXIX.

Isabel of Urgel. Issue:

4 — **John**.

4 — **Joana** (b. 3 Feb 1452; d. 14 May 1490), a nun.

4 — **John II/João II the Perfect**[1] (b. 3 or 4 May 1455, Lisbon; d. 25 Oct 1495, "not without suspicion of poison"; bur. Batalha), only surviving son, King of Portugal 1481–1495; m. at Setubal 18 Jan 1471 **Leonor** (b. 2 May 1458; d. 17 Nov 1525; bur. Lisbon), eldest daughter of **Ferdinand** (b. 1433; d. 1470), Duke of Vizen/Vizeu, and **Beatrice of Portugal** (d. 1506) (daughter of **John** (b. 1400; d. 1442)[2]).

3 — **Ferdinand** (b. 1433; d. 8 Sep 1470), Duke of Vizen; m. **Beatrice of Portugal** (d. 1506), daughter of **John**, brother of **Duarte I**. For historical interest, issue included[3]:

4 — **Manuel I**[4] (b. 31 May[5]/1 Jun 1469,[6] Alconchette; d. 13 Dec 1521, Belem) King of Portugal 1495–1521; m. (1) at Valencia Oct 1497 **Isabel** (b. 2 Oct 1470; d. 24/25 Aug 1498, Saragossa; bur. Saragossa or Toledo), daughter of **Ferdinand II** (d. 1516), King of Aragon, and his wife, **Isabel I** (d. 1501), Queen of Castile; m. (2) at Alcazar de Sol 30 Oct 1500 **Maria** (b. 29 Jun 1482; d. 7 Mar 1517), the sister of his first wife. Issue of second marriage

---

[1] **John II** (d. 1495) found the sailing route to the East Indies and ordered a survey made of the African coast to the Cape of Good Hope. (Anderson, *Royal Genealogies*, Table CCCCLXIX)

[2] **John** was the son of **Joao I/John I** and **Philippa of Lancaster**.

[3] Anderson, *Royal Genealogies*, Table CCCCLXIX.

[4] During the reign of **Manuel I** (1495–1521), the first East Indian voyage was accomplished, and Portugal became involved in trade with Africa and the the distant parts of Asia. His reign has been referred to as the Golden Age of Portugal.

[5] Anderson, *Royal Genealogies*, Table CCCCLXIX.

[6] *KQE*, pg. 15.

(seven sons, three daughters[1]) included:

   5 — **John III** (b. 6 Jun 1502, Lisbon; d. 11 Jun
   1557, Lisbon; bur. Belem), King of Portugal;
   m. 1525 **Catharin** (d. 1577 or 1578), daughter of
   Phillip I, King of Spain.
   5 — **Isabella of Portugal** (b. 4 Oct 1503;
   d. 1 May 1539) m. 1526 **Charles V** (d. 1556),
   Holy Roman Emperor, Emperor of Austria, and (as
   Charles I) King of Spain, son of **Philip I**, King of
   Spain.
Manuel I, as above, husband of **Maria**, m. (3) at
Lisbon 7 Mar 1519 **Leonor** (b. 24 Nov 1498,
Brussels; d. 18 Feb 1558, Talavera), daughter of
Philip I, King of Castile, and his wife, **Juana**, Queen
of Castile. Issue included[2]:
   5 — **Leonor/Eleonora** (b. 1458; d. 1525)
   m. **John II** (b. 1455; d. 1495), King of Portugal
   1481–1495, son of **Alfonso V** (d. 1481), King of
   Portugal, and **Isabel**.
   5 — **John** (d. 22 Aug 1484), Duke of Viseo.
   5 — **James** (k. 22 Aug 1482, slain by his brother-
   in-law, **John II** (d. 1495), for conspiring against
   him), Duke of Viseo.
   5 — **Isabel**, wife of **Ferdinand**, Duke of Bragança.
3 — **Philip** (d. aged 10).
3 — **Eleonora of Portugal** (b. 8 Sep 1434; d. 1 Sep
1467) m. at Naples 8 Mar 1452 **Frideric/Frederick III**
(b. 21 Sep 1415; d. 19 Aug 1493), Holy Roman
Emperor, King of the Germans.[3] Their issue included:
   4 — **Maximilian I** (b. 23 Mar 1459; d. 12 Jan 1519),
   Holy Roman Emperor; m. **Marie** (d. 1482), daughter

---

[1] *KQE*, pg. 15; Anderson, *Royal Genealogies*, Table CCCCLXIX;
Crankshaw, *The Hapsburgs*, Genealogical Tables.

[2] Anderson, *Royal Genealogies*, Table CCCCLXIC.

[3] Crankshaw, *The Hapsburgs*, Genealogical Tables. An illustration in
this book shows a detail from a fresco painted by Pintoricchio of the
meeting of **Frederick III** and **Eleanor of Portugal**.

of **Charles the Bold** (d. 1477), Duke of Burgundy.

3 — **Catharin** (d. 12 Jun 1463), a nun.

3 — **Joanna Posthuma** (b. Mar 1439; d. 13 Jun[1]/
17 Jan 1475, Tora) m. 1455 **Henry IV** (b. 5 Jan 1425,
Valladolid; d. 11 Dec 1474), King of Castile and Leon,
son of **Juan II** (d. 22 Jul 1454), King of Castile and
Leon, and his wife, **Maria of Aragon** (d. Feb 1445).

2 — **Pedro** (b. 1392; k. 20 May 1449), Duke of Coimbra;
m. 1428 **Isabel of Urgel**, daughter of **James**, Count of
Urgel. Issue[2]:

3 — **Peter** (d. 30 Jun 1466), Constable of Portugal.

3 — **John** (d. 1457), Duke of Coimbria; m. **Charlotta**,
daughter of **John III**, King of Cyprus.

3 — **Philippa**, a nun.

3 — **Beatrix** m. **Adolph** de Cleve, Lord of Ravenstein.

3 — **James** (d. 27 Aug 1459), Bishop of Lisbon,
Cardinal 1456.

3 — **Isabel** (b. 1432; d. 2 Dec 1455, Evora;
bur. Batalha), wife of **Alfonso V**.

2 — **Prince Henry the Navigator** (b. 1394; d. 1460), Duke
of Vizen, Grand Master of the Order of Christ (1394).

2 — **Isabel** (b. 1397; d. 17 Dec 1472) m. 10 or Jan 1429/
1430 as his third wife **Philip the Good**[3] (d. 15 Jun 1467),
Duke of Burgundy, son of **John the Fearless** (assassinated
10 Sep 1419[4]), Duke of Burgundy and Count of Flanders,
and his wife, **Margaret of Bavaria/Margaret of Holland**
(d. 1422/1432) (daughter of Albert of Bavaria, regent of
Hainault, Holland and Zeeland).[5] Issue[6]:

---

[1] *KQE*, pg. 44.

[2] Anderson, *Royal Genealogies*, Table CCCCLXIX.

[3] On 10 Feb 1429, **Philip the Good** founded the Order of the Golden
Fleece at Bruges, similar to the Order of the Garter. His first wife was
Michelle of France (d. 1422). He m. (2) 1424 **Bonne of Artois**, who
died about a year later. (Vaughan, *Philip the Good*, pgs. 57, 132)

[4] Vaughan, *Philip the Good*, pg. 1.

[5] **John the Fearless** (d. 1419) was the grandson of **John the Good**
(d. 1364), King of France (Cartellieri, *The Court of Burgundy*, Table

(continued...)

3 — **Charles the Bold** (b. 10 Nov 1433; k. 5 Jan 1477,
Battle of Nancy; bur. St. George's Church, Nancy),
Duke of Burgundy, K.G., an ancestor of the Spanish
House of Hapsburg; m. (1) 1439 **Catharin of Valois**
(d. 1446), daughter of **Charles VII**, King of France; no
issue; m. (2) 1454 **Isabella of Bourbon** (d. 1465),
daughter of his father's sister, **Agnes**, and her husband,
Charles I (d. 1456), Duke of Bourbon[1]; there was
issue; m. (3) 1468 **Margaret of York** (b. 3 May 1446,
Fotheringhay; d. 28 Nov 1503, Malines; bur. Church of
the Cordeliers, Malines), youngest daughter of **Richard
Plantagenet** (ex. 1460), Duke of York, and sister of
Edward IV and **Richard III**, KINGS OF ENGLAND;
no issue.
   3 — **Catharin** m. **Humbert**, Lord of Queille.
   3 — **John**, Provost of St. Audun.
   3 — **Mary**, a nun.
   3 — **Cornelia** m. **Adrian**, Lord of Mornay.
2 — **John** (b. 1400; d. Oct 1442), Constable of Portugal,
Grand Master of the Order of St. James; m. **Isabel of
Portugal** (d. 1445). Issue[2]:
   3 — **James** (d. 1443), Grand Master of the Order of

---

[5] (...continued)
"France, Burgundy, Orleans"). Vaughan, *Valois Burgundy*, Table 1
"The Valois Dukes of Burgundy" and Table 2 "The Succession to
Brabant and to Hainault, Holland, and Zeeland"; Vaughan, *Philip the
Bold*, table on pg. 82.

[6] Anderson, *Royal Genealogies*, Table CCCLX. Vaughan states that
Philip the Good had no issue by either his first or second wife, but by
his third wife, he had three sons born between 1431 and 1433. Only the
third son, **Charles**, survived. **Philip** also had a number of illegitimate
children. Exactly how many is not yet known, and Vaughan warns that
the number has been "exaggerated by the devious enthusiasm" of
genealogists, perhaps on behalf of particular clients with "aristocratic
aspirations." (Vaughan, *Philip the Good*, pgs. 132–135)

[1] Vaughan, *Valois Burgundy*, Table 3 "Burgundy and Bourbon";
Philip the Good, pg. 342.

[2] Anderson, *Royal Genealogies*, Table CCCCLXIX.

St. James, Constable of Portugal.
3 — **Isabel** (b. 1430; d. 15 Aug 1496, Arevalo;
bur. Miraflores, nr Burgos) m. at Madrigal Aug 1447
John II (b. 6 Mar 1405; d. 22 Jul 1454, Valladolid),
King of Castile.
3 — **Beatrice of Portugal** (d. 1506), as above, wife of
Fernando (b. 1433; d. 8 Sep 1470), Duke of Vizen.
3 — **Philippa** (d. unm).
2 — **Ferdinand** (b. 1402; d. 1443, a hostage in Tangiers),
Grand Master of Avis.
1 — **Elizabeth of Lancaster** (b. bef 21 Feb 1363/1364[1];
d. 24 Nov 1425; bur. Burford Church, Salop) m. (1) (diss. abt
1383/aft 24 Sep 1383[2]) at Kenilworth 24 Jun 1380[3] as his
first wife[4] **John Hastings** (d. 30/31 Dec 1389, Woodstock,
fatally injured while practicing for a jousting tournament[5];
bur. (1) church of the Friars Preachers, Hereford, (2) in or
aft March 1391/1392 church of the Friars Minors (Grey Friars),
London), 3rd Earl of Pembroke; no issue; m. (2) "at or near
Plymouth"[6] 24 Jun 1386/1384 **John de Holand**[7]

---

[1] Armitage-Smith, *John of Gaunt*, pg. 94, states that **Elizabeth of
Lancaster** was "b. ? 1364." According to Burke's *Royal Family*,
pg. 199, she was born "*ante* 21 Feb 1363."

[2] *CP*, Pembroke section.

[3] The *CP*, Exeter section, states that **Elizabeth of Lancaster** was
"affianced" to **Hastings**, that **Hastings** was under the age of 14 in 1386,
and that **Elizabeth** probably was older than **Hastings**. There was no true
marriage and no issue.

[4] **John Hastings** m. (2) as her first husband **Philippa Mortimer**
(b. 21 Nov 1375, Ludlow; d. 24/25 Sep 1401, Halnaker, Sussex;
bur. Boxgrove, nr Lewes), daughter of **Edmund II de Mortimer**
(d. 1381), 3rd Earl of March. (Burke's *Royal Family*, pg. 199; *CP*,
Pembroke section; *CP*, March section)

[5] *CP*, Pembroke section.

[6] CP, Exeter section.

[7] **John de Holand** was half-brother of **Richard II**, KING OF
ENGLAND (Burke's *Royal Family*, pg. 199).

(b. abt 1352/aft 1350; ex. by mob 9 or 10 Jan 1399/1400,[1]
Pleshy, Essex; bur. Collegiate Church, Pleshy, Essex), Earl of
Huntingdon, 1st Duke of Exeter, K.G., third son[2] of **Thomas
de Holand** (d. 1360), 1st Earl of Kent, by his wife **Joan**
(d. 1385), the Fair Maid of Kent (only daughter of **Edmund of
Woodstock** (ex. 1330), Earl of Kent). Issue (three sons, two
daughters[3]):

   2 — **Richard de Holand** (d. 3 Sep 1400). No issue.[4]

   2 — **Edward de Holand**.

   2 — **John de Holand** (b. 18 or 29 Mar 1395/1396,
Dartington, Devonshire; d. 5 Aug 1447; bur. (1) Church of
St. Katherine by the Tower, (2) Regent's Park, (3) 1951,
the Tower of London[5]), second son,[6] Constable of the
Tower, Earl of Huntingdon, Duke of Exeter, K.G., K.B.;
m. (1) lic. 24 Oct 1429[7]/bef 15 Jul 1427[8] **Anne Stafford**
(d. 20 or 24 Sep 1432[9]; bur. (1) Church of St. Katherine

---

   [1] **John de Holand** was involved in a conspiracy to overthrow
Henry IV, his brother-in-law, and restore **Richard II**, his own half-
brother, to the throne.

   [2] *DNB*, "Holland, John, Duke of Exeter and Earl of Huntingdon
(1352?-1400)"; *Sureties* 90-7.

   [3] *DNB*, "Holland, John, Duke of Exeter and Earl of Huntingdon
(1352?-1400)"; Burke's *Royal Family*, pg. 199.

   [4] Ramsay, *Lancaster and York*, Vol. I, Table IV, gives a death date
of 1416.

   [5] **John de Holand** (d. 1447), **Anne de Mortimer** (his first wife), and
Anne Montagu (his third wife) were buried together in the Church of
St. Katherine by the Tower. According to Wilson, *The Tower of London*,
pgs. 69-70, St. Katherine's Hospital was demolished in 1825 when
building was begun on St. Katherine's Docks. The "remains and
benignly smiling effigies" of Holand and the two wives were moved to
Regent's Park, then moved again in 1951 to the Tower.

   [6] CP, Exeter section.

   [7] *DNB*, "Holland, John, Duke of Exeter and Earl of Huntingdon
(1395-1447)."

   [8] CP, Exeter section.

   [9] **Anne** is believed to have died soon after the birth of her husband's
son and heir, **Henry**. (*DNB*, "Holland, John, Duke of Exeter and Earl of
Huntingdon (1352-1400)")

by the Tower, (2) Regent's Park, (3) 1951, the Tower of London), daughter of **Edmund de Stafford** (d. 1403), 5th Earl of Stafford, and his wife, **Anne** (d. 1438) (daughter of **Thomas of Woodstock**). **Anne Stafford** was the widow (no issue) of **Edmund IV de Mortimer** (b. 4/6 Nov 1391, the New Forest; d. of the plague 18/19 Jan 1424/1425, Trim, co. Meath), 5th Earl of March. Issue:

3 — **Henry de Holand** (b. 27 Jun 1430, Tower of London; d. Sep 1475, found dead in the English Channel), only son by his first wife, [1] Duke of Exeter, Earl of Huntingdon, Constable of the Tower, Admiral of England, Ireland, and Aquitaine; m. (div. 12 Nov 1472 [2]) bef 30 Jul 1447 [3] **Anne Plantagenet** (b. 10 Aug 1439, Fotheringhay; d. 14 Jan 1475/1476; bur. St. George's Chapel, Windsor), daughter of **Richard Plantagenet** (ex. 1460), 3rd Duke of York, and his wife, **Cecily Sweet Cis Neville** (d. 1495) (daughter of **Ralph Neville** (d. 1425), 1st Earl of Westmorland). Issue (only child [4]):

4 — **Anne de Holand** (b. abt 1455; d. 1475/liv. Jan 1472/1473 or bef 6 Jun 1474 or "soon after" 26 Aug 1467) m. at Greenwich as his first wife [5] Oct 1466

---

[1] *CP*, Exeter section.

[2] **Anne** m. (2) **Thomas Seint Leger** or **Selenger**, who was beheaded at Exeter abt 8 Nov 1483. He and his wife were buried in a chantry which he founded in 1481 in the Chapel of St. George at Windsor. They had a daughter, **Anne**, who married **George Manners**, Lord Ros, of Belvoir. (CP, Exeter section)

[3] The match between **Anne** and **Henry de Holand** was agreed upon by their fathers in August 1445. (Johnson, *Duke Richard of York 1411–1460*, pg. 68)

[4] *CP*, Dorset section, Exeter section.

[5] **Thomas Grey** (d. 1501) m. (2) bef Apr 1475 as her first husband **Cecily Bonville** (aged 13 in 1474; d. 12 Apr/bef 2 Jun 1530/12 May 1529, Shacklewell in Hackney; bur. Astley, co. Warwick), Baroness Harington, Baroness Bonville, daughter and heir of **William Bonville** (d. 1461), Lord Harington, and his wife, **Catherine Neville** (daughter of
(continued...)

Thomas Grey (b. 1451; d. 20 Sep 1501; bur. Astley, co. Warwick), 1st Marquess Dorset, Lord Ferrers of Groby, K.G., son and heir of **John Grey** (k. 17 Feb 1460/1461, Second Battle of St. Albans) and his wife, **Elizabeth Woodville** (daughter of **Richard Woodville** and queen consort of **Edward IV**). No issue.[1]

3 — **Anne de Holand** (d. 26 Dec 1486), only sister[2] of **Henry de Holand**; m. (1) bef 18 Feb 1440/1441 **John Neville** (d. 7 Mar 1449/1450; bur. Haltemprice, co. York), Lord Neville, son of **Ralph Neville** (d. 1484), 2nd Earl of Westmorland; no issue; m. (2) bef 5 Sep 1452 **John Neville** (b. abt 1410; k. 29 Mar 1461, Battle of Towton), Lord Neville, uncle of her first husband; there was issue[3]; m. (3) as his second wife[4] **James Douglas** (d. aft 22 May 1491), 9th Earl of Douglas.[5]

John de Holand (d. 1447), Earl of Huntingdon, Duke of Exeter, as above, husband of **Anne Stafford**, m. (2) (license 20 Jan 1432) **Beatrice of Portugal**[6] (d. 23 Oct 1439, Bordeaux[7]; bur. Arundel), illegitimate daughter ("probably legitimated") of **John I/João I**, King of

---

[5] (...continued)
Richard Neville (ex. 1460), Earl of Salisbury). Their son, **Thomas Grey** (d. 1550), was betrothed to **Anne St. Leger**. (St. Aubyn, *The Year of Three Kings 1483*, pg. 24; *CP*, Dorset section, Wiltshire section, Bonville section)

[1] *CP*, Dorset section.

[2] *CP*, Exeter section, wherein is stated that she "has always been erroneously represented by genealogists as his half-sister, and da. of Anne (de Mountagu)...."

[3] *CP*, Neville section.

[4] **James Douglas'** first wife was **Margaret**, Maid of Galloway.

[5] *CP*, Neville section, Westmorland section. The *DNB*, "Douglas, James, ninth Earl of Douglas (1426–1488)," which gives a death date for **James Douglas** as 14 Jul 1488, states "a single record is supposed to prove" this marriage between **Anne Holand** and **James Douglas**.

[6] Armitage-Smith, *John of Gaunt*, pg. 308. **Beatrix** had a brother, also illegitimate, **Alfonso**, Count of Barcellos, Duke of Bragança, from whom descended the House of Bragança.

[7] CP, Exeter section, Arundel section.

Portugal, by **Doña Inez**[1] and the widow[2] of **Thomas FitzAlan** (b. 13 Oct 1381; d. 13 Oct 1415; bur. Collegiate Church of Arundel[3]), Earl of Arundel; no issue; m. (3) **Anne Montagu** (d. 28 Nov 1457; bur. (1) Church of St. Katherine by the Tower, (2) Regent's Park, (3) 1951, the Tower of London), eldest daughter of **John Montagu** (b. abt 1350; d. ex. Jan 1399/1400, Cirencester; bur. (1) Cirencester, (2) 1420 Bisham), 3rd Earl of Salisbury,[4] and his wife **Maud Francis** (d. bef 5 1424) (daughter of **Adam Francis**, Mayor of London[5]); there was issue.[6]

2 — **Constance Holand** (aged 4 in Oct 1391; d. 12 or 14 Nov 1437; bur. Church of St. Katherine by the Tower) m. (1) (papal disp. Oct 1391[7]) **Thomas de Mowbray** (b. 17 Sep 1385; ex. without trial 8 Jun 1405, his head being fixed on Bootham Bar; bur. Grey Friars, York), Earl of Norfolk, Duke of Norfolk, Earl Marshal; no issue; m. (2) bef 24 Feb 1412/1413 **John Grey** (d. 27 Aug 1439) of Ruthin, son of **Reynold Grey** (d. 18 Oct 1440), Lord Grey, of Ruthin, and his first wife, **Margaret Roos** (d. 3 Sep or 12 Nov 1448) (daughter of **Thomas de Roos**

---

[1] The name of the mistress is given as **Agnes Perez** in Anderson, *Royal Genealogies*, Table CCCCLXIX. The *CP*, Exeter section, gives the name as **Inez Pires**, and the Arundel section states **Inez Perez**.

[2] **Thomas FitzAlan** m. at Lambeth 26 Nov 1405 **Beatrice of Portugal** but died without issue. He was the son of **Richard III FitzAlan** and his wife, **Elizabeth de Bohun**. (*CP*, Arundel section)

[3] CP, Exeter section; *DNB*, "FitzAlan, Thomas, Earl of Arundel and Surrey (1381-1415)."

[4] *DNB*, "Holland, John, Duke of Exeter and Earl of Huntingdon (1352?-1400)"; *DNB*, "Holland, John, Duke of Exeter and Earl of Huntingdon (1395-1337)."

[5] *CP*, Salisbury section.

[6] Reference *CP*, Exeter section, pg. 211, footnote (a), wherein is listed simply, "his sons, Lowes (the eldest), Edmond, Philip, Harry, and John, fitz Lowes: his daughters, Margaret (the eldest), Elizabeth, Alice, and Margaret (the youngest)."

[7] *CP*, Norfolk section.

of Hemsley, co. York). Issue included:

3 — **Edmund Grey** (b. 26 Oct 1416; d. 22 May 1490)
of Ruthin, Earl of Kent; m. bef 1458/1459 **Katherine
Percy** (b. 28 May 1423), daughter of **Henry de Percy**
(b. 3 Feb 1392/1393; k. 22 May 1455, First Battle of
St. Albans), 2nd Earl of Northumberland, only son of
Henry Hotspur Percy (d. 1403) and his wife, **Eleanor
Neville** (d. 1463) (daughter of **Ralph Neville** (d. 1425),
1st Earl of Westmorland). For historical interest, two of
their issue were:

4 — **Anthony Grey** (d. bet. 15 May and 27 Nov
1480; bur. Abbey of St. Albans), first son; m. **Joan
Woodville,** daughter of **Richard Woodville** (d. 1469),
1st Earl Rivers, and his wife, **Jacquetta of
Luxembourg** (d. 30 May 1472), Duchess of Bedford
(daughter of **Pierre de Luxembourg,** Count of
St. Pol, Conversano, and Brienne). **Joan Woodville**
was sister of **Elizabeth Woodville,** queen consort of
Edward IV, KING OF ENGLAND. No issue. [1]

4 — **George Grey** (d. 16 Dec 1503, Ampthill),
second son, Earl of Kent; m. (1) in or aft 1483 **Anne
Woodville** (d. 30 Jul 1489; bur. Warden,
Bedfordshire), daughter of **Richard Woodville,** 1st
Earl Rivers, and his wife, **Jacquetta of Luxembourg,**
and the widow of **William Bourchier** (d. aft 12 Feb
1482/1483); **Anne Woodville** was sister of **Elizabeth
Woodville,** queen consort of **Edward IV,** KING OF
ENGLAND; m. (2) on or bef 1 Oct 1490 **Catherine
Herbert** (d. bef 8 May 1504), daughter of **William
Herbert** (ex. 27 Jul 1469, Battle of Northampton;
bur. Tintern Abbey), 1st Earl of Pembroke, and his
wife **Anne Devereux** (liv. 25 Jun 1486). [2]

2 — A daughter of **Elizabeth of Lancaster** and **John de
Holand** died at a young age and without issue[3]; she

---

[1] *CP*, Grey section, Kent section.
[2] *CP*, Kent section.
[3] *CP*, Oxford section.

"almost certainly"[1] m. **Richard de Vere** (b. prob. 1385; d. 15 Feb 1416/1417; bur. (1) Earls Colne, (2) 1935 St. Stephen's Chapel, Bures), Earl of Oxford, K.G., son of **Aubrey de Vere** (d. 23 Apr 1400), Earl of Oxford, and his wife, **Alice FitzWalter** (daughter of **John FitzWalter** (d. 18 Oct 1361; bur. Dunmow Priory[2]), 2nd Baron FitzWalter, and his wife **Eleanor Percy**).

Elizabeth of Lancaster (d. 1425), as above, m. (3) bef 12 Dec 1400 **John Cornwall**[3] (b. "at sea in St. Michael's Mount Bay, Cornwall"[4]; d. 11 Dec 1443; bur. Chapel of Black Friars by Ludgate), Lord Fanhope, 1st Baron Fanhope of Fanhope and Milbroke of Milbroke, K.G. Issue[5]:

   2 — **Constance** (d. bef 1429) m. as his first wife (or was contracted to)[6] **John d'Arundel** (b. 14 Feb 1407/1408; d. 12 Jun 1435 at Beauvais, from injuries received May 1435 at the siege of Gerberoy, in the Beauvaisis; bur. (1) Grey Friars, Beauvais, (2) 15 Feb 1435/1436,

---

[1] *CP*, Oxford section.

[2] *CP*, FitzWalter section.

[3] Descended from an illegitimate son of **Richard of Cornwall** (d. 1271), Earl of Cornwall and King of the Romans. (Burke's *Royal Family*, pg. 199)

[4] *CP*, Fanhope section, wherein he is described as the son and heir of **John Cornwall** "by a niece of the Duke of Brittany." **John Cornwall** (d. 1443) had an only and illegitimate son, **John Cornwall**, who died unmarried in the lifetime of his father, "being slain at the siege of Meaux, Dec. 1421," aged 17.

[5] *CP*, Arundel section.

[6] **John d'Arundel** (d. 1435) m. (2) **Maud Lovell** (d. 19 May 1436), widow of **Richard Stafford** (d. abt 1427) and daughter of **Robert Lovell** and his wife, **Elizabeth Bryene** (daughter and coheir of **Guy Bryene**). This **Guy Bryene** was "1st s. and h. ap. of Sir Guy de Bryene [Lord Bryene]." **John d'Arundel** and **Maud Lovell** had an only child, **Humphrey FitzAlan** (b. 30 Jan 1429; d. unm. 24 Apr 1438), Earl of Arundel, Duke of Touraine. **Humphrey FitzAlan** had a half-sister, **Avice Stafford** (b. 4 Dec 1423; d. 3 Jun or 3 Jul 1457), who m. **James Butler** (ex. 1 May 1461, Newcastle, after Battle of Towton), Earl of Wiltshire and Ormond. (*CP*, Arundel section, Ormond section; *DNB*, "FitzAlan, John VI, Earl of Arundel (1408–1435)")

Arundel), Earl of Arundel, Duke of Touraine, son of **John
FitzAlan d'Arundel** (d. 21 Apr 1421), Lord Maltravers,
Earl of Arundel, and **Eleanor Berkeley** (d. 1 Aug 1455;
bur. Arundel) (daughter of **John Berkeley** of Beverstone,
co. Gloucester).

1 — **John** (b. 1362/1364(?); d. yng; bur. St. Mary's Church,
Leicester).

1 — **Edward** (b. 1365/1368; d. yng; bur. St. Mary's Church,
Leicester).

1 — **John** (b. bef 4 May 1366; d. yng; bur. St. Mary's Church,
Leicester). [1]

1 — **Henry IV of Bolingbroke** (b. 4 Apr 1366, Bolingbroke
Castle; d. 20 Mar 1413, Jerusalem Chamber, Westminster
Abbey; bur. Canterbury Cathedral), from whom descended the
House of Lancaster, KING OF ENGLAND, 1st Duke of
Hereford, 2nd Duke of Lancaster; m. (1) at Arundel
Castle 1380/1381 **Mary de Bohun** (d. aged 3 or 4 in 1372;
4 Jul 1394, Peterborough Castle; bur. 6 Jul 1394, Leicester[2]).
Issue:

2 — Son (b. Apr 1382; d. yng).

2 — **Henry V of Monmouth**, KING OF ENGLAND
(b. 9 Aug 1387, Monmouth; d. 31 Aug 1422, Bois de
Vincennes, France; bur. Chapel of the Confessor,
Westminster Abbey); m. in the Church of St. John, Troyes,
Trinity Sunday, 2 Jun 1420(?) (1) **Catherine of Valois** [3]

---

[1] Tauté lists two **Johns** who died young.

[2] Ramsay, *Lancaster and York*, Vol. I, pg. 158. Ramsay gives the
year of marriage as 1380 and adds that "the patent for the marriage is
dated 27 July."

[3] **Queen Catherine**, widow of **Henry V** (d. 1422), and **Owen Tudor**
(d. 1461) (**Owen ap Meredyth ap Tydier**) had issue:

1 — **Edmund Tudor** (d. 1456), Edmund of Hadham, Earl of Richmond;
m. **Margaret Beaufort** (d. 1509), daughter of **John Beaufort**
(d. 27 May 1444), Duke of Somerset, son of **John Beaufort** (d. 1410)
and grandson of **John of Gaunt** and **Katherine de Roet**. (**Margaret
Beaufort** later married **Thomas Stanley**, 1st Earl of Derby.) Issue of
Edmund Tudor and **Margaret Beaufort**:

(continued...)

(b. 1401; crowned 24 Feb 1421; d. 1437/1438), daughter of **Charles VI**, King of France. Only issue:

    3 — **Henry VI**, KING OF ENGLAND (b. 6 Dec 1421, Windsor; d. 21–22 May 1471), Henry of Windsor, Duke of Cornwall; m. **Margaret of Anjou** (d. 1482), daughter of **René of Anjou**. Issue:

        4 — **Edward** (b. 13 Oct 1453; k. 4 May 1471, Battle of Tewkesbury), Prince of Wales; betrothed[1] August 1470 to **Anne Neville** (b. 1454; d. 1485), daughter of **Richard Neville the Kingmaker** (d. 1471), and his wife, **Anne de Beauchamp** (d. 1492) (only daughter of **Richard de Beauchamp** (d. 1439), 13th Earl of Warwick, and his second wife). No issue.

2 — **Thomas Plantagenet/Thomas of Lancaster** (b. bef 1 Oct 1388, Kenilworth; k. 22 Mar 1421, Battle of Baugé), Duke of Clarence, K.G.; m. 1412 **Margaret Holand** (d. 30 Dec 1439), "widow of his father's half-brother, **John Beaufort** (d. 1410), 1st Earl of Somerset," and daughter of **Thomas de Holand** (d. 1397), K.G., 2nd Earl of Kent, and his wife (m. 1364), **Alice FitzAlan**

---

[3] (…continued)

    2 — **Henry VII**, KING OF ENGLAND (reigned 1485–1509).

1 — **Jasper Tudor** (d. 1495 without legitimate issue), Jasper of Hatfield, Earl of Pembroke, Duke of Bedford, K.G.; m. (2) bef Nov 1485 as her second husband **Katherine Woodville** (d. 1497), daughter **Richard Woodville** (ex. 12 Aug 1469), 1st Earl Rivers, and his wife, **Jacquetta of Luxembourg** (d. 30 May 1472), and the sister of **Elizabeth**, queen consort of **Edward IV**, KING OF ENGLAND.

1 — **Thomas of Westminster**, a monk at Westminster.

1 — A daughter who became a nun.

1 — **Jacina**, "said to have married" **Reginald, Lord Grey de Wilton**.

    Historians have not determined whether **Queen Katherine** and **Owen Tudor** were legally married. The *CP*, Richmond section, states that it is "likely" they were married about 1429.

(*DNB*, "Tudor, Owen (d. 1461)"; Ramsay, *Lancaster and York*, Vol. II, pg. 320)

[1] They never married. **Anne Neville** later became the wife of **Richard III**, KING OF ENGLAND.

(d. 17 Mar 1415/1416 [1]) (daughter of **Richard II Copped Hat FitzAlan** (d. 1375), 5th Earl of Arundel). No issue.
2 — **John of Bedford** (b. 20 Jun 1389; d. 15 Sep 1435, Rouen), Duke of Bedford, Earl of Kendal, Regent of France, Protector of England 1422–1435, K.G.; m. (1) at church of St. John, Troyes, 17 Apr 1432 **Anne of Burgundy** (d. 14 Nov 1432, from a fever she caught while tending the sick [2]), daughter of **John the Fearless** (d. 1419), Duke of Burgundy, and his wife, **Margaret of Bavaria** (d. 1422/1423); no issue [3]; m. (2) at Thérouenne 20 or 22 Apr 1433 **Jacquetta of Luxembourg-St. Pol** [4] (d. 30 May 1472), daughter of the Count of St. Pol. He had no surviving issue. [5]
2 — **Humphrey of Gloucester** (b. Aug/Sep 1390; d. 23 Feb 1447, Bury St. Edmunds [6]), youngest son, Duke of Gloucester, Regent of England 1420–1421, Protector of England 1422 and 1427–1429, K.G., the good Duke [7];

---

[1] *CP*, Kent section.

[2] Williams, *My Lord of Bedford 1389–1435*, pgs. 221–222. Her death left **John of Bedford** in "utter desolation." Williams states that the contemporary opinion of **Bedford's** second marriage coming so soon after the death of his first wife was that this second union was "based on political expediency" and was necessary to strengthen England's position in France.

[3] Williams, *My Lord of Bedford 1389–1435*, pg. 222.

[4] **Jacquetta of Luxembourg** m. (2) **Richard Woodville/Wydville** (ex. 1469), 1st Earl Rivers, K.G. They were parents of **Elizabeth Woodville** (d. 1492), who m. (1) **John Grey** (k. 1461, Second Battle of St. Albans), Lord Ferrers; m. (2) **Edward IV**, KING OF ENGLAND.

[5] *CP*, Kendal section.

[6] "Duke **Humphrey** died in captivity under mysterious circumstances" (St. Aubyn, *The Year of Three Kings 1483*). Another author has reminded us that when anyone died in captivity, the circumstances were usually considered suspicious.

[7] So called because of his "patronage of learning." **Humphrey** was instrumental in the development of the library of Oxford University. (St. Aubyn, *The Year of Three Kings 1483*; Walker, *To Dine with Duke Humphrey*)

m. (1) (div. [1]) 1422 **Jacqueline of Bavaria** [2] (d. 1436), Countess of Holland, Duchess of Hainault, daughter of **William VI** (d. 1417), Count of Hainault, Holland and Zeeland, Duke of Bavaria, and his wife, **Margaret** (d. 1441), Countess of Hainault (daughter of **Philip the Bold** (d. 1404)); no issue; m. (2) (div. 1441) 1428/bef 1431 **Eleanor Cobham** [3] (d. 7 Jul 1452/1454), daughter of **Reginald Cobham**; no legitimate issue. [4]

2 — **Blanche** (b. 1392, Peterborough Castle; d. 21 May 1409, Germany) m. 6 Jul 1402 as his first wife **Louis/ Ludwig II/III Barbatus** (d. 20 Dec 1436 or 1439), Duke of Bavaria, Elector Palatine of the Rhine. Issue [5]:

   3 — **Rupert Anglicus** (b. 1406; d. 1426).

2 — **Philippa** (b. 4 Jul 1394; d. 5 Jan 1430, Chapel of St. Anna in the Convent of Vadstena) m. 26 Oct 1404 [6] **Eric VII** of Pomerania (d. 1459), King of Denmark, Sweden, and Norway, K.G. No issue. [7]

---

[1] Previté-Orton states that they were divorced 1426; *KQB*, pg. 86, states the marriage was annulled in 1428.

[2] **Jacqueline of Bavaria/Hainault** was married four times: (1) the Dauphin of France (d. 1417); (2) (div.) **John**, Duke of Brabant (d. 1427); (3) (sep. about 1426) **Humphrey** (d. 1447), Duke of Gloucester; and (4) **Franz of Borselen** (d. 1472). (Cartellieri, *The Court of Burgundy*, Table "France, Burgundy, Orleans")

[3] **Eleanor Cobham** had been a lady in waiting to **Humphrey's** first wife and became his mistress after he left his wife in the Flemish territories and returned to England (Walker, *To Dine with Duke Humphrey*, pg. 12–13). She has been described as "a marvellously fair and pleasant woman." (*CP*, Gloucester section)

[4] *KQB*, pg. 86. **Humphrey of Gloucester** had illegitimate issue. *Ancestral* 1A states that some believe (without proof) that **Eleanor**, as his mistress, may have been the mother of **Arthur** and of **Antigone** (b. bef 1428). The latter m. 3 Jan 1434/1435 **Henry Grey** (b. abt 1419; d. 13 Jan 1449/1450), Earl of Tankerville. (Walker, *To Dine with Duke Humphrey*, pg. 13)

[5] Anderson, *Royal Genealogies*, Table CCLXX.

[6] Ramsay, Vol. I, pg. 159, citing Green, *Lives of the Princesses of England*, Vol. III, pg. 387.

[7] Anderson, *Royal Genealogies*, Table CLXXXVII.

Henry IV, KING OF ENGLAND, as above, m. (2) 3 Apr 1402 by proxy, then 7 Feb 1403 in Winchester Cathedral in person **Joan of Navarre**[1] (d. 2, 9, or 10 Jul 1437, Havering-atte-Bower, Essex; bur. Canterbury Cathedral[2]), second daughter of **Charles II the Bad**, King of Navarre, and **Joan of France**. No issue.

1 — **Isabel** (b. abt 1368; d. yng).

* * *

John of Gaunt m. (2) at Roquefort, Guienne, or St. Andrew[3] Sep 1371 **Constance/Costanza** (b. 1354, Castro Kerez[4]; d. 24 Mar 1394[5]), from whom descended the kings of Castile and Aragon, titular Queen of Castile and Leon, second daughter of **Peter I/Pedro I the Cruel of Castile** (b. 30 Aug 1334; k. 23 Mar 1369) by his mistress, **Maria de Padilla**.[6]

---

[1] **Joan of Navarre** (b. abt 1370, Pamplona) m. (1) 11 Sep 1386 **John V the Valiant de Montfort** (d. 1 Nov 1399), Duke of Brittany. According to the *KQB*, pg. 87, they were parents of nine children. The *DNB*, "Joan or Joanna of Navarre (1370?-1437)," states they had eight: **John** (d. 1442), Duke of Brittany; **Arthur**, Comte de Richemonte; **Gilles** (d. 1412); **Richard** (d. 1438), Comte d'Estampes; **Joanna** (b. and d. 1387); **Marie** (d. 1446), Duchess of d'Alencon; **Blanche** (d. yng), Comtesse d'Armagnac; and **Margaret** (d. yng), Vicomtesse de Rohan.

[2] *CP*, Richmond section.

[3] Armitage-Smith, *John of Gaunt*, pg. 93.

[4] Armitage-Smith, *John of Gaunt*, pg. 94.

[5] Armitage-Smith, *John of Gaunt*, pg. 357, states 24 Mar and adds that another source states 25 Mar 1394. This was the same year that saw the deaths of **Queen Anne** (wife of **Richard II**, **John of Gaunt's** nephew) and **Mary de Bohun**, wife of **Henry of Bolingbroke/ Henry IV**, **John of Gaunt's** son.

[6] **Pedro I** claimed he and **Maria de Padilla** had been secretly married (Burke's *Royal Family*, pg. 199). Other issue of this couple includes **Alfonso** (b. 1351; d. 1362); **Beatrix** (b. 1353; d. 1368); and **Isabel** (b. abt 1355/1356, Morales/Tordesillas, Castile; d. 23 Nov 1392/ 1393; bur. Church of the Dominican Friars, King's Langley, Hertfordshire), who in 1372 married **Edmund of Langley** (d. 1402). (Armitage-Smith, *John of Gaunt*, pg. 300)

Ancestors of Constance of Castile

```
                               ┌Alfonso XI, King of Castile and Leon
                    ┌Pedro I, King of Castile and Leon (d. 1369)
                    │          └Maria, daughter of Alfonso IV of Portugal
    Constance of Castile (d. 1394)
                    │        ┌
                    └Maria de Padilla
                             └
```

Issue of John of Gaunt and Constance

1— **Catherine**[1] (b. by 31 Mar 1373,[2] Hertford; d. 2 Jun 1418; bur. Toledo) from whom descended the Kings of Castile and Aragon; m. 1388/1393[3] **Henry III/Enrique III the Infirm** (b. 4 Oct 1379, Burgos; d. 25/26 Dec 1406, Toledo; bur. Toledo), King of Castile and Leon, elder son of **Juan I** (d. 9 Oct 1390), King of Castile and Leon, and his first wife, **Leonor** (daughter of **Pedro of Aragon**).[4] Issue[5]:

  2 — **Maria** (b. 14 Nov 1401; d. 4 Sep 1458, Valencia) m. 12 Jun 1415 her cousin **Alfonso V** (b. 1394; d. 27 Jun 1458), King of Aragon, son of **Ferdinand I the Just** (d. 2 Apr 1416),[6] King of Aragon. No issue.[7]

  2 — **Catalina/Catharin** (b. 1406; d. 1439/1440) m. 1420 as his first wife her cousin **Enrique/Henry of Aragon**

---

[1] After **Pedro I the Cruel** was murdered 23 Mar 1369 by **Henry of Trastamara**, **John of Gaunt** became a claimant to the throne of Castile in right of his wife. He failed in his bid for that throne, but his claims were passed on to his daughter, **Catherine**. (Previté-Orton, Table 24; *KQE*, pg. 43)

[2] According to Burke's *Royal Family*, pg. 200, **Catherine** was born between 6 Jun 1372 and 31 Mar 1373.

[3] *KQE*, pg. 43, and Burke's *Royal Family*, pg. 200, state **Catherine** and **Henry III the Infirm** were married 1393; Armitage-Smith, *John of Gaunt*, gives the date as 1388. Silva-Vigier, *This Moste Highe Prince...John of Gaunt*, pg. 283, states that Constanza visited "her daughter and son-in-law in 1388-9."

[4] Armitage-Smith, *John of Gaunt*, pg. 300.

[5] Armitage-Smith, *John of Gaunt*, pg. 300; Anderson, *Royal Genealogies*, Table CCCCLXI.

[6] *KQE*, pg. 39.

[7] *KQE*, pg. 39.

(d. 1445), Master of Santiago/Duke of Villena, her cousin, and son of **Ferdinando I the Just** (d. 1416), King of Aragon.[1]

2 — **Juan II/John II** (b. 6 Mar 1405, Toro; d. 22 Jul 1454, Valladolid), King of Castile and Leon 1406–1454; m. (1) 20 Oct 1418 **Maria of Aragon** (d. Feb 1445, Villacastin), daughter of **Ferdinand I**, King of Aragon and Sicily, and **Leonor of Albuquerque**. Issue (one son, two daughters[2]):

3 — **Catharin** (d. inf.).
3 — **Eleanora** (d. inf.).
3 — **Henry IV/Enrique IV** (b. 5 Jan 1425; d. 11 Dec 1474, Madrid), King of Castile and Leon 1454–1474; m. 15 Sep 1440 (annulled 1453) **Blanca of Aragon** (b. 1420; d. 1464), daughter of **Juan II**, King of Navarre and Aragon, and his first wife, **Blanca of Navarre**; m. (2) at Cordoba 21 May 1455 **Joana** (b. Mar 1439; d. 13 Jun 1475), daughter of **Duarte I/ Edward**, King of Portugal, and **Leonor of Aragon**.

Juan II, as above, husband of **Maria of Aragon**, m. (2) at Madrigal Aug 1447 **Isabel of Portugal** (b. 1430; d. 15 Aug 1496; bur. Miraflores, nr Burgos), daughter of **John**, Prince of Portugal, and **Isabel of Bragança**. Issue (one son, one daughter[3]):

3 — **Alphonso** (b. 17 Dec 1453; d. 5 Jul 1468).
3 — **Isabella I** (b. 23 Apr 1451; d. 26 Nov 1504), Queen of Castile and Leon 1474–1504; m. 18 Oct 1469 **Ferdinand V** (d. 1516), King of Aragon, son of **Juan II**, King of Aragon.[4] They were ancestors of the Spanish House of Hapsburg.[5] Issue included[6]:

[1] Ryder, *Alfonso the Magnanimous*, pg. 9.
[2] *KQE*, pg. 43.
[3] *KQE*, pg. 43.
[4] *KQE*, Table 4, pg. 184.
[5] Armitage-Smith, *John of Gaunt*, pg. 300.
[6] Weightman, *Margaret of York, Duchess of Burgundy 1446–1503*, Table 4 "Selected Genealogy of the Habsburg Rulers of Burgundy."

4 — **Catherine of Aragon** (d. 1536) m. **Henry VIII,**
KING OF ENGLAND.
1 — **John of Gaunt** (b. 1374, Ghent; d. yng).

* * *

John of Gaunt m. (3) at Lincoln 13 Jan 1396 **Katherine de
Roet** or **Roelt** (b. 1350; d. 10 May 1403,[1] Lincoln[2];
bur. Lincoln Cathedral), from whom descended the House of
Tudor and the kings of Scotland.

Katherine was daughter of Payn de Roet, Kt., of Hainault,
and widow of Hugh Swynford, Kt. (aged 33 abt 1366;
k. 11 Nov 1371, Gascony,[3] while fighting in Aquitaine),
whom she married in 1366 (when he was received into the
service of John of Gaunt) or in 1367/1368. Hugh Swynford was
from an old Saxon family, whose main seat was the manor of
Kettlethorpe, co. Lincoln.[4]

Katherine and Hugh Swynford had a daughter, Blanche
Swynford (b. 1367) (to whom John was godfather), and a son,
Thomas Swynford (b. 1368; d. 1432), whom John placed in his
son's household. Thomas was about two years younger than the
future Henry IV and developed a life-long attachment to him.[5]

After Hugh's death, Katherine received her husband's
property and lived both at Kettlethorpe and at John of Gaunt's
home in Lincoln. At Kettlethorpe, Katherine had a deer park,
and Silva-Vigier remarks that remnants of the deer park, the
gateway to the manor, and the moat can still be seen.[6]

Katherine was sister of Philippa de Roet, wife of poet
Geoffrey Chaucer.[7] Both Philippa and Geoffrey were in

---

[1] *CP*, Somerset section; *CP*, Lancaster section.

[2] Armitage-Smith, *John of Gaunt*, pg. 389.

[3] Silva-Vigier, *This Moste Highe Prince...John of Gaunt*, pgs. 159,
128.

[4] Silva-Vigier, *This Moste Highe Prince...John of Gaunt*, pg. 160.

[5] Silva-Vigier, *This Moste Highe Prince...John of Gaunt*, pg. 156.

[6] Silva-Vigier, *This Moste Highe Prince...John of Gaunt*, pg. 160.

[7] Armitage-Smith, *John of Gaunt*, pgs. 390–391, 461. See also
chapters, "Royal Connections of Poet Geoffrey Chaucer" and "Some

(continued...)

service to the royal household. Katherine probably entered the position of governess to the children of John of Gaunt and Blanche about 1362 or 1363, the same time as Philippa and Geoffrey entered the services of Queen Philippa and Edward III. [1]

It is uncertain when Katherine became the mistress of John of Gaunt. It could have been about the time of Hugh Swynford's death in 1371 or it could have been between the time of Blanche's death in Oct 1368 and July 1370. Silva-Vigier is of the opinion that neither John nor Katherine would put aside their loyalty to Blanche. [2] Silva-Vigier also states that when seeking the Pope's confirmation of their marriage thirty years later, that Katherine and John confessed that their relationship had begun during the life of her husband and during John's second marriage, which he consented to for reasons of state, as he had hoped to secure the crown of Castile. [3] The birth date of their first son, John Beaufort, is known from a grant to be 1372.

In a time when marriages were made for political and financial conveniences, extramarital relationships between lord and servant were not unusual, could be typical, and were "quite admissible." [4] However, Katherine was no common mistress; John showed "open and unashamed love" [5] toward her. After John and Katherine were married and she became, as a result, socially higher than the other ladies of the court, Katherine experienced their jealousy. This was to be expected: Katherine of low birth had married the king's son, the richest and most eligible bachelor in the kingdom and one of the most powerful men in England. A chronicler, remarking on the resulting

---

[7] (...continued)
Royal Descendants of Payn de Roet." **Katherine de Roet Swynford** is the subject of Anya Seton's novel, *Katherine*.

[1] Silva-Vigier, *This Moste Highe Prince...John of Gaunt*, pg. 104.

[2] Silva-Vigier, *This Moste Highe Prince...John of Gaunt*, pgs. 126–128.

[3] Silva-Vigier, *This Moste Highe Prince...John of Gaunt*, pg. 128.

[4] Silva-Vigier, *This Moste Highe Prince...John of Gaunt*, pg. 127.

[5] Silva-Vigier, *This Moste Highe Prince...John of Gaunt*, pg. 155.

jealousy and rudeness shown toward Katherine, states, however, that "the lady herself was a woman of such bringing up and honourable demeanour that envy could not in the end but give place to well deserving."[1]

About 1382, Katherine retired from her position as governess to John of Gaunt's daughters and went to the estates he had given her in Lincolnshire and Nottingham.[2] Their four illegitimate children, three sons and a daughter, were collectively called the Beauforts.

The name Beaufort was taken from their "their father's castle in Champagne [not Anjou], which devolved on him through his 1st wife, Blanche of Lancaster."[3] The village was located between Chalons and Troyes and since 1689 has been called Montmorency, Aube. The name of the castle and lordship, Beaufort, would not interfere with the titles which belonged to John of Gaunt's legitimate son, Henry Bolingbroke. Beaufort castle, leased to John Wyn, was betrayed in 1369 to the French and later sold by John of Gaunt to Philip the Bold, Duke of Burgundy. Though the Beauforts were named after this lost French possession and though "romantic legend"[4] names the castle as their birthplace, they were probably born at Katherine's home of Kettlethorpe in Lincoln, where money, wood for fuel and building, wine, and deer were delivered while John of Gaunt was out of England.[5]

In January 1396, John of Gaunt married Katherine de Roet Swynford, and in September of the same year, Boniface IX issued a bull which confirmed the marriage and made their issue legitimate. An act of Parliament confirmed their legitimacy, allowing them due property rights and enabling "their promotions to the ranks of the nobility."[6]

---

[1] Silva-Vigier, *This Moste Highe Prince...John of Gaunt*, pg. 166.

[2] Armitage-Smith, *John of Gaunt*, pgs. 390–391.

[3] *CP*, Somerset section.

[4] Jones and Underwood, *The King's Mother*, pg. 18.

[5] Silva-Vigier, *This Moste Highe Prince...John of Gaunt*, pgs. 160–163, 175, 222, 348.

[6] Jones and Underwood, *The King's Mother*, pg. 20.

Richard II issued letters patent dated 9 Feb 1397 declaring the children legitimate.[1] His successor, Henry IV, son of John of Gaunt by his first wife, confirmed the legitimization in 1407 but added the phrase *excepta dignitate regali*, which barred his half-brothers from succession to the crown.[2] "It was, however, debatable whether the reservation could legally negate the rights created by the original grant."[3]

Issue by Katherine de Roet

1 — **John Beaufort** (b. abt 1370/1373; d. 16 Mar 1409/1410,[4] in St. Catherine's Hospital by the Tower; bur. Chapel of St. Michael in Canterbury Cathedral[5]), Earl of Somerset, Marquess of Dorset, K.G., from whom descended the House of Tudor and kings of Scotland; m. (1) bef 23 Apr 1399[6] as her first husband[7] **Margaret Holand** (b. 1385; d. 30/31 Dec 1439, London; bur. Chapel of St. Michael in Canterbury Cathedral), third daughter of **Thomas de Holand** (d. 1397), 2nd Earl of

---

[1] Armitage-Smith, *John of Gaunt*, pg. 392.

[2] Armitage-Smith, *John of Gaunt*, pgs. 391–392.

[3] Harris, *Edward Stafford, Third Duke of Buckingham, 1478–1521*, pgs. 25–26.

[4] Date from *Ancestral* 1-32 and *CP*, section Somerset. The *DNB*, "Beaufort, John, first Earl of Somerset and Marquis of Dorset and of Somerset (1373?–1410)," also gives a death date of 16 Mar and adds, "not, as all the peerages say, on 21 March."

[5] Jones and Underwood, *The King's Mother*, pg. 25.

[6] Burke's *Royal Family*, pg. 200, states that **John Beaufort** and **Margaret Holand** were married "*ante* 23 April 1399," the same date given by the *DNB*, "Beaufort, John, first Earl of Somerset and Marquis of Dorset and of Somerset (1373?–1410)." The marriage date according to *Ancestral* 47-33 is bef 28 Sep 1397.

[7] **Margaret Holand** m. (2) 1412 **Thomas Plantagenet** (k. 1421, Battle of Baugé; bur. Chapel of St. Michael in Canterbury Cathedral), Duke of Clarence, second son of **Henry IV**, KING OF ENGLAND, by his first marriage.

Kent. Issue (three sons and two daughters[1]):

2 — **Henry Beaufort** (b. Oct 1401; d. 25 Nov 1418), 2nd Earl of Somerset.

2 — **John Beaufort** (b. bef 25 Mar 1404; d. 27 May 1444; bur. Wimborne Minster[2]), Earl of Somerset, 1st Duke of Somerset, Earl of Kendal; m. 1439 **Margaret de Beauchamp**[3] (b. 1385; d. bef 3 Jun 1482/8 Aug 1482) of Bletsoe, only daughter of **John de Beauchamp** (d. 1412), 3rd Baron Beauchamp of Bletsoe, and his wife, **Edith Stourton** (daughter of **John Stourton**). Margaret de Beauchamp was also the sister and heiress of **John de Beauchamp** (d. yng),[4] 4th Baron Beauchamp of Bletso, and the widow of **Oliver St. John** (d. 1437) of Bletso.[5] Issue:

---

[1] *DNB*, "Beaufort, John, first Earl of Somerset and Marquis of Dorset and Somerset (1373?–1410)." **John Beaufort** had an illegitimate daughter, **Thomasine/Tacine Beaufort** (liv. May 1461), who m. by 6 Oct 1447 **Reynold Grey** (d. 22 Feb 1493), 7th Lord Grey of Wilton (*Ancestral* 207-37). Some sources show a **Thomas Beaufort** (d. 1431/1432) as a son of **John Beaufort** (d. 1410).

[2] *DNB*, "Beaufort, Margaret (1443–1509)," states that her parents were buried at Wimborne Minster, "beneath the stately monument she erected to their memory." The *CP*, Somerset section, mentions the tomb with its effigies.

[3] By her marriage to **Oliver St. John** (d. 1437), **Margaret de Beauchamp** was mother of **Edith St. John** who married **Geoffrey Pole** and had issue of **Richard Pole**. This **Richard Pole** m. **Margaret Plantagenet**, the Countess of Salisbury, who was executed in 1541 by **Henry VIII**. **Margaret de Beauchamp** m. (3) **Leo/Lionel**, Lord Welles, 6th Baron Welles (k. 29 Mar 1461, Towton; bur. at Methley with his first wife), K.G., K.B. (Burke's *Royal Family*, pg. 200; *CP*, Somerset section; *CP*, Welles section; W. Schenk, *Reginald Pole, Cardinal of England*, pg. 172; Jones and Underwood, *The King's Mother*, Table 2.)

[4] *CP*, Beauchamp (of Bletsoe) section.

[5] Issue of **Margaret Beauchamp** and **Oliver St. John** (d. 1437), briefly:

1 — **Edith St. John** m. **Geoffrey Pole** (will proved 21 Mar 1474/1475).

1 — **John St. John** of Bletsoe m. **Alice Bradshaw**.

1 — **Mary St. John** m. **Richard Frogenhall**.

(continued...)

3 - **Margaret Beaufort**[1] (b. Apr 1441/1443, Bletso,
Bedfordshire; d. 5 Jul 1509, Westminster Palace;
bur. Westminster Abbey), Countess of Richmond and
Derby; heiress of her father; less than two years old
when her father died[2]; m. (1) (div. bef 1453[3]) **John de
la Pole** (b. 27 Sep 1442; d. bet. 29 Oct 1491 and 27 Oct
1492[4]), 2nd Duke of Suffolk, K.G., son of **William de
la Pole** (ex. 2 May 1450) and his wife, **Alice Chaucer**
(only child of **Thomas Chaucer** and granddaughter of
poet **Geoffrey Chaucer**[5]); no issue;
m. (2) 1455 **Edmund Tudor**[6] (b. abt 1430, Hadham,
Bedfordshire/Hertfordshire; d. 3 Nov 1456, Carmarthen;

---

[5] (...continued)
1 — **Elizabeth St. John** (liv. 1489; d. bef 3 Jul 1494) m. (1) as his
second wife **William la Zouche** (d. 25 Dec 1462), Lord Zouche of
Haryngworth; m. (2) as his third wife **John le Scrope** (d. 17 Aug 1498),
Lord Scrope of Bolton.
1 — **Oliver St. John** of Lydiard Tregoze m. **Elizabeth Bigod**.
(Jones and Underwood, *The King's Mother, Lady Margaret Beaufort*,
Table 2; *CP*, Zouche section, Salisbury section)
  [1] See chapter, "The Beaufort Women."
  [2] *DNB*, "Beaufort, Margaret (1443–1509), countess of Richmond and
Derby."
  [3] According to Pearsall, *The Life of Geoffrey Chaucer*, pg. 282, this
was not an actual marriage between **John de la Pole** and **Margaret
Beaufort** but a planned marriage, which was cancelled for political
reasons after the murder/execution in 1450 of the prospective
bridegroom's father, **William de la Pole**, Duke of Suffolk. The
bridegroom's mother, **Alice Chaucer**, thought it wise to marry her son
into the house of York, rather than the house of Lancaster; thus the
bridegroom married **Elizabeth**, second daughter of **Richard Plantagenet**
(d. 1460), Duke of York, and sister of the future **Edward IV** and
Richard III.
  [4] *CP*, Suffolk section.
  [5] See chapter, "Some Royal Connections of Poet Geoffrey Chaucer."
  [6] Half-brother of **Henry VI**. (*DNB*, "Beaufort, Margaret
(1443–1509), Countess of Richmond and Derby")

bur. St. David's Cathedral/Grey Friars, Carmarthen [1]), Earl of Richmond, eldest son of **Owen Tudor** and **Queen Katherine of Valois** (widow of **Henry V**, KING OF ENGLAND). Issue:

4 — **Henry VII** (b. posthumously 28 Jan 1456/1457; d. 21 Apr 1509, Richmond Palace; bur. Henry VII's Chapel, Westminster Abbey), KING OF ENGLAND, reigned 1485–1509; m. **Elizabeth of York** (d. 1503), [2] daughter of **Edward IV**, KING OF ENGLAND (reigned 1461–1470, 1471–1483).

Margaret Beaufort, as above, wife of **Owen Tudor**, m. (3) 1459 **Henry Stafford** (d. 1481 [3]), Lord Stafford, second son of **Humphrey Stafford** (b. 1402; d. 1460), 1st Duke of Buckingham; no issue; m. (4) in 1482 [4] as his second wife **Thomas Stanley** (d. 29 Jul 1504, Lathom), 1st Earl of Derby, Constable of England, K.G.

---

[1] On the dissolution of the monasteries in 1536, **Edmund Tudor's** body was removed to St. David's Cathedral. (*DNB*, "Tudor, Edmund, Earl of Richmond, known as Edmund of Hadham (1430?–1456)")

[2] The marriage of **Henry VII** of the Lancastrian branch of the royal family and **Elizabeth of York** of the Yorkist branch of the royal family was one that joined the two warring factions and ended the Wars of the Roses. The white York rose and the red Lancaster rose were overlaid to form the Tudor rose, which became the symbol of the Tudor era. For many historians, **Henry VII's** defeat of **Richard III** at the Battle of Bosworth (1485) marks the end of the medieval period of English history.

[3] The year of Henry Stafford's death has been seen as 1471 (*CP*, Suffolk section, John de la Pole (d. 1492); *CP*, Richmond section; Rawcliffe, *The Staffords, Earls of Stafford and Dukes of Buckingham 1394–1521*, pg. 22). Ramsay, *Lancaster and York*, Vol. I, Table III, gives a death date of 1481–1482. Hogrefe, *Women of Action in Tutor England: Nine Biographical Sketches*, pg. 139, gives 1481 as the year of death. Cooper, *Memoir of Margaret, Countess of Richmond and Derby*, pg. 17, states that Henry Stafford "appears to have died in 1482, as his will was proved on the 4th May in that year" and that the will "is dated 2 Oct 1481."

[4] Coward, *The Stanleys: Lords Stanley and Earls of Derby, 1385–1672*, pg. 11.

This was a marriage for political and social convenience; no issue.

2 — **Edmund Beaufort** (b. abt 1406; k. 22 May 1455, First Battle of St. Albans; bur. the chapel of the Blessed Virgin in the Abbey Church[1]), 2nd Duke of Somerset, 4th Earl of Somerset, Marquess of Dorset, Count of Mortain, K.G.; m. (2) abt 1431/1435/bef 7 Mar 1437/1438[2] **Eleanor de Beauchamp**[3] (b. 1407/1408 Edgenoch/Wedgenock, co. Warwick; d. 4–6 Mar 1466/1467, Baynard's Castle, London), second daughter of **Richard de Beauchamp** (d. 1439), Earl of Warwick, K.G., by his first wife, **Elizabeth Berkeley** (b. abt 1386; d. 28 Dec 1422) (daughter of **Thomas de Berkeley** (d. 13 Jul 1417), Lord Berkeley[4]). Issue[5]:

3 — **Henry Beaufort** (b. abt Apr 1436[6]/26 Jan 1436; ex. 15 May 1464, Battle of Hexham; bur. Hexham Abbey), 2nd Duke of Somerset.[7] Unm.

---

[1] "His blood was the first shed in the Wars of the Roses, which proved fatal to his sons, and ended the male line of the **Beauforts**." (*DNB*, "Beaufort, Edmund (d. 1455), Duke of Somerset"; *CP*, Somerset section)

[2] *CP*, Ros section.

[3] **Eleanor de Beauchamp** m. (1) **Thomas de Ros** (d. 18 Aug 1430), 9th Baron de Ros; (3) **Walter Rokesley**, Esq. (bur. Croyland, co. Lincoln). (*Ancestral* 87-34, 1-33; *CP*, Somerset section, Ros section)

[4] This **Thomas de Berkeley** "may bee called Thomas the Magnificent."

[5] In part, from Jones and Underwood, *The King's Mother, Lady Margaret Beaufort*, Table 1.

[6] *CP*, Somerset section, wherein is stated that at the First Battle of St. Albans (22 May 1455), he was "sore hurt that he might not go" and was "caryede hom in a cart." The same section also gives the place of burial as Hexham Abbey.

[7] **Henry Beaufort** (ex. 15 May 1464), 2nd Duke of Somerset, had an illegitimate son by **Joan Hill**:

4 — **Charles Somerset** (b. abt 1460; d. 15 Apr 1526; bur. Beaufort Chapel, St. George's Chapel, Windsor), Lord Herbert of Ragland, Earl of Worcester; m. (1) 2 Jun 1492 **Elizabeth Herbert**, only daughter and

(continued...)

3 — **Edmund Beaufort** (b. bef 1440; ex. 6 May 1471, Tewkesbury, two days after the Battle of Tewkesbury; bur. the Abbey Church), 3rd Duke of Somerset. Unm.

3 — **John Beaufort** (k. 4 May 1471, Battle of Tewkesbury; bur. the Abbey Church (Tewkesbury?)).

---

[7] (...continued)
heir of **William Herbert** (d. 16 Jul 1491), Earl of Huntingdon, and his first wife, **Mary Woodville** (daughter of **Richard Woodville**, 1st Earl Rivers, and **Jacquetta of Luxembourg** and the sister of **Elizabeth**, queen consort of **Edward IV**, KING OF ENGLAND). Issue:

5 — **Henry Somerset** (d. 26 Nov 1549, aged abt 53; bur. Chepstow), "only son by first wife," Earl of Worcester; m. (1) **Margaret Courtenay** (b. 1479, Eltham, Kent; d. bef 15 Apr 1526/15 Nov 1527, Tiverton, Devon; bur. 3 Dec 1527, Tiverton), daughter of **William Courtenay** (b. abt 1475; d. 9 Jun 1511, Greenwich, of pleurisy; bur. Black Friars' in London), Earl of Devon, and his wife, **Katherine Plantagenet**, youngest daughter of **Edward IV**, KING OF ENGLAND; no issue; m. (2) bef 1527 **Elizabeth Browne** (d. bet 20 Apr and 23 Oct 1565), daughter of **Anthony Browne**, Kt., and his wife, **Lucy Neville** (daughter of **John Neville** (k. 14 Apr 1471, Battle of Barnet), Marquess of Montagu, Earl of Northumberland). **Henry Somerset** was present at both the coronation and the trial of **Queen Anne Boleyn**. (*CP*, Worcester section; Montagu section)

5 — **Elizabeth** (d. 1545) m. **William Brereton** (ex. 1536).
Charles Somerset, as above, husband of **Elizabeth Herbert**, m. (2) **Elizabeth West**, daughter of **Thomas West**, 8th Lord de la Warr, and his first wife, **Elizabeth Mortimer** (daughter of **Hugh Mortimer** of Mortimer's Hall, Hampshire). Issue (according to the *CP*, Worcester section, "three children"):

5 — **Charles Somerset**, captain of the Rysbank at Calais.
5 — **George Somerset** of Bedmundsfield in Suffolk.
Charles Somerset, as above, husband of **Elizabeth West**, m. (3) **Eleanor Sutton** (d. bef 1549), daughter of **Edward "Sutton or Dudley,"** 5th Lord Dudley, and his wife, **Cecily** (daughter of **William Willoughby**). No issue.
(*DNB*, "Woodville or Wydeville, Richard, first Earl Rivers (d. 1469)"; *DNB*, "Somerset, Charles, Earl of Worcester (1460?–1526)"; Ives, *Anne Boleyn*, Table "The Nobility of Henry VIII's Court"; *CP*, Worcester section, Somerset section)

3 — **Thomas Beaufort** (d. yng bef 1463).

3 — **Margaret Beaufort** (d. spring 1474)
m. (1) **Humphrey Stafford** (d. aft 22 May 1455/1458,[1]
in the lifetime of his father), son of **Humphrey Stafford**
(d. 10 Jul 1460, Battle of Northampton), Earl of
Stafford, and **Anne Neville** (d. 20 Sep 1480) (daughter
of **Ralph Neville**, 1st Earl of Westmorland). Issue (two
sons):

> 4 — **Henry Stafford** (b. 4 Sep 1455; ex. 2 Nov 1483,
> Salisbury[2]; bur. the Grey Friars), 2nd Duke of
> Buckingham; m. **Katherine Woodville**[3] (d. 1497),
> daughter of **Richard Woodville** (ex. 12 Aug 1469)
> and **Jacquetta of Luxembourg** (d. 30 May 1472) and
> the sister of **Edward IV's** queen consort, **Elizabeth
> Woodville** (d. 1492).

> 4 — **Humphrey Stafford.**[4]

Margaret Beaufort, as above, wife of **Humphrey
Stafford**, m. (2) **Richard Dayrell/Darell**, Kt., of
Lillingstone Dayrell, Buckinghamshire.

3 — **Eleanor Beaufort** (d. 16 Aug 1501), "eldest da." of
her father, Countess of Wiltshire; m. (1) "possibly" Apr

---

[1] **Humphrey Stafford** was "gretly hurt" in the First Battle of
St. Albans, 22 May 1455, and died "soon afterward" (*DNB*, "Stafford,
Humphrey, first Duke of Buckingham (1402–1460)." Harris, *Edward
Stafford: Third Duke of Buckingham, 1478–1521*, pgs. 234–235, 19,
states that he died of the plague in 1458.

[2] **Henry Stafford**, despite his family ties through marriage with the
family of **Edward IV**, had supported **Richard III** in his usurpation of
the throne in the summer of 1483. By October, **Richard** had branded
Henry Stafford a traitor. He was quickly captured, tried, and executed.

[3] **Katherine Woodville** m. (2) bef Nov 1485 **Jasper Tudor**
(d. 21 Dec 1495), Duke of Bedford, who died without legitimate issue;
m. (3) as his first wife **Richard Wingfield** (d. 22 Jul 1525), K.G. (*CP*,
Buckingham section)

[4] Harris, *Edward Stafford: Third Duke of Buckingham, 1478–1521*,
pg. 19.

1458 as his second wife **James Butler** or **Botiller**[1]
(b. abt 1420; ex. 1 May 1461, Newcastle, having been
captured after the Battle of Towton, 29 Mar 1461[2]), 5th
Earl of Ormond and 1st Earl of Wiltshire, K.G.; no
issue[3]; m. (2) abt 1465/in or bef 1470 **Robert Spencer**,
Kt. (b. abt 1435; liv. 13 Mar 1492/liv. 1502).[4] Issue
(two daughters)[5]:

   4 — **Catherine Spencer** (bur. 19 Oct 1542, Beverley)
   m. bef 1502 **Henry Algernon Percy** (d. 19 May
   1527; bur. Beverley), Earl of Northumberland.[6]

   4 — **Margaret [not Eleanor] Spencer** (b. abt 1472)
   m. abt 1490 **Thomas Cary** (b. abt 1460) of Chilton
   Foliot, Wiltshire.

3 — **Elizabeth Beaufort** (d. bef 1492) m. **Henry Lewes/
FitzLewis** (d. May 1480) of Horndon, Essex, Kt. Their
daughter:

   4 — **Mary FitzLewis** m. bef Oct 1480 as his second
   wife **Anthony Woodville** (b. abt 1440; d. 25 Jun
   1483), 2nd Earl Rivers.[7]

3 — **Margaret/Mary Beaufort** m. _ **Burgh**.

3 — **Anne Beaufort** m. **William Paxton/Paston II**,

---

[1] **James Butler** m. (1) bef 4 Jul 1438 **Avice Stafford** (b. 4 Dec
1423, Woodford, Dorset; d. 3 Jun or 3 Jul 1457), daughter of **Richard
Stafford** (d. abt 1427) and **Maud Lovell** (d. 1436). (*CP*, Ormond
section)

[2] His head was "smete of, and send unto London to be sette uppon
London Brygge." (*CP*, Ormond section)

[3] *CP*, Ormond section.

[4] *Ancestral* 1-34.

[5] *CP*, Ormond section.

[6] *CP*, Northumberland section. **Henry Percy** (d. 30 Jun 1537), a son
of **Henry Algernon Percy** and **Catherine Spencer**, may have intended
to marry **Anne Boleyn** before **Henry VIII** noticed her.

[7] *CP*, Rivers section, wherein **Mary FitzLewis** is described as "da.
and h."; Jones and Underwood, *The King's Mother, Lady Margaret
Beaufort*, Table 1.

Kt.[1] (b. 1436; d. 1496), son of **Justice William Paston I** (b. 1378; d. 13/14 Aug 1444) and his wife, **Agnes Berry** (daughter of **Edmund Berry**).[2] Issue (he left two daughters and coheirs[3]):

4 — **Mary Paston** (b. 19 Jan 1469/1470; d. abt Christmas 1489, in the lifetime of her father, "of measles" at the Court at Westminster), the eldest; m. as his first wife **Ralph Neville**[4] (d. 1498, in the lifetime of his father; bur. Brancepeth), Lord Neville, only son of **Ralph Neville** (d. 6 Feb 1498/1499, "it is said of grief for his son's death"), 3rd Earl of Westmorland, Hornby Castle, co. York), and his wife, **Isabel Booth**,[5] daughter of **Roger Booth** and niece of **Lawrence Booth**, Archbishop of York.[6]

4 — **Agnes Paston**.

4 — **Elizabeth Paston**.

4 — **Margaret Paston** (b. 19 Jul 1474, d. inf).

3 — **Joan Beaufort** (liv. with no issue 1492[7]) m. (1) **Robert Howth**, Lord of Howth in Ireland;

---

[1] Virgoe, *Private Life in the Fifteenth Century*, pgs. 32, 267, wherein **William Paston II** is described as "a successful lawyer." His father is described both as **Justice Paston** (Bennett, *The Pastons and Their England*, pgs. 1–3) and **William Paston** of Norfolk, Justice of the Commons Pleas (*CP*, Westmorland section).

[2] Virgoe, *Private Life in the Fifteenth Century*, pg. 22; *DNB*, "Paston, William (1378–1444), judge."

[3] *CP*, Westmorland section. There are numerous books on this great letter-writing family of England. *The Pastons and Their England* by H. S. Bennett is suggested as an introduction.

[4] **Ralph Neville** m. (2) **Edith Sandys** (d. 22 Aug 1529 of the "gret sykenesse"), daughter of **William Sandys** and **Margaret Cheney** (daughter of **John Cheney** of Shurland, in the Isle of Sheppey, Kent). (*CP*, Westmorland section)

[5] *DNB*, "Neville, Ralph, fourth Earl of Westmorland (1499–1550)," gives her name as **Margaret** or **Matilda**. The *CP*, Westmorland section, gives her name as **Isabel** and states that she was "said to be" the niece of **Lawrence Booth**, Archbishop of York.

[6] *CP*, Westmorland section.

[7] Burke's *Royal Family*, pg. 200.

m. (2) **Richard Fry, Kt.**

3 — **Isabel** (bur. Oct 1453, Chapel of St. Michael in Canterbury Cathedral).

2 — **Thomas Beaufort** (b. 1405; d. 1431/1432), Earl of Perche. No issue. [1]

2 — **Joan/Jane Beaufort** (d. 15 Jul 1445, Dunbar Castle; bur. with her first husband in the Carthusian Church, Perth), Queen of Scots; m. (1) at the Church of St. Mary Overy (Southwark Cathedral [2]) 2/12/13 Feb 1424 **James I** (b. bef 1 Aug/Dec 1394, Dunfermline; crowned 21 May 1424; murdered 21 Feb 1437; bur. Carthusian Church, Perth), King of Scots 1406–1437, [3] third son of **Robert III**, King of Scots, and **Annabella Drummond**. Issue [4]:

3 — **Margaret** (b. 1424, Linlithgow, Scotland; d. 16 Aug 1445, Châlons; bur. (1) Châlons Cathedral, (2) St. Leon of Thouars) m. at Tours 24 Jun 1436 as his first wife **Louis XI** (b. 3 Jul 1423, Bourges; d. 24/30 Aug 1483; bur. Notre-Dame de Cléry, Montils), the Dauphin of France; **Margaret** died before her husband became king of France. No issue.

3 — **Alexander** (b. 16 Oct 1430, Holyrood; d. yng), Duke of Rothesay, twin to **James II**.

---

[1] Burke's *Royal Family*, pg. 200. Harriss, *Cardinal Beaufort*, pg. 204, mentions "the cardinal's nephews, Edmund, count of Mortain, and Thomas, count of Perche...." Ramsay, *Lancaster and York*, Vol. I, Table III, shows a "Thomas Beaufort d.s.p.?" as issue of **John Beaufort** (d. 1410). Jones and Underwood, *The King's Mother, Lady Margaret Beaufort*, Table 1, identifies a **Thomas**, Count of Perche, who died 1431.

[2] Donaldson, *Scottish Kings*, pg. 65.

[3] Donaldson in *Scottish Kings* states that **Joan** and **James I** were crowned at Scone on 2 May 1424. The *DNB*, "Jane or Johanna (d. 1445), queen of Scotland," gives the date as 21 May. "His love for his wife never wavered. Almost alone of Scottish kings, he had no mistress and no bastards" (*DNB*, "James I (1394–1437), king of Scotland").

[4] Donaldson, *Scottish Kings*, pgs. 74–75; Burke's *Royal Family*, pg. 319.

3 — **James II**, King of Scots (b. 16 Oct 1430[1];
crowned 25 Mar 1437, Holyrood, "in the Parliament of
Edinburgh"[2]; reigned 1437–1460; k. 3 Aug 1460, when
a cannon burst during a siege of Roxburgh Castle"[3];
bur. Holyrood); m. at Holyrood 2 Jul 1449 **Mary of
Gueldres** (d. 1463), daughter of **Arnold**, Duke of
Guelders. Issue[4]:

> 4 — **James III** (b. May 1452, St. Andrews Castle[5];
> crowned 10 Aug 1460, Kelso Abbey; murdered[6]
> after the Battle of Sauchieburn nr Bannockburn,
> 11 Jun 1488; bur. Cambuskenneth Abbey) m. at
> Holyrood 13 Jul 1469 **Margaret of Denmark**
> (d. 14 Jul 1486, Stirling; bur. Cambuskenneth
> Abbey), daughter of **Christian I**, King of Denmark.
> 4 — **Alexander Stewart** (b. abt 1454/bef 8 Jul 1455;
> d. 1485(?), Paris, killed in a tournament accident;
> bur. Church of Celestins, Paris), Duke of Albany,
> Earl of March; m. (1) (div. 2 Mar 1477/1478)
> **Catherine Sinclair**, daughter of **William Sinclair**,
> Earl of Orkney and Caithness, by his wife, **Elizabeth
> Douglas** (daughter of **Archibald Douglas**, 4th Earl of
> Douglas); m. (2) in France on or aft 16 Jan 1478/
> 1479 **Anne** (d. 13 Oct 1512, La Rochette in Savoy;
> bur. Carmelite Monastery, La Rochette in Savoy),
> daughter of **Bertrand de la Tour**, Count of Bologne
> and Auvergne.[7]

---

[1] *DNB*, "James I (1394–1437), king of Scotland."

[2] *DNB*, "James II (1430–1460), king of Scotland."

[3] *Webster's Biographical Dictionary*, 1962, "James II."

[4] Donaldson, *Scottish Kings*; Bingham, *Kings and Queens of Scotland*, Table 4 "The House of Stewart"; Ross, *Monarchs of Scotland*, pg. 84; *DNB*, "James II (1430–1460), king of Scotland"; Burke's *Royal Family*, pg 319.

[5] Burke's *Royal Family*, pg. 319, states that **James III** was not born at Stirling on 10 Jul 1451, as was formerly accepted. *CP*, Rothesay section, states that **James** was b. 20 Jul 1451.

[6] Burke's *Royal Family*, pg. 319.

[7] *CP*, Albany section.

4 — **David Stewart** (b. abt 1455; d. bef 18 Jul 1457), Earl of Moray.

4 — **John Stewart** (b. abt Jul 1457; d. 1497), Earl of Mar. Unm.

4 — **Margaret Stewart** "had issue by" **William Crichton**, 3rd Lord Crichton.

4 — **Mary Stewart** (d. 1460) m. (1) bef 26 Apr 1467 **Thomas Boyd** (d. abt 1473), Master of Boyd, Earl of Arran; m. (2)[1] bef Apr 1474 **James Hamilton** (d. 16 Nov 1479), 1st Lord Hamilton.

3 — **Elizabeth/Isabel** (d. 1494) m. 30 Oct 1442 **Francis I** (d. 1450), Count of Montfort, Duke of Bretagne/Brittany.

3 — **Joan/Janet** (b. abt 1428; liv. 16 Oct 1486), who was deaf and dumb; m. bef 15 May 1459 **James Douglas** (d. bef 22 Oct 1493), Lord Dalkeith/1st Earl of Morton, son of **James Douglas**, called by some 2nd Lord Dalkeith, and his wife, **Elizabeth Giffard** (daughter of **James Giffard** of Sheriffhall).[2]

3 — **Eleanor** (d. 1480) m. 12 Feb 1449 **Archduke Sigismund of Austria** (d. 26 Oct 1496).

3 — **Mary** (d. 20 Mar 1465; bur. Sandenburg at ter Veere in Zealand) m. at ter Veere in Zealand 1444 as a child to **Wolfram von Borselen/Wolfart van Borssele** (d. 29 Apr 1487, Ghent; bur. Sandenburg), Lord of Camp-Vere in Zealand, Count of Grandpré, Earl of Buchan in Scotland, son of **Hendrick van Borssele**, Count of Grandpré in Champagne, Heer van der Veere in Zealand.[3]

3 — **Annabella** m. (1) ("diss by div") 14 Dec 1447 **Louis** (d. Apr 1482), Count of Geneva, son of **Louis**, Duke of Savoy; m. (2) ("diss by div" 24 Jul 1471) bef 10 Mar 1459 **George Gordon** (d. by 30 Jan 1502/

---

[1] Bingham, *Kings and Queens of Scotland*, Table 4.

[2] *DNB*, "James I (1394–1437), king of Scotland"; *CP*, Morton section.

[3] *CP*, Buchan section.

1503), 2nd Earl of Huntley, lord high chancellor of
Scotland.[1] Issue (four sons, six daughters[2]) included:
    4 — **William Gordon**, ancestor of Lord Byron.
    4 — **Katherine Gordon** m. (1) **Perkin Warbeck**[3]
    (ex. 23 Nov 1499), imposter, pretender to the crown,
    and impersonator of **Edward IV's** second son,
    Richard, Duke of York; m. (2) **Matthew Cradock**.
Joan Beaufort, as above, Queen of Scotland,
m. (2) bef 21 Sep 1439 **James Stewart**, "the Black 'Rider'
or Knight of Lorne."[4] Issue[5]:
    3 — **John Stewart** of Balveny (b. abt 1440; d. 15 Sep
    1512; bur. Dunkeld Cathedral), Earl of Atholl;
    m. (1) 1459/1460, **Margaret** (d. in or bef 1475), "the
    fair maid of Galloway," only daughter of **Archibald**, 5th
    Earl of Douglas; m. (2) bef 19 Apr 1475 **Eleanor
    Sinclair** (d. 21 Mar 1518), daughter of **William
    Sinclair**, Earl of Orkney and Caithness.[6]
    3 — **James Stewart** (d. bet Jan 1497 and Jan 1499/1500)
    Hearty James, Earl of Buchan; m. bef 1 Mar 1466/1467
    Margaret Ogilvy, daughter and heir of **Alexander
    Ogilvy** of Auchterhouse.[7]
    3 — **Andrew Stewart**, Bishop of Moray.
  2 — **Margaret Beaufort**, second and youngest daughter;
m. aft 1421 **Thomas Courtenay** (b. 1414; d. 3 Feb 1457/

---

[1] Donaldson, *Scottish Kings*, pg. 75; *DNB*, "Gordon, George, second
Earl of Huntly (d. 1502?)." Though **George Gordon** is said by some
sources to have died abt 8 Jun 1501, the *DNB* article states that he was
living 11 Jul 1502 and died between then and 30 Jan 1502/1503.
[2] *DNB*, "Gordon, George, second Earl of Huntly (d. 1502?)."
[3] **Perkin Warbeck** was acknowledged by **Edward IV's** sister,
Margaret, and accepted by France and Scotland as **Richard IV**. He
landed in Cornwall and proclaimed himself king. He was taken prisoner
and confessed to the imposture and was imprisoned in the Tower. He
was hanged after attempting to escape.
[4] *DNB*, "Jane or Johanna (d. 1445), queen of Scotland."
[5] Bingham, *Kings and Queens of Scotland*, pg. 63.
[6] *CP*, Atholl section.
[7] *CP*, Buchan section.

1458, Abingdon Abbey), Earl of Devon,[1] son of **Hugh de Courtenay** (d. 16 Jun 1422). Issue[2]:

   3 — **Thomas de Courtenay** (b. 1432; ex. 3 Apr 1461, York, after being taken prisoner at the Battle of Towton, 29 Mar 1461), Earl of Devon. Unm.

   3 — **Henry de Courtenay** (ex. 17 Jan 1468/1469 for treason).

   3 — **Joan de Courtenay** (b. 1447) m. (1) **Roger Clifford** (ex. 1485); m. (2) **William Knyvett** and had issue.

   3 — **Elizabeth de Courtenay** (b. 1449) m. **Hugh Conway** (liv. 1471/1472, aged 22).

   3 — Three died young.

1 — **Henry Beaufort** (b. abt 1375; d. 11 Apr 1447; bur. Winchester Cathedral), second son, Bishop of Winchester, Cardinal, Chancellor, 2nd Earl of Somerset, Bishop of Lincoln, Bishop of Winchester, Dean of Wells, Chancellor of Oxford University, Chancellor of England.[3]

1 — **Thomas Beaufort** (b. abt Jan 1377[4]; d. 31 Dec 1426,[5]

---

[1] *DNB*, "Beaufort, John, first Earl of Somerset and Marquis of Dorset and of Somerset (1373?–1410)."

[2] *CP*, Courtenay section, Devon section.

[3] *CP*, Somerset section. **Henry Beaufort** had illegitimate issue of a daughter, **Joan/Jane Beaufort** (b. "prob. winter" 1391/1392), by **Alice FitzAlan** (d. 17 Mar 1415/1416), daughter of **Richard II Copped Hat FitzAlan** (d. 24 Jan 1375/1376), Earl of Arundel. This **Joan/Jane Beaufort** m. **Edward Stradling** (b. abt 1389), Kt., of St. Donat's, county of Glamorgan. **Edward Stradling** had a younger brother, **William Stradling**, whose daughter, **Gwenlian Stradling**, m. **Anthony Woodville** (d. 1483). They were parents of **Margaret Woodville**, who married **Robert Poyntz** (d. 1520), Kt. (*Ancestral* 60-32, 234-31, 234-32, 234-33, 234-34, 234-35; *CP*, Kent section).

Henry Beaufort was one of the judges who condemned **Joan of Arc** and participated when she was burned at the stake in Rouen 30 May 1431. He ordered that her ashes be gathered and thrown into the river so that they would not become the focal point of "popular veneration." (Harriss, *Cardinal Beaufort*, pg. 209)

[4] Armitage-Smith, *John of Gaunt*, pg. 389.

[5] *CP*, Somerset section.

Greenwich manor; bur. Bury St. Edmunds), Duke of Exeter, Earl of Dorset, Chancellor of England, K.G.; m. **Margaret Neville**, daughter of **Thomas Neville**, Kt., of Hornby, Lincolnshire. "Left no issue."[1]

2 — **Henry Beaufort** (d. yng).

1 — **Joan Beaufort** (b. abt 1379; d. 13 Nov 1440, Howden, Yorkshire; bur. in Lincoln Cathedral[2]) from whom descended the House of York; m. (1) bef 30 Sep 1394 (betrothed in 1386; married in 1392[3]) **Robert de Ferrers** (b. 1373; d. bef 29 Nov 1396),[4] 2nd Baron Ferrers of Wemme, son of **Robert de Ferrers** (aged 25 and more in 1375; d. 24 or 31 Dec 1380) and his wife **Elizabeth Botiller** (d. 19 Jun 1411) (daughter of **William le Botiller** of Wem and Oversley).[5] Issue:

    2 — **Mary de Ferrers** (b. bef 1394; d. 25 Jan 1457/1458), Lady of Oversley; m. **Ralph Neville** (d. 26 Feb 1457/1458), second son of **Ralph Neville** (d. 1425), 1st Earl of Westmorland, by his first wife, **Margaret Stafford**.[6] Issue:

        3 — **John Neville** (d. 17 Mary 1481/1482) m. **Elizabeth Newmarch**, daughter of **Robert Newmarch** of Wormsley.

    2 — **Elizabeth de Ferrers** (b. bef 1395/aged 18 or more in 1411[7]; d. 1434; bur. Church of the Black Friars, York), Lady of Wem; m. abt 28 Oct 1407 **John de Greystoke** (b. bef 1389; d. 8 Aug 1436), Lord Greystoke, Baron of Greystoke, son of **Ralph de Greystoke** (b. 18 Oct 1353,

---

[1] *DNB*, "Beaufort, Sir Thomas (d. 1427), Duke of Exeter"; Burke's *Royal Family*, pg. 200. *CP*, Somerset section, indicates that he died without surviving issue.

[2] **Joan's** effigy appears on her husband's tomb at Staindrop. (*CP*, Westmorland section; *DNB*, "Neville, Ralph, sixth Baron Neville of Raby and first Earl of Westmorland (1364–1425)")

[3] Harriss, *Cardinal Beaufort*, pg. 6.

[4] *Ancestral* 62-34; *CP*, Somerset section.

[5] *CP*, Ferrers section, Table "Ferrers of Chartley."

[6] *Ancestral* 2-33, 10-33. See also chapter, "Issue of the First Marriage of Ralph Neville."

[7] *CP*, Greystoke section.

Kirkby Ravensworth, co. York; d. 6 Apr 1418), Lord Greystoke, and **Katharine Clifford** (d. 23 Apr 1413) (daughter of **Roger de Clifford**, Lord Clifford, and **Maud Beauchamp**).[1] Issue[2]:

3 — **Ralph de Greystoke** (aged 22 or more in Aug 1436; d. 1 Jun 1487; bur. Kirkham Monastery), Lord Greystoke; m.[3] (1) **Elizabeth/Isabel FitzHugh**, daughter of **William FitzHugh** (d. 22 Oct 1452), Lord FitzHugh, and his wife, **Margery de Willoughby** (daughter of **William Willoughby** (d. 4 Dec 1409), Lord Willoughby of Eresby, co. Lincoln); m. (2)[4] "in the chapel within the manor house of Lord Greystoke at Hinderskelf" aft 20 Sep 1483 **Beatrice Hawclyf or Hatcliff/Awtecliffe**[5] of Hinderskelfe.[6]

3 — **Eleanore de Greystoke**.

3 — **Thomas de Greystoke**.

3 — **Richard de Greystoke**.

3 — **William de Greystoke**.

Joan Beaufort, as above, wife of **Robert de Ferrers**, m. (2) bef 20 Feb 1396/1397 (Nov 1396[7]) as his second wife[8] **Ralph Neville** (b. abt 1364; d. 21 Oct 1425, Raby Castle[9]), 6th Lord Neville of Raby Castle,[10] 1st Earl of

---

[1] *Ancestral* 62-35; *CP*, Greystoke section.

[2] *CP*, Greystoke section.

[3] A papal dispensation was necessary because they were "related in the 4th-4th degree of consanguinity." The dispensation was dated 1 Jul 1436. (*CP*, Greystoke section)

[4] The *CP*, Greystoke section, states that there may have been another wife named **Elizabeth** or **Isabel** between the two wives listed above.

[5] **Beatrice Hawclyf** m. (2) **Robert Constable** (d. 22 Nov 1501), son of **Robert Constable** of Flamborough. (*CP*, Greystoke section)

[6] *CP*, Greystoke section.

[7] Harriss, *Cardinal Beaufort*, pg. 7.

[8] See chapter, "Issue of the First Marriage of Ralph Neville."

[9] *CP*, Somerset section.

[10] Armitage-Smith, *John of Gaunt*, pg. 389.

Westmorland,[1] K.G.[2] Issue:
  2 — **Richard Neville** (b. 1399[3]; ex. 31 Dec 1460,
  Pontefract Castle, after the battle of Wakefield; bur. 1463
  with the Earls of Salisbury at Bisham Priory, Berkshire[4]),
  eldest son, Earl of Salisbury, K.G.; m. abt Feb 1420/
  1421 **Alice Montagu** (d. bef Feb 1463/bet 3 Apr and 9 Dec
  1462[5]), only child of **Thomas de Montagu** (d. 3 Nov
  1428, siege of Orleans), 4th Earl of Salisbury.[6] Issue[7]:
    3 — **Richard Neville the Kingmaker** (b. 22 Nov 1428;
    k. 14 Apr 1471, Battle of Barnet; bur. Bisham Abbey,
    Berkshire), Earl of Warwick and Salisbury; m. **Anne de
    Beauchamp** (b. abt Sep 1426, Caversham; d. "shortly

---

[1] **Ralph de Neville** was on 29 Sep 1397 created Earl of
Westmorland. This act raised **Joan Beaufort** to the rank of countess and
was more a reflection of **Richard II's** favour toward his uncle, **John of
Gaunt**, than toward the **Nevilles** (Harriss, *Cardinal Beaufort*, pg. 7).
Ralph de Neville later played a prominent role in forcing the abdication
of **Richard II** and securing the throne for his wife's half-brother,
Henry IV (*CP*, Westmorland section).
  [2] The greater part of the information concerning the **Neville** family
was taken from individual articles on the **Nevilles** in the *DNB*.
  [3] **Richard Neville** was knighted in 1420. He was 26 years of age in
1425, when he married **Alice Montagu**, who had just reached her
eighteenth year. She was the only child of **Thomas de Montagu**
(d. 1428), 4th Earl of Salisbury (*Warwick the Kingmaker*, pgs. 22–23).
Ramsay, *Lancaster and York*, Vol. II, Table I, gives the year of birth as
1400.
  [4] According to the *DNB*, "Neville, Richard, Earl of Warwick and
Salisbury (1428–1471)," Bisham Abbey was destroyed during
Henry VIII's dissolution of the monasteries. During the years of
dissolution, tombs were often desecrated and destroyed and the bones
scattered.
  [5] *CP*, Salisbury section.
  [6] **Thomas Montagu** (d. 1428), Earl of Salisbury, m. (2) **Alice
Chaucer**, daughter of **Thomas Chaucer**, son of the poet **Geoffrey
Chaucer**. There was no issue of this second marriage. However, he left
a natural son, **John**. (*DNB*, "Montacute or Montagu, Thomas de, fourth
Earl of Salisbury (1388–1428)")
  [7] *CP*, Salisbury section.

before" 20 Sep 1492[1]), only daughter of **Richard de Beauchamp** (d. 1439), 13th Earl of Warwick, and his second wife, **Isabel le Despenser**[2] (b. 1400; d. 1439) (daughter of **Thomas le Despenser** (ex. 1400), 6th Baron le Despenser, Lord of Glamorgan and Morgannoc). Issue (two daughters):

4 — **Isabel Neville** (b. 5 Sep 1451, Warwick Castle; d. Dec 1476,[3] Warwick Castle; bur. Tewkesbury Abbey) m. 1469 **George** (b. October 1449, Dublin, Ireland; ex. 17 or 18 Feb 1478, Tower of London[4]), Duke of Clarence, brother of **Richard III**, KING OF ENGLAND.[5]

4 — **Anne Neville** (b. 11 Jun 1454/1456, Warwick Castle; d. 16 Mar 1485, Westminster Palace; bur. Westminster Abbey), QUEEN OF ENGLAND, betrothed Aug 1470 to **Edward** (k. 4 May 1471, after the battle of Tewkesbury), Prince of Wales, only son of **Henry VI**, KING OF ENGLAND; m. 12 Jul 1472 **Richard III** (reigned 1483–1485; k. 22 Aug 1485, Battle of Bosworth), KING OF ENGLAND.[6]

3 — **Thomas Neville** (k. 30 Dec 1460, Battle of Wakefield) m. at Tattershall, Lincolnshire, Aug 1453 **Maud Stanhope** (d. 30 Aug 1497), widow of **Robert**

---

[1] *CP*, Warwick section.

[2] **Isabel le Despenser** was the widow of **Richard de Beauchamp** (b. abt 1397; d. Mar 1422), Earl of Worcester, son of **William de Beauchamp** (d. 1411), Lord Abergavenny.

[3] Exact day of **Isabel Neville's** death seen as 21 Dec (Ramsay, *Lancaster and York*, Vol. II, Table II) and 12 Dec.

[4] Ramsay, *Lancaster and York*, Vol. II, Table II.

[5] Their daughter, **Margaret Plantagenet**, Countess of Salisbury, was beheaded 27 May 1541 on order of **Henry VIII**, KING OF ENGLAND, despite the fact she was nearing the age of seventy. Their son, **Edward Plantagenet**, was also executed by **Henry VIII**, simply because he was of the blood royal.

[6] The only issue of **Anne** and **Richard III** was a son, **Edward Plantagenet** (b. abt 1476; d. 9 Apr 1484), Prince of Wales, Earl of Salisbury, who died in the lifetime of his parents.

Willoughby (d. 25 Jul 1452), 6th Lord Willoughby de
Eresby, and daughter of **Richard Stanhope** (d. 1436)
and his wife, **Maud Cromwell** (sister of **Ralph
Cromwell** (d. 1454)).[1] No issue.
3 — **John Neville** (b. abt 1431; k. 14 Apr 1471, Battle
of Barnet; bur. Bisham Abbey), Baron Montagu,
Marquis of Montagu, Earl of Northumberland;
m. 25 Apr 1457 **Isabel/Elizabeth Ingaldesthorpe**
(d. 20 May 1476; bur. Bisham),[2] daughter of **Edmund
Ingaldesthorpe** and his wife **Joan Tibetot/Tiptoft** (sister
and heir of **John Tibetot** (ex. 18 Oct 1470), Earl of
Worcester, and daughter of **John**, Lord Tibetot.[3]
3 — **George Neville** (d. 1476), Bishop of Exeter,
Archbishop of York, Lord Chancellor.
3 — **Joan Neville** (d. bef 9 Sep 1462; bur. Arundel)
m. **William FitzAlan** (also **Mautravers**) (b. 23 Nov
1417[4]; d. 1487, aged 71; bur. Arundel), Earl of
Arundel.[5]
3 — **Cecily Neville** (d. 28 Jul 1450; bur. 31 Jul 1450 in
Lady Chapel of Tewkesbury Abbey) m. (1) 1434 **Henry
de Beauchamp** (b. 22 Mar 1424,[6] Hanley Castle;
d. 11 Jun 1446, Hanley Castle; bur. Tewkesbury
Abbey), Duke of Warwick, Count of Aumale;
m. (2) lic. 3 Apr 1449 as his first wife **John Tiptoft**
(b. 8 May 1427; ex. 18 Oct 1470, Tower Hill[7]), Earl of
Worcester, son of **John Tiptoft** (d. 27 Jan 1442/1443),

---

[1] *DNB*, "Neville, Richard, Earl of Salisbury (1400–1460)"; *CP*,
Willoughby section.

[2] **Isabel/Elizabeth Ingaldesthorpe** m. (2) 25 Apr 1472 **William
Norreys** (attainted 1484) and had issue. (*CP*, Montagu section)

[3] *CP*, Montagu section; Worcester section.

[4] Ramsay, *Lancaster and York*, Vol. II, Table II.

[5] *CP*, Arundel section.

[6] Ramsay, *Lancaster and York*, Vol. II, Table II.

[7] *CP*, Warwick section; Worcester section. **John Tiptoft** (d. 1470) is
sometimes referred to as the "Butcher of England." The *CP*, Worcester
section, references a biography, *John Tiptoft* by Miss R. J. Mitchell,
published in 1938.

1st Lord Tiptoft, and his second wife, **Joyce Cherleton** (b. abt 1403; d. 22 Sep 1446).

3 — **Alice Neville** (liv. 22 Nov 1503) m. **Henry FitzHugh** (b. abt 1429[1]; d. 8 Jun 1472), Lord FitzHugh of Ravensworth Castle, son of **William FitzHugh** and **Margery de Willoughby**.

3 — **Eleanor Neville** (bur. St. James's, Garlickhithe, London) m. aft 10 May 1457[2]/1459[3] as his first wife[4] **Thomas Stanley** (b. abt 1435; d. 29 Jul 1504, Lathom; bur. Burscough Abbey, nr Ormskirk), 1st Lord Stanley, 1st Earl of Derby. Issue of six sons, four daughters.[5]

3 — **Catherine Neville** (d. bet 22 Nov 1503 and 25 Mar 1504; will directed burial at Ashby-de-la-Zouch), fifth daughter, betrothed bef 10 May 1459 to **William Bonville** (d. bef 17 Feb 1461/31 Dec 1460, slain at battle of Wakefield with his father), Lord Harington; there was issue[6]; m. (2) bef 6 Feb 1461/1462 **William Hastings** (aged 24 or more in 1455; ex. 13 Jun 1483, the Tower; bur. St. George's Chapel, Windsor[7]), Lord Hastings, son of **Leonard Hastings** (d. 20 Oct 1455) and his wife, **Alice Camoys** (daughter of **Thomas Camoys**, Lord Camoys).[8]

3 — **Margaret Neville** (d. aft 20 Nov 1506; bur. Colne Priory) m. aft 1459 as his first wife **John de Vere III**

---

[1] Ramsay, *Lancaster and York*, Vol. II, Table II.

[2] *CP*, Derby section.

[3] Bagby, *The Earls of Derby*, pg. 10.

[4] **Thomas Stanley's** second wife was **Margaret Beaufort** (d. 1509), mother of **Henry of Richmond** and daughter of **John Beaufort**. It was a marriage of politics and convenience, and there was no issue. **Lord Stanley** was instrumental in the defeat of **Richard III** at Bosworth, a victory that put **Margaret Beaufort's** son on the throne as **Henry VII**.

[5] Pollard, *The Stanleys of Knowsley: A History of the Noble Family*.

[6] Ramsay, *Lancaster and York*, Vol. II, Table II.

[7] **Hastings** was executed on orders of **Richard**, Duke of Gloucester, probably as part of **Richard's** plot to take the throne of England from his young nephew, **Edward V**.

[8] *CP*, Hastings section.

(b. 8 Sep 1442; d. 10 Mar 1513, Hedingham Castle; bur. Colne Priory[1]), 13th Earl of Oxford. No surviving issue.[2]

2 — **William Neville** (d. 9 Jan 1462/1463; bur. Guisborough Priory), sixth son by second wife, Baron of Fauconberg, Lord Fauconberg, Earl of Kent; m. bef 28 Apr 1422 as her first husband[3] **Joan Fauconberge** (b. 18 Oct 1406, Skelton; d. 11 Dec 1490, "having survived all her children") of Skelton Castle, Cleveland, daughter and heir of the last Baron Fauconberg, **Thomas Fauconberg/Faucomberge** (d. 9 Sep 1407), and his second wife, **Joan Brounflete** (d. 4 Mar 1408/1409) (daughter of **Thomas Brounflete**). Issue (no legitimate surviving male issue[4])[5]:

3 — **Joan Neville** (aged 30 or more in 1463) m. **Edward Bedhowing/Bethom/Bethum** (d. 22 Feb 1472). No issue.

3 — **Elizabeth Neville** (aged 22 or more in 1463) m. as his first wife **Richard Strangeways** (d. 13 Apr 1488) of West Harlsey, Co. York.

3 — **Alice Neville** (aged 26 or more in 1463) m. **John**

---

[1] "He was *bur.* with his 1st wife under the same tomb, destroyed *circa* 1730...." (*CP*, Oxford section)

[2] *CP*, Oxford section.

[3] Described as "a fool and idiot from birth." **Joan Fauconberge** m. (2) "within two months of her husband's death," a **John Berwyke**. (*CP*, Fauconberge section)

[4] Ramsay, *Lancaster and York*, Vol. II, Table I. According to the *DNB*, "Neville, William, Baron Fauconberg and afterwards Earl of Kent (d. 1463)," **William Neville** had an illegitimate son, **Thomas Fauconberg**, called the Bastard of Fauconberg. The *CP*, Fauconberge section, names this son as **Thomas Fauconbridge** and describes him as, "one of his [Neville's] bastard sons...." This illegitimate son was captured after an unsuccessful plot to restore **Henry VI** to the throne in May 1471. He was beheaded and his head set upon London Bridge.

[5] *CP*, Fauconberge section.

Conyers[1] (d. 26 Jul 1469, Battle of Edgcote Field) of Hornby Castle, Yorkshire, son of **John Conyers** (d. bef 14 Mar 1489/1490) and **Margaret Darcy** (d. bet. 20 Mar and 20 Apr 1469).[2]

2 — **George Neville** (d. 30 or 31 Dec 1469; bur. Well, co. York), Baron Latimer, third son, heir of his half-uncle, **John**, Lord Latimer; m. in or bef Feb 1436/1437 as her first husband[3] **Elizabeth Beauchamp** (aged 22 in 1439; d. bef 2 Oct 1480; bur. Beauchamp Chapel of St. Mary's, Warwick), daughter of **Richard de Beauchamp** (d. 1439), Earl of Warwick, by his first wife, **Elizabeth Berkeley** (b. abt 1386; d. 28 Dec 1422) (daughter of **Thomas de Berkeley** (d. 13 Jul 1417), Lord Berkeley, and his wife, **Margaret**, daughter of Warin, Lord L'Isle[4]). Issue:

3 — **Henry Neville** (k. 26 Jul 1469, Battle of Edgecot nr Banbury; bur. Beauchamp Chapel, Warwick) m. **Jane** or **Joan Bourchier** (d. 7 Oct 1470), daughter of **John Bourchier** (d. 16 or 21 May 1474, bur. Chertsey Abbey, Surrey), 1st Lord Berners, and his wife, **Margery/Margaret Berners**[5] (d. 18 Dec 1475) (daughter of **Richard Berners** of West Horsley, Surrey, and his wife **Philippe Dalyngridge**, daughter of **Edward Dalyngridge**[6]).

2 — **Robert Neville** (b. 1404; d. 8/9 Jul 1457; bur. Durham Cathedral), fifth son, Bishop of Salisbury,

---

[1] Identified with the "mysterious personage" of Robin of Redesdale. (*DNB*, "Neville, William, Baron Fauconberg and afterwards Earl of Kent (d. 1463)")

[2] *CP*, Fauconberge section.

[3] **Elizabeth Beauchamp** (d. 1480) m. (2) **Thomas Wake** (d. 20 May 1476), Esquire, of Blisworth. (*CP*, Latimer section)

[4] *Ancestral* 87-33.

[5] **Margery Berners** was the widow of **John Ferreby** (his will was dated 1 Oct and proved 12 Nov 1441). (*CP*, Berners section)

[6] *CP*, Latimer section, Berners section. In her will, **Joan Bourchier** mentions her brothers, **Humphrey Bourchier** and **Thomas Bourchier**, and her sister, **Elizabeth Bourchier**, Lady Welles.

Bishop of Durham.[1]

2 — **Edward Neville**[2] (d. 18 Oct 1476;
bur. "apparently" at priory church at Abergavenny), sixth
and youngest son, 1st Baron of Bergavenny/Abergavenny,
K.G.; m. (1) (bef Oct 1424) **Elizabeth de Beauchamp**
(b. 16 Sep 1415, Hanley Castle, Worcestershire; "said to
have died" 18 Jun 1448; bur. Carmelites, Coventry[3]), only
child of **Richard de Beauchamp**[4] (b. 1397; d. 18 Mar
1422, from injuries received at the siege of Meaux in
France), Earl of Worcester, K.B., and his wife, **Isabel le
Despenser** (d. 1439) (daughter of **Thomas le Despenser**
(ex. 1400), 6th Baron le Despenser, Lord of Glamorgan and
Morgannoc, and his wife, **Constance** (d. 1416) (daughter of
Edmund of Langley, Duke of York (d. 1402)[5]).[6] Issue:

   3 — **Richard Neville** (d. in the lifetime of his father;
bur. Staindrop Church, "the ancient Neville mausoleum
by the gates of Raby Castle").

   3 — **George Neville** (b. abt 1420, "said to have been
born at Raby"; d. 20 Sep 1492; bur. Lewes Priory,
Sussex), second son, Baron of Abergavenny;
m. (1) **Margaret Fenne** (d. 28 Sep 1485), daughter of
Hugh Fenne, Treasurer of the Household to Henry VI[7];
m. (2) as her fourth husband **Elizabeth**[8] (d. 1500).[9]

---

  [1] The *DNB*, "Neville, Robert (1404–1457), bishop of Salisbury and
Durham," suggests that three recipients in his will, **Thomas Neville**,
Ralph, and their sister **Alice**, may have been his issue.

  [2] The majority of the information concerning **Edward Neville**
(d. 1476) and his family has been taken from the *DNB*, "Neville,
Edward (d. 1476), first Baron of Bergavenny or Abergavenny."

  [3] *CP*, Abergavenny section.

  [4] **Richard de Beauchamp** was the son of **William de Beauchamp**
(d. 1411), K.G., and **Joan FitzAlan**.

  [5] *CP*, York section.

  [6] *DNB*, "Neville, Edward (d. 1476), first Baron of Bergavenny or
Abergavenny."

  [7] *Sureties* 48-9.

  [8] She was widow of **John Stokker** of St. George's, Eastcheap;
Richard Naylor (will pr. 1483), citizen of London; and **Robert Bassett**,
Lord Mayor of London 1475-1476. (*CP*, Abergavenny section)

Edward Neville, as above, husband of **Elizabeth de Beauchamp**, m. (2) **Catherine Howard**[1] (liv. 29 Jun 1478), daughter of **Robert Howard** (b. abt 1383; d. 1436), Kt., and his wife (m. abt 1420), **Margaret Mowbray** (daughter of **Thomas de Mowbray** (b. 22 Mar 1365/1366; d. 22 Sep 1399[2]), Duke of Norfolk) and sister of **John Howard** (d. 22 Aug 1485, Battle of Bosworth), 1st Duke of Norfolk. Issue of this second marriage[3]:

> 3 — **Ralph Neville**. No issue.
> 3 — **Edward Neville**. No issue.
> 3 — **Margaret Neville** (d. 30 Sep 1506; bur. Cobham) m. as his second wife **John Brooke** (b. 1444; d. 9 Mar 1511/1512), Baron Cobham, Lord Cobham, son of **Edward Brooke** and **Elizabeth Tuchet**. For historical interest, their son:
>> 4 — **Thomas Brooke** (d. 19 Jul 1529; bur. Cobham), Lord Cobham; m. (1) **Dorothy Heydon**, daughter of **Henry Heydon** and **Anne Boleyn** (daughter of **Geoffrey Boleyn** and **Anne Hoo**) and had issue of thirteen children, including[4]:

---

[1] According to the *DNB*, "Neville, Edward (d. 1476), first Baron of Bergavenny or Abergavenny," **Edward** was excommunicated for marrying **Catherine** because of their "illicit relations during his [first] wife's lifetime" and because "they were within the third degree of consanguinity." However, the Pope was "persuaded to grant a dispensation [dated 15 Oct 1448] for the marriage." (*CP*, Abergavenny section)

[2] *Ancestral* 16-34 through 16-32.

[3] *DNB*, "Neville, Edward (d. 1476), first Baron of Bergavenny or Abergavenny."

[4] d'Angerville, *Living Descendants of Blood Royal (in America)*, pg. 24.

5 — **Elizabeth Brooke** m. (1) **Thomas Wyatt**
(b. 1503; d. 10 Oct 1542) of Allington Castle in
Kent, poet.
Thomas Brooke (d. 1529), as above, m. (2) **Dorothy
Southwell**; no issue; m. (3) **Elizabeth Hart**
(liv. 31 Mar 1552); no issue. [1]
3 — **Anne Neville**.
3 — **Catherine Neville** m. **Robert Tanfield**.
2 — **Joan Neville**, a nun.
2 — **Catherine Neville** (d. aft 1478/liv. 1483) m.
(1) **John V de Mowbray** (b. 1392; d. 19 Oct 1432,
Epworth; bur. priory at Epworth), 2nd Duke of Norfolk;
m. (2) bef 27 Jan 1441/1442 **Thomas Strangeways**;
m. (3) after 1442 as his second wife **John Beaumont**
(d. 10 Jul 1460, Battle of Northampton), Viscount
Beaumont, K.G., Constable of England 1445–1450, Great
Chamberlain, son of **Henry Beaumont** (d. Jun 1413;
bur. Sempringham, co. Lincoln), Lord Beaumont, and
Elizabeth Willoughby (d. "shortly before" 12 Nov 1428)
(daughter of **William Willoughby** (d. 4 Dec 1409), Lord
Willoughby of Eresby, and his first wife, **Lucy Strange**
(liv. 28 Apr 1398; bur. "probably" Spilsby), daughter of
Roger, 5th Lord Strange of Knockin); m. (4) aft 1464 when
she was aged 80 to the 20-year-old **John Woodville**
(ex. 12 Aug 1469, Kenilworth, with his father, **Richard
Woodville**, 1st Earl Rivers), brother-in-law of **Edward IV**,
KING OF ENGLAND. [2] Issue by first husband (only son

---

[1] *CP*, Cobham section.

[2] The marriage of **Catherine Neville** and **John Woodville** was one of
many in which the **Woodvilles** were placed in powerful and affluent
families in England (*DNB*, "Mowbray, John (V), second Duke of
Norfolk (1389–1432)"); *CP*, Beaumont section. Ramsay, *Lancaster and
York*, Vol. II, Table I, lists the husbands of **Catherine Neville** thus:
(1) **John Mowbray I**; (2) **John Beaumont**, Viscount Beaumont;
(3) **John Woodville**. The *CP*, Beaumont section, lists the husbands thus:
(1) **John Mowbray I**; (2) **Thomas Strangways**; (3) **John Beaumont**;
(4) **John Woodville**.

and heir[1]):

 3 — **John VI de Mowbray**[2] (b. 12 Sep 1415; d. 6 Nov
1461; bur. Thetford Priory), only son, 3rd Duke of
Norfolk, K.G.; m. "as early as 1424"[3] **Eleanor
Bourchier** (d. Nov 1474; bur. Thetford Priory), daughter
of **William Bourchier** (d. 28 May 1420), Count of Eu in
Normandy, and his wife, **Anne Plantagenet** (d. 1438)
(daughter of **Thomas of Woodstock**, Duke of
Gloucester, son of **Edward III**). **Eleanor** was sister of
Henry Bourchier (d. 1483), Earl of Essex.

 2 — **Anne Neville** (d. 20 Sep 1480; bur. Pleshy, Essex)
m. (1) bef 18 Oct 1424 **Humphrey Stafford** (k. 10 Jul
1460, Battle of Northampton; bur. Grey Friars at
Northampton), 1st Duke of Buckingham, son of **Edmund
Stafford** (d. 1403), Earl of Stafford, and his wife, **Anne**[4]
(d. 16 Oct 1438) (daughter of **Thomas of Woodstock**
(murdered 8 Sep 1397), Duke of Gloucester). For issue, see
chapter, "Edward III 1327–1377." **Anne Neville**
m. (2) bef 25 Nov 1467 as his second wife **Walter Blount**
(b. abt 1420; d. 1 Aug 1474; bur. chapel of the Apostles in
the Church of the Grey Friars, London), 1st Baron
Mountjoy. No issue of this marriage.[5]

 2 — **Eleanor Neville** (d. 1463) m. (1) aft 23 May 1412
Richard le Despenser (b. 30 Nov 1396; d. 7 Oct 1414,
Merton, Surrey; bur. Tewkesbury Abbey), Lord le
Despenser; no issue; m. (2) **Henry de Percy** (b. 3 Feb
1392/1394; k. 22 May 1455, Battle of St. Albans), 2nd Earl

---

[1] *CP*, Norfolk section.

[2] The *CP*, Norfolk section, states that his monogram contains all the
letters, *John Mowbray, Norf*, and is reproduced in the *Paston Letters*,
Vol. I. **John de Mowbray** and **Eleanor Bourchier** had an only son,
John de Mowbray (d. 16 or 17 Jan 1475/1476, Framingham Castle,
Suffolk), Duke of Norfolk, who was father of **Anne Mowbray**
(d. 1481), five-year-old bride of **Richard**, Duke of York (second son of
Edward IV, KING OF ENGLAND).

[3] *CP*, Norfolk section.

[4] **Anne** later married **William Bourchier** (d. 1420), Count of Eu.

[5] *CP*, Mountjoy section.

of Northumberland, K.G., the only son of **Henry Hotspur Percy** (d. 1403). Issue by second marriage (twelve children[1]):

3 — **Henry de Percy** (b. 25 Jul 1421, Leconfield, Yorkshire; k. 29 Mar 1461, Battle of Towton Field; bur. "it is believed" in the church of St. Dionys/Denis at York), Kt., Earl of Northumberland, Lord Poynings; m. on or bef 25 Jun 1435 **Eleanor Poynings**[2] (b. abt 1422; d. Feb 1483/1484), daughter of **Richard de Poynings** (k. 10 Jun 1429 nr Orleans; will directed burial in Poynings churchyard), Lord Poynings, and his second wife, **Eleanor Berkeley** (d. 1 Aug 1455[3]) (widow of **John de Arundel** (b. 1 Aug 1385; d. 21 Apr 1421), Lord Maltravers, and daughter of **John Berkeley** of Beverstone, co. Gloucester).[4]

3 — **Thomas de Percy** (b. 29 Nov 1422, Leckonfield, co. York; d. 10 Jul 1460, Battle of Northampton), Lord Egremont.[5]

3 — **George de Percy** (b. 1424), a prebendary of Beverley.

3 — **Ralph de Percy** (d. 25 Apr 1464, Battle of Hedgely Moor), seventh son. Unm.[6]

3 — **Richard de Percy** (d. 29 Mar 1461, Battle of Towton).

3 — **William de Percy** (b. 1428; d. 1462), Bishop of Carlisle.

3 — Three sons (d. yng).

3 — **Joan de Percy** (bur. Whitby Abbey), a nun.

---

[1] *DNB*, "Percy, Henry, second Earl of Northumberland (1394–1455)." The *CP*, Northumberland section, states there were nine sons.

[2] By his marriage with **Eleanor Poynings**, **Henry de Percy** acquired the baronies of Poynings, Fitzpaine, and Bryan. (*DNB*, "Percy, Henry, second Earl of Northumberland (1394–1455)")

[3] *CP*, Poynings section.

[4] *CP*, Poynings section, Arundel section, Northumberland section.

[5] *CP*, Egremont section.

[6] *DNB*, "Percy, Sir Ralph (1425–1464)."

3 — **Katherine de Percy** (b. 28 May 1423, Leconfield)
m. bef Jan 1458/1459 **Edmund Grey** (b. 26 Oct 1416;
d. 22 May 1490), Lord Grey of Ruthin, Earl of Kent,
son and heir of **John Grey** (d. 27 Aug 1439), K.G., and
his wife, **Constance Holand** (d. 12 or 14 Nov 1437;
bur. Church of St. Katherine by the Tower) (daughter of
John Holand (ex. 10 Jan 1399/1400), Duke of Exeter).
3 — **Anne de Percy** (d. 1522) m. (1) **Thomas
Hungerford**; (2) **Laurence Rainsford**; (3) **Hugh
Vaughan.**
2 — **Cecily Sweet Cis Neville** (b. 3 May 1415, Raby
Castle; d. 31 May 1495, Berkhamsted Castle;
bur. Fotheringhay), youngest daughter; m. bef 18 Oct 1424
Richard Plantagenet (b. 20 Sep 1411/1412; ex. 30/31 Dec
1460, Battle of Wakefield; bur. (1) Pontefract,
(2) Fotheringhay), Duke of York, Earl of March and Ulster,
the Protector, only son of **Richard of Cambridge**
(b. abt 1375; ex. 5 Aug 1415, Southampton; bur. "God's
House" in Southampton), Earl of Cambridge, and his first
wife, **Anne Mortimer** (d. bef 1415) (daughter of **Roger VI
de Mortimer** (k. 15 Aug 1398), 4th Earl of March and
Ulster, and his wife **Eleanor de Holand** (d. 1405), daughter
of **Thomas de Holand** (d. 1397), 2nd Earl of Kent). The
issue of **Cecily Sweet Cis Neville** and **Richard Plantagenet**
(eight sons, four daughters) are listed in chapter,
"Edward III 1327-1377." Briefly, for reference, they are:
3 — **Anne Plantagenet** (d. 1475/1476).
3 — **Henry** (d. yng).
3 — **Edward IV** (d. 1483), KING OF ENGLAND.
3 — **Edmund** (d. 1460), Earl of Rutland.
3 — **Elizabeth** (d. 1503/1504).
3 — **Margaret of York** (d. 1503).
3 — **William** (d. yng).
3 — **John** (d. yng).
3 — **George** (d. 1478), Duke of Clarence.
3 — **Thomas** (d. yng).
3 — **Richard III** (d. 1485), KING OF ENGLAND.
3 — **Ursula** (d. yng).

2 — **Cuthbert Neville.** No issue.[1]
2 — **Henry Neville.** No issue.[2]
2 — **Thomas Neville.** No issue.[3]

Possible Illegitimate Issue of John of Gaunt

1 — **Blanche,**[4] daughter of **Marie de St. Hilaire,** who was a maid of honour or lady-in-waiting in the service of **Queen Philippa**), and "probably the daughter of a Hainault knight, Jean, called Vilain de Saint-Hilaire and Dame Mahaut de Wasnes"[5]; m. 1381 **Thomas Morieux/Morrieux.**

John of Gaunt
(d. 1399)

---

[1] Ramsay, *Lancaster and York*, Vol. II, Table I.
[2] Ramsay, *Lancaster and York*, Vol. II, Table I.
[3] Ramsay, *Lancaster and York*, Vol. II, Table I.
[4] Armitage-Smith, *John of Gaunt*, pg. 460, describes this **Blanche** as a "mysterious daughter" whose parentage is referenced only in a passage in the writings of the chronicler, **Froissart**. Gardner in *The Life and Times of Chaucer*, pg. 113, remarks that **John of Gaunt** "took care of both mother and daughter ever afterward." Silva-Vigier, *This Moste Highe Prince...John of Gaunt*, pg. 165, describes **Thomas Morrieux** as son-in-law of **John of Gaunt** and names his companion as "Blanche, John's daughter by Mairie St Hilaire."
[5] Silva-Vigier, *This Moste Highe Prince...John of Gaunt 1340–1399*, pgs. 72–73.

Some Genealogy of Harold II

Harold Godwinson, though descended from the Kings of Wessex, [1] was not considered to be of the English royal bloodline, yet in 1066, he was elected, consecrated, and crowned King of England. In less than a year, he lost crown, country, and life.

Harold had for possibly twenty years or more a common-law or hand-fast wife known as Edith Swan-Neck by whom he had issue. It was she who came after Harold's last and fatal battle "to find the mutilated corpse and to identify her lover by markings known only to herself." [2]

In an effort to aid in the understanding of the personal relationships of Harold's genealogy, the story of England and Normandy in 1066 is briefly given here.

1066: King Edward, King Harold, King William

In 1064, Harold Godwinson, Earl of Wessex, in traveling from England to the continent, found himself (probably not by design) in the court of William the Bastard, Duke of Normandy, where his status as an honored captive in William's household was implicitly understood. In order to be released to return home to England, Harold had to make a solemn oath on a chest or altar to support William's claim as Edward the Confessor's successor to the throne of England. William, Duke of Normandy, was distantly related to the childless King Edward, being great-grandson of Richard I, Duke of Normandy,

---

[1] *Ancestral* 1B-14 through 1B-23.
[2] Butler, *1066: The Story of a Year*, pg. 66.

grandfather of King Edward.

Harold's sister was Edward's queen, and Harold himself, a member of one of the most powerful noble families in England, was the right hand man of the king. And because King Edward had led a life of celibacy and had no issue to succeed him, Harold could very well have aspired to the throne soon to be vacated by the aging Edward.

William I, Harold II Godwinson, and Edward the Confessor

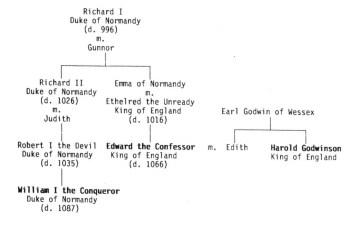

That knowledge, along with Harold's physical proximity to the English court, probably spurred William to insist on the oath from Harold; and Harold's desire to return to England probably spurred him to give it. The tradition is that after the oath was made, William revealed the contents of the chest or altar and Harold paled to see the holy relics on which he had sworn his oath. To break his word would place his soul in deadly peril.

But the oath was made and Harold returned to England. Soon afterwards, in a move to gain the support of Eadwine, the Earl of Mercia, Harold married the Earl's sister, Edith/Ealdyth/Aldgyth, widow of Gruffydd, the troublesome Welsh prince.

On 5 Jan 1066, Edward the Confessor died, having named Harold as his successor and putting in his care both queen and kingdom.

Though he was not of the royal family, Harold's kingship was constitutional: "...he received it by bequest of his predecessor, by election in the national assembly, and by consecration."[1] However, some believed that Harold, having sworn the oath on relics to support William's claim to the crown, was a usurper who had sacrificed his soul. Harold's supporters claimed the oath was made under duress and thus was no oath. Edward was buried in Westminster Abbey and there, too, the same day was Harold crowned King of England.

Douglas suggests that the haste with which the coronation took place indicated that Harold's taking of the throne was "premeditated, and that he feared opposition."[2] However, the truth may have been more that "...the perilous circumstances of the time demanded quick action." Immediate and strong leadership was needed; thus, the chief descendant of the old Saxon house, young Edgar, was not considered. The witan elected the experienced and powerful Harold.

According to Butler, the coronation coming so soon after the burial of the king was not considered indecent haste. "Until the king was buried, the king could not be crowned, and by custom the office of the coronation took place during a festival of the church, when the time was holy, and the witan were gathered to debate the [affairs] of state."[3]

William in Normandy, hearing of the death of the king and the crowning of Harold, prepared for his invasion of England.

In October 1066, William, sailing in his new ship, the *Mora*, led his army across the English Channel and landed at Pevensey. Harold, in battle with Tostig in the north of England, hurried south to defend his realm. On October 14, the two armies met at Hastings, and by nightfall William's standard flew in victory over the battlefield where Harold's body lay

---

[1] *DNB*, "Harold (1022?–1066)."
[2] Douglas, *William the Conqueror*, pg. 182.
[3] Butler, *1066: The Story of A Year*, pg. 30.

mutilated and unrecognized until identified by his lover, Edith Swan-Neck.

Harold's mother offered William her son's weight in gold for the return of his body, but William refused, "declaring that [Harold] should be buried on the short of the land which he sought to guard." [1] It is believed that William Malet, at the Conqueror's bidding, buried Harold's body on the shore and marked the grave with a pile of stones and that Harold's body was later moved to Waltham Abbey. There, it was buried in front of the high altar where it remained until the grave was destroyed at the dissolution of the abbey.

On Christmas Day 1066, William the Conqueror, claiming the crown of England by conquest, was crowned in Westminster Abbey, ending a year of three kings. [2]

---

[1] *DNB*, "Harold (1022?–1066)."

[2] Other years of three monarchs: 1483 (Edward IV, Edward V, Richard III), 1553 (Edward VI, Lady Jane Grey, Mary I), and 1936 (George V, Edward VIII, George VI). Edward V and Edward VIII were never crowned.

A Kinship Through Marriage
of Harold II and William I

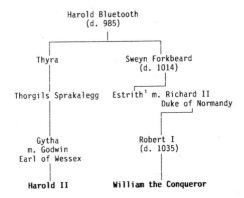

The Genealogy

Harold Godwinson, KING OF ENGLAND, Earl of East
Anglia (abt 1045–1053), Earl of Wessex (abt 1053–1066), son
of **Godwin**[2] (d. 1053), Earl of Wessex, and **Gytha** (believed
to be the daughter of **Thurgils Sprakalegg**[3]); *b.* abt 1022;
d. 14 Oct 1066, Battle of Hastings/Senlac; *bur.* (1) "the cliffs

---

[1] Cannon and Griffiths, *The Oxford Illustrated History of the British
Monarchy*, Table II, where **Estrith** is shown as the second wife of
Richard II, Duke of Normandy but not as the mother of **Robert I**.
Sweyn Forkbeard was also the father of **Harold IV** (d. 1019), King of
Denmark, and **Cnut the Great**, King of all the English.

[2] **Godwin** was son of **Wulfnoth** (d. 1015). **Godwin's** daughter,
Edith (d. 1075; bur. Westminster Abbey), was queen of **Harold's**
predecessor, King **Edward the Confessor** (1042–1066), who died
without issue (it is said that he practiced a life of chastity). (Butler,
1066: The Story of a Year, Tables 3, 7; *Ancestral* 1B-22)

[3] **Thurgils Sprakalegg** is possibly issue of **Styrbiörn**, son of **Olaf**,
King of Sweden, and his wife, **Thrya**, daughter of **Harald Blatand**,
King of Denmark 935–985 (Butler, *1066: The Story of A year*, Table 2;
Ancestral 1B-22). Stuart, *Royalty for Commoners*, Line 368, notes that
"recent research questions the relationship of Jarl Thorkill [Thorgils
Sprakalaeg] to Gytha."

of Fairlight"[1] nr Senlac, (2) Waltham Abbey); *m.* **Alditha**,[2] daughter of **Aelfgar**, Earl of Mercia, Earl of East Anglia, and his wife, **Alveva**. **Alditha** was widow of **Gruffydd** (k. 1063), King of Wales.

Issue

1 — **Harold**(?) (liv. 1098).
1 — **Ulf**(?) (liv. 1087, Normandy), perhaps a twin with **Harold**.[3]

Illegitimate Issue

Eadgyth Swanneshals (Edith of the Swan's Neck or **Edith Swan-Neck)**, "at most **[Harold's]** common law wife,"[4] is believed to be the mother of the following[5]:
1 — **Godwin** (liv. 1068).
1 — **Edmund**.
1 — **Magnus**.

---

[1] Butler, *1066: The Story of a Year*, pg. 253–254.

[2] **Alditha** was the widow of **Gruffydd** (k. Aug. 1063, "executed by his own followers") (Butler, *1066: Story of a Year*, pg. 59), King of Wales, "the Welsh prince whose bloody head Earl Harold had sent as a trophy to **Edward** [the Confessor, KING OF ENGLAND]." Concerning issue of **Alditha** and **Gruffydd**: "It seems likely that a daughter at least had been born" (Butler, *1066: The Story of a Year*, pgs. 71–72). **Alditha** was also sister of **Edwin** (d. 1072), Earl of Mercia, **Morkere**, Earl of Northumbria, and possibly **Lucia**, who married **Ivo Taillebois** (Butler, *1066: The Story of a Year*, Table 5).

[3] Of this **Ulf** being a twin with **Harold**, *DNB*, "Harold (1022?–1066)," states that there "seems to be no evidence; he may have been a son of Edith Swan-neck, or of some third woman." Whitelock, *The Anglo-Saxon Chronicle*, Table 11, shows **Ulf** ("alive in 1087") as being a son of **Edith Swanneck**.

[4] "...for possibly more than twenty years, he may have been faithful to one woman, Edith Swan-Neck, she was at most his common-law wife, and their union was unrecognised by the Church." (Butler, *1066: The Story of a Year*, pg. 57)

[5] Butler, *1066: The Story of a Year*, pgs. 57, 312.

1 — **Gunhild**, a nun at Wilton.

1 — **Gytha**[1] m. abt 1070 **Vladimir II** (b. 1053; d. 19 May 1125), Prince of Kiev, son of **Vsevolod I**, Prince of Kiev, and grandson of **Jaroslav I** (d. 20 Feb 1053), Grand Prince of Kiev.

The Blood of Harold Returns to the English Throne

Of the five children of Harold and Edith Swan-Neck, Gytha, their daughter, transmitted the blood of her parents to the royal lines of Russia and the kings of Europe. Presented here are two lines in which the blood of Harold II, King of England, returns to the throne of England.

Gytha and **Vladimir II** were parents of[2]:

2 — **Mstislas II/Mystislaw I Harold**[3] (b. 1076; d. 15 Apr 1132), Grand Prince of Kiev; m. (2) daughter (d. 1168) of **Dmitri I** of Novogorod. They were parents of:

   3 — **Euphrosine** (b. abt 1130; d. 1175/1176) m. **Geza II**, King of Hungary. They were parents of:

      4 — **Bela III** (b. abt 1148; d. 18/23 Apr 1196), King of Hungary; m. abt 1171 **Agnes/Anne de Châtillon** (d. 1184). They were parents of:

         5 — **Andrew II** (b. 1176; d. abt 7 Mar/21 Sep 1235), King of Hungary; m. (2) 1215 **Yolande de Courtenay** (d. 1233), daughter of **Peter de Courtenay** (d. bef 1218) and **Yolande of Flanders** (d. Aug 1219). They were parents of:

---

[1] "…through [Gytha], the blood of **Harold Godwinson** would be preserved in the royal lines of Russia and the kingdoms of the north" (Butler, *1066: The Story of a Year*, pg. 142). **Gytha** and **Vladimir** had a son, "named seemingly Harold, through whose daughters the blood of Harold Godwinson, and probably of Edith Swan-Neck, reached the veins of the Scandinavian kings, and thence, centuries later, of the kings of England" (Butler, *1066: The Story of a Year*, pg. 269; *KQB*, pg. 223).

[2] *Ancestral* 1B-24; 242-7, 8, 9, 10; 103-27 through 34; Stuart, *Royalty for Commoners*, Lines 240-29 and 240-28; 51-29 descending thru 51-23.

[3] Stuart, *Royalty for Commoners*, Line 240-29.

6 — **Yolande** (d. 1255[1]) m. **James I** (d. 1276),
King of Aragon. They were parents of:
   7 — **Isabella of Aragon** (d. 1271) m. **Philip III**
   the Bold (b. 1245; d. 1285), King of France.
   They were parents of:
      8 — **Philip IV** the Fair (b. 1268,
      Fontainebleau; d. 29 Nov 1314), King of
      France; m. 1284 **Jeanne of Navarre**
      (b. 1272; d. 1305), daughter of **Henry I** of
      Navarre. They were parents of:
         9 — **Isabella of France** (d. 1357)
         m. **Edward II**, KING OF ENGLAND.
In February 1308, Isabella of France, wife of the ill-fated
Edward II, was crowned Queen of England. This descendant of
Harold came to be called the She-Wolf of France, and she
brought back his blood to the throne of England with a
vengeance. Pushed aside by her husband in his preference for
his favorite, Piers Gaveston, she became romantically involved
with Roger de Mortimer, Earl of March, and their intrigues
resulted in the deposition and assassination of the king.

5 — **Andrew II** (d. abt 7 Mar 1235), King of Hungary, as
above, m. (1) bef 1203 **Gertrude von Meran** (d. 1213/1214),
daughter of **Berthold IV**, Duke of Meran. They were parents
of[2]:
   6 — **Bela IV** (d. abt 1275), King of Hungary; m. **Marie**,
   daughter of **Theodore Lascaris I**, Emperor. They were
   parents of:
      7 — **Stephen V** (d. 1 Aug 1272), King of Hungary;
      m. **Elizabeth**, daughter of **Kuthen**, Prince of Kumans.
      They were parents of:
         8 — **Marie of Hungary** (d. Mar 1323) m. **Charles II**
         (d. abt 6 May 1309), King of Naples. They were
         parents of:

---

[1] *KQE*, pg. 38.
[2] Stuart, *Royalty for Commoners*, Lines 78, 88, 70; *Ancestral* 103-28
through 103-34.

9— **Margaret of Naples** m. **Charles** (d. 1325),
Count of Valois, son of **Philip III** the Bold
(b. 1245; d. 1285), King of France, and himself a
descendant of **Harold** through his mother, **Isabella
of Aragon**. They were parents of:
    10 — **Jeanne of Valois** (d. abt 1342[1])
    m. abt 1305 **William III** (d. 1337), Count of
    Hainault and Holland. They were parents of:
        11 — **Philippa of Hainault** (b. 24 Jun 1311;
        d. abt 15 Aug 1369) m. **Edward III, KING
        OF ENGLAND**, himself a descendant of
        Harold through his mother, **Isabella of
        France**.

Philippa of Hainault, wife of Edward III, has been
described as amiable, popular, motherly, and kind-hearted.

Siblings of Harold II

- Edith (d. 18 Dec 1075; bur. Westminster Abbey)
  m. Edward the Confessor, King of England.
- Gunhild (a nun in Flanders).
- Swegen (d. abt 1052 on a pilgrimage[2]).
- Tostig (d. 25 Sep 1066, Battle of Stamford Bridge), Earl of
  Northumbria; m. Judith, daughter of Baldwin IV, Count of
  Flanders.
- Gyrth (d. 14 Oct 1066, Battle of Hastings), Earl of East
  Anglia.
- Leofwine (d. 14 Oct 1066, Battle of Hastings), Earl of
  Kent.
- Wulfnoth (liv. Normandy 1087).[3]

---

[1] *Ancestral* 103-33 indicates a death date of about 1352 as does
Turton's *Plantagenet Ancestry*, Chart 2; *KQB*, pg. 223, gives a death
date of 1342; Stuart, *Royalty for Commoners*, Line 70-23, states that
Jean of Valois was b. abt 1294 and d. 7 Mar 1342.

[2] Whitelock, *The Anglo-Saxon Chronicle*, Table 11.

[3] Siblings from Butler, *1066: The Story of a Year*, Table 3.

Sources:

Butler, Denis, *1066: The Story of a Year*, Anthony Blond Ltd., London, 1966.

Cannon, John & Griffiths, Ralph, *The Oxford Illustrated History of the British Monarchy*, Oxford University Press, Oxford and NY, 1988.

Douglas, David C., *William the Conqueror*, University of California Press, Berkeley & L.A., 1964.

Stephen, Sir Leslie, and Lee, Sir Sidney, eds., *Dictionary of National Biography*, Oxford University Press, London, 1964.

Stuart, Roderick W., *Royalty for Commoners*, Genealogical Publishing Co., Inc., Baltimore, MD, 1992.

Turton, Lt.-Col. W. H. Turton, D.S.O., *The Plantagenet Ancestry*, Genealogical Publishing Co., Inc., Baltimore, MD, 1993.

Weis, Frederick Lewis, *Ancestral Roots of Sixty Colonists*—6th ed., Genealogical Publishing Co., Inc., 1990.

Whitelock, Dorothy, ed., *The Anglo-Saxon Chronicle*, Rutgers University Press, New Brunswick, NJ, 1961.

Williamson, David, *Debrett's Kings and Queens of Britain*, Dorset Press, New York, 1992.

Williamson, David, *DeBrett's Kings and Queens of Europe*, Salem House Publishers, Mass., 1988.

Issue of Isabelle of Angoulême and Hugh de Lusignan

As the widow of John, King of England, Isabelle of Angoulême married in 1220[1] Hugh X le Brun de Lusignan, Count of la Marche, son of Hugh IX de Lusignan (d. 1219, Damietta).

Before marrying John, Isabelle had been betrothed to either Hugh X or his father. Snellgrove[2] believes it was the father who originally was to have married the young Isabelle. Instead, John took the girl for his wife, an act of betrayal on the part of a lord toward his vassal. Many writers attribute this action to John's lust, but any contemporary baron with wife or daughter would know that John did not need the sanctity of marriage to assuage his lust for any woman. Rather, politically and strategically, the marriage was a wise move: the "towns [of Angoumois] dominated the passage from Poitiers to Bordeaux,

---

[1] Snellgrove, *The Lusignans in England 1247–1258*, pg. 12. The *CP*, Pembroke section, gives the date for the marriage as being between 10 Mar and 22 May 1220. Burke's *Royal Family* gives a date of about 1220.

[2] Snellgrove, *The Lusignans in England 1247–1258*, pgs. 9, 10, 13, wherein his sources are quoted. The reader should note that scholars are not in agreement on the causes of the quarrels between John and the Lusignans. The events presented here are taken from Snellgrove's article and present, for a large part, the generally accepted facts. Cazel and Painter (pg. 86) note, "The *Histoire des ducs de Normandie* goes so far as to make John in 1205 tell Isabelle that she caused him to lose his lands." Other viewpoints for the rebellions against John may be found in the sources listed at the end of this chapter.

and from the central mountains of France to the sea."[1] Too, if the betrothal between Hugh IX de Lusignan of la Marche and the daughter of Aymer of Angoulême were allowed to continue, the eventual uniting of the two counties would give Hugh de Lusignan a powerful position in the region. John's political security would be threatened, and Hugh could prove to be a contending factor in the friction between John and Philip Augustus, King of France.

However, as politically wise a marriage as it seemed, the difficulty of the situation came with the fact that John's marriage to Isabelle required the breaking of the betrothal between her and the Count of la Marche, an act which was considered John's betrayal of the Lusignans, a powerful and illustrious family. In 1201, John went further in his damage to the Lusignans by taking Hugh's county and giving it to Isabelle's father, Count Aymer, then taking possession of the Norman lands of Hugh IX's brother, Ralph de Lusignan.

The Lusignans appealed to Philip Augustus, who called for John to appear in trial before him. John essentially thumbed his nose at the French king and went his own way. Hugh IX was then joined in rebellion by other powerful Poitevin vassals. As a result, the following year, Philip Augustus confiscated John's French fiefs,[2] and John suffered loss of "possessions and prestige on the continent."

In 1202, in what was perhaps his finest military hour, John raced to Mirabeau Castle, where his mother was besieged by the rebels. He won the castle, rescued his mother, and captured a majority of the rebels, including, to his great pleasure, no doubt, Hugh IX and and his brother, Geoffrey de Lusignan, whose heroic battle skills had earned him a reputation much like that of Richard I the Lion-Heart. Captured also were John's own nephew and rival for the English throne, Arthur of Brittany, who would die in imprisonment at his uncle's hands.[3] John's foe, Hugh IX, was imprisoned by the king at Caen but,

---

[1] Warren, *King John*, pgs. 67–68, 219.
[2] Hallam, *The Plantagenet Chronicles*, pg. 263.
[3] See chapter, "The Disappearance of Arthur."

to the amazement of many, was released the following year.

Finally, on 25 May 1214, Hugh IX was reconciled with John, who, desiring to strengthen his position in the Aquitaine, gave his daughter Joan (b. 1210; d. 1238) to be betrothed to Hugh IX's son, Hugh X. Joan was sent to live under the supervision of the Lusignan family until she was old enough to marry.

In 1218, Hugh IX joined the Third Crusade. He died in Damietta the following year. His son, Hugh X, was his successor.

After John's death (1216), Isabelle returned to Angoulême, and Hugh X in 1220 repudiated Joan (broke the betrothal) and married Isabelle.

As stated above, Snellgrove believes it was in fact the father to whom Isabelle was betrothed. He quotes Delisle, who writes that Hugh, "the ninth of that name, came into possession of the county of La Marche before 1190. But in 1200 he declared himself against King John who had kidnapped his fiancée. He left for Damietta in 1218 and died there in 1219."[1] Snellgrove quotes as "conclusive evidence," a letter dated June 1235 from Gregory IX (1227-1241) in which he commanded "the archbishop of Tours, the archbishop of Chartres, and Master Peter de Columpton, canon of Chartres, to inquire and enlighten the pope touching a reported marriage of the Count of la Marche with Queen Isabella, notwithstanding a contract of marriage made by his father with the said queen, and a contract of marriage by him with her daughter."[2]

---

[1] Delisle, L., "Mémoire sur une lettre inédite addressęe à la reine Blanche par un habitant de la Rochelle," *Bibliothèque de l'Ecole des Chartes*, 4th series, II, 1856, pg. 539. "Hugh IX prit possession du comité de la Marche avant 1190, ... Il se declara en 1200, contre Jean sans Terre, qui lui avait enlevé Isabelle d'Angoulême, sa fiancée." (Snellgrove, *The Lusignans in England 1247-1258*, pg. 13)

[2] The Pope's request is puzzling. It is difficult to believe that the Pope is only in 1235 hearing rumors of a marriage that took place in 1220, especially considering the prominence of the powerful Lusignans, the hostility and trouble that Isabelle caused among her second husband's

(continued...)

One of Snellgrove's sources[1] states that Hugh IX was married to Matilda, daughter of Vulgrin, Count of Angoulême. When he married her and whether she was the mother of Hugh X is uncertain and probably doubtful: Matilda's father was half-brother of Isabelle's father, a relationship which would cause Hugh X and Isabelle to be too closely related for marriage, and there was no mention in letters or betrothal agreements of the necessary papal dispensation for the marriage of either Joan or her mother Isabelle to either Hugh X or his father. It appears that this is a question that has not been answered.

Snellgrove adds that Hugh IX had an uncle, Geoffrey de Lusignan, who was captured by John at Mirabeau; an uncle, Aumary, who was King of Jerusalem; and a younger brother, Ralph de Lusignan (d. 1 May 1219[2]), Count of Eu.

The following information on the issue (five sons, "probably" three daughters[3]) of Isabelle (d. 1246) and Hugh X (d. 1246) has been gathered from several sources. Where issue

---

[2] (...continued)
people and the court of the French king (according to Matthew Paris, many French and Poitevins thought she should be called Jezebel rather than Isabelle), the prominent parts played by both Isabelle and her husband in Poitevin intrigues during the reign of Henry III of England, and the fact that the previous pope, Honorius III (1216–1227), not only threatened her with excommunication but corresponded with her husband concerning detainment of the rejected Joan, who should have been returned to England and who was being held as a hostage or bargaining lever in Isabelle's dealings with her son, Henry III, King of England.

[1] L. Delisle in *Bibliothèque de l'Ecole des Chartes*, 4th Series, II (1856), 539, in which he states, "Il avait épousé Mathilde, fille de Vulgrin, comte d'Angoulême, laquelle vivait encore au mois d'août 1233.... Il fut père de Hugue X." As translated, he married Matilda, daughter of Vulgrin, Count of Angoulême; she survived him and lived to August 1233; he was father of Hugh X.

[2] *CP*, Eu section.

[3] *DNB*, "Isabella of Angoulême (d. 1246)," states there were "probably" three daughters and lists **Margaret** and **Alicia**. Snellgrove, *The Lusignans in England 1247–1258*, Table 2, names the four daughters listed in above text.

of further generations proves historically interesting, information has been included but should not be considered inclusive.

1 — **Hugh XI le Brun de Lusignan** (b. 1220; d. 1250, while on Crusade with **Louis IX**, King of France), Count of la Marche, Count of Angoulême; m. Jan 1235/1236 **Yolande de Dreux** (b. 1218; d. 10/16 Oct 1272), daughter of **Peter (Mauclerk) of Dreux/Pierre de Dreux**, Duke of Brittany. They were parents of:

    2 — **Alice de Lusignan** m. (div. 18 Jul 1271) spring 1253 as his first wife **Gilbert de Clare** (b. 2 Sep 1243, Christ Church, Hampshire; d. 7 Dec 1295, Monmouth Castle; bur. 22 Dec 1295, Tewkesbury), Earl of Gloucester, "the Red Earl." [1]

    2 — **Hugh XII de Lusignan** (d. 1270), Count of la Marche; m. 29 Jan 1253/1254 **Joanne de Fougéres**. They were parents of:

        3 — **Guy de Lusignan** (d. 1308).

        3 — **Hugh XIII de Lusignan**, Count of la Marche.

1 — **Guy de Lusignan**, Count of Angoulême, Lord of Cognac.

1 — **Aymer de Lusignan de Valence** (d. 4 Dec 1260), Bishop of Winchester (elected 4 Nov 1250). [2]

1 — **William of Valence/de Lusignan** [3] (b. aft 1225, Cistercian Abbey of Valence nr Lusignan(?); d. 18 May 1296 [4]; bur. Westminster Abbey), fourth son, Lord of Valence, Montignac, Bellac, Rancon, and Champagnac, styled Earl of Pembroke, but according to the *CP*, Pembroke section, was not

---

[1] *Ancestral* 117-30; 63-30; *CP*, Gloucester section, March [England] section. **Gilbert de Clare** m. (2) **Joan of Acre** (d. 1307) and had issue of a son and three daughters.

[2] Nicolas, *The Historic Peerage of England*, pg. 576. According to the *DNB*, "Aymer," **Aymer** was "barely 23 at the time of his election to the bishopric of Winchester in 1250."

[3] "Valence near Lusignan was probably his birthplace." (*Westminster Abbey: Official Guide*, pg. 82)

[4] *DNB*, "William de Valence, titular Earl of Pembroke (d. 1296)," states **William** died 13 Jun.

created Earl nor was he ever invested with the Earldom;
m. 13 Aug 1247 **Joan de Munchensy/Muntchensesy**
(d. bef 20 Sep 1307), daughter of **Warin de Munchensy**
(d. 1255), Lord of Swanscombe, "co-heiress of the Pembroke
lands."[1] They were parents of:[2]

   2 — **Isabel de Valence** (d. 5 Oct 1305; bur. Coventry
   Priory) m. at Braxted aft 28 Jun 1275 as his first wife **John
   de Hastings** (d. 10 Feb 1312/1313), Lord Bergavenny.

   2 — **Margaret de Valence** (bur. 24 Mar 1275/1276,
   Westminster Abbey).

   2 — **Agnes de Valence** (d. 1310) m. (1) as his second wife
   Maurice FitzGerald (d. 1268), 3rd Baron of Offaly; no
   issue; m. (2) **Hugh de Balliol**; m. (3) **John d'Avesnes**.[3]

   2 — **Joan de Valence** m. **John Comyn** (d. 1306) of
   Badmoc/Lord of Badenoch.

   2 — **John de Valence** (d. Jan 1276/1277; bur. Westminster
   Abbey), first son. No issue.

   2 — **William de Valence** (d. 16 Jun 1282, "in a battle
   between **Gilbert de Clare** and the Welsh," nr Llandeilo,
   co. Carmarthen), second son. No issue.

   2 — **Aymer de Valence** (b. abt 1270; d. 23 Jun 1324,
   France; bur. 1 Aug, Westminster Abbey, nr main altar),
   Lord of Valence, Montignac, Bellac, Rancon, and
   Champagnac, Earl of Pembroke, third son; m. (1) **Beatrice
   de Clermont-Nesle** (d. bef 14 Sep 1320), third daughter of
   Ralph de Clermont, Lord of Néele and Brios, Constable of
   France, and his first wife **Alice** (first daughter of **Robert de
   Dreux**, Lord of Beu); no issue; m. (2) in Paris 3 or 5 Jul
   1321 **Marie of St. Pol** (d. 16 or 17 Mar 1377, Denny;
   bur. Denny), daughter of **Guy de Châtillon**, Count of
   St. Pol, and his wife **Mary of Brittany** (d. 3 May 1339)

---

[1] According to the *CP*, Pembroke section, her mother, **Joan**, was the
youngest of the five daughters of **William the Marshal**, 4th Earl of
Pembroke.

[2] *CP*, Pembroke section; *DNB*, "William de Valence, titular Earl of
Pembroke (d. 1296)."

[3] *CP*, Kerry section, Table "The Geraldines."

(daughter of **John of Dreux/John II of Britanny**
(d. 18 Nov 1305; bur. Carmelite Church, Ploernel), Earl of
Richmond, Duke of Brittany, Earl of Richmond); no issue.
Marie of St. Pol survived her husband about fifty years;
she was the founder of Pembroke College, Cambridge, and
Denny Abbey.

1 — **Margaret de Lusignan** m. (annulled 1245) **Raymond VII**
of Toulouse; m. (2) **Geoffrey de Chateaubriand**.

1 — **Alice de Lusignan** (d. 9 Feb 1255/1256) m. Aug 1247
John de Warenne (b. in or aft Aug 1231; d. abt Michaelmas
1304, Kennington nr London; bur. Lewes Priory[1]), Earl of
Surrey. They were parents of:

   2 — **William de Warenne** (d. 15 Dec 1286) m. "probably"
   Jun 1285 **Joan** (d. on or bef 23 Nov 1293[2]; bur. Lewes),
   daughter of **Robert de Vere** (d. bef 7 Sep 1296[3]), Earl of
   Oxford, and his wife, **Alice de Sanford** (d. 7 Sep 1312).[4]

1 — **Isabella de Lusignan** (d. 1299) m. (1) **Geoffrey de
Rancon**, Lord of Taillebourg; m. (2) **Maurice V de Craon**
(d. 1282/liv. 1290), Lord of Craon. They were parents of:

   2 — **Maurice VI** (d. 1292), Lord of Craon; m. **Mahaut de
   Malines** (d. 1306). They were parents of:

      3 — **Amaury III** (d. 1332), Lord of Craon;
      m. (1) **Isabella de Ste. Maure**; m. (2) **Beatrice de
      Roucy**.

1 — **Agatha de Lusignan** m. **William de Cauvigny**, Lord of
Chateauroux.

1 — **Geoffrey de Lusignan**, Lord of Ste. Hermine and Jarnac;
m. **Joan**, daughter of **John**, Viscount of Chatellerault.[5]

---

[1] *CP*, Surrey section.

[2] "…having attended a tournament at Croydon, where he is said to
have been ambushed and cruelly slain by his rivals." (*CP*, Surrey
section)

[3] *CP*, Oxford section.

[4] *CP*, Surrey section.

[5] Snellgrove, *The Lusignans in England 1247-1258*, pg. 24.

Sources:

Barber, Richard, *The Devil's Crown: Henry II, Richard I, John*, British Broadcasting Corporation, London, 1978.

Bateman, Somerset, B.A. (London), *Simon de Montfort: His Life and Work*, Cornish Brothers Ltd, Birmingham, 1923.

Burke's Peerage, *Burke's Guide to the Royal Family*, Burke's Peerage Limited, 1973.

Cazel, Fred A., Jr., and Painter, Sidney, "The Marriage of Isabelle of Angoulême," The English Historical Review, Vol. LXIII, 1948, pgs. 83–89.

Cokayne, G. E., *The Complete Peerage*, St Catherine Press, London.

Hallam, Elizabeth, ed., *The Plantagenet Encyclopedia*, Grove Weidenfeld, NY, 1990.

Nicolas, Sir Nicholas Harris, edited by William Courthope, *The Historic Peerage of England*, J. Murray, London, 1867.

Prestwich, Michael, *Edward I*, University California Press, Berkeley, 1988.

Richardson, H. G., "The Marriage and Coronation of Isabelle of Angoulême," The English Historical Review, Vol. LXI, No. 241, September, 1946, pgs. 289–314.

Snellgrove, Harold S., "The Lusignans in England 1247–1258," The University of New Mexico Publications in History, Number Two, The University of New Mexico Press, Albuquerque, 1950.

Stephen, Sir Leslie, and Lee, Sir Sidney, eds., *Dictionary of National Biography*, Oxford University Press, London, 1964.

Vale, Malcolm, *The Angevin Legacy and the Hundred Years War 1250-1340*, Basil Blackwell,1990.

Warren, W. L., *King John*, University of California Press, Berkeley, 1978.

Weis, Frederick Lewis, *Ancestral Roots of Sixty Colonists*—6th ed., Genealogical Publishing Co., Inc., Baltimore, 1990.

Westminster Abbey: Official Guide, Jarrold and Sons Limited, Norwich, 1988.

Issue of Malcolm III
and St. Margaret

On 2 Aug 1100, William II Rufus, King of England, was killed by a hunting arrow in the New Forest, and his youngest brother, Henry I, rushed to secure the royal treasury and claim the throne of England. There were those who believed that Robert Curthose, Rufus' older brother, should have succeeded Rufus, but Robert was away on crusade in the Holy Land.

Henry's reasons for claiming the throne included the fact that he was the only son of William I the Conqueror who was "born in the purple," that is, while his father was king. He gained support from the English by issuing a charter of liberties, which promised to do away with some of the undesirable exactions of his brother's and father's reigns. He gained further support of the English by marrying Edith Matilda of Scotland, daughter of Malcolm III Canmore (d. 1093), King of Scots, and St. Margaret (canonized in 1250). Edith Matilda was a descendant of Alfred the Great and granddaughter of Edmund II Ironside (d. 1016), King of England. Their marriage brought back to the throne the ancient royal bloodline of the kings of England and thus gained popular support for the new king.

Like Edith Matilda, her siblings and many of their issue would play prominent roles in English history. Some of those siblings and other relations are shown here.

Issue of **Malcolm III** and **St. Margaret** (further generations are listed where of historical interest):
1 — **Edward** (d. 16 Nov 1093, nr Jedburgh, after Battle of Alnwick).

1 — **Edmund I**, King of Scots 1094–1097.
1 — **Ethelred**, Abbot of Dunkeld.
1 — **Edgar**, King of Scots 1097–1107.
1 — **Alexander I the Fierce**, King of Scots 1107–1124;
m. **Sibylla** (d. 1122), illegitimate daughter of **Henry I**, KING
OF ENGLAND. No issue.
1 — **David I the Saint** (b. abt 1080; d. 24 May 1153, Carlisle;
bur. Dunfermline), King of Scots 1124–1153, Earl of
Huntingdon; m. in 1113 **Matilda of Huntingdon** (d. 1130 or
1131; bur. Scone[1]), widow of **Simon de St. Liz**, Earl of
Huntingdon. They were parents of:
  2 — **Henry of Huntingdon** (b. abt 1114; d. 12 Jun 1152;
  bur. Kelso), Earl of Huntingdon and Northumberland;
  m. **Ada de Warenne** (d. 1178), daughter of **William de
  Warenne** (d. 1138), Earl of Surrey, and his wife, **Isabel de
  Vermandois** (d. 13 Feb 1131; bur. Lewes) (daughter of
  Hugh Magnus (d. 1101)). They were parents of:
    3 — **Malcolm IV the Maiden** (b. 1141; d. unm. 9 Dec
    1165, Jedburgh,[2] aged 23 years), King of Scots
    1153–1165.
    3 — **William the Lion** (d. 4 Dec 1214), King of Scots
    1164–1214; m. 1186[3] **Ermengarde de Beaumont**. They
    were parents of:
      4 — **Alexander II** (d. 6 Jul 1249), King of Scots
      1214–1249; m. (1) **Joan of England**, daughter of
      John, KING OF ENGLAND; no issue; m. (2) **Marie
      de Coucy** of the French nobility, daughter of
      Enguerrand III de Coucy.[4] They were parents of:
        5 — **Alexander III** (k. March 1286, in a fall from
        the cliffs), King of Scots 1249–1286; m. (1) Dec
        1251 **Margaret of England** (d. 1275), daughter of
        Henry III, KING OF ENGLAND; m. (2) at

---

[1] *CP*, Huntingdon section.
[2] *DNB*, "Malcolm IV (The Maiden) (1141–1165)."
[3] Bingham, *Kings and Queens of Scotland*, pg. 27.
[4] **Marie de Coucy** m. (2) **John de Brienne** (d. 1296), son of the
King of Jerusalem.

Jedburgh Abbey 1 Nov 1285 **Yolande de Dreux** (d. 1323), daughter of **Robert IV**, Count of Dreux.
    4 — **Margaret** (d. 1259; bur. Church of the Black Friars, London) m. at York Jun 1221 as his third wife **Hubert de Burgh** (d. 12 May 1243, Banstead, Surrey; bur. Church of the Black Friars, London), Earl of Kent. [1]
    4 — **Isabella** (bur. Black Friars, London) m. May 1225 **Roger Bigod** (b. 1212 or 1213; d. 3 or 4 July 1270; bur. 10 Jul, Thetford), Earl of Norfolk. [2] No issue.
    4 — **Marjorie/Margaret** (d. 17 Nov 1244; bur. Church of the Preaching Friars) m. at Berwick **Gilbert Marshal** (d. 27 Jun 1241, Hertford Priory, from injuries received in a tournament; entrails bur. at Hertford Priory, body bur. Temple Church, London), Earl of Pembroke, third son of **William Marshal** (d. 14 May 1219, Caversham; bur. Temple Church, London). [3]
    3 — **David** (d. 17 Jun 1219, Yardley, Northants; bur. Sawtrey Abbey), Earl of Huntingdon; m. 26 Aug 1190 **Maud** (d. abt 6 Jan 1233), daughter of **Hugh Kevelioc**, Earl of Chester.
1 — **Edith Matilda** m. **Henry I**, KING OF ENGLAND.
1 — **Mary of Scotland** (d. 31 May 1115/1116; bur. Abbey of St. Savior, Bermondsey, London) m. **Eustace III** (d. 1125), Count of Boulogne. They were parents of:
    2 — **Matilda of Boulogne** m. **Stephen**, KING OF ENGLAND.

---

[1] *CP*, Kent section.
[2] *CP*, Norfolk section.
[3] *CP*, Pembroke section.

Sources:

Barlow, Frank, *William Rufus*, University of California Press, Berkeley and Los Angeles, 1983.

Bingham, Caroline, *Kings and Queens of Scotland*, Dorset Press, NY, 1976.

Cokayne, G. E., *The Complete Peerage*, St Catherine Press, London, 1912.

Crystal, David, ed., *The Barnes & Noble Encyclopedia*, Barnes & Noble Books, New York, 1990.

Ross, Stewart, *Monarchs of Scotland*, Facts On File, NY, 1990.

Stephen, Sir Leslie, and Lee, Sir Sidney, eds., *Dictionary of National Biography*, Oxford University Press, London, 1964.

Tauté, Anne, compiler, *Kings and Queens of Great Britain* wall chart, 1990.

The Beaufort Women

The tendency of families to continue a name in issue eventually leads to confusion and possibly errors for searchers attempting to follow family lines. This section has been added in an attempt to clarify two of those names, Margaret Beaufort and Joan Beaufort.

There are several Margaret Beauforts, two better known than the rest. To increase the confusion, not only are the two women *from* the same family, they married *into* the same family: their fathers were brothers and they married brothers.

A similar situation exists with the Joan Beauforts. Two Joans described here have the relationship of aunt and niece: they are daughter and granddaughter of John of Gaunt.

The Beauforts are John of Gaunt's issue by his third wife, Katherine de Roet Swynford, whom he married long after the four Beauforts were born. In fact, all the women described here were descendants of John of Gaunt and Katherine de Roet Swynford.

Margaret Beaufort, Mother of Henry VII

Margaret Beaufort (b. 31 May 1443[1]/1441, Bletsoe in Bedfordshire[2]; d. 29 Jun 1509; bur. Westminster Abbey), Countess of Richmond and mother of Henry VII, King of England, was the daughter of John Beaufort (d. 1444), Earl of

---

[1] *CP*, Suffolk section, footnote to John de la Pole (d. 1492); *CP*, Richmond section.

[2] Cooper, *Memoir of Margaret, Countess of Richmond and Derby*, pgs. 1–2.

Somerset, Earl of Kendal, and Duke of Somerset, and his wife,
Margaret Beauchamp (d. 1482). John Beaufort was the son of
John Beaufort (d. 1410), son of John of Gaunt. Margaret
Beauchamp was widow of Oliver St. John (d. 1437) and
daughter and heiress of John Beauchamp, Kt., (d. 1412) of
Bletso, 3rd Baron Beauchamp, and his wife, Edith Stourton. [1]

Margaret was about two years old when her father died. His
title of Duke of Somerset passed to his brother, Edmund
Beaufort (d. 1455).

Margaret was the ward of William de la Pole until his death
(ex. 2 May 1450, English Channel). A marriage was considered
between her and his son, John de la Pole (d. abt 1492). [2]
However, plans were changed, and the actual marriage never
took place, often being described as a marriage dated between
28 Jan and 7 Feb 1449/1450 and a divorce taking place before
1453. According to the *CP*, Suffolk section, "This child-
marriage was dissolved before 24 Mar 1452/3." There was no
issue. Note the approximate ages of the children during these
events. [3]

After William de la Pole's death, Henry VI granted her

---

[1] Cooper, *Memoir of Margaret, Countess of Richmond and Derby*,
pg. 3.

[2] John de la Pole's mother was Alice Chaucer, granddaughter of the
poet, Geoffrey Chaucer.

[3] "In the Middle Ages consent was regarded as being the essence of
marriage. Bethrothal was deemed to be just as binding as vows made in
church..." (St. Aubyn, *The Year of Three Kings 1483*, pg. 150). "By the
ancient canon law, a contract for marriage might be valid and perfect
without the church ceremony..." (Sharon Turner as quoted by Halsted,
The Life of Margaret Beaufort, pg. 132. The copy of the Halsted book
which your compiler referenced had no bibliography to give specifics of
Sharon Turner's book, listing only "iii p. 463.") Margaret, being under
the age of twelve, could publically and legally refuse to be bound by a
marriage contract. Either Margaret or John de la Pole, on reaching
puberty, could dissolve such a marriage if they chose not to consummate
it (Seward, *The Wars of the Roses*, pg. 28).

wardship to brothers Edmund and Jasper Tudor.[1]

When she was about nine, she was betrothed to Edmund Tudor, Earl of Richmond. They were married in 1455 when Margaret was about twelve. On 3 Nov 1456 Edmund Tudor died of the plague,[2] and on the following 28 Jan, in Pembroke Castle, Wales, Margaret gave birth to Henry, Earl of Richmond and the future Henry VII, King of England. Though Margaret was married several times, Henry VII was her only child.[3]

Margaret next married by 10 Jul 1460[4] Henry Stafford (d. 4 Oct 1481[5]; bur. Pleshey[6]), a younger son of Humphrey

---

[1] Hogrefe, *Women of Action in Tudor England: Nine Biographical Sketches*, pgs. 138–139. Edmund Tudor, Earl of Richmond, and Jasper Tudor were the sons of the Welshman, Owen Tudor (ex. 1461, Hereford, after the Battle of Mortimer's Cross) and Katherine of Valois (d. 1437). Owen Tudor was master of the queen's wardrobe, and Katherine of Valois was Queen of England and widow of Henry V. Edmund and Jasper were, therefore, half-brothers of Henry VI. Whether Katherine of Valois and Owen Tudor were legally married, as they claimed, has not been proven or disproven.

[2] Edmund Tudor, Earl of Richmond, died "probably at Carmarthen Castle" (*CP*, Richmond section) and was buried at the house of Grey Friars at Carmarthen "from whence [in 1536] at the dissolution of that monastery his remains were removed to the cathedral church of St. David...." (Cooper, *Memoir of Margaret, Countess of Richmond and Derby*, pg. 10). He has been described as "Father and Brother to Kings" (*CP*, Richmond section).

[3] Margaret Beaufort was "the progenitrix of all English Sovereigns from the accession of Henry VII." (St. Aubyn, *The Year of Three Kings 1483*, pg. 189)

[4] Cooper, *Memoir of Margaret, Countess of Richmond and Derby*, pg. 12, notes that in the will of Humphrey Stafford (b. 1402; k. 10 Jul 1460, Battle of Northampton), 1st Duke of Buckingham, the Duke "bequeaths to his son Henry and his daughter Margaret countess of Richmond his wife, the sum of four hundred marks." The Duke's will "appears to have been made but a short time previously to his death."

[5] The year of Henry Stafford's death has been seen as 1471 (*CP*, Suffolk section, John de la Pole (d. 1492); *CP*, Richmond section; Rawcliffe, *The Staffords, Earls of Stafford and Dukes of Buckingham 1394–1521*, pg. 22; Harris, *Edward Stafford: Third Duke of*

(continued...)

Stafford, 1st Duke of Buckingham, and his wife, Anne Neville
(d. 20 Sep 1480). Anne Neville was daughter of Ralph Neville
(d. 1425), 1st Earl of Westmorland, and his second wife, Joan
Beaufort (daughter of John of Gaunt and Katherine de Roet
Swynford). There was no issue of the marriage between
Margaret and Henry Stafford.

The Yorkist victory at Tewkesbury 4 May 1471 resulted in
the capture of Henry VI. He was imprisoned in the Tower
where he was summarily murdered by the Yorkist faction,
leaving Margaret's son, now fifteen years old, as the head of
the house of Lancaster. It was the time of the wars of the
Roses, the Lancastrians versus the Yorkists, and Yorkist
Edward IV currently held the throne. To secure the safety of
young Henry, his uncle, Jasper Tudor, took him across the
Channel to the continent. He would be gone for fourteen years.

His mother maintained careful communication with her son
but cooperated with the Yorkist powers by taking in 1482/
1483 [1] Thomas Stanley (d. 1504), [2] Edward IV's trusted

---

[5] (...continued)
Buckingham, 1478–1521, pg. 235). Ramsay, *Lancaster and York*, Vol. I,
Table III, gives a death date of 1481 1482. Hogrefe, *Women of Action in
Tudor England: Nine Biographical Sketches*, pg. 139, gives 1481 as the
year of death. Cooper, *Memoir of Margaret, Countess of Richmond and
Derby*, pg. 17, states that Henry Stafford "appears to have died in 1482,
as his will was proved on the 4th May in that year" and that the will "is
dated 2 Oct 1481." Again, Jones and Underwood, who believe Stafford
died in 1471, state in their book, *The King's Mother, Lady Margaret
Beaufort*, pg. 97, that "the will was contested and not proved until over
a decade later."
[6] Jones and Underwood, *The King's Mother, Lady Margaret
Beaufort*, pg. 58.
[1] *CP*, Suffolk section. The date of marriage between Margaret
Beaufort and Thomas Stanley has also been seen as bef Oct 1473.
Coward, *The Stanleys: Lords Stanley and Earls of Derby 1385–1672*,
pg. 11; St. Aubyn, *The Year of Three Kings 1483*, pg. 126; Halsted, *The
Life of Margaret Beaufort*, pg. 110; and the *CP*, Derby section, state that
Margaret Beaufort and Thomas Stanley were married in 1482. However,
a footnote in the *CP*, Richmond section, states, "*Rolls of Parl.*, vol. vi,
(continued...)

minister, as her third husband (or fourth husband if the "marriage" between her and John de la Pole is counted). Thomas Stanley was third cousin of the Countess. Both were

---

[1] (...continued)

p. 77. The date '1482' given for this marriage *ante, sub* Derby, should be corrected accordingly [to 1473]." Jones and Underwood, *The King's Mother*, pgs. 144–145, draws attention to the marriage date descrepancy and states a preference for the earlier date, adding that Margaret negotiated the marriage settlement "very much on her own terms." According to Cooper's *Memoir of Margaret, Countess of Richmond and Derby*, pg. 17, Henry Stafford, husband of Margaret Beaufort, "appears to have died in 1482, as his will was proved on the 4th May in that year. By this will, which is dated the 2nd October, 1481...." Cooper continues, "From a saving clause in the act of resumption of 1473 it would seem that the countess of Richmond had been married to lord Stanley at that period. There can however be little doubt that the clause in question was added many years after the act itself first received the sanction of the legislature" and adds the reference of above, *Rot. Parl.* vi, 77. Note a previous footnote concerning the death date of Henry Stafford.

[2] Thomas Stanley's first wife was Eleanor Neville (Bagley in *The Earls of Derby 1485–1985*, states they were married in 1459). She was the daughter of Richard Neville (ex. 30 Dec 1460, Pontefract), Earl of Salisbury, and Alice Montagu. Eleanor's death date is elusive, but it appears she was dead before Nov 1482 and was buried in St. James's, Garlickhithe, London. According to the *DNB* article, "Stanley, Thomas, first Earl of Derby (1435–1504)," Thomas Stanley and Eleanor Neville were married before 1460 and Eleanor died "between 1464 and 1473."

Eleanor Neville was the sister of Cecily Sweet Cis Neville, mother of Richard III, King of England. Eleanor Neville's mother, Alice Montagu, was daughter of Thomas Montagu (d. 3 Nov 1428), 4th Earl of Salisbury, who married as his second wife and her second husband (no issue) Alice Chaucer (grandddaughter of the poet, Geoffrey Chaucer).

According to Crawford, *Letters of the Queens of England 1100–1547*, pg. 147, the mothers of Henry VII and Richard III, "held each other in great respect and in her will Cecily left the countess a beautiful breviary [prayer book] bound in gold." It was greatly due to Margaret Beaufort's efforts that her son and the granddaughter of Cecily were wed, thus bringing about the recognized end of the wars of the Roses.

descended from Richard II Copped Hat FitzAlan and Eleanor
Plantagenet. [1] It is probable that a papal dispensation was
therefore necessary, but if that was the case, it does not appear
to have survived. [2]
One wonders about the complexity of politics behind the
marriage of Margaret Beaufort and Thomas Stanley. Lord
Stanley's "political attitude was from the first ambiguous." [3]
Crawford [4] suggests that Margaret Beaufort "protected herself"
by her marriage with Thomas Stanley, as she could safely keep
her estates for her son, "provided Henry returned from exile."
Edward IV, quite aware of his Lancastrian rival, may have felt
more secure on the throne by having practically in hand the
well-beloved mother of "the King's great rebel and traitor,"
where she could be watched for treasonous activity. [5] In fact,
soon after Edward IV's sudden and unexpected death (9 Apr
1483) and the usurpation of his throne by his brother,
Richard III, Margaret was accused of being "deeply engaged in
Buckingham's uprising" [6] against the new king and was

---

[1] Richard II Copped Hat FitzAlan (d. 1375/1376) m. Eleanor
Plantagenet (d. 1372). Issue:
1 — Alice FitzAlan m. Thomas Holand (d. 1397), 2nd Earl of Kent.
   2 — Margaret Holand m. John Beaufort (d. 1410), Earl of
Somerset, Marquess of Dorset.
      3 — John Beaufort, Duke of Somerset, m. Margaret Beauchamp.
         4 — Margaret Beaufort, Countess of Richmond.
1 — Richard III FitzAlan, Earl of Arundel, m. Elizabeth de Bohun.
   2 — Elizabeth FitzAlan m. Robert Goushill.
      3 — Joan Goushill m. Thomas Stanley, 1st Lord Stanley.
         4 - Thomas Stanley, 2nd Lord Stanley, 1st Earl of Derby.
(Cooper, *Memoir of Margaret, Countess of Richmond and Derby*,
pg. 19)
[2] Halsted, *The Life of Margaret Beaufort*, pg. 110; Tytler, *Tutor
Queens and Princesses*, pgs. 146–147.
[3] *DNB*, "Stanley, Thomas, first Earl of Derby (1435?–1504)."
[4] Crawford, *Letters of the Queens of England 1100–1547*, pg. 145.
[5] St. Aubyn, *The Year of Three Kings 1483*, pg. 193.
[6] *DNB*, "Stanley, Thomas, first Earl of Derby (1435?–1504)."

declared guilty of treason by an Act of Parliament.[1] However, the new king on his unstable throne, in need of powerful friends, had the attainder remitted, put Margaret in the custody of her husband, and charged Stanley with keeping her isolated in order to prevent any communication with her son.

That 1483 uprising in favor of the Earl of Richmond failed. Henry Stafford, 2nd Duke of Buckingham, who, "from causes, which appear never to have been accurately ascertained,"[2] had suddenly turned against Richard III, was captured, tried, and on Sunday, 2 Nov 1483, beheaded in the market-place of Salisbury.

Margaret Beaufort continued to work discreetly, gathering support for the return of her son. It was her hope to marry him to the daughter of Edward IV, thus uniting the houses of Lancaster and York and securing the throne and peace.

On 22 August 1485, the armies of Henry of Richmond met the armies of Richard III on Bosworth Field. The factor that swung the Battle of Bosworth to a Lancastrian victory was the last minute move made by Margaret Beaufort's husband, Thomas Stanley, and his brother, William, to direct all their men against Richard III, killing the king and winning the crown for his stepson, Henry, Earl of Richmond. The traditional story is that after the battle, Richard's crown was found in a hawthorn bush and that Thomas Stanley placed the crown on Henry of Richmond's head.[3] On 27 Oct 1485, Henry of

---

[1] Hogrefe, *Women of Action in Tudor England: Nine Biographical Sketches*, pg. 140. "When Parliament met in January 1484, about a hundred people were attainted, many of whom were later pardoned, and only some dozen rebels lost their heads. The royal clemency was remarkable.... It even extended to Margaret Beaufort...." (St. Aubyn, *The Year of Three Kings 1483*, pg. 193).

[2] Cooper, *Memoir of Margaret, Countess of Richmond and Derby*, pg. 22. It has been suggested that Buckingham planned to eventually take the throne for himself (Cheetham, *The Life and Times of Richard III*, pgs. 136–138).

[3] "The device of a crown on a hawthorn bush was later incorporated into the design of the East Window of Henry VII's Chapel at

(continued...)

Richmond was crowned Henry VII and Lord Stanley was
created by charter Earl of Derby. [1]

If it is true that Margaret had tears in her eyes at the
coronation of her son, it is not because of fear, as one source
suggests, but more because of pride and happiness, and perhaps
relief that years of fear for her son's safety were behind her.
Her work had come to successful fruition.

Margaret Beaufort's last marriage was one of political
convenience only. While Lord Stanley was still living, "she
secured from him a promise to let her adopt a chaste life and
made a vow of chastity," [2] in which she did with "all my
hearte promise from henceforth the chastity of my bodye,"
beseeching God that he would accept her promise "to the
remedye of my wretched lyfe and relief of my sinfull
soule...." [3] She was declared a 'femme sole' and had total
control over her own property: "Her husband's financial rights
were scrupulously respected but she took over the practical
management of her estates." [4]. She renewed her vow after Lord
Stanley's death. She spent much of the remainder of her life
making endowments and benefactions. According to Bishop
Fisher, the Countess kept a dozen poor men and women in her
home, (where she perhaps resided occasionally), feeding and
clothing them, caring for them in their sicknesses, "and when it
pleased God to call ony of them out of this wretched worlde,
she wolde be present to see them departe and to lerne to deye,
and lykewyse bring them unto the erthe." [5]

---

[3] (...continued)
Westminster Abbey." St. Aubyn, *The Year of Three Kings 1483*,
pg. 217.

[1] *CP*, Derby section.

[2] Hogrefe, *Women of Action in Tudor England: Nine Biographical
Sketches*, pg. 144.

[3] Cooper, *Memoir of Margaret, Countess of Richmond and Derby*,
pgs. 97–98.

[4] Crawford, *Letters of the Queens of England 1100–1547*, pg. 148.

[5] From his *Mornynge Remembrance*, as quoted in Cooper, *Memoir of
Margaret, Countess of Richmond and Derby*. John Fisher, Bishop of
(continued...)

Despite her married status, she was treated as a "femme sole," and managed her estates and finances herself.[1]

She was an extremely wealthy lady who knew the importance of education, and a large portion of her wealth went to universities and colleges and the printing of books. She had translated or translated herself books from French to English. She was a patron of three printers, Caxton, Pynson, and Wynkyn de Worde,[2] who styled himself as "Printer unto the most excellent princess my lady the king's grandame," the king by Worde's time being her grandson, Henry VIII. She was, as well, a patron of musicians and composers, and she contributed funds toward the education of students in the universities. She founded Christ's College and St. John's and used her own properties to supply revenues for the new institutions.

Margaret Beaufort, mother of Henry VII and Countess of Richmond and Derby, was buried in Henry VII's Chapel in

----

[5] (...continued)

Rochester, was Margaret Beaufort's confessor. He, like Sir Thomas More, was fatally caught up in the political turbulence resulting from Henry VIII's fascination with Anne Boleyn and his determination to annul his marriage with Katherine of Aragon (d. January 1536). Fisher's sentence of a traitor's death was commuted to beheading. He was executed on Tower Hill 22 Jun 1535. Born in 1459, he was at least 76 years old when he died. His head was displayed on London Bridge, and his body was buried without ceremony in the churchyard of Allhallows Barking. It was later moved to the church of St. Peter ad Vincula in the Tower of London, where it was buried beside the body of Sir Thomas More. His portrait was painted by Holbein. (*DNB*, "Fisher, John (1459–1435), Bishop of Rochester")

[1] Crawford, *Letters of the Queens of England 1100–1547*, pg. 148.

[2] William Caxton (abt 1421–1491), English printer and translator; Richard Pynson (b. Normandy; d. 1529–1530), arrived in England about 1490, naturalized 26 Jul 1513, on accession of Henry VIII appointed printer to the king; Jan Van Wynkyn of Worth (de Worde) in Alsace (d. 1534–1535; bur. the church of St. Bride in Fleet Street), also called Johannes Wynkyn, an apprentice of William Caxton (Wynkyn succeeded to Caxton's business and materials). (*DNB* articles, "Caxton, William (1422?–1491)"; "Pynson, Richard (d. 1530)"; "Worde, Wynkyn de (d. 1534?)")

Westminster Abbey. Her tomb effigy by Torrigiano[1] is
considered one of the finest in the Abbey.

Margaret Beaufort, Mother of the Executed Henry

Margaret Beaufort (d. spring 1474), mother of the executed
Henry Stafford, 2nd Duke of Buckingham, was the daughter of
Edmund Beaufort (d. 1455), 2nd Duke of Somerset, and
Eleanor Beauchamp (d. 1467/1468). Eleanor Beauchamp was
the second daughter of Richard de Beauchamp (d. 1439), 5th
Earl of Warwick, and his first wife, Elizabeth Berkeley
(d. 1422) (the daughter of Thomas, Lord Berkeley).[2]
Edmund was the brother of John Beaufort (d. 1444), Duke
of Somerset, who was father of Margaret Beaufort (mother of
Henry VII). When John Beaufort died, Edmund Beaufort
became the 2nd Duke of Somerset.
Margaret married (1) Humphrey Stafford (d. 1458 of the
plague[3] in the lifetime of his father). He was the son of
Humphrey Stafford (b. 1402; d. 1460), 1st Duke of
Buckingham, and his wife, Anne Neville (d. 20 Sep 1480),
daughter of Ralph Neville, 1st Earl of Westmorland, and his
second wife, Joan Beaufort (daughter of John of Gaunt and
Katherine de Roet Swynford).
Humphrey Stafford (d. 1458) was the older brother of

---

[1] The Florentine Renaissance sculpture, Pietro Torrigiano
(1472-1528), also created the tomb effigies of Henry VII and his wife,
Elizabeth of York. Elizabeth was "the last of the House of York to wear
the English Crown" and the first to be buried in Henry VII's newly-
completed Chapel. (*Westminster Abbey: Official Guide*, pg. 72)

According to Halsted, *Life of Margaret Beaufort*, pg. 219, Thomas
Stanley (d. 29 Jul 1504, Lathom) had ordered a tomb with effigies of
himself and both his wives in the priory church of Burscough, near
Lathom, where, in accordance with his wishes, "they were ordered to be
prayed for, and had in perpetual remembrance, and where, in accordance
with his last testament, dated July, in 1504, he was himself interred."

[2] *Ancestral* 87-33.

[3] Harris, *Edward Stafford, Third Duke of Buckingham, 1478-1521*,
pg. 19.

Henry Stafford (d. 1481), who married Margaret Beaufort, mother of Henry VII.

Margaret and Humphrey Stafford had Henry Stafford (b. abt 1454; ex. 1483 by Richard III), 2nd Duke of Buckingham, who married Katherine Woodville (d. 1497), sister of Elizabeth Woodville, Edward IV's queen consort.[1] The Woodvilles were considered upstarts by the old nobility, and despite Henry Stafford's marriage to the queen's sister, he actively supported Richard III as he took political control from the Woodvilles and usurped the crown from Edward IV's young son and heir, Edward V. Henry Stafford, as Richard III's man, received many honors, position, and properties.

Richard III was crowned in July 1483. By October, the new king had proclaimed Henry Stafford a traitor, and the 2nd Duke of Buckingham had fled northward in disguise. Historians still debate causes for the abrupt change in the relationship between the king and the Duke. Possible reasons could have centered around money, promises, properties, positions or offices, or the probable murder of Edward IV's two sons, the princes in the Tower.

In the same month, there were several uprisings—commonly called Buckingham's rebellion—in favor of Henry of Richmond. There were unsuccessful, being put down by Richard's men.

Henry Stafford, 2nd Duke of Buckingham, was captured and tried and on Sunday, 2 Nov 1483, beheaded in the market-place of Salisbury.

Margaret Beaufort, Sister of the Queen of Scots

A lesser known Margaret Beaufort was the second daughter of John Beaufort (d. 1410), 1st Earl of Somerset and Marquess

---

[1] Katherine Woodville m. (2) bet 2 Nov 1483 and 7 Nov 1485 Jasper Tudor (b. abt 1431; d. 21 or 26 Dec 1495), Earl of Pembroke and Duke of Bedford, second son of Owen Tudor (d. 1461) by Catherine of Valois; no issue; m. (3) Richard Wingfield (d. 1525), son of John Wingfield of Letheringham, Suffolk, and his wife, Elizabeth (daughter of John FitzLewis of West Horndon, Essex. (*DNB*, "Wingfield, Sir Richard (1469?–1525)")

of Dorset, and his wife Margaret Holand (d. 1429), daughter of Thomas Holand (d. 1397), 2nd Earl of Kent. This Margaret Beaufort would, therefore, be sister of Joan Beaufort, Queen of Scots.

Margaret married after 1421 Thomas de Courtenay (b. 1414; d. 3 Feb 1458, Abbey of Abingdon), 5th Earl of Devon (1414–1458), by whom she was mother of Thomas de Courtenay (b. 1432; beheaded 3 Apr 1461 at York after Battle of Towton 29 Mar; unm.), 6th Earl of Devon[1]; John de Courtenay (beheaded or killed 4 May 1471, Battle of Tewkesbury[2]; unm.; bur. Tewkesbury), 7th Earl of Devon; Henry de Courtenay (beheaded 17 Jan 1468/1469, Salisbury; unm.[3]); Joan Courtenay (b. 1477), who married (1) Roger Clifford (beheaded 1485), (2) William Knyvett; and Elizabeth de Courtenay (b. 1449), who married Hugh Conway (liv. 1471/1472, aged 22).[4]

Joan Beaufort, Daughter of John of Gaunt

Joan Beaufort (b. abt 1379; d. 13 Nov 1440, Howden, Yorkshire; bur. Lincoln Cathedral) was the youngest child and only daughter of John of Gaunt and Katherine de Roet Swynford.

Joan m. (1) Robert de Ferrers (b. 1373; d. bef 29 Nov 1396[5]), 2nd Baron Ferrers of Wemme, by whom she had issue of two daughters.

She m. (2) Ralph Neville (d. 1425), 6th Lord Neville of Raby, 1st Earl of Westmorland. They had a large family, which included Cecily Sweet Cis Neville (d. 1495), who married Richard Plantagenet (ex. 1460), 3rd Duke of York. Cecily Neville and Richard Plantagenet were parents of Edward IV and Richard III.

---

[1] *CP*, Devon section.
[2] Hallam, *The Plantagenet Encyclopedia*, pg. 56.
[3] *CP*, Devon section.
[4] Lodge, *The Genealogy of the Existing British Peerage*, pgs. 107–109.
[5] *CP*, Ferrers of Chartley section, Table "Ferrers of Chartley."

Joan Beaufort, Queen of Scots

Joan Beaufort (d. 1445), Queen of Scots, was the daughter of John Beaufort (d. 1410), Earl of Somerset, and Margaret Holand. Margaret Holand was daughter of Thomas de Holand (d. 1397), 2nd Earl of Kent.

Joan was the sister of Henry Beaufort (d. 1418[1]); John Beaufort (d. 1444), 1st Duke of Somerset; Edmund Beaufort (d. 1455), 2nd Duke of Somerset; and Margaret Beaufort who married Thomas Courtenay.

Her father's parents were John of Gaunt and Katherine de Roet Swynford.

In the month of May 1423 at Windsor, James I, uncrowned King of Scots, fell in love with Joan. From the age of eleven or twelve till the age of twenty-nine or thirty, James I (b. Jul 1394; d. 1437), son of Robert III, King of Scots, and Annabella Drummond, had been held as an honored prisoner in England. Despite his status as prisoner, he was given an education and allowed to take part in court life. As a poet, he recorded his love for Joan in his poem, *The Kingis Quair*. The match was considered suitable and politically beneficial, and James and Joan, "whose place in his affections was never contested,"[2] were married 12/13 Feb 1424 in the church of St. Mary Overy. By April, they were in Scotland, and on 2 May[3]/21 May[4] they were crowned at Scone. "His love for his wife never wavered. Almost alone of Scottish kings, he had no mistress and no bastards."[5]

James I was murdered 21 Feb 1437, and his murderers were "executed [by order of Queen Joan] with a barbarity which was deemed unusual even in that age." James' heart was "sent to the Holy Land and brought back in 1443 from Rhodes

---

[1] Storey, *The End of the House of Lancaster*, Table I.

[2] Bingham, *The Stewart Kingdom of Scotland*, pg. 47.

[3] Donaldson, *Scottish Kings*, pg. 65.

[4] Burke's *Royal Family*, pg. 319; *DNB*, "James I (1394–1437), king of Scotland."

[5] *DNB*, "James I (1394–1437), king of Scotland."

by a knight of St. John, and presented to the Carthusians."[1]
James I's six-year-old son was crowned as James II, King of
Scots, at Holyrood.

By 21 Sep 1439, Joan had married James Stewart, "the
Black 'Rider,' or Knight of Lorne." They had three sons—John
Stewart (b. abt 1440; d. 15 Sep 1512; bur. Dunkeld
Cathedral[2]), Earl of Atholl; James "Hearty James" Stewart
(d. bet. Jan 1497 and Jan 1499/1500[3]), Earl of Buchan; and
Andrew Stewart, Bishop of Moray.[4]

Joan died 15 Jul 1445 at Dunbar Castle and was buried with
her first husband in the Carthusian Church at Perch.[5]

Other Joan Beauforts

Another Joan Beaufort was the daughter of Edmund
Beaufort (d. 1455), 2nd Duke of Somerset, and his wife,
Eleanor de Beauchamp. This Joan ("liv sp 1492") was sister of
Margaret Beaufort, mother of the executed Henry Stafford. She
m. (1) Robert Howth, Lord of Howth in Ireland;
m. (2) Richard Fry, Kt.

Still another Joan Beaufort was the illegitimate daughter of
Henry Beaufort (d. 11 Apr 1447[6]), Bishop of Winchester,
Chancellor of England, and one of the four illegitimate children
of John of Gaunt. This Joan's mother was Alice FitzAlan
(b. abt 1373/1375), daughter of Richard FitzAlan (d. 24 Jan
1375/1376), Earl of Arundel. Joan (b. 1392) m. Edward
Stradling (d. in Jerusalem), Kt., of St. Donat's, county of
Glamorgan, Knight of the Sepulchre 1476.[7]

---

[1] *DNB*, "James I (1394–1437), king of Scotland."
[2] *CP*, Atholl section.
[3] *CP*, Buchan section.
[4] Bingham, *Kings and Queens of Scotland*, pg. 63.
[5] Bingham, *Kings and Queens of Scotland*, pgs. 60–63; Table 4 "The
House of Stewart."
[6] *CP*, Somerset section.
[7] *DNB*, "Beaufort, Henry (d. 1447), bishop of Winchester and
cardinal"; *Ancestral* 60-32, 234-31, 234-32, 234-33, 234-34, 234-35;
d'Angerville, *Living Descendants of Blood Royal (in America)*, pg. 563.

The Beaufort Women

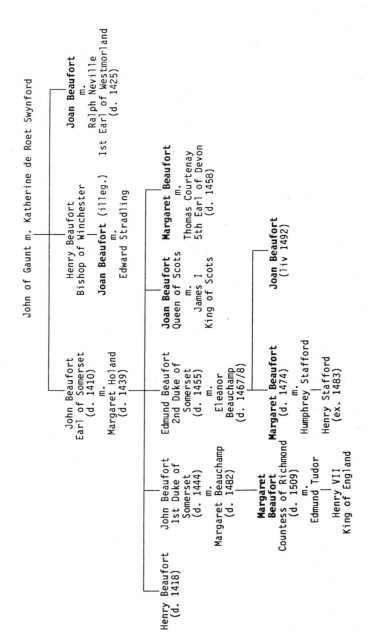

John of Gaunt m. Katherine de Roet Swynford

Henry Beaufort
Bishop of Winchester
|
Joan Beaufort (illeg.)
m.
Edward Stradling

Joan Beaufort
m.
Ralph Neville
1st Earl of Westmorland
(d. 1425)

John Beaufort
Earl of Somerset
(d. 1410)
m.
Margaret Holand
(d. 1439)

Edmund Beaufort
2nd Duke of
Somerset
(d. 1455)
m.
Eleanor
Beauchamp
(d. 1467/8)

Joan Beaufort
Queen of Scots
m.
James I
King of Scots

Margaret Beaufort
m.
Thomas Courtenay
5th Earl of Devon
(d. 1458)

Joan Beaufort
(liv 1492)

Henry Beaufort
(d. 1418)

John Beaufort
1st Duke of
Somerset
(d. 1444)
m.
Margaret Beauchamp
(d. 1482)

Margaret Beaufort
(d. 1474)
m.
Humphrey Stafford
|
Henry Stafford
(ex. 1483)

Margaret
Beaufort
Countess of Richmond
(d. 1509)
m.
Edmund Tudor
|
Henry VII
King of England

Sources:

Bagley, J. J., *The Earls of Derby 1485-1985*, Sidgwick & Jackson, London, 1985.
Bingham, Caroline, *Kings and Queens of Scotland*, Dorset Press, New York, 1976.
Burke, Sir Bernard, and Burke, Ashworth P., *A Genealogical and Heraldic History of the Peerage and Baronetage, The Privy Council, Knightage and Companionage*, 69th Edition, Harrison and Sons, London, 1907.
Burke's Peerage, *Burke's Guide to the Royal Family*, Burke's Peerage Limited, London, 1973.
Cokayne, G. E., *The Complete Peerage*, St Catherine Press, London, 1912.
Cooper, Charles Henry, F.S.A., *Memoir of Margaret, Countess of Richmond and Derby*, Deighton Bell and Co., London, 1874.
Coward, Barry, *The Stanleys, Lords Stanley and Earls of Derby 1385-1672: The origins, wealth and power of a landowning family*, printed for the Chetham Society, Manchester, 1983.
Crawford, Anne, *Letters of the Queens of England 1100-1547*, Alan Sutton Publishing Ltd, Phoenix Mill, 1994.
Donaldson, Gordon, *Scottish Kings*, Barnes & Noble Books, New York, 1967.
Hallam, Elizabeth, Ed., *The Plantagenet Chronicles*, Weidenfeld & Nicolson, NY, 1986.
Halsted, Carolyn, *The Life of Margaret Beaufort, Countess of Richmond and Derby*, Smith, Elder, and Co., Cornhill, London, 1845.
Harris, Barbara J., *Edward Stafford, Third Duke of Buckingham, 1478-1521*, Stanford University Press, Stanford, California 1986.
Hogrefe, Pearl, *Women of Action in Tudor England: Nine Biographical Sketches*, Iowa State University Press, Ames, Iowa, 1977.
Lodge, Edmund, *The Genealogy of the Existing British Peerage*, Saunders & Otley, London, 1832.
Pearsall, Derek, *The Life of Geoffrey Chaucer: A Critical Biography*, Blackwell, Oxford UK & Cambridge USA, 1992.
Rawcliffe, *The Staffords, Earls of Stafford and Dukes of Buckingham 1394-1521*, Cambridge University Press, Cambridge, 1978.
St. Aubyn, Giles, *The Year of Three Kings 1483*, Collins, London, 1983.
Stephen, Sir Leslie, and Lee, Sir Sidney, eds., *Dictionary of National Biography*, Oxford University Press, London, 1964.
Storey, R. L., *End of the House of Lancaster*, Stein and Day, NY, 1967.

Tytler, Sarah, *Tudor Queens and Princesses*, Barnes and Noble Books, New York, 1993.

Weis, Frederick Lewis, *Ancestral Roots of Sixty Colonists*—6th Ed., Genealogical Publishing Co., Inc., Baltimore, 1990.

Westminster Abbey: Official Guide, Jarrold and Sons Limited, Norwich, 1988.

Some Royal Descendants
of Payn de Roet

Payn de Roet, a knight of Hainault, was probably a widower when he went to England in the company of Philippa of Hainault, bride of Edward III, King of England. He had worked as an official of protocol in the household of Marguerite, Empress of Germany and Countess of Hainault, Queen Philippa's sister.[1] His name has been seen as Payn, Payne, Paon, and Panneto.

He was the father of Elizabeth de Roet, eldest daughter, who was placed in a convent in 1349 when she was about thirteen. A daughter, Philippa de Roet, was in the service of Queen Philippa and married Geoffrey Chaucer.[2] A son, Walter de Roet, was in the service of Edward, the Black Prince, son and heir of Edward III. A third daughter, Katherine de Roet, married as her first husband Hugh Swynford (d. 1372) and had issue. Katherine was governess to the children of John of Gaunt and his first wife, Blanche of Lancaster (d. 1369). About 1371, she became the mistress of John of Gaunt and had four children by him, collectively called the Beauforts:

- John Beaufort (d. 1410), 1st Earl of Somerset
- Henry Beaufort (d. 1447), Bishop of Winchester
- Thomas Beaufort (d. 1426), Duke of Exeter, Earl of Dorset
- Joan Beaufort (d. 1440), Countess of Westmorland

One of Payn de Roet's great-granddaughters, Joan Beaufort, was Queen of Scots. Another great-granddaughter, Cecily Sweet

---

[1] Howard, *Chaucer, His Life, His Works, His World*, pg. 91.
[2] See chapter, "Some Royal Connections of Poet Geoffrey Chaucer."

Cis Neville, was mother of two kings of England—Edward IV and Richard III. A great-great-grandson, John de la Pole, was named by Richard III as his heir to the throne of England.

Other descendants in England include Henry VIII, Queen Elizabeth the Great, George I, Queen Victoria, and Queen Elizabeth II.

Payn de Roet was buried in Saint Paul's Cathedral. His tombstone indicates that he held a position in the college of heralds as "Guienne King of Arms."[1] His tomb inscription from Weever's *Ancient Funerary Monuments of Great Britain* (1767) refers to Philippa as Anne, and names Hugh Swynford as Otes Swynford. The engraving also lists Payn de Roet's descendants as being eight kings, four queens, and five princes of England; six kings and three queens of Scotland; and two cardinals; as well as various Dukes, Duchesses, and other nobilities of both these kingdoms and other kingdoms.[2]

Sources:

Armitage-Smith, Sydney, *John of Gaunt*, Barnes & Noble, Inc., NY, 1964.

Cokayne, G. E., The Complete Peerage, St. Catherine Press, London.

Harris, Barbara J., *Edward Stafford: Third Duke of Buckingham*, 1478-1521, Stanford University Press, Stanford, CA, 1986.

Howard, Donald R., *Chaucer: His Life, His Works, His World*, Fawcett Columbine, NY, 1987.

Silva-Vigier, Anil, *This Moste Highe Prince...John of Gaunt 1340–1399*, The Pentland Press, Ltd., Edinburgh, 1992.

---

[1] Howard, *Chaucer: His Life, His Works, His World*, pg. 91.
[2] Silva-Vigier, *This Moste Highe Prince...John of Gaunt*, pg. 348.

Some Royal Descendants of Payn de Roet

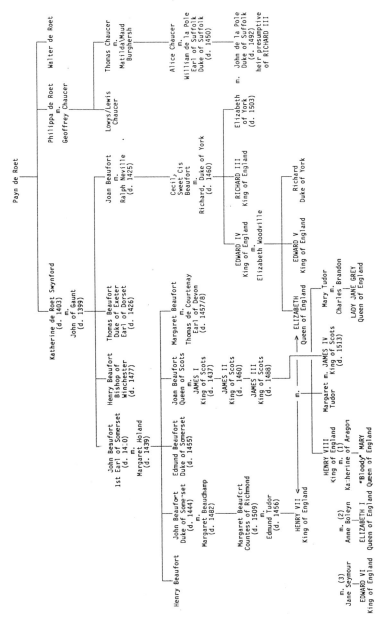

Some Royal Connections
of Poet Geoffrey Chaucer

Geoffrey Chaucer (b. abt 1340; d. 1400), best known as the author of *The Canterbury Tales*, was the brother-in-law of John of Gaunt, son of Edward III, King of England.[1] Chaucer's wife, Philippa de Roet (d. prob. 1387), was the sister of John of Gaunt's mistress, Katherine de Roet Swynford, who later became his third wife.[2] For many years, Chaucer enjoyed the patronage as well as the friendship of John of Gaunt. In fact, according to the *DNB*, he held pensions from both John of Gaunt and the crown.[3]

Geoffrey Chaucer's father was vintner John Chaucer (b. abt 1312; d. 1366[4]), who is known to have been in attendance on the Edward III and his queen, Philippa of Hainault, in their 1338 expedition to Flanders and Cologne. John Chaucer was the son of Robert Chaucer (b. abt 1288; d. 1314 or 1315) of Ipswich and London.[5] John Chaucer's

---

[1] Chaucer's *The Book of the Duchess* was written on the occasion of the death of Blanche (d. Sep 1369), Duchess of Lancaster, first wife of John of Gaunt. (Howard, *Chaucer: His Life, His Works, His World*, pg. 506)

[2] Katherine became the mistress of John of Gaunt about 1370, after the death of his first wife. They were married in 1396 (Pearsall, *The Life of Geoffrey Chaucer*, Appendix II).

[3] *DNB*, "Chaucer, Geoffrey (1340?–1400)."

[4] Pearsall, *The Life of Geoffrey Chaucer*, pg. 12.

[5] Robert Chaucer was the son of Andrew de Dynyngton of Ipswich, also known as A. le Taverner (d. abt 1288). Andrew married Isabella Malyn, daughter of Walter Aurifaber, and had issue Robert Malyn who

(continued...)

mother was Maria, who was married first "to one Heyroun"[1] and had issue of Thomas Heyroun (d. 1349 of the plague). She married secondly Robert Chaucer, just mentioned, and had John Chaucer, father of the poet. She married thirdly Richard Chaucer (d. 1349 of the plague), cousin[2] of Robert Chaucer and a vintner, who became step-grandfather of Geoffrey Chaucer. Pearsall adds that this Richard Chaucer had a brother Simon who died in 1336.[3]

Robert Chaucer had a sister Agnes who married (1) Walter de Westhale; married (2) Geoffrey Stace. By her first marriage she had issue of Joan and Sibyl. Sibyl married William de Knapton and had issue of Agnes.

John Chaucer was "married at least twice," his first wife being "probably" Joan de Esthalle, according to the *DNB*. He also married (late 1330s[4]/bef 1343) Agnes de Copton (d. prob. 1381), daughter of John de Copton and niece of Hamo de Copton.[5] The date of the marriage of John and Agnes is not known, but Joan was alive in 1331 and Agnes was wife of John Chaucer in 1349. John Chaucer died in 1366, and, according to the *DNB*, Geoffrey Chaucer's "widowed mother soon after

---

[5] (...continued)
to us is known as Robert (le) Chaucer (d. 1314 or 1315). According to Pearsall, *The Life of Geoffrey Chaucer*, pg. 12 and Table 1, in which Pearsall acknowledges the information of Lister M. Matheson, Robert was known as Robert Malyn, Robert le Chaucer, Robert Malyn le Chaucer, Robert of Ipswich, and Robert de Dynyngton. Pearsall, pg. 12, explains Robert's name change by referencing "a recent study by Lister Matheson." When Robert's employer, John le Chaucer ("a mercer"), was killed in a brawl (1302), Robert inherited the business and took his employer's surname. Robert seems to have done well for himself: he was in the king's service in 1305.

[1] *DNB*, "Chaucer, Geoffrey (1340?-1400)." Also seen as Heyron and Heron. Pearsall, *The Life of Geoffrey Chaucer*, Table 1, shows Maria married to a John Heyron.

[2] Pearsall, *The Life of Geoffrey Chaucer*, pg. 12.

[3] Pearsall, *The Life of Geoffrey Chaucer*, pg. 14.

[4] Pearsall, *The Life of Geoffrey Chaucer*, pg. 12.

[5] Chute, *Geoffrey Chaucer of England*, pgs. 22 and 23, states that Agnes was Agnes de Northwell by her first marriage.

married one 'Bartholomew Attechapel,'" or Chappel.[1] John Chaucer was a wealthy vintner who rendered military and civilian services to the king.

Silva-Vigier[2] notes that a John Chaucer was an active participant in support of Edward III as he seized control of power from Roger Mortimer in 1327 and that a John Chaucer was in military service in Flanders in 1338 with Edward III.

The earliest record of Geoffrey Chaucer is 1357. He was in the service of Elizabeth de Burgh, Countess of Ulster, wife of Lionel of Antwerp, Duke of Clarence (d. 1368), son of Edward III.[3] Queen Philippa had also placed in Elizabeth's service a girl from her native Hainault, Philippa de Roet. She was daughter of Payn de Roet, a knight of Hainault who came to England with the company of Philippa of Hainault. It is most likely that Geoffrey and Philippa first met at court.

Payn de Roet (probably a widower when he accompanied Philippa of Hainault to her wedding in England) had another daughter, Katherine, who was governess of the children of John of Gaunt and later the third wife of John of Gaunt. He also had a son, Walter, who was in the service of the Black Prince, Edward III's first son and heir. Elizabeth, a third daughter of Payn de Roet, was placed in a convent when she was about thirteen years old (1349).[4]

Geoffrey Chaucer's career with the English court is often overshadowed by his literary achievements. He was not a professional poet; he was employed by the king in various official capacities. He served in Prince Lionel's household (1357–1358), was captured and ransomed while serving with Edward III in France (1359–1360), served as a valet in the king's household (1367), held several official posts, made

---

[1] Pearsall, *The Life of Geoffrey Chaucer*, pg. 12.

[2] Silva-Vigier, *This Moste Highe Prince...John of Gaunt*, pg. 64.

[3] Miller, Barnes and Noble Encyclopedia, CompuServe.

[4] Payn de Roet's tombstone in Saint Paul's indicates that he held a position in the college of heralds as "Guienne King of Arms." (Howard, *Chaucer: His Life, His Works, His World*, pg. 91; Silva-Vigier, *This Moste Highe Prince...John of Gaunt*, pg. 104)

diplomatic trips to the Continent (including Italy) (1370–1378), was "comptroller of customs on wool and hides at London" (1374–1386) and of petty customs (1382–1386), was knight of the shire for Kent (1386), and served as clerk of the king's works (1389–1391).[1]

Geoffrey Chaucer and Philippa de Roet (d. bet 18 Jun and 7 Nov 1387[2]) were married by 1374, possibly "before 12 September 1366,"[3] when a Philippa Chaucer was known to be a lady of the chamber to Edward III's queen, Philippa of Hainault.

Geoffrey Chaucer and his wife, Philippa, had a son Lewis ("litel Lowys, my sone"[4]) (b. 1381[5]) for whom Chaucer compiled "The Treatise on the Astrolabe." Lewis has been described as "the boy sent to Oxford about 1390 at the age of ten."[6] A Lewis Chaucer is noted as bearing arms in 1403. Nothing more is known about Lewis.

It is believed that Thomas Chaucer[7] (b. abt 1361[8]/1367[9]; d. 14 Mar 1434; bur. Ewelme Church, Oxfordshire) was also the son of Geoffrey Chaucer and his wife. Thomas Chaucer's tomb at Ewelme Church in Oxfordshire, bears among its various coats of arms those used by his mother, Philippa de

---

[1] *The Columbia-Viking Desk Encyclopedia*, Third Edition, The Viking Press, NY, 1968, "Chaucer, Geoffrey."

[2] Pearsall, *The Life of Geoffrey Chaucer*, pg. 143.

[3] Pearsall, *The Life of Geoffrey Chaucer*, pg. 49.

[4] *DNB*, "Chaucer, Geoffrey (1340?–1400)."

[5] Howard, *Chaucer: His Life, His Works, His World*, pg. 506.

[6] Howard, *Chaucer: His Life, His Works, His World*, pg. 93.

[7] Howard, *Chaucer: His Life, His Works, His World*, pg. 93, states that the Chaucers had "as it appears from scanty and often mysterious records," four children. On pg. 506 he states, "The Chaucers had, it appears from the records, three children." The truth seems to be that only Thomas is known for certain to be son of Geoffrey. According to Pearsall (*The Life of Geoffrey Chaucer*, pg. 12), Thomas was "the only child born to them of whom there is definite knowledge, though there is seventeenth-century evidence of a sister called Katherine."

[8] *DNB*, "Chaucer, Geoffrey (1340?–1400)."

[9] Howard, *Chaucer: His Life, His Works, His World*, pg. 93; *DNB*, "Chaucer, Thomas (1367?–1434)."

Roet, quartered by those used by his wife, Maud Burghersh.
One would expect to see his father's arms taken for his own and
quartered with those of his mother. Some writers have taken
Thomas's choice of arms to mean that he was the illegitimate
son of Philippa de Roet by John of Gaunt. However, Howard
points out the fact that Thomas's mother's coats of arms were
"more prestigious" than those of his father, and that Thomas
"was a snob, not a bastard." Too, John of Gaunt's generosity
and responsibility toward those around him are well known and
demonstrated by the fortunes his four illegitimate children by
Katherine de Roet Swynford. Pearsall states that if Thomas
Chaucer were the son of John of Gaunt, he certainly received
"paltry" attention from the man who was supposed to be his
father. He adds that even if Thomas Chaucer were illegitimate,
the choice of heraldic markings is a far cry from proving his
sire to be John of Gaunt.

Thomas Chaucer was speaker of the House of Commons
1407, 1410, 1411, and 1414. He served as butler to Richard II,
Henry IV, Henry V, and Henry VI and fought at Agincourt in
1417. He was "reputed to be immenseley rich." [1]

There is the possibility of two other children born to
Geoffrey Chaucer and his wife. Howard lists an Elizabeth
"Chausier," who entered the convent at Barking Abbey in
1381. The expense of her admission to the nunnery was paid by
John of Gaunt. [2] In fact, Silva-Vigier [3] states that the registers
of John of Gaunt show a dowry of £50 to enable Geoffrey and
Philippa's daughter, Elizabeth Chaucer, to enter the nunnery.

---

[1] Hallam, *The Plantagenet Encyclopedia*, pg. 48.

[2] John of Gaunt was generous towards his retainers. If Elizabeth was
the daughter of Geoffrey and Philippa Chaucer, paying for Elizabeth's
admission into the convent would have been in character for John of
Gaunt: Elizabeth's mother, Philippa, had been in the service of Elizabeth
of Ulster, wife of John's brother, Lionel (in fact, Elizabeth may have
been named after her or perhaps after Philippa's oldest sister, Elizabeth);
Philippa had also been in the service of John's mother, the Queen; and
in 1371, she entered the service of John's second wife, Costanza.

[3] Silva-Vigier, *This Moste Highe Prince...John of Gaunt 1340-1399*,
pg. 164.

An Elizabeth Chausier, possibly the same person, has been
mentioned as living in 1397.

An Agnes Chaucer was a damsel-in-waiting at Henry IV's
coronation in 1399. Howard suggests that this individual, being
born as late at the mid-1380s, might have been Geoffrey
Chaucer's granddaughter rather than daughter.[1] And though
the *DNB* states that Chaucer was not an uncommon name in
fourteenth century London, it should be remembered that
Henry IV was son of John of Gaunt; the relationship of the
Chaucer family with that of John of Gaunt is such that one
would not be surprised to see a Chaucer listed as taking part in
the coronation of Henry IV.

The above mentioned Thomas Chaucer, son of Geoffrey and
Philippa, was the king's butler for almost thirty years, was a
wealthy squire of Ewelme, a vintner, a diplomat, a justice of
the peace, sheriff of Oxfordshire (appt. 1400), and a member of
parliament and served five times as speaker of the House of
Commons.[2] He entered the service of John of Gaunt in 1386
and remained with him for life. He was chief butler to
Richard II and Henry IV. He received the manor of Woodstock
and other properties from Queen Philippa. He was present at
the battle of Agincourt. Henry IV appointed him constable of
Wallingford Castle for life. The powerful Beauforts, the
illegitimate issue of John of Gaunt and Katherine de Roet
Swynford, were his cousins.

Thomas married Maud/Matilda Burghersh (d. 4 May 1437;
bur. Ewelme Church), second daughter and coheiress of John
de Burghersh (d. 21 Sep 1391[3]), Lord Kerdeston,[4] of
Ewelme, and his wife, Ismania de Hanham, daughter of Simon

---

[1] *Chaucer: His Life, His Works, His World*, pg. 93.

[2] Kingsford, *Prejudice and Promise in 15th Century England*, Barnes
and Noble, NY, 1962. pg. 148.

[3] Metcalfe, *Alice Chaucer, Duchess of Suffolk, c1404–1475*, pg. 2;
CP, Kerdeston section, wherein the death date for Maud Burghersh, wife
of Thomas Chaucer, is given as Apr 1437.

[4] *CP*, Suffolk section.

de Hanham.[1] John de Burghersh (d. 1391) was the son of John
de Burghersh (d. 30 Jun 1349) and Maud de Kerdeston
(d. 20 May 1349), daughter of William, Lord Kerdeston, who
died without legitimate male issue in 1361.[2] Chute adds that
the father of Maud Burghersh (d. 1437) was a nephew of Henry
Burghersh (d. 1341), Bishop of Lincoln, and she was the niece
of Lady Joan Mohun.[3]

Thomas and Maud were parents of an only child, Alice
Chaucer (b. 1404[4]; d. 20 May 1475). Alice was married three
times. Her first husband, John Philip,[5] was killed 2 Oct 1415
at Harfleur and buried 20 Oct 1415 at Kidderminster. Alice was
about ten years old at that time. Metcalfe (pg. 14) states Philip
was buried in the parish Church of St. Mary and All Saints at
Kidderminster "by the side of his second wife, Maud."
Metcalfe adds without details, "Sir John was also related to the
Burghersh family...."

Alice married secondly before Nov 1424 as his second wife
Thomas de Montagu, 4th Earl of Salisbury,[6] who died 3 Nov

---

[1] Ismania was the widow of John Ralegh. She m. (3) Lawrence
Berkerolles. (*CP*, Kerdeston section)

[2] *CP*, Kerdeston section.

[3] Chute, *Geoffrey Chaucer of England*, pg. 231.

[4] Metcalfe, *Alice Chaucer, Duchess of Suffolk, c1404–1475*, pg. 2.

[5] Seen also as Phelip. She was Philip's third wife. "...possibly they
were affianced only." (*CP*, Salisbury section, Kerdeston section)

[6] Thomas de Montagu's first wife (m. 1399) was Eleanor de Holand
(d. 1405; bur. Bisham), daughter of Thomas Holand (d. 1397), 2nd Earl
of Kent. Their daughter, Alice de Montagu, married Richard Neville
(ex. 31 Dec 1460, battle of Wakefield), Earl of Salisbury, and became
mother of Richard Neville the Kingmaker (d. 1471) (*Ancestral* 78-35;
DNB, "Montacute or Montagu, Thomas de, fourth Earl of Salisbury
(1388-1428)"). Thomas de Montagu's mass was held 29 Nov 1428 at
Saint Paul's in London. He was buried at Bisham. In his will he made
arrangements for a tomb for himself and both his wives ("Lady Alianor"
and "Lady Alice...if she will") in a chapel which was to be built behind
the high altar at Bisham. His will also stated that his beloved wife (Alice
Chaucer) would every day serve food and drink to three poor people
"with her own hands," (*CP*, Salisbury section), though Metcalfe (*Alice*

(continued...)

1428 in France from injuries received at the siege of Orleans. There was no issue of either marriage.

In 1430/1431 (royal license 11 Nov 1430[1]), when Alice was twenty-four, she married her third husband, William de la Pole (b. 16 Oct 1396, at Cotton, co. Suffolk[2]; beheaded in the English Channel 2 May 1450[3]), Earl of Suffolk, Duke of Suffolk. He was the second son of Michael de la Pole (b. in or bef 1367; d. 18 Sep 1415 "of the flux" at the siege of Harfleur; bur. Wingfield), 2nd Earl of Suffolk, and his wife, Catherine Stafford (d. 8 Apr 1419; bur. Wingfield with her husband) (daughter of Hugh de Stafford (d. 1386), Earl of Stafford, "who was of royal descent"[4]). They founded Wingfield College and built the almshouses in Suffolk. In his will, William de la Pole called Alice his "best loved wife" and added, "for above all the earth my singular trust is in her."[5]

William de la Pole and Alice Chaucer had John de la Pole (b. 27 Sep 1442; d. bet 29 Oct 1491 and 27 Oct 1492; bur. Wingfield), 2nd Duke of Suffolk and Earl of Suffolk, who married[6] in 1458[7] Elizabeth (b. 22 Apr 1444, Rouen;

---

[6] (...continued)
Chaucer, Duchess of Suffolk, c1404–1475, pg. 17) adds that he allowed "alternative arrangements" should the request prove inconvenient for Alice. It should be noted that caring for the poor was a common duty among the well-to-do.

[1] *CP*, Salisbury section, Suffolk section.

[2] Bigham, *The Chief Ministers of England 920–1720*, pg. 164, adds that Thomas de Montagu (d. 1428), Earl of Salisbury and second husband of Alice Chaucer, was William de la Pole's "old commander." Clive (pg. xxxii) states that William de la Pole, 4th Earl and 1st Duke of Suffolk, was descended from merchants "and not landed gentry."

[3] Alice was charged with treason after her husband's death but was later acquitted by her peers. (Metcalfe, *Alice Chaucer, Duchess of Suffolk, c1404–1475*, pgs. 37–38)

[4] Chrimes, *Fifteenth Century England 1399–1509*, pg. 87.

[5] Kerr, *A Guide to Medieval Sites in Britain*, pg. 111.

[6] John de la Pole m. (1) bet 28 Jan and 7 Feb 1449/1450 Margaret Beaufort, only daughter of John Beaufort (d. 1444), Duke of Somerset. However, this was a child marriage and was dissolved before 24 Mar 1452/1453. (*CP*, Suffolk section)

d. bet. 7 Jan 1502/1503 and 3 May 1504; bur. Wingfield with her husband[1]), the second daughter of Richard (d. 1460), Duke of York, and his wife Cecily Sweet Cis Neville[2] (d. 1495) and the sister of the future Edward IV and Richard III.

Alice Chaucer is credited by the *DNB* with two other children, William and Anna, but no other information concerning them is given.

It is believed that John de la Pole and Elizabeth of York had seven sons,[3] who were great-great-grandsons of Geoffrey Chaucer:

● John de la Pole (b. abt 1462; d. 16 Jun 1487, Battle of Stoke), Earl of Lincoln, eldest son, was declared by Richard III as his heir presumptive to the English throne.[4] He married (1) Margaret FitzAlan, daughter of Thomas FitzAlan (d. 1524), 12th Earl of Arundel (no issue) and (2) the daughter and heiress of John Golafre (no issue).

● Edward de la Pole, Archdeacon of Richmond.

● Edmund de la Pole (b. 1471–72), Duke of Suffolk, was beheaded in the Tower by Henry VIII in the spring of 1513[5]; he m. bef 10 Oct 1496 Margaret Scrope (d. Feb 1514/1515),

---

[7] (...continued)

[7] According to the *CP*, Lincoln section, John de la Pole married Edward IV's sister, Elizabeth, "in or before Aug. 1461."

[1] *CP*, Suffolk section.

[2] Cecily Neville was the youngest daughter of Joan Beaufort (daughter of John of Gaunt) and her second husband, Ralph Neville (d. 1425), Earl of Westmorland.

[3] *CP*, Vol. 12, Pt. 1, Appendix I, "The Sons of John (de la Pole), 2nd Duke of Suffolk, by Elizabeth (of York), Sister of Edward IV and Richard III." The ordering of sons is suggested by this article.

[4] John de la Pole, Earl of Lincoln, was fourth in descent from Philippa de Roet Chaucer while Richard III's competitor for the throne, the Earl of Richmond (Henry VII), was in exactly the same degree of relationship to Philippa's sister, Katherine Swynford. When Henry VII was victorious over Richard III at Bosworth 22 Aug 1485, Katherine became the ancestress of all the future sovereigns of England." Halsted, *The Life of Margaret Beaufort, Countess of Richmond and Derby*, pgs. 135–136.

[5] Because of their royal blood and Yorkist descent, the de la Poles were considered a serious threat to both Henry VII and Henry VIII.

daughter of Richard Scrope,[1] and his wife, Eleanor Washbourne.

- Humphrey de la Pole (b. 1 Aug 1474; d. bef 15 Feb 1513) seems to have had an ecclesiastical career, serving, among other positions, as Rector of Leverington, co. Cambridge, and Prebendary in St. Paul's.
- William de la Pole (b. abt 1478; d. "probably before" 20 Nov 1539, when the male line of his race became extinct") was arrested in 1502 for "alleged complicity" in a projected rebellion and was sent to the Tower. He received a general pardon from Henry VIII on that king's accession but was not released from his imprisonment, dying, "it is said," in the Tower. He had no issue.
- Geoffrey de la Pole, unless confused with his brother, Humphrey.
- Richard de la Pole (d. 24 Feb 1525, Pavia) styled himself the Duke of Suffolk and was called "the White Rose" and "the pretender to the throne." As grandson of Richard, Duke of York, he claimed the crown of England and allied himself with the supportive French king. As a valid threat to the king, he was taken seriously, and he was considered "the King's dreaded enemy." Wolsey had been involved in plans for the abduction or assassination of Richard in 1515. Richard de la Pole died unmarried, in the French defeat at Pavia.

Pearsall states there were four daughters. Catherine, the eldest, married William, Lord Stourton (b. abt 1457; d. 17 Feb 1523/1524[2]), and Elizabeth, the youngest, married Henry Lovel (d. 13 Jun 1489), 2nd (and last) Lord Morley of the Lovel name.[3] Neither had issue. Pearsall states that "around 1539 the male line of the de la Poles became extinct, and with it Geoffrey Chaucer's descendants."[4]

Alice Chaucer, Duchess of Suffolk and granddaughter of

---

[1] Sir Richard Scrope was second son of Henry Scrope, Lord Scrope, of Bolton. (*CP*, Suffolk section)

[2] *CP*, Stourton section.

[3] *DNB*, "Pole, John de la, second Duke of Suffolk (1442–1491)."

[4] Pearsall, *The Life of Geoffrey Chaucer*, pg. 284.

Geoffrey Chaucer, died 20 May 1475 at Ewelme and was buried 9 June at Ewelme Church, which she and her husband had rebuilt, in Oxfordshire. She was one of the first women members of the Order of the Garter. Her tomb of ornately carved alabaster is extant and depicts her wearing the Garter on her left arm.[1]

Geoffrey Chaucer, died 25 October 1400. At the time of his death he was a tenant of Westminster Abbey, having rented a house which was located in the garden of the Lady Chapel, Westminster.[2] As a tenant of the Abbey, he was buried in the Abbey, initially near the door of the Chapel of St. Benedict. According to Pearsall, this area in the church was beginning to be used for the burial of those who had been monastic officials. The *Westminster Abbey: Official Guide*, pg. 93, states that a leaden plate bearing Chaucer's epitaph written by a poet laureate, Sirigonus of Milan, hung on a pillar near his grave, and for 150 years, this was his only memorial. In 1556, Nicholas Brigham, a minor poet, erected a new tomb against the east wall of the south transept. The tomb is extant.

Chaucer continued to be recognized by poets and those who loved poetry. When Edmund Spenser died in 1599, he was at his request buried near Chaucer, and that area of Westminster Abbey came to be known as Poet's Corner.

---

[1] Uden, *A Dictionary of Chivalry*, pg. 47; Beltz, *Memorials of the Most Noble Order of the Garter*, pg. ccxxiii. Alice Chaucer's tomb, as well as those of her father, Thomas Chaucer, and her grandfather, Geoffrey Chaucer, are pictured in Pearsall's *The Life of Geoffrey Chaucer: A Critical Biography*.

[2] The *DNB* notes that Henry VII's Chapel now occupies the space where the Lady Chapel stood.

Some Relations of Poet Geoffrey Chaucer

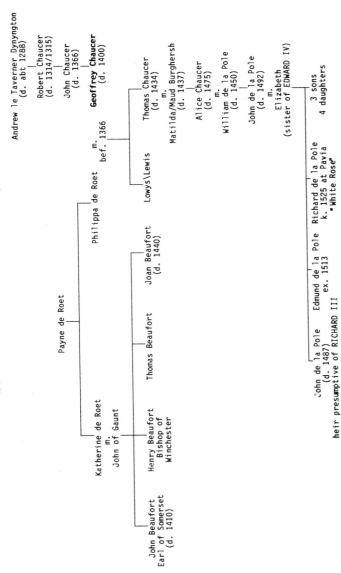

Sources:

Armitage-Smith, Sydney, *John of Gaunt*, Barnes & Noble, Inc., NY, 1964.

Bigham, Hon. Clive, *The Chief Ministers of England 920–1720*, E. P. Dutton and Co., 1923.

Chrimes, Ross, Griffiths, eds., *Fifteenth Century England 1399–1509*, Manchester University Press, NY, 1972.

Chute, Marchette, *Geoffrey Chaucer of England*, E. P. Dutton and Co., 1958.

Clive, Mary, *This Sun of York: A Biography of Edward IV*, Alfred A. Knopf, NY, 1974.

Cokayne, G. E., The Complete Peerage, St. Catherine Press, London, 1912.

Coulton, G. G., *Chaucer and his England*, Russell & Russell, Inc., New York, 1957.

Gardner, John, *The Life and Times of Geoffrey Chaucer*, Alfred A. Knopf, NY, 1977.

Howard, Donald R., *Chaucer: His Life, His Works, His World*, Fawcett Columbine, NY, 1987.

Kerr, Nigel and Mary, *A Guide to Medieval Sites in Britain*, Paladin Grafton Books, London, 1989.

Kingsford, C. L., *Prejudice and Promise in 15th Century England*, Barnes and Noble, NY, 1962.

Metcalfe, Carol A., *Alice Chaucer, Duchess of Suffolk, c1404–1475*.

Pearsall, Derek, *The Life of Geoffrey Chaucer: A Critical Biography*, Blackwell, Oxford UK & Cambridge USA, 1992.

Silva-Vigier, Anil, *This Moste Highe Prince...John of Gaunt 1340–1399*, The Pentland Press, Ltd., Edinburgh, 1992.

Stephen, Sir Leslie, and Lee, Sir Sidney, eds., *Dictionary of National Biography*, Oxford University Press, London, 1964.

Uden, Grant, *A Dictionary of Chivalry*, Thomas Y. Crowell, NY, 1968.

Weis, Frederick Lewis, *Ancestral Roots of Sixty Colonists*, Genealogical Publishing Co., Inc., Baltimore, MD, 1976.

Westminster Abbey: Official Guide, Jarrold and Sons Limited, Norwich, 1988.

Issue of First Marriage of Ralph Neville

Ralph Neville (d. 1425), 1st Earl of Westmorland, is best known in genealogy as the husband of Joan Beaufort, daughter of John of Gaunt.[1] Joan was his second wife and the mother of fourteen of his twenty-three children. Ralph Neville's first wife (m. bef 1370) was Margaret Stafford (d. 9 Jun 1396; bur. Brancepeth, co. Durham[2]), daughter of Hugh de Stafford (b. abt 1342; d. 10 Oct 1386), 2nd Earl of Stafford, and his wife, Philippa de Beauchamp (d. bef 6 Apr 1386). Ralph Neville's issue of his first marriage were "thrown into the shade by the offspring of his more splendid second alliance which brought royal blood into the family."[3]

Issue of **Ralph Neville** and **Margaret Stafford**[4] (nine children):

1 — **John Neville** (b. in or bef 1387; d. bef 20 May 1420)[5] m. (license 29 Aug 1394) **Elizabeth de Holand** (d. 4 Jan 1422/ 1423; bur. Greyfriars, London), daughter of **Thomas de Holand** (d. 1397), Earl of Kent.

1 — **Ralph Neville** of Oversley (d. 26 Feb 1457/1458), second

---

[1] For issue of Ralph Neville and Joan Beaufort, see chapter "The Marriages of John of Gaunt."

[2] *CP*, Westmorland section.

[3] *DNB*, "Neville, Ralph, sixth Baron Neville of Raby and first Earl of Westmorland (1364–1425)."

[4] *DNB*, "Neville, Ralph, sixth Baron Neville of Raby and first Earl of Westmorland (1364–1425)."

[5] *CP*, Neville section, Westmorland section. **John Neville's** son, **Ralph Neville** (b. 1408; d. 1484), became the 2nd Earl of Westmorland.

son; m. **Mary de Ferrers**[1] (b. 1393/bef. 1394; d. 25 Jan 1457/1458), Lady of Oversley, daughter and co-heiress of **Robert de Ferrers** (d. bef 29 Nov 1396), Baron Ferrers of Wem in Shropshire, and his wife, **Joan Beaufort** (d. 13 Nov 1440) (daughter of **John of Gaunt**).

1 — **Mathilda Neville** (d. Oct 1438; bur. church of the Friars Preachers, Scarborough) m. bef 6 Aug 1400 **Peter/Piers de Mauley** (b. abt 1378; d. 6 Sep 1415; bur. St. John's, Bridlington), Lord Mauley, son of **Piers de Mauley** (d. bet. Jan 1377/1378 and Mar 1382/1383) and his wife, **Margery de Sutton**.[2]

1 — **Philippa Neville** (liv. 8 Jul 1353; d. bef her husband) m. **Thomas de Dacre** (b. 27 Oct 1387, Naworth Castle, Brampton, Cumberland; d. 5 Jan 1457/1458; bur. Lanercost Priory), Lord Dacre of Gilsland, son of **William de Dacre** (d. 20 Jul 1399; bur. Lanercost Priory), Lord Dacre.[3]

1 — **Alice Neville** m. (1) **Thomas Grey** of Heton; m. (2) **Gilbert Lancaster**.

1 — **Elizabeth Neville**, a nun.

1 — **Anne Neville** m. **Gilbert Umfreville** of Kyme.

1 — **Margaret Neville** (d. bet. 4 Mar 1463 and 3 Mar 1464; bur. Church of the Austin Friars at Clare, Suffolk) m. (1) bef 31 Dec 1413 **Richard le Scrope** (b. 31 May 1394; d. 29 Aug 1420), Lord le Scrope of Bolton, son of **Roger le Scrope** (d. 3 Dec 1403) and his wife, **Margaret Tibetot** (daughter of **Robert Tibetot** (d. 13 Apr 1372), Lord Tibetot); m. (2) bef 5 Nov 1427 **William Cressener** of Sudbury, Norfolk.[4]

1 — **Anastasia Neville** (prob. d. inf).[5]

---

[1] **Mary de Ferrers'** sister, **Elizabeth de Ferrers**, (b. bef 1395; d. 1434; bur. York), was the Lady of Wem. She married **John de Greystoke** (d. 8 Aug 1436).

[2] *CP*, Mauley section.

[3] *CP*, Dacre section.

[4] *CP*, Scrope section.

[5] *CP*, Westmorland section.

Sources:

Cokayne, G. E., *The Complete Peerage*, St Catherine Press, London, 1912.
Stephen, Sir Leslie, and Lee, Sir Sidney, eds., *Dictionary of National Biography*, Oxford University Press, London, 1964.
Storey, R. L., *End of the House of Lancaster*, Stein and Day, NY, 1967.

The Poles
and the de la Poles

The Poles and the de la Poles were two separate families. The de la Poles were descended from William de la Pole (d. 1329), a merchant of Hull. This family increased their political and social standing by marrying heiresses, the most notable heiress (and last before their downfall) being Elizabeth, sister of Edward IV, King of England. Elizabeth's son, John de la Pole[1] (d. 1487), Earl of Lincoln, was named by Richard III as heir presumptive to the throne, so the climb of approximately 150 years up the social and political ladder almost culminated in the ultimate success.

The Pole family, on the other hand, was descended from Geoffrey Pole (will proved 21 Mar 1474/1475[2]) who married Edith St. John. She was a descendant of Magna Charta Surety, William Malet, and half-sister of Margaret Beaufort, mother of Henry VII.[3]

Both the later de la Poles and Poles could trace their lines back to Richard (ex. 1460), Duke of York: the de la Poles through York's daughter, Elizabeth, and the Poles through York's son, George, Duke of Clarence (of malmsey fame[4]).

---

[1] See chapter, "Some Royal Connections of Poet Geoffrey Chaucer."

[2] *CP*, Salisbury section.

[3] *Sureties* 57. The mother of Edith St. John was Margaret de Beauchamp (d. 1482), who m. (1) Oliver de St. John (d. 1437); (2) John Beaufort (d. 1444), Duke of Somerset; m. (3) Leo/Lionel, Lord Welles (d. 1461). (*CP*, Welles section) See chapter, "The Beaufort Women."

[4] In January 1478, he was tried on charges of high treason, found guilty by his brother, Edward IV, and sentenced to death. It is said he

(continued...)

Both families were persecuted by Henry VII and Henry VIII who saw the royal descendants as threats to their thrones. As a result, both houses had members who were executed for the slightest reasons. [1]

Henry VIII's cruelty seemed to peak with his passion. Cardinal (Reginald) Pole's mother, the Countess of Salisbury, at age sixty-eight was beheaded by Henry, who may very well have been venting his rage with the Cardinal on the old woman: Cardinal Pole would not support Henry's decision to divorce his first queen, Katherine of Aragon, and marry Anne Boleyn.

The threat of the Pole family was felt as late as 1562 by Henry VIII's daughter, Elizabeth I, when Arthur Pole, "conspirator," was found guilty of treason for conspiring to pretend to the crown. His brother Edmund, who encouraged his activities, was also judged a traitor. Both were imprisoned in the Tower, where "probably in 1570" they died.

"It seemed as if the house of York were to be extirpated to secure the Tudor throne." [2]

---

[1] Note the life of Edward, son of George, Duke of Clarence. See chapter, "Edward III."

[2] *DNB*, "Pole, Edmund de la, Earl of Suffolk (1472?-1513)."

The Poles and the de la Poles

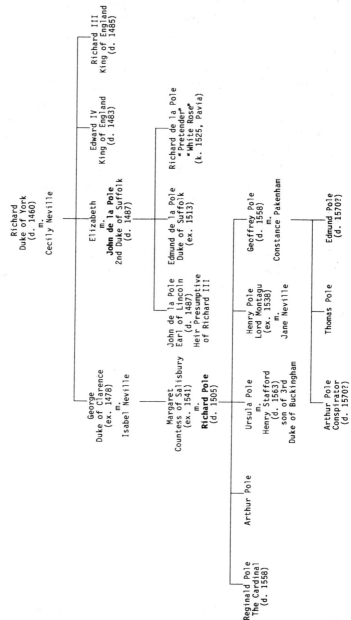

Some Ancestors of the de la Poles

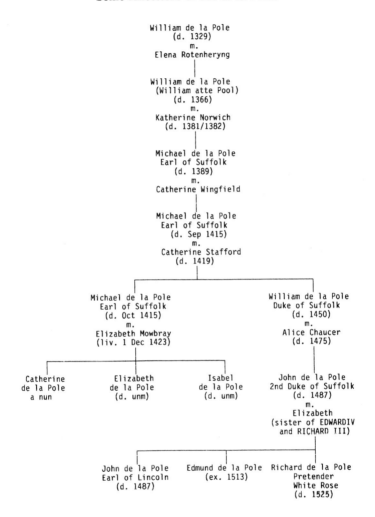

William de la Pole
(d. 1329)
m.
Elena Rotenheryng

William de la Pole
(William atte Pool)
(d. 1366)
m.
Katherine Norwich
(d. 1381/1382)

Michael de la Pole
Earl of Suffolk
(d. 1389)
m.
Catherine Wingfield

Michael de la Pole
Earl of Suffolk
(d. Sep 1415)
m.
Catherine Stafford
(d. 1419)

Michael de la Pole
Earl of Suffolk
(d. Oct 1415)
m.
Elizabeth Mowbray
(liv. 1 Dec 1423)

William de la Pole
Duke of Suffolk
(d. 1450)
m.
Alice Chaucer
(d. 1475)

Catherine
de la Pole
a nun

Elizabeth
de la Pole
(d. unm)

Isabel
de la Pole
(d. unm)

John de la Pole
2nd Duke of Suffolk
(d. 1487)
m.
Elizabeth
(sister of EDWARD IV
and RICHARD III)

John de la Pole
Earl of Lincoln
(d. 1487)

Edmund de la Pole
(ex. 1513)

Richard de la Pole
Pretender
White Rose
(d. 1525)

Sources:

Cheetham, Anthony, *The Life and Times of Richard III*, Cross River Press, New York, 1992.

Cokayne, G. E., *The Complete Peerage*, St Catherine Press, London.

Fuller, Thomas & Freeman, John, *The Worthies of England*, George Allen & Unwin Ltd, London, 1952.

Harris, Barbara J., *Edward Stafford: Third Duke of Buckingham, 1478-1521*, Stanford University Press, Stanford, CA, 1986.

Stephen, Sir Leslie, and Lee, Sir Sidney, eds., *Dictionary of National Biography*, Oxford University Press, London, 1964. Specifically:

DNA, "Pole, Authur (1531-1570?), conspirator."

DNB, "Pole, Edmund de la, Earl of Suffolk (1472?-1513)."

DNB, "Pole, Sir Geoffrey (1502?-1558)."

DNB, "Plantagenet, George, Duke of Clarence (1449-1478)."

DNB, "Pole, Sir Henry, Baron Montague or Montacute (1492?-1539)."

DNB, "Pole, John de la, second Duke of Suffolk (1442-1491)."

DNB, "Pole, Margaret, Countess of Salisbury (1473-1541)."

DNB, "Pole, Michael de la, called in English Michael atte Pool, Earl of Suffolk (1330?-1389)."

DNB, "Pole, Michael de la, second Earl of Suffolk (1361?-1415)."

DNB, "Pole, Reginald (1500-1558), cardinal and archbishop of Canterbury."

DNB, "Pole, Richard de la (d. 1525), pretender to the crown."

DNB, "Pole, Sir William de la, called in English William atte Pool (d. 1366)."

DNB, "Pole, William de la, fourth Earl and first Duke of Suffolk (1396-1450)."

Williams, Neville, *Henry VIII and His Court*, The MacMillan Company, NY, 1971.

Some Ancestors of Anne Boleyn and Elizabeth I

This is one of many lines that lead to **Anne Boleyn** and her daughter, **Elizabeth I the Great**. It contains names of some of the most prominent families in medieval English history.

1 — **Blanche de Brienne**, Lady of Loupeland, daughter of **Jean de Brienne** (d. 1296) and **Jeanne, Dame de Chateau du Loir**, daughter of **Geoffrey IV**, Vicomte de Chateaudun; m. **William de Fiennes** (d. 11 Jul 1302, battle of Courtrai).[1] They were parents of:

2 — **Margaret de Fiennes** (d. 7 Feb 1333/1334) m. abt 1285 **Edmund de Mortimer** (b. 1261; d. 17 Jul 1304; bur. Wigmore), Baron Mortimer of Wigmore. They were parents of:

3 — **Roger de Mortimer** (b. 25 Apr 1287; ex. 29 Nov 1330, Tyburn), Baron of Wigmore, 1st Earl of March; m. **Joan de Geneville** (b. 2 Feb 1285/1286; d. 19 Oct 1356), daughter of **Piers de Geneville** (d. bef 8 Jun 1292).[2] They were parents of:

4 — **Katherine de Mortimer** (d. bet. 4 Aug and 6 Sep 1369[3]; bur. St. Mary's, Warwick) m. aft 22 Feb 1324/1325

---

[1] *Ancestral* 120-31; *CP*, Mortimer section.

[2] *Ancestral* 135-32. The **Genevilles** were descendants of **Magna Charta Surety Hugh Bigod** (d. 1224/1225), Earl of Norfolk, and **Jeanne de Lusignan** (d. 1322/23), a descendant of **Louis VI**, King of France.

[3] *CP*, Warwick section.

(dispensation 19 Apr 1319[1]) **Thomas de Beauchamp**
(b. "probably" 14 Feb 1313/1314, Warwick Castle; d. 13 Nov
1369, of the plague, Calais; bur. St. Mary's, Warwick), a First
Founder K.G., Earl of Warwick.[2] They were parents of:
5 — **William Beauchamp** (b. aft 1344; d. 8 May 1411), Baron
Abergavenny; m. **Joan FitzAlan** (b. 1375; d. 14 Nov 1435[3]),
daughter of **Richard III FitzAlan** (b. 1346; ex. 21 Sep 1397),
Earl of Arundel and Surrey, and **Elizabeth de Bohun** (d. 3 Apr
1385) (daughter of **William de Bohun** (b. 1310/1312; d. Sep
1360) and **Elizabeth de Badlesmere** (b. 1313; d. 1355/
1356)).[4]
6 — **Joan Beauchamp** (d. 3 or 5 Aug 1430; bur. 8 Aug, chapel
of St. Thomas Acon, London) m. abt 28 Aug 1413 as his first
wife **James Butler** (b. abt 1390/1392; d. 23 Aug 1452), Earl of
Ormond, The White Earl.[5] They were parents of:
7 — **Thomas Butler** (d. 3 Aug 1515), 7th Earl of Ormond;
m. (1) unknown.[6] They were parents of:
8 — **Margaret Butler** (b. 1465; d. bet. 30 Sep 1539 and
20 Mar 1539/1540) m. 1485 **William Boleyn**. They were
parents of:
9 — **Thomas Boleyn** (b. abt 1477; d. 12 Mar 1538/1539,
Hever, Kent)), Earl of Wiltshire, Earl of Ormond[7]; m. by
1506 **Elizabeth Howard**[8] (d. 3 Apr 1537, Abbot of Reading's

---

[1] According to the *CP*, Warwick section, "the marriage was planned
to end a feud between the Beauchamp and Mortimer families."
[2] *CP*, Warwick section.
[3] *CP*, Abergavenny section.
[4] *Ancestral* 15-30; Tauté; *Ancestral* 15-30, 31; 65-34. **William de
Bohun** (d. Sep 1360) was son of **Humphrey VIII de Bohun**
(d. 1321/1322), Earl of Hereford and Essex, and his wife (m. 1302)
Elizabeth Plantagenet (d. 1316), daughter of **Edward I**, KING OF
ENGLAND.
[5] *Ancestral* 120-36, 7-33.
[6] *Ancestral* 120-37, 38.
[7] *Ancestral* 120-39.
[8] *Ancestral* 22-36. Lofts in *Anne Boleyn*, pg. 11, states, "Of Anne's
early life so little is known that there is argument even about whether her
(continued...)

Palace beside Baynard's Castle), daughter of **Thomas Howard,** 2nd Duke of Norfolk, and his wife, **Elizabeth Tylney** (daughter of **Frederick Tylney**).[1] Issue:

> 10 — **George Boleyn** (ex. 17 May 1536, as part of **Henry VIII's** plot to rid himself of his queen, **Anne Boleyn**; bur. Chapel of St. Peter ad Vincula, Tower of London), Viscount Rochford; m. in or bef 1526 **Jane Parker** (ex. 13 Feb 1541/1542, Tower Green) with **Henry VIII's** fifth queen, **Katherine Howard**), daughter of **Henry Parker**, Lord Marley, and his wife **Alice St. John** (daughter of **John St. John** of Bletsoe).[2]

> 10 — **Mary Boleyn** (d. 30 Jul 1543), older daughter, mistress of **Henry VIII**, KING OF ENGLAND, before the king noticed her younger sister, **Anne**; m. 31 Jan 1520/1521 **William Cary** (b. abt 1495; d. 22 Jun 1528, of sweating sickness), a gentleman of the Privy Chamber to the **Henry VIII**.

> 10 — **Anne Boleyn** (b. "probably" 1501 or 1502, Blicking Hall, Norfolk or Hever Castle, Kent; ex. 19 May 1536, Tower of London; bur. Chapel Royal of St. Peter ad Vincula, Tower of London[3]), QUEEN OF ENGLAND; m. (div. 17 May 1536) 25 Jan 1533 as his second wife **Henry VIII**, KING OF ENGLAND. Surviving issue:

>> 11 — **Elizabeth I** (b. 7 Sep 1533, Greenwich Palace; crowned 15 Jan 1559, Westminster Abbey; d. 24 Mar 1603, Richmond Palace; bur. Westminster Abbey[4]), the Virgin QUEEN OF ENGLAND, never married. No issue.

---

[8] (...continued)
mother died when she was a child, or whether she outlived her by two years. What evidence there is—a sentence in a letter and a few words on a tombstone, suggest that Elizabeth Howard lived on until 1538, and that the stepmother of humble origin is part of the myth."

[1] *CP*, Ormond section.
[2] *CP*, Ormond section.
[3] *KQB*, pg. 121.
[4] *KQB*, pg. 130.

Sources:

Cokayne, G. E., *The Complete Peerage*, St Catherine Press, London.

Lofts, Norah, *Anne Boleyn*, Coward, McCann & Geoghegan, Inc., NY, 1979.

Starkey, David, ed., *Rivals in Power: Lives and Letters of the Great Tudor Dynasties*, Grove Weidenfeld, New York, 1990.

Stephen, Sir Leslie, and Lee, Sir Sidney, eds., *Dictionary of National Biography*, Oxford University Press, London, 1964. Specifically:
DNB, "Boleyn, George, Viscount Rochford (d. 1536)."
DNB, "Boleyn, Sir Thomas, Earl of Wiltshire (1447–1539)."

Tauté, Anne, compiler, *Kings and Queens of Great Britain* wall chart, 1990.

Weis, Frederick Lewis, *Ancestral Roots of Sixty Colonists*, 6th ed., Genealogical Publishing Co., Inc., 1990.

Williams, Neville, *All the Queen's Men: Elizabeth I and Her Courtiers*, The MacMillan Company, New York, 1972.

Williamson, David, *Debrett's Kings and Queens of Britain*, Dorset Press, New York, 1992.

Events and Instances

The Papal Prohibition of the Marriage of William the Conqueror

The exact date of the marriage of William the Conqueror, Duke of Normandy, and Matilda of Flanders is not known. It is believed to have occurred between 1050 and the end of 1053, when Matilda appears on a charter as William's consort.[1] It is known that the marriage was considered in or before 1049 and was forbidden by Pope Leo IX on the grounds that the couple was "within the forbidden degrees."[2] It is not known whether William and Matilda were within the prohibited degrees of consanguinity (blood relationship) or affinity (relationship by marriage).[3] The exact relationship that caused that response from the Pope has been surmised in several forms.

A relationship would be brought about by the second marriage of Matilda's grandfather, Baldwin IV of Flanders, who by his first marriage to Ogiva[4] was grandfather of Matilda. His second marriage was to the sister[5] of Duke

---

[1] Douglas, *William the Conqueror*, pg. 391.

[2] Douglas, *William the Conqueror*, pg. 392.

[3] Bush in *Memoirs of the Queens of France*, pg. 96, uses the term *spiritually allied* or *spiritual alliance* in describing the relationship wherein Robert, King of France, having stood as godfather to Bertha's child by her previous marriage, was considered *spiritually allied* to Bertha. He later married Bertha but was forced to dissolve the marriage because the laws of the church did not permit marriage between two who were spiritually allied. See chapter, "The Interdict."

[4] Ogiva was daughter of Richard, duke of the Ardennes. (Douglas, *William the Conqueror*, pg. 393)

[5] Butler, *1066: The Story of a Year*, Tables 4 and 7, show her name as Eleanor.

Robert I (father of William) and created an affinity between William and Matilda. Douglas states, "This marriage, if it occurred, might perhaps have been made to serve as a reason for the ban."

A Possible Relationship Between William and Matilda

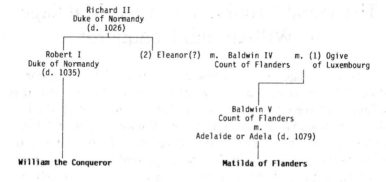

Previté-Orton, Table 13, indicates a marriage between Richard III (d. 1027), Duke of Normandy and brother of William's father, and Adelaide/Adela, daughter of Robert II the Pious (King of France), and mother of Matilda of Flanders. This marriage (or contract of marriage) would have brought about a relationship between William and Matilda. However, Douglas[1] states that it has not been proven that there was a contract of marriage between Duke Richard and Adelaide/Adela and that had there been a marriage, the bride would have been too young to consummate the marriage in the Duke's lifetime.

A Second Possible Relationship
Between William and Matilda

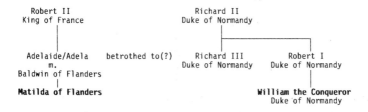

```
    Robert II                      Richard II
  King of France                 Duke of Normandy
       |                               |
       |                      _____|_____
       |                     |                   |
  Adelaide/Adela  betrothed to(?)  Richard III      Robert I
       m.                    Duke of Normandy   Duke of Normandy
 Baldwin of Flanders                                    |
       |                                                |
 Matilda of Flanders                           William the Conqueror
                                                Duke of Normandy
```

Another possible relationship might exist in the two daughters of Robert II the Pious, King of France. The names of these two daughters are difficult to separate and agree upon. The *KQE*[2] mentions simply "2 das" as female issue of Robert II the Pious. Douglas names the mother of Matilda of Flanders and the wife of Baldwin V as *Adela*. Bush[3] names the two daughters of Robert II as *Adele*, who married Robert, Duke of Normandy (or Robert-le-Diable), and *Adelaide*, who married Baldwin V. Previté-Orton refers to the wife of Baldwin V of Flanders as *Adelaide*. *Ancestral* 163-22 and 162-22 names Baldwin V's wife *Adele of France*. Stuart[4] names the wife of Baldwin V as *Adele* and *Adela*. Though the names differ, the

[1] Douglas, *William the Conqueror*, pg. 392.
[2] *KQE*, pg. 65.
[3] Bush, *Memoirs of the Queens of France*, pg. 106.
[4] Stuart, *Royalty for Commoners*, 73-33 and 140-32.

point is, they were sisters, and one married Baldwin V, father
of Matilda, and the other is said to have married Duke Robert,
father of William. If there were a marriage between Duke
Robert and the sister of Baldwin V's wife, it would have put
William and Matilda within the forbidden degrees of
consanguinity and could have been the cause of the papal
prohibition of their marriage.

Another Possible Relationship
Between William and Matilda

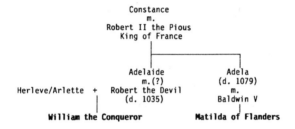

Despite the ban and the close degree of consanguinity or
affinity ("if it existed"[1]), William and Matilda married, and
Douglas remarks that "the ecclesiastical opposition to the match
must have sensibly increased the difficulties of Duke William
within his own duchy."

Finally, in 1059, Pope Nicholas II removed the ban to
William's marriage under the condition that the husband and
wife would found and support a monastic house at Caen.
Matilda founded the Abbey of the Holy Trinity (the Abbaye-
aux-Dames), a twin with William's Abbey of St. Stephen (the
Abbaye-aux-Hommes).

---

[1] Douglas, *William the Conqueror*, pg. 76.

The Iron Cutters

It is said by chroniclers that on 14 October 1066, Ivo de Taillefer, Norman troubadour, having crossed the channel from Normandy into England with Duke William's invading forces, asked William if he might lead the first charge against the Englishmen. Granted his request, Taillefer brandished his sword overhead, raised his voice in inspiring songs of Charlemagne and Roland, and spurred his mount forward up the hill to the place where Harold's army waited. A Latin poem on the battle of Hastings was written by Guy, Bishop of Amiens, and in it he mentioned this minstrel, whom he named as Incisor Ferri, who "continued singing and juggling with his sword until he was slain" by Harold's army. [1]

On 6 June 1944, Dwight David Eisenhower, having offered simply with his presence his own songs of war, commanded the fighting men who crossed the channel from England to attack the beaches of Normandy.

Some historians state that the instance with Ivo de Taillefer never actually happened, that it was a myth. One would like to think this incident was, in fact, true, if only because of the coincidence of the names involved: Taillefer (or Incisor Ferri) and Eisenhower—they translate to Iron Cutter: he who hews an army to pieces.

Sources:

Bruce, John Collingwood, *The Bayeux Tapestry: The Battle of Hastings and the Norman Conquest*, Dorset Press, New York, 1987.
Camp, Anthony J., *My Ancestors Came with the Conqueror: Those Who*

---

[1] Camp, *My Ancestors Came with the Conqueror*, pg. 19.

Did and Some of Those Who Probably Did Not, Genealogical
    Publishing Co., Inc., 1990.
Douglas, David C., *William the Conqueror*, University of California
    Press, Berkeley & L.A., 1964.
Grand LaRousse Encyclopedia, Librairie Larousse, Paris, 1964.
Llewellyn, Sam, *Small Parts in History*, Barnes & Noble Books, New
    York, 1985.
Mansion, J. E., *Harrap's Standard French and English Dictionary*,
    Harrap, London, 1989.
Wahrig, Gerhard, *Das Grosse Deutsche Wörterbuch*, Bertelsmann
    Lexikon-Verlag, Gütersloh, 1968.
Webster's Biographical Dictionary, G. & C. Merriam Co., Publishers,
    Springfield, Mass., 1962.

The Death of William Rufus

William Rufus was crowned William II, King of England, on 26 September 1087 in Westminster Abbey. He was the third (second surviving) and reportedly favorite son of William I the Conqueror, King of England, and his wife, Matilda of Flanders. It was his father's decision to leave the crown of England to William. To his oldest son, Robert Curthose, he left the Duchy of Normandy. Henry, the youngest son, received money.

William Rufus ruled almost thirteen years. His style of living required large amounts of money, and, more often than not, that money came from church revenues. He earned the contempt of the churches and churchmen; and the monastic writers, believing that William Rufus abused the churches, left poor character references of him. William of Malmesbury, a Benedictine monk, wrote of the king's abuse of the church, adding that "he did nothing that was not bad." The Anglo-Saxon Chronicle describes Rufus' rule as "harsh and fierce" and states that "everything that was hateful to God and to righteous man was the daily practice in this land during his reign. Therefore he was hated by almost all his people and abhorrent to God."[1] Their opinions of Rufus have been instrumental in establishing him as a poor king and ruler. Though he was an able soldier and a capable administrator, he cared more for his power, comforts, and pleasure than he did for the welfare of his people.

On a late afternoon in August 1100, William Rufus, his brother Henry, and a small group of men went deer hunting in the New Forest. With them was the chief huntsman, a man who

---

[1] Hallam, *The Plantagenet Encyclopedia*, pgs. 208–209.

knew the area and whose job it was to accompany the king during the hunt. Beaters circled through the forest, scaring the deer ahead of them toward the clearing where the huntsmen were positioned. As a deer entered the clearing, an arrow was released. It hit William Rufus in the chest, killing him. The arrow was commonly believed to have come from the bow of Walter Tirel, who was hunting nearby.[1] Tirel, knowing he would be blamed for killing the king, raced to his horse and fled. He would later state on his death-bed, "invoking God's judgment on his soul, that he was innocent of the deed."[2]

William Rufus's body was loaded onto a cart and taken back to camp. The next day it was carried into Winchester where he was buried "out of reverence for the regal dignity"[3] in the cathedral but "with little ceremony."[4] The *DNB* adds, "...no religious service accompanied or followed the burial." It is said that the clergy refused him the last rites.

Many believe the king's death was an accident. However, others believe Henry was involved in a conspiracy to murder his brother and secure the throne. It has been suggested by some historians that almost any one of his subjects would have been glad to kill Rufus. There was, however, never a serious investigation into his death. "When such an evident sinner perished, there was no need at all to look beyond the avenging hand of God."[5]

Today a small obelisk called the Rufus Stone marks the spot in the New Forest where the king fell.

---

[1] *DNB*, "Tirel or Tyrrell, Walter."

[2] Barlow, *William Rufus*, pg. 424.

[3] *DNB*, "William II (d. 1100), king of England."

[4] *KQB*, pg. 47; Cannon and Griffiths, *Oxford Illustrated History of the British Monarchy*, pg. 656.

[5] Barlow, *William Rufus*, pg. 425.

Sources:

Barlow, Frank, *William Rufus*, University of California Press, Berkeley and Los Angeles, 1983.

Cannon, John & Griffiths, Ralph, *The Oxford Illustrated History of the British Monarchy*, Oxford University Press, Oxford and NY, 1988.

Delderfield, Eric R., *Kings and Queens of England and Great Britain*, Taplinger Publishing Co., NY, 1970.

Grinnel-Milne, Duncan, *The Killing of William Rufus: An Investigation in the New Fortest*, Augustus M. Kelley Publishers, NY, 1968.

Hallam, Elizabeth, ed., *The Plantagenet Encyclopedia*, Grove Weidenfeld, NY, 1990.

Morris, Jean, *The Monarchs of England*, Charterhouse, NY, 1975.

Seymour, William, *Sovereign Legacy*, Doubleday & Co., Inc., Garden City, NY, 1980.

Stephen, Sir Leslie, and Lee, Sir Sidney, eds., *Dictionary of National Biography*, Oxford University Press, London, 1964.

Williamson, David, *Debrett's Kings and Queens of Britain*, Dorset Press, New York, 1992.

The Wreck of the *White Ship*

In 1120, Henry I, King of England, "the Lion of Justice," despite having a large number of illegitimate children, had legitimate issue of only a son, William (b. 1103), and a daughter, Matilda, more often known as Matilda FitzEmpress or the Empress Matilda. Some historians add a second son, Richard, whom other historians treat as illegitimate issue.[1]

William was commonly called William Audelin or the Atheling (the Prince) because his mother, Edith Matilda of Scotland, was of the old English blood royal. He was recognized as his father's heir by the Norman barons in 1115 and by the English in 1116. He was betrothed in February 1113 to the young daughter of Fulk V, Count of Anjou, and they were married in Lisieux in Normandy in June 1119.

As a future duke of Normandy, William the Atheling owed homage to Louis VI, King of France, an obligation he fulfilled in 1120, and in November of that year, he was in Barfleur with his father, preparing to sail home to England. On the evening of the 25th, William the Atheling sailed in a new ship that had been built by Thomas FitzStephen and was first offered as a gift to Henry, who requested that it be offered to his son.

Henry's ship sailed safely across the Channel, but William's ship was wrecked off Barfleur and all drowned, save one man, whose tale is the only story we have for the accident. Ordericus Vitalis identifies him as Berold, butcher of Rouen, adding that he was the poorest man of the company and wore a sheepskin

---

[1] "Henry's benefactions to the Church caused the monkish historians to palliate his sins and to find excuses for his lust...." (CP, Vol. 11, Appendix D, pg. 121)

dress, which kept him alive throughout the cold night of the wreck.

According to the witness, the passengers and crew of the *White Ship* (*Blanche-Nef*) had been "drinking and making merry." The ship hit a rock in the waters outside Barfleur and sank. Though the Atheling was safely put into a small boat and rowed away from the wreck, he insisted on returning to save his half-sister, the Countess of Perche, whose cries he had heard. Everyone swam to his boat, overcrowded it, and it sank. The Atheling drowned with them. The pilot of the ship heard of the loss of the Atheling, "abandoned himself to his fate," and sank to his death. The one survivor was rescued the following day.

No one dared be the bearer of such news to the king. According to Ordericus Vitalis, a plan was devised whereby "a boy threw himself at the king's feet, weeping bitterly; and upon his being questioned as to the cause of his sorrow, the king learnt from him the shipwreck of the *Blanche-Nef*" and the loss of his son and heir. Many other relatives and friends were lost to Henry, including his illegitimate(?) son, Richard, and his illegitimate daughter, Matilda, Countess of Perche.

In 1122, Henry, still hoping for male issue, married Adeliza/Adelaide of Louvain, daughter of Geoffrey, Count of Louvain. By December 1126, when there still was no issue of the marriage, Henry designated his daughter, Matilda FitzEmpress, as his heir and married her to Geoffrey Plantagenet, Count of Anjou and Maine, two unpopular moves that, upon Henry's death, threw England into nineteen years of civil war, undoing his years of strong government and royal justice.

Sources:

Cokayne, G. E., *The Complete Peerage*, St Catherine Press, London, Vol. 11, Appendix D, pg. 121.

Delderfield, Eric R., *Kings and Queens of England and Great Britain*, Weathervane Books, New York, 1972.

Hallam, Elizabeth, ed., *The Plantagenet Encyclopedia*, Grove Weidenfeld, NY, 1990.

Innes, Arthur D., ed., *A Source Book of English History for the Use of Schools*, Vol. I, Cambridge at the University Press, 1912.

Stephen, Sir Leslie, and Lee, Sir Sidney, eds., *Dictionary of National Biography*, Oxford University Press, London, 1964.

Williamson, David, *Debrett's Kings and Queens of Britain*, Dorset Press, New York, 1992.

"A Time When Christ and His Saints Slept"

The story of the rivalry between Stephen and his cousin, the Empress Matilda, for the crown of England might be considered a romantic and colorful episode of English history had not it had such a devastating effect on the country. In reality, it was a family feud that affected and infected the country with lawlessness, starvation, cruelty, and death. Those that suffered the most were the innocent common people.

The Empress Matilda (she was widow of the German Emperor Henry V) was the only surviving legitimate issue of Henry I, King of England, and his queen, Matilda of Scotland. As such, she had been chosen by her father as heir to his throne, and three times he had had the barons swear to accept and support her as their ruler. Yet when Henry died on 1 Dec 1135, the Empress Matilda's cousin, Stephen of Blois (one of those who had promised to accept her as Henry's heir), hurried to England and claimed the crown in right of the fact that he was Henry's favorite nephew and the grandson of William the Conqueror. Stephen was a charming and gallant man, and the people of London accepted him. Many of the barons decided to support him and, therefore, broke their oaths, saying that the oaths the support Matilda had been extracted from them against their will and, furthermore, they did not want to be ruled by a woman. Too, they knew that if Matilda came to the throne, her husband, Geoffrey of Anjou, would be in the position of king, and this was not acceptable situation to the English barons. They, therefore, supported Stephen and at Christmastime 1135 in Westminster Abbey, saw him crowned King of England.

In 1139, the Empress Matilda, supported by the barons who

honored their oaths to Henry, arrived in England to challenge Stephen, and for the remainder of Stephen's reign there was civil war in England between the two factions. Stephen was so involved in defending his throne, he had no time or resources to maintain the laws of the land, and men made their own laws, robbed, abused, and killed their neighbors, tortured passersby for the little gold they might be carrying, and in general wreaked havoc across the country. Livestock and crops were stolen or destroyed, and people starved. As charming as Stephen might have been, he proved an inept and ineffectual ruler. One author describes Stephen as having been "miscast as king" and writes, "He reigned, but did not rule." [1] His queen, Matilda of Boulogne, was a great aid to him and served as leader of his army when he was captured by the Empress Matilda. Queen Matilda negotiated for her husband's release, and the Empress Matilda, who actually had the victory (and the crown) in her pocket, agreed (for whatever reason) to return the queen's husband to her in exchange for her own illegitimate half-brother and commander, Robert, Earl of Gloucester.

The story reads like a game of chess, the king and queen being cornered or captured, being protected by the knights, the chase continuing, and the common people, like pawns, being sacrificed in the struggle to win the contest for the crown.

The Empress Matilda lost her brother and commander, Robert of Gloucester, and retired to Normandy, and her son Henry (now aged 21, who had been two years old when Stephen was crowned) crossed to England to state his claim to the throne. In 1153, the Treaty of Westminster was signed, by which it was agreed that Stephen would continue to rule until his death and that the Empress Matilda's son, Henry, would be his heir to the throne.

The following year, on 25 Oct 1154, Stephen died, ending a reign that had been described in the *Anglo-Saxon Chronicle* as a time when "Christ and his saints slept." Henry succeeded with no opposition and in Westminster Abbey on 19 Dec 1154 was crowned Henry II.

---

[1] Andrews, *Kings & Queens of England & Scotland*, pgs. 38–39.

The first years of Henry II's reign were spent in restoring peace to England. The Empress Matilda stayed in Normandy, living near Rouen. Her last 13 years were spent in good works: she founded several religious houses, was a benefactress to hospitals, churches, and monasteries, and in her last will arranged for a distribution of her wealth to the poor.

The table illustrates the family connections among the principle players in the wars of Stephen's reign.

Principle Players in the Wars of Stephen's Reign

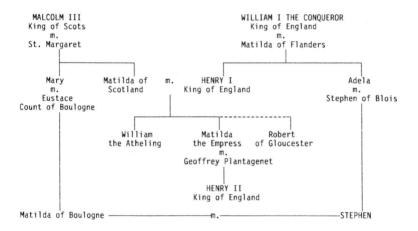

Sources:

Davis, R. H. C., *King Stephen 1135-1154*, Longman, London, 1980.
Potter, Jeremy, *Pretenders: Claimants to the Throne*, Constable, London, 1987.
Stephen, Sir Leslie, and Lee, Sir Sidney, eds., *Dictionary of National Biography*, Oxford University Press, London, 1964. Specifically: *DNB*, "Matilda, Maud, Mold, Aethelic, Aaliz (1102-1167)."
Williamson, David, *Debrett's Kings and Queens of Britain*, Dorset Press, New York, 1992.

Twice Crowned But Never King

Henry the Young King was the second son of Henry II and Eleanor of Aquitaine, but after the death in 1156 of his older brother, William, he became the recognized heir to the throne of England.

He was betrothed as an infant in September 1158 to Margaret, daughter of Louis VII of France and his second wife, Constance of Castile (d. 1160).[1] Margaret was about six months old at that time.[2] They were married at Neubourg 2 Nov 1160 at the command of Henry II in order that he might gain control of the French lands that were Margaret's dowry. At the time of the marriage, Margaret was about two years old; Henry was about five.[3] Young Henry was afterward placed in the care of Thomas Becket, his father's chancellor, until 1162 or 1163, when he received the fealty of his father's barons and the homage of the Welsh princes and the king of Scots. He did homage himself for the lands he held under the French king.

As early as 1162, Henry II had planned to have the young Henry crowned king in order to guarantee the succession of his heir. There were two probable reasons for this decision. First, Henry II's mother, daughter of Henry I, had received the fealty of her father's barons and their recognition of her as his heir. Yet, uncrowned and unannointed, she was abandoned by many who preferred not to be ruled by a woman. They favored, instead, her cousin, Stephen, who usurped the Crown on the

---

[1] See chapter, "The Marriages of Louis VII of France."

[2] Moore, *The Young King, Henry Plantagenet (1155–1183)*, pg. 30.

[3] Kelly, *Eleanor of Aquitaine and the Four Kings*, pgs. 105–106, wherein Margaret's birthdate is given as "early in 1158."

death of his uncle, the king.[1] Second, there were no solid
traditions of primogeniture at that time, that is, the oldest son
did not necessarily have the right or expectancy to inherit.
Henry II was concerned that on his death there should be a
smooth and peaceful transition of the crown from his head to
his son's. Thus, the coronation of young Henry was planned.[2]

The see of Canterbury at this time was vacant and it was
this see that held the right to crown an English king. Becket
was appointed to fill the see in June 1162, but the schism that
developed between the king and the Archbishop resulted in the
delay of the coronation.

Henry pulled political strings and on 14 Jun 1170[3] at
Westminster, young Henry was crowned by the Archbishop of
York. The royal accounts attest to the expense of the regalia of
the prince and the celebratory feasts.[4] At the coronation

---

[1] Lodge, *The Genealogy of the British Peerage*, pg. 2.

[2] Stephen, Henry I's predecessor, had attempted to secure the
succession for his own son, Eustace, in 1152. Even in an age when
primogeniture (the right of the first-born to inherit) was not yet
established in England, this was an innovative idea which met the
resistance of the church: neither the Archbishop of Canterbury nor the
Pope would crown a successor while the king lived. Stephen was
eventually forced to treat with Henry and to make Henry his successor.
This was a move that cut Stephen's son from the succession, and Eustace
pitched a royal fit across Cambridgeshire, "ravaging the countryside on
every hand," until in August he came to the monastery at Bury
St. Edmunds. Though received with honour, Eustace demanded money
from the monastery to pay his soldiers. When it was denied, he ravaged
their lands and crops. A week later, Eustace was suddenly dead,
apparently from something he had eaten. The chronicler, Gervase of
Canterbury, in the manner of the day, ascribed the death as being the
vengeance of St. Edmund. (Appleby, *The Troubled Reign of King
Stephen 1135-1154*, pgs. 190-191; Ross, *The Monarchy of Britain*,
pg. 19; Piper, *Kings & Queens of England and Scotland*, pg. 41;
Andrews, *Kings and Queens of England & Scotland*, pgs. 38-39)

[3] Moore, *The Young King, Henry Plantagenet (1155-1183)*, pg. 5.
Warren, *Henry II*, pg. 111, gives the date of the ceremony as 24 May
1170.

[4] Kelly, *Eleanor of Aquitaine and the Four Kings*, pg. 143.

banquet, the king himself, as if to underline the new status of his son, served at the Young King's table. The Archbishop of York is credited with remarking to young Henry that it was a rare honor for a Prince to be served by a king, whereupon young Henry returned that it was not so remarkable for the son of a count to serve the son of a king. [1]

Two years later, on 27 Aug 1172 at Winchester, at the insistence of Louis VII, who wanted to see his daughter secure in her position as future queen, there was a second coronation. Margaret was crowned queen and Henry, beside her, was again crowned king. [2]

Over the course of the next eleven years, the Young King, desiring and denied his own lands to maintain himself and his queen in what he felt was proper estate, was in and out of opposition with his father, who, it seemed, was determined to keep his son dependant on him.

Henry II had had his sons recognized in their lordships in order that there might be peaceful succession after his death. Now the sons wanted to rule these lands and to profit from them financially. Henry II saw that the Young King showed "neither taste nor desire for responsibility." After the Young King's coronation, attempts had been made to involve and train him in the duties that would be expected and required of him, but "administration bored him." [3]

Each time his father refused him lands to rule, the young Henry would fly to the court of the French king, who delighted in playing son against father. In his last revolt, the "selfish, faithless, unprincipled" son took his fury out on the common people, the monastery of Grandmont, and the shrines of Rocamadour and while doing so was "struck down by fever." On 11 Jun 1183, he died, penitent, dressed in a hair-shirt and lying on a bed of ashes. His life has been described as one of

---

[1] Kelly, *Eleanor of Aquitaine and the Four Kings*, pg. 143; Meade, *Eleanor of Aquitaine: A Biography*, pg. 263. Henry I was the son of Matilda FitzEmpress and Geoffrey Plantagenet, Count of Anjou.

[2] Kelly, *Eleanor of Aquitaine and the Four Kings*, pg. 170.

[3] Warren, *Henry II*, pgs. 117–118, 580–581.

"the meanest ingratitude" and "the basest perfidy" and his
popularity ascribed to his "princely liberality."[1] "He had the
sort of charm that makes even gross irresponsibility seem
nothing more than the mischievousness of a lively boy."[2]

In accordance with his wishes, his eyes, brains, and
intestines were buried in the monastery of St. Martial, and his
body was taken for burial to the cathedral church of Rouen.

In transit, the body was seized by the people of Le Mans,
who buried it in their own cathedral, perhaps because of the
revenue and patronage his tomb might bring to the church. The
people of Rouen, equally desirous of having the Young King's
tomb in their church, threatened to take the body by force.
Henry II intervened and ordered that the body be moved to
Rouen for burial as his son had requested.

The Young King and his wife, Margaret, had one child who
was born and died in 1177.

Sources:

Andrews, Allen, *Kings & Queens of England & Scotland*, Marshall
    Cavendish Publications Limited, London, 1976.
Appleby, John T., *The Troubled Reign of King Stephen 1135–1154*,
    Barnes & Noble Books, New York, 1995.
Barber, Richard, *The Devil's Crown: Henry II, Richard I, John*, British
    Broadcasting Corporation, London, 1978.
Kelly, Amy, *Eleanor of Aquitaine and the Four Kings*, Harvard
    University Press, Cambridge, Mass., 1950.
Lodge, Edmund, *The Genealogy of the Existing British Peerage*,
    Saunders & Otley, London, 1832.
Meade, Marion, *Eleanor of Aquitaine: A Biography*, Hawthorn Books,
    Inc., New York, 1977.
Moore, Olin H., Ph.D., *The Young King, Henry Plantagenet
    (1155–1183), in History, Literature and Tradition*, The Ohio State
    University: University Studies, Vol. II, No. 12, Columbus, Ohio,
    1924.

---

[1] Moore, *The Young King, Henry Plantagenet (1155–1183)*,
pgs. 26, 25.
[2] Warren, *King John*, pg. 31.

Piper, David, *Kings & Queens of England and Scotland*, The Leisure Circle Limited, Middlesex, 1980.

Ross, Josephine, *The Monarchy of Britain*, William Morrow and Company, Inc., NY, 1982.

Stephen, Sir Leslie, and Lee, Sir Sidney, eds., *Dictionary of National Biography*, Oxford University Press, London, 1964.

Warren, W. L., *Henry II*, University of California Press, Berkeley and Los Angeles, 1973

Warren, W. L., *King John*, University of California Press, Berkeley, 1978.

Rosamunde: Rose of the World

Rosamunde, beloved mistress of Henry II, King of England, was daughter of the Norman knight, Walter de Clifford (d. perhaps 1190) of Bredelais on the Welsh border, and his wife, Margaret, believed to have been the daughter of Ralph de Tony.

It is uncertain when Rosamunde became the mistress of Henry. Given-Wilson and Curteis suggest it may have been 1173, the same year that Henry imprisoned Eleanor, his queen, for intriguing with her sons against her husband. At that time, Henry was living openly with Rosamunde, and Giraldus Cambrensis[1] wrote that while some called her *Rosa-mundi*, Rose of the World, she was actually *Rosa-immundi*, the Rose of Unchastity.

In 1176, Rosamunde died of an illness—not, as some legends have it, by the hand of Queen Eleanor, who was locked away at the time. She was buried in Godstow Nunnery, which received gifts from Osbert FitzHugh ("apparently" Rosamunde's brother-in-law), Walter de Clifford (her father), and Henry, who ordered that a shrine be erected to her.[2]

The chroniclers report that in 1191, while visiting Godstow, St. Hugh, Bishop of Lincoln, found Rosamunde's tomb "set in

---

[1] Giraldus Cambrensis was the literary name of Giraldus de Barri (1146?-1220), Welsh historian, geographer, and ecclesiastical scholar. In 1176, he was elected to the bishopic of St. David's but was rejected by Henry. His 1196 election to the same position was rejected by the Archbishop of Canterbury. His father was Norman; and his mother was "a princess of the Welsh royal family." (*Webster's Biographical Dictionary*, "Giraldus or Gerald de Barri")

[2] Warren, *Henry II*, pg. 119.

the middle of the church choir before the altar, and adorned with silken hangings, lamps, and waxen candles." Amazed that such a harlot should be so buried, he ordered her body to be moved outside the church, "lest virtuous women, beholding her burial place decked like a shrine, should be led to fear not at all the consequence of sin."[1] The body was probably moved to the chapter-house. The tomb's inscription reportedly read,

> Hic jacet in tumulo Rosa mundi non Rosa munda:
> Non redolet sed olet quæ redolere solet.

Montgomery[2] offers a translation:

> This tomb doth here enclose
> The world's most beauteous Rose—
> Rose passing sweet erewhile,
> Now nought but odor vile.

Meade[3] offers a less reverent translation:

> Here lies the rose of the world, not a clean rose;
> She no longer smells rosy, so hold your nose.

Her grave seems to have remained undisturbed until the Reformation when "Rosamunde's tumbe at Godstowe nunnery was taken up a-late. It is a stone with this inscription, 'Tumba Rosamunde.'" According to a later report, "this stone was broken into pieces; but tradition still pointed out 'her stone coffin....'"[4]

The historical facts have spawned various fictional accounts of Eleanor's vengeance, including the story of how Eleanor, following a silken thread caught on Henry's boot, found Rosamunde's Woodstock residence hidden away in a bower or

---

[1] Kelly, *Eleanor of Aquitaine*, pg. 151.
[2] Montgomery, *The Leading Facts of English History*, pg. 94.
[3] Meade, *Eleanor of Aquitaine*, pg. 236.
[4] *DNB*, "Clifford, Rosamond (Fair Rosamond)(d. 1176?)."

labyrinth and how she caused Rosamunde to bleed to death in a hot bath or killed her with a dagger or poisoned cup.

"Rosamunde was undoubtedly Henry II's favourite mistress, but she was not his only one. He was the father of at least three illegitimate children, and it is very unlikely that Rosamunde was the mother of any of them."[1]

However, "there was no one to match her in his affections...." Rosamunde had been the great love in Henry's life.[2]

Sources:

Given-Wilson, Chris & Curteis, Alice, *The Royal Bastards of Medieval England*, Routledge & Kegan Paul, London, 1984.

Hallam, Elizabeth, ed., *The Plantagenet Chronicles*, Weidenfeld & Nicolson, NY, 1986.

Kelly, Amy, *Eleanor of Aquitaine and the Four Kings*, Harvard University Press, Cambridge, Mass., 1950.

Meade, Marion, *Eleanor of Aquitaine*, Hawthorn Books Publishers, Inc., NY, 1977.

Montgomery, D. H., *The Leading Facts of English History*, Ginn & Company, Publishers, Boston, 1900.

Stephen, Sir Leslie, and Lee, Sir Sidney, eds., *Dictionary of National Biography*, Oxford University Press, London, 1964.

Warren, W. L., *Henry II*, University of California Press, Berkeley and Los Angeles, 1973.

Webster's Biographical Dictionary, G. & C. Merriam Co., Publishers, Springfield, Mass., 1962.

---

[1] Given-Wilson and Curteis, pg. 9.
[2] Warren, *Henry II*, pgs. 601-602, 119.

The Interdict

One of the most tedious chores thrust upon a medieval king was the constant wrestling which must be done with the pope, and in an age of deeply religious and superstitious beliefs, the Pope carried a great deal of weight. Simply a threat of excommunication was often enough to bring kings to their knees, and if that didn't work, there was always the interdict.

King John of England experienced both in 1209, and in 1213 he surrendered his kingdom to the pope and received it back again as a fief. [1]

What was this interdict and what did it mean to the king and his people?

Warren[2] describes it as "a general strike of the clergy" which stopped "all the comforts of religion." The churches were closed; there were no marriages, no Christian burials, no burials in consecrated ground, no sacraments, no tolling of church bells; pictures in churches were covered and the statues wrapped in black cloth and put away on beds of ashes and thorns. It was hoped the king would be pressured by the suffering of his innocent people: the innocent suffered with the guilty and, thus, the guilty received no sympathy from the innocent.

In a translation of the law which was published by Pepin le Bref[3] at the Council of Verberie (755), it is stated that a

---

[1] Bridgwater, *The Columbia-Viking Desk Encyclopedia*, 1968, "John, 1166–1216."

[2] Warren, *King John*, pg. 164.

[3] Pepin le Bref (b. 714(?); d. 768), or Pepin the Short, king of Franks; also Pepin III, king of Germany. He was the son of Charles

(continued...)

person who has been excommunicated shall not enter a church nor drink nor eat with other Christians; in this particular situation, the king shall be considered as nothing more than a simple person, and no one should drink or eat with him or give him the kiss of peace nor join with him in prayer nor greet him; and if anyone voluntarily communicates with him, then he should be excommunicate himself.[1]

Robert II (d. 1031), King of France, was forced by an interdict to put aside his much-loved wife, Bertha, because he was the godfather of one of Bertha's children by her previous husband. This meant they were spiritually allied, and marriage was not permitted between spiritual allies.

The "tenderly attached" couple would not submit to the judgement of Rome and be separated, so the pope proclaimed that Robert should be cursed along with his children, his cattle, and his possessions; that no one was to befriend him; no priest was to pray for him; no one was to assist him on his deathbed; that should he die, his entrails would burst from his stomach but no one should bury him or "throw a little earth upon his miserable remains"; his name should be dishonored and his memory forgotten; and "the Aurora of another life shall never dawn to rejoice his spirit."[2] Innocent probably had similar words for John.

Two sacraments were allowed in this interdict of 1209 in England: the baptism of infants and the confession of the dying. No clear cut lines had been drawn and exactly what was allowed by the pope was unclear; liberties, undoubtedly, were taken by the church on behalf of the people. Warren[3] reports that there were "no signs of popular discontent: it must have been very worrying to pastors, and disturbing to the pope." He adds that as the interdict progressed, the parish clergy began

---

[3] (...continued)
Martel and the father of Charlemagne. (Webster's Biographical Dictionary, 1962, "Pepin the Short")

[1] Bush, *Memoirs of the Queens of France*, pgs. 97–98.

[2] Bush, *Memoirs of the Queens of France*, Vol. I, pgs. 96–101.

[3] Warren, *King John*, pg. 171.

taking up secular work or took to spending a good deal of their now-free time in the taverns and became a problem to their diocesans when the Interdict finally ended.

John, faced with baronial revolt and invasion from France, finally was reconciled with the pope in July 1213, and the interdict was lifted.

Sources:

Bridgwater, William, Editor-in-chief, *The Columbia-Viking Desk Encyclopedia*, Viking Press, New York, 1953.

Bush, Mrs. Annie Forbes, *Memoirs of the Queens of France with Notices of the Royal Favorites*, Vol. I, Henry Colburn, Publisher, London, 1843.

Cannon, John & Griffiths, Ralph, *The Oxford Illustrated History of the British Monarchy*, Oxford University Press, Oxford and NY, 1988.

Warren, W. L., *King John*, University of California Press, Berkeley, 1978.

Webster's Biographical Dictionary, G. & C. Merriam Co., Publishers, Springfield, Mass., 1962.

The Disappearance of Arthur

In 1199, John succeeded his brother, Richard I the Lion-Heart, to the throne of England. This succession was questioned by those who believed that John's nephew, Arthur of Brittany, was the true successor, being the son of John's elder brother, Geoffrey, who had died 19 Aug 1186. [1]

This Arthur, Count of Brittany, born 29 Mar 1187, after his father's death, was named specifically by Richard I as his heir should he die childless, which he did. However, many were against having Arthur as king because, not having grown up in England, he would be a continental stranger ruling England with foreign ways.

Anjou, Maine, and Touraine supported Arthur as Geoffrey's heir. Philip II, King of France, knighted the boy and invested him with Richard's French possessions. When John arrived on the continent to claim those possessions, Arthur led an uprising against John in Poitou in which he took the castle of Mirabel/Mirabeau[2] and captured England's dowager queen, Eleanor of Aquitaine, John's mother. On 1 Aug 1202, John's forces attacked the castle, freed his mother, and captured Arthur, whom John placed in the care of William de Braose. [3]

---

[1] *DNB*, "Arthur, Duke or Count of Brittany (1187–1203)."

[2] Hallam, *The Plantagenet Encyclopedia*, pg. 21.

[3] William de Braose "publicly refused to retain charge of the prince, suspecting that his life was in danger." William's wife, Maude de St. Valerie (or de Haye), later refused to give her sons to King John as hostages for their father's good behavior, either insinuating by her remarks or blatantly stating that King John had murdered Arthur. She and her eldest son, John, paid heavily for this: they were captured and

(continued...)

The following year, Arthur was moved to Rouen.

John was known to be at Rouen on 3 Apr 1203 when, according to a contemporary chronicler,[1] Arthur, aged about sixteen, was murdered, if not by John's hands, then on his command.

The chronicler states that John, "in a fit of frenzy," struck Arthur dead and threw his body into the Seine where it was recovered by fishermen and given burial in the priory of Ste. Marie des Prez, near Bec. Another chronicler states simply that Arthur disappeared and was buried in a secret place; others, that John had Arthur murdered.

Duncan,[2] referencing French historians, writes that John took Arthur by force during the night, put him in a boat, stabbed him, and threw his body into the Seine. Another historian states that the prince, in an attempted escape, jumped from the wall of the castle and was drowned in the river. Still another suggests that the imprisoned Arthur died of mental grief.

The *DNB* states that we have "no more definite conclusion than that in April 1203 Arthur suddenly disappeared, and that his disappearance was contrived by John." It also adds that Arthur "never asserted his right" to the crown of England.[3]

Geoffrey and Constance of Brittany also had a daughter, Eleanor, Maid of Brittany, who was among those captured at Mirabel. Eleanor was John's prisoner until her death of old age in 1241. Though a prisoner, she appears to have been treated well by John, receiving gifts, an allowance, fine clothing, and "ornamented saddles and reins,"[4] which indicates that her confinement was not a close one.

---

[3] (...continued)
imprisoned in Windsor Castle where they were starved to death. (*DNB*, "Braose, William de (d. 1211)"; Warren, *King John*, pgs. 185–187)

[1] The author of the "Annales Margam."

[2] *The Dukes of Normandy*, pg. 327.

[3] *DNB*, "Arthur, duke or count of Brittany (1187–1203)."

[4] Warren, *King John*, University of California Press, Berkeley and Los Angeles, 1978, pg. 83.

Sources:

Duncan, Jonathan, Esq. B.A., *The Dukes of Normandy, from the Time of Rollo to the Expulsion of King John by Philip Augustus of France*, Joseph Rickerby, Sherbourn Land, and Harvey and Darton, Gracechurch Street, London, 1839.

Hallam, Elizabeth, ed., *The Plantagenet Encyclopedia*, Grove Weidenfeld, NY, 1990.

Stephen, Sir Leslie, and Lee, Sir Sidney, eds., *Dictionary of National Biography*, Oxford University Press, London, 1964.

Warren, W. L., *King John*, University of California Press, Berkeley and Los Angeles, 1978.

The Eleanor Crosses

Eleanor of Castile (d. 1290), daughter of Ferdinand III of Castile and his second wife, Joanna, was queen of Edward I, King of England. Although their marriage (Oct 1254, at the Cistercian monastery of Las Huelgas near Burgos in Spain) was mainly one of political importance, it was a successful and affectionate marriage, and the couple reportedly were seldom apart from one another, the queen even joining her husband on Crusade 1270–1274.

In the summer of 1290, Eleanor, while traveling with her husband, became ill and was lodged at Harby/Hadby in Nottinghamshire, where she died 28 Nov.

As was the custom, her body was embalmed. Her heart was buried in the Dominican Blackfriars in London; her entrails at Lincoln Cathedral. Both burials had elaborate tombs of gilt-bronze. (Both tombs were eventually destroyed, the latter during the Commonwealth period.[1])

On 4 Dec, the funeral procession left for London, stopping for the night in Lincoln, Grantham, Stamford, Geddington, Northampton (at Hardingstone), Stony Stratford, Woburn, Dunstable, St. Albans, Waltham, Westcheap in London, and Charing, all being locations of castles or major monasteries. The grief-stricken king ordered the erection of a memorial cross in each of the twelve towns to mark the ceremony of the funeral procession. The crosses were constructed between 1291 and 1294 at the king's expense.

Seven hundred years later, of the twelve original crosses, three survive: Waltham Cross (near London), Hardingstone

---

[1] Parsons, *Eleanor of Castile 1290–1990*, pgs. 71, 72.

Cross (Northampton), and Geddington Cross (Northamptonshire). The crosses at Charing and Cheapside were both
destroyed by Parliamentary soldiers in 1643. The present cross
at Charing is a replacement.

The Eleanor crosses, while varying individually, were
basically vertical monuments layered in wedding cake manner: a
solid base supported a tier designed with niches in which were
statues of the queen; this tier, in turn, supported a shaft. The
tops of the shafts are now broken off; they may have been
topped with crosses or crowns or ended in pyramidal tips.
There was various detailed ornamentation, such as flowers,
foliage, rosettes, and shields of arms, all accented with gables
and finials. It appears most of the monuments sit atop a
pyramid of steps. A 1735 sketch shows the Waltham Cross to
be approximately forty feet high.

On 17 Dec 1290 Eleanor was buried at Westminster Abbey,
where her tomb and effigy "of remarkable beauty" can still be
seen.

Sources:

Jenner, Michael, *Journeys into Medieval England*, Michael Joseph,
    London, 1991.
Kerr, Nigel and Mary, *A Guide to Medieval Sites in Britain*, Paladin
    Grafton Books, London, 1989.
Parsons, David, ed., *Eleanor of Castile 1290-1990*, Paul Watkins,
    Lincolnshire, 1991.
Stephen, Sir Leslie, and Lee, Sir Sidney, eds., *Dictionary of National
    Biography*, Oxford University Press, London, 1964. Specifically:
    DNB, "Eleanor of Castile (d. 1290)."
Strong, Roy, *Lost Treasures of Britain*, Viking, London, 1990.

Edward II: King Deposed
and Murdered

Edward II came to the throne on the death of his father, Edward I, who has been described as a "great soldier and wise statesman" of strong character and a faithful husband. Edward I seems to have been everything his son was not, and this situation only magnified the lack of kingly abilities in Edward II.

His predilection for favorites is evident in his more than generous treatment of Piers Gaveston and, later, the father and son Despensers. Gaveston had such an undesirable influence on the young Edward, that Edward I had him exiled in February 1307. However, as soon as the king died (7 Jul 1307), Gaveston was royally recalled and in August of the same year was created Earl of Cornwall. [1]

In January 1308, Edward travelled to France to wed Isabella, [2] daughter of Philip IV, king of France, and left Gaveston as regent of England in his absence, much to the disgust of the barons. Edward and Isabella returned to England and their coronation 25 February 1308, [3] in which Gaveston carried St. Edward's crown. It is said that he was more richly dressed than either the king or queen.

---

[1] *CP*, Cornwall section; Hutchinson, *Edward II*, pg. 53.

[2] Hutchinson, *Edward II*, pg. 55, states that Isabelle was sixteen years old and Edward, twenty-three at the time of the marriage. *KQB*, pgs. 77–78, states that Isabella was born 1295, making her about thirteen when she was married. Whether sixteen or thirteen, she was hardly the She-Wolf she would become toward the close of Edward's reign.

[3] *CP*, Cornwall section; Hutchinson, *Edward II*, pg. 55.

In 1309, Gaveston was given as his wife, Margaret de Clare (d. 1342), the daughter of Gilbert de Clare (d. 1295), Earl of Gloucester, and Edward's own niece.

Edward's continuing preference for Gaveston over his new bride was evident (Philip IV's wedding presents to Edward had been "promptly" passed on to Gaveston[1]), and Gaveston, with his arrogance and his control over the king, became increasingly intolerable to the barons. He has been described as a foreign upstart[2]; a man who was "brave and accomplished, but foolishly greedy, ambitious, ostentatious, and imprudent"[3]; and an "immoral pervert."[4] In May of the same year, in answer to the barons' "Declaration of 1308,"[5] Edward II was forced to issue letters patent which stripped Gaveston of his titles and required that he leave England. Edward made him lieutenant of Ireland/Chief Governor of Ireland (Jun 1308 to Sep 1309),[6] a position he occupied with success for a year before returning to England.

In October 1311, under baronial pressure, Gaveston was "condemned to perpetual exile" and commanded to leave the country by 1 November. He left 3 November and was back in the king's apartments before the end of the year. The following month, the king restored to him his titles and properties. In accordance with the ordinances, the Archbishop excommunicated Gaveston; the barons armed for civil war.

Gaveston was forced to flee. He surrendered from Scarborough Castle on 19 May 1312 and became the prisoner of Aymer de Valence (d. 1324), Earl of Pembroke; John de Warenne (d. 1347), Earl of Surrey; Guy de Beauchamp (d. 1315), Earl of Warwick; and Henry de Percy (Baron Percy) (d. 1314). In June, Warwick took Gaveston from Pembroke's

---

[1] *KQB*, pg. 77; Hutchinson, pg. 57.
[2] Hutchinson, *Edward II*, pg. 72.
[3] *DNB*, "Gaveston, Piers, Earl of Cornwall (d. 1312)."
[4] Hutchinson, *Edward II*, pg. 72.
[5] Hutchinson, *Edward II*, pg. 58.
[6] *CP*, Cornwall section.

guards and imprisoned him in the dungeon of Warwick Castle until he was handed over on 19 June[1] to Thomas (d. 1321/ 1322), Earl of Lancaster,[2] Humphrey de Bohun (d. 1321/ 1322), Earl of Hereford, and Edmund de FitzAlan (d. 1326), Earl of Arundel. Gaveston was taken to Blacklow Hill where "a Welsh soldier ran him through the body with his sword, and another struck off the head..."[3] Warwick refused "either to be present or to take charge of the corpse."[4]

The following year, the void left in Edward's life by the death of Gaveston was filled by Hugh the younger le Despenser, son of Hugh the elder le Despenser, Earl of Winchester. Both Despensers were supporters of the king, the younger being King's Chamberlain. The Despensers proved worse than Gaveston: they were more arrogant, more greedy, and more in control of the king. They, too, were condemned under baronial pressure "to perpetual exile and to disinheritance."[5] They, too, rebounded. In 1324, they "intrigued against the Queen" and "induced Edward to deprive her of her estates."[6] For Isabella, who for almost twenty years had lived with her husband's "abnormalities and eccentricities,"[7] it must have been the last straw.

In 1325, Edward, "in a fit of stupidity,"[8] sent Isabella as an ambassador to her brother Charles IV, King of France. Here she began or resumed her liason with Roger de Mortimer, a Marcher baron, who had (with her assistance?) in 1323 escaped from the Tower of London where he and his uncle had been imprisoned. It was decided to summon her son, the young Edward (III) to France to do homage for his continental lands.

---

[1] *CP*, Warwick section; Lancaster section.

[2] Thomas, Earl of Lancaster, Leicester, Derby (1298-1322), Lincoln and Salisbury (1311-1322). (Hutchinson, *Edward II*, pg. 179)

[3] Hutchinson, *Edward II*, pg. 72.

[4] *CP*, Warwick section; Hutchinson, *Edward II*, pg. 73; *DNB*, "Gaveston, Piers, Earl of Cornwall (d. 1312)."

[5] Hutchinson, *Edward II*, pg. 107.

[6] *KQB*, pg. 76.

[7] Costain, *The Three Edwards*, pg. 213.

[8] Morris, *The Monarchs of England*, pg. 91.

King Edward, in another fit of stupidity, allowed his son, "his most valuable weapon," to join the queen in France.

Isabella did not return to her husband in England, despite his pleas, accusations, and threats. She demanded, instead, the removal of the Despensers. When this was not accomplished, she settled in at her brother's court until Charles requested she leave: he could not countenance her overt affair with Roger de Mortimer.

Isabella's entourage moved to Hainault, where she was welcomed by the Count and his family, which included the future wife of Edward III. Here Isabella bartered for an army to accompany her back to England, and part of the bargaining probably included the condition that one of the Count's three daughters would marry the prince and become the future queen consort of England.

In September of 1326, Isabella, Mortimer, and the prince landed with their forces in Suffolk. They were supported by such a majority of the barons that King Edward fled London. Hugh the elder le Despenser was captured and hanged. Hugh the younger was arrested and given a sham trial before suffering a traitor's death. It is said Isabella watched as he was hanged, disemboweled, and quartered. An illustration captioned "Isabella and the execution of Hugh le Despenser" is printed in Hutchinson (pg. 102) and shows the sexual mutilation of the younger Despenser.

The king was captured and imprisoned in Kenilworth Castle, where in January 1327, a deputation from Parliament informed him of the decision for his deposition and added that the young prince had requested his father's consent before taking the crown. Edward II had no choice but to agree and abide by the measure which had been passed.

In the meantime, Mortimer and Isabella took control of the new king's reign. Among Mortimer's first actions were those which created knighthoods for three of his sons,[1] raised his barony to an earldom, and gave him custody of various lands and monies.[2]

---

[1] *CP*, March section.
[2] Costain, *The Three Edwards*, pg. 221.

Edward continued a prisoner in Kenilworth, but, as with any deposed monarch, he became a rallying point for discontents, and there was concern that he might be the subject of a rescue attempt. He was thus sent to Berkeley Castle, where his accommodations proved less comfortable. It was attempted to starve him to death or to have him die as a result of the unsanitary conditions of his cell, but his constitution proved too strong.

During a September night, 1327, Edward II was murdered at Berkeley Castle on the orders, it is believed, of Isabella and her lover, Roger de Mortimer. John de Maltravers (Mautravers), Edward de Gurney, and William Ogle, are traditionally held to have been the murderers of Edward II,[1] who was killed "by the contemporary method of execution for a proved sodomite...." In short, they burned out his entrails with a red-hot poker. This particular method of murder was convenient for Mortimer and Isabella, as it left no marks on the body and death appeared natural. It has traditionally been said that the cries of the tormented man reached far outside the castle to the village people.[2]

He was buried at Gloucester Cathedral, where his son ordered an alabaster effigy to mark his burial place. A cult following grew up around Edward II and brought plentious

---

[1] As to the fate of the men involved: William Ogle was "condemned but escaped and died abroad." Edward de Gurney was arrested in Italy but died (1332) while being taken back to England for trial; his corpse, it is said by chroniclers, was beheaded at sea, but Costain states, "there was no foundation" for such belief, adding that the captured Gurney "took sick and died" in Gascony as he was being taken back to England. John de Maltravers seems to have suffered no penalties, performing in the king's service in Flanders and dying in 1364/1365. Thomas de Berkeley of Berkeley Castle (a son-in-law of Mortimer and a brother-in-law of Maltravers) pled ignorance of the murder and served the king loyally until his death in 1361. (Hutchinson, *Edward II*, pg. 143; *DNB*, "Maltravers, John, Baron Maltravers (1290?–1365)"; Costain, *The Three Edwards*, pg. 252–253)

[2] Murray, *The Kings and Queens of England*, pg. 171; Costain, *The Three Edwards*, pgs. 225–226.

offerings to the cathedral from those who made pilgrimages to his tomb.

Isabella and Mortimer ruled England through the young King Edward III until October 1330 when Edward took the government into his own hands. Mortimer was arrested, tried, and condemned to be executed. On 29 Nov 1330, he was hanged at Tyburn and his body left on the gallows two days and two nights. It has commonly been believed that he suffered the traitor's death, but the *CP*, March section, states, "It does not appear that he was beheaded and quartered, as sometimes asserted."[1]

Isabella was "firmly retired"[2] or "obliged to take up residence"[3] at Castle Rising in Norfolk, where her standard of living was "in accordance with her royal rank."[4] She died 22 August 1358, aged sixty-three. She was buried in Grey Friars Church in London in the robes of the Poor Clares, having taken the vows of the order of Santa Clara. It is said a small casket containing the heart of her husband was buried with her, prompting one writer to surmise that though Isabella could not have Edward's heart during life, she now possessed it for all eternity.[5]

---

[1] The *CP*, March section, indicates that Mortimer was buried in the Church of the Grey Friars at Shrewsbury, but in a footnote adds that Mortimer may initially have been buried in the Grey Friars, London, and then have been transferred by his widow to Wigmore Abbey.

[2] Hallam, *Four Gothic Kings*, pg. 231.

[3] *KQB*, pg. 79.

[4] Costain, *The Three Edwards*, pg. 261.

[5] *KQB*, pg. 79; Lofts, *Queens of England*, pg. 60. Costain in *The Three Edwards*, pg. 264, suggests that Isabella, after thinking about the past for twenty-eight years, had a "sincere desire to do this much penance." However, Strickland in *Lives of the Queens of England*, describes this as Isabella's "characteristic hypocrisy."

Sources:

Chaplais, Pierre, *Piers Gaveston: Edward II's Adoptive Brother*, Clarendon Press, Oxford, 1994.

Cokayne, G. E., *The Complete Peerage*, St Catherine Press, London.

Costain, Thomas B., *The Three Edwards*, Doubleday & Company, NY, 1958.

Hallam, Elizabeth, ed., *Four Gothic Kings*, Weidenfeld & Nicolson, NY, 1987.

Hutchinson, Harold F., *Edward II*, Stein and Day Publishers, New York, 1972.

Lofts, Norah, *Queens of England*, Doubleday & Company, Inc., Garden City, NY, 1977.

Morris, Jean, *The Monarchs of England*, Charterhouse, NY, 1975.

Murray, Jane, *The Kings and Queens of England: A Tourist Guide*, Charles Scribner's Sons, NY, 1974.

Stephen, Sir Leslie, and Lee, Sir Sidney, eds., *Dictionary of National Biography*, Oxford University Press, London, 1964.

Strickland, Agnes, *Lives of the Queens of England*, London, 1840-1848.

Williamson, David, *Debrett's Kings and Queens of Britain*, Dorset Press, New York, 1992.

First Founder Knights
of the Order of the Garter

The date of the founding of the institution of the Knights of the Order of the Garter is unknown. Suggested dates have included 1344, 1347, 1348, 1349, and 1351. Froissart, the chronicler, gives a date of 1344. Beltz takes the date from Froissart and asserts the date of the first feast of the Knights of the Order as 23 April 1344, the date most commonly given. The *CP*, however, believes the correct year to be 1348.

The exact purpose of the establishing of the Knights of the Order of the Garter is just as uncertain as the exact date. It has been suggested that the chilvaric order was to have been an emulation of the Knights of the Round Table and was to be housed in Edward III's new building of St. George's Chapel at Windsor. The twenty-five founder knights were selected by the king. The motto, "Honi soit qui mal y pense," translates to "Evil (or dishonor) to him who thinks ill of it." Determining to what the motto refers requires only more speculation.

The Order may have been intended as a unifying, supportive factor in Edward's claim to the French throne. Or it may have been something as simple and elegant as another level of exclusiveness and ceremony meant to build and maintain spirit and morale.

The ensign and habit of the Order consists of the Mantle, the Surcoat, the Hood, and the Garter. The garter was made of a blue fabric, such as silk, velvet, or taffata, embroidered with gold and "silk of various colours." [1] It was fastened by a gold or silver buckle on the left leg below the knee. In the case of a

---

[1] Beltz, pg. l–li; Wurts, *Magna Charta*, pg. 221.

woman wearing the garter, the garter was worn on the left arm. [1]

The *CP* [2] quotes from Sir Harris Nicolas [3] that "the deficiency of materials for the ancient History of the Order renders it more than probable that many knights may have been elected whose names are not recorded, and it is not impossible that a few are erroneously supposed to have received its honours." He adds that it is misleading to number the knights for this very reason.

The twenty-five men listed here are usually described as the "original" Knights of the Garter; however, "the twenty-five original knights were described on the plates of their arms, pleonastically, as 'First Founders,' to distinguish them from the successors to their stalls in the royal chapel, who, by the statutes, were to be named, 'Founders.'" [4] The listing is based on the *CP*, Vol. II, Appendix B, "The Order of the Garter," and Beltz, *Memorials of the Most Noble Order of the Garter*.

First Founder Knights of the Order of the Garter

Edward of Woodstock (b. 15 Jun 1330, Woodstock; d. 8 Jun 1376, Palace of Westminster; bur. Canterbury Cathedral), the Black Prince, Prince of Wales, son of **Edward III**, King of England.

Henry of Grosmont [5] (b. 1299(?), Castle of Grosment/ Grosmont, Monmouthshire; d. 24 Mar/13 May 1361 [6] "of the

---

[1] As noted in the chapter, "Some Royal Connections of Poet Geoffrey Chaucer," Alice Chaucer, one of the first women members of the Order of the Garter, is shown in her tomb effigy as wearing the garter on her left arm.

[2] *CP*, Vol. II, Appendix B, "The Order of the Garter."

[3] *History of the Orders of Knighthood*, Vol. II, pg. 54.

[4] Beltz, pg. cxlix.

[5] Beltz, pgs. 19–25. "...his name being second on the list, following that of the Prince of Wales" (*CP*, Lancaster section).

[6] Beltz, pg. 25, and *CP*, Lancaster section, give the death date as 24 Mar; *DNB*, "Henry of Lancaster, first Duke of Lancaster (1299?–1361)," gives the death date as 13 May.

pestilence" [plague], Leicester; bur. "collegiate church of Newarke in that town"), 4th Earl of Lancaster, 1st Duke of Lancaster, Earl of Derby, Lincoln and Leicester, only son of Henry of Lancaster (d. 1345), Earl of Lancaster and Leicester, and Maud Chaworth (d. 1322) (or de Cadurcis); m. abt 1337 Isabel, daughter of Henry Beaumont, 1st Lord Beaumont, by whom he had two daughters: Maud (aged 22 in 1361; d. 10 Apr 1362) (widow at age 6 of Ralph Stafford, eldest son of Ralph, Earl of Stafford) m. 1352 William V, Duke of Bavaria, Count of Holland and Zeeland (no issue); and Blanche (aged 14 in 1361) m. John of Gaunt, son of Edward III.

Thomas de Beauchamp (d. 13 Nov 1369 of the plague, Calais, aged 55; bur. St. Mary's, Warwick), Earl of Warwick, son of Guy de Beauchamp (d. 1315), Earl of Warwick, and his wife, Alice de Toeni (sister and heir of Robert de Toeni, Baron of Flamsted); m. aft 22 Feb 1324/1325 Katherine Mortimer (d. 1369), eldest daughter of Roger de Mortimer (ex. 29 Nov 1330), 1st Earl of March, by whom he had seven sons and four daughters. [1]

Jean/John de Grailly (d. 1377; bur. Notre Dame), Captal de Buch, Vicomte de Benauges, son of Peter Sire de Grailly, Vicomte de Benanges and Castillon, and his wife, Assalide (sister of Peter of Bordeaux, Captal of Buch and Lord of Puy-Paulin); m. Nov 1350 Rose d'Albret, legitimated daughter of Bernard Sire d'Albret; no issue. He had an illegitimate son, John de Grailly (d. bet. 17 Jun and 10 Jul 1400, perhaps in England; will requested burial in the "Church of the convent of Carmelites at Bordeaux, of which city he was mayor"). [2]

Ralph Stafford (b. 24 Sep 1301; d. 31 Aug 1372; bur. Tonbridge), Lord Stafford, Earl of Stafford, son of Edmund Stafford (b. 15 Jul 1273; d. bef 12 Aug 1308), Lord Stafford, and Margaret Basset (daughter of Ralph Basset, Lord Basset of Draiton); m. (1) abt 1326 or 1327 Katherine, daughter of John Hastang of Chebsey, co. Stafford; m. (2) bef 6 Jul 1336 Margaret Audeley (d. 7 Sep 1347; bur. Tonbridge with her

---

[1] Beltz, pgs. 25–27.
[2] Beltz, pgs. 28–33.

mother and father), daughter and heir of Hugh de Audeley
(d. 1347), Earl of Gloucester, and his wife, Margaret de Clare
(d. 9 Apr 1342) (widow of Piers de Gaveston (d. 1312), Earl of
Cornwall, and daughter of Gilbert de Clare (d. 7 Dec 1295),
Earl of Gloucester and Hertford, and his wife Joan of Acre
(d. 23 Apr 1307)). [1]

William de Montagu (b. 20/25 Jun 1328, Donyatt,
Somerset; d. 3 Jun 1397; bur. Bisham; will directed burial in
the conventual church of the Priory of Bustleham-Montacute,
Berkshire), 2nd Earl of Salisbury, son of William Montagu
(d. 30 Jan 1343/1344), 1st Earl of Salisbury, last surviving
founder [2]; m. (1) (div. in or bef Oct 1349) Joan of Kent,
daughter of Edmund of Woodstock, Earl of Kent;
m. (2) possibly 1349 Elizabeth (b. 1343; d. 14-16 Jan 1414/
1415), eldest of three daughters and coheir of John Mohun
(d. 1375) of Dunster, a First Founder, and his wife Joan,
(daughter of Bartholomew Burghersh the elder). Their only
child, William de Montagu (d. 6 Aug 1382), m. Elizabeth
FitzAlan (d. 14 Jan 1414/1415) but had no issue. [3]

Roger de Mortimer (b. 11 Nov 1328, Ludlow; d. suddenly
26 Feb 1359-1360, Rouvray, Burgundy (Côte d'Or);
bur. (1) France, (2) Wigmore), Earl of March, son of Edmund
Mortimer (d. 1331/1332) and Elizabeth de Badlesmere [4]
(d. 8 Jun 1355) (daughter of Bartholomew de Badlesmere "le
Riche" (ex. 1322) and sister of Giles de Badlesmere, Lord
Badlesmere); m. Philippa de Montagu (d. 5 Jan 1381;
bur. Bisham), daughter of William Montagu (d. 30 Jan

---

[1] Beltz, pgs. 33-36; *CP*, Stafford section, Cornwall section.

[2] *CP*, Salisbury section.

[3] William de Montagu (d. 1397) was "the last survivor of the
Founders of the Order." His father died in 1343 "of consequences
received at the Windsor jousts." His only child, William Montagu, was
"slain at a tilting match at Windsor by the Earl his father, on the 6th
August 1382." (Beltz, pgs. 33, 39)

[4] Elizabeth de Badlesmere m. (2) William de Bohun (d. Sep 1360),
Earl of Northampton. (*CP*, Mortimer section)

1343/1344), 1st Earl of Salisbury, and sister of one of the First Founders.[1]

John de Lisle (aged 24 and more in 1342; d. 14 Oct 1355/ 1356 "being killed in a raid made by Prince Edward from Bordeaux to Narbone," "wounded by a quarrel shot from a cross bow"[2]), Lord Lisle of Rougemont, son of Robert de Lisle (d. 1342), Lord Lisle of Rougemont; m. bef 16 Dec 1332 Maud (liv 1376/1377), daughter of Henry de Grey, by whom he had Robert Lisle (d. 1399), Lord Lisle; John de Lisle, who died without issue; William Lisle of Cameldon and Shefford, who died without issue; and Elizabeth, who m. William de Aldeburgh, Lord Aldeburgh.[3] Robert Lisle (d. 1399) may have had issue. According to "a pedigree copied in the Visitation book of Somersetshire, Anno 1623, he had a son, Sir William Lisle, seated at Waterpery, Com. Oxon."[4]

Bartholomew Burghersh the younger (d. 5 Apr 1369; will directed burial in the Lady Chapel of Walsingham Abbey[5]), Lord Burghersh, son of Bartholomew Burghersh the elder (d. 3 Aug 1355), 2nd Lord Burghersh, and his wife, Elizabeth de Verdun (d. 1360) (daughter and coheir of Theobald de Verdun, Lord Verdun); m. (1) bef 10 May 1335 Cicely, daughter and heir of Richard de Weyland, by whom he had his only daughter and heir, Elizabeth (d. 1409) (who m. Edward le Despenser (d. 1375), Lord le Despenser); m. (2) bef. Aug 1366 Margaret Badlesmere (d. 1 Jul 1393), widow of _ Pichard; she m. as her third husband William de Burchester.[6]

John Beauchamp (d. 2 Dec 1360), son of Guy Beauchamp (d. 12 Aug 1315), Earl of Warwick, and brother of Thomas Beauchamp (d. 13 Nov 1369), Earl of Warwick, also a First Founder.[7] Unm.

---

[1] *CP*, Salisbury section.
[2] *CP*, Lisle section; Beltz, pg. 43.
[3] Beltz, pgs. 42–44.
[4] Beltz, pgs. 42–44.
[5] *CP*, Burghersh section, pg. 426; Beltz, pg. 46.
[6] Beltz, pgs. 45–47.
[7] Beltz, pgs. 47–48; *DNB*, "Beauchamp, Thomas de, Earl of Warwick (d. 1401)."

John Mohun of Dunster (d. 15 Sep 1375[1]/d. bet. 14 Apr 1375 and 4 Apr 1376[2]; bur. Bruton priory), son and heir of John de Mohun (d. 1322), 1st Lord Mohun (d. in or abt 1330), and Christian[3]/Sibilla[4] de Segrave (daughter of John de Segrave); m. bef Sep 1342 Joan Burghersh (d. 4 Oct 1404; bur. in the chantry chapel which she had endowed in Christ Church, Canterbury), daughter of Bartholomew Burghersh the elder (d. 1355) and Elizabeth de Verdon (daughter and coheir of Theobald de Verdon). Joan Burghersh was sister of Bartholomew Burghersh the younger, also a First Founder. John Mohun left no sons. By his wife he had three daughters: Elizabeth Mohun (d. without surviving issue, 1414/1415) m. as his second wife William de Montagu (d. 1397), 2nd Earl of Salisbury, also a First Founder; Philippa (d. 1431, no surviving issue) m. (1) Walter FitzWalter (d. 1386), (2) John Golofrey/ Golafre (d. 1396), and (3) Edward (d. 1415), Duke of York, K.G., grandson of Edward III; and Matilda or Maud (d. bef 1376/ or 1400/1401) m. John Strange (d. 1397), Lord Strange of Knockin in Shropshire and had issue of Richard Strange, Lord Strange of Knokin.[5]

Hugh de Courtenay (b. 22 Mar 1326/1327; d. bef 2 Sep 1349, in the lifetime of his father), one of the six sons of Hugh de Courtenay (b. 12 Jul 1303; d. 2 May 1377[6]), Earl of Devon, and his wife, Margaret de Bohun (m. 11 Aug 1325; d. 16 Dec 1391) (daughter of Humphrey VIII de Bohun (d. 16 Mar 1321/1322), Earl of Hereford and Essex, and his wife, Elizabeth Plantagenet (d. 5 May 1316)); m. 1341 Elizabeth[7] and had issue Hugh de Courtenay (d. 20 Feb 1373/

---

[1] *CP*, Mohun section; *DNB*, "Mohun, John de (1320–1375)."

[2] Beltz, pg. 50.

[3] *CP*, Mohun section.

[4] Beltz, pg. 49.

[5] Beltz, pgs. 50–51; *DNB*, "Mohun, John de (1320–1375)"; *CP*, Mohun section.

[6] *CP*, Devon section; Beltz, pg. 394.

[7] According to the *CP*, Devon section (pg. 325, footnote c), this Elizabeth (d. 23 Sep 1375) is "said to have been (but doubtless through

(continued...)

1374), who m. (1) bef May 1361 Margaret de Bryan
(d. "shortly after" 1361), daughter of Guy de Bryan (d. 1390);
m. (2) Maude/Matilda de Holand (d. bef 13 Apr 1392),
daughter of Thomas de Holand (d. 1360), 1st Earl of Kent, also
a First Founder.[1]

Thomas Holand, 1st Earl of Kent (d. in Normandy 26 or
28 Dec 1360; bur. in the Church of the Grey Friars at
Stamford), second son of Robert Holand of Holand in
Lancashire (d. 1328 nr Henley, Oxfordshire) and Maud la
Zouche (daughter of Alan la Zouche of Ashby); m. Joan the
Fair Maid of Kent (d. "apparently" 8 Aug 1385, Wallingford
Castle, Berkshire), daughter of Edmund of Woodstock, Earl of
Kent,[2] by whom he had two sons and two daughters: Thomas
de Holand, 2nd Earl of Kent (d. 1397); John de Holand
(b. aft 1350; ex. 9 or 10 Jan 1399/1400), Earl of Huntingdon
and Duke of Exeter; Joan de Holand (d. 1384), second wife of

---

[7] (...continued)
confusion with her son's 1st wife) da. of Sir Guy de Bryan of Tor
Bryan, Devon," who was "summoned to parliament" in 1350, also a
K.G. (51st elected). (Beltz, pg. cliv, gives Bryan's death date as 17 Aug
1390.)

   This Elizabeth is elusive. According to the *CP*, Mowbray section
(pg. 383 and footnote j), Elizabeth, widow of Hugh de Courtenay
(d. 1349), was "da. of John (de Vere or Veer) [d. 1359/1360], Earl of
Oxford," and Maud de Badlesmere. Elizabeth m. (2) John de Mowbray
(d. 4 Oct 1361), Lord Mowbray; m. (3) bef 18 Jan 1368/1369 William
de Cosynton (liv. 6 Jul 1380), son of de Stephen Cosynton. Her death
date is given as "Aug. or Sep. 1375."

   The *CP*, Oxford section (pg. 223-224, footnote n) lists the issue of
John de Vere (d. 23 or 24 Jan 1360) as four sons and three daughters:
Margaret, Maud, and Elizabeth. The names of Elizabeth's three
husbands are listed in footnote as they are given here.

   The *DNB*, "Vere, John de, seventh Earl of Oxford (1313-1360),"
states that the Earl had "four sons and at least one daughter." A
daughter Elizabeth is not mentioned, though Margaret and Maud are
listed. The *DNB*, "Mowbray, John (II) de, ninth Baron (d. 1361)," does
not mention a marriage with Elizabeth.

[1] Beltz, pgs. 51-54.
[2] *CP*, Kent section; Beltz, pgs. 55-57.

John de Montfort IV (b. "probably" Nov or Dec 1339;
d. 1–2 Nov 1399, Nantes; bur. Nantes cathedral[1]), Duke of
Brittany, K.G.; and Maud de Holand (d. bef 13 Apr 1392)
m. abt 1365 as her first husband and his second wife Hugh de
Courtenay (d. 20 Feb 1373/1374), Lord Courtenay, son of
Hugh de Courtenay, First Founder, no issue; m. (2) Waleran de
Luxemburg (d. 19 Apr 1415, Castle of Ivoi, Luxemburg),
Count of Ligny and St. Paul/St. Pol.[2]

John Grey of Rotherfield (b. 9 Oct 1300, Rotherfield;
d. 1 Sep 1359, Rotherfield), son of John (d. 17 Oct 1311),
Lord Grey de Rotherfeld, and Margaret (daughter of William de
Odingsells); m. (1) bef 1 Mar 1311/1312 Catherine, daughter
and coheir of Bryan FitzAlan, Lord FitzAlan of Bedale, and
Maud; m. (2) Avice Marmion (liv. 20 Mar 1378/1379),
daughter of John de Marmion and sister of Robert de
Marmion.[3]

Richard FitzSimon (d. aft 1347–1348), son of Hugh
FitzSimon; m. Anne Conquest, by whom he had Adam
FitzSimon.[4]

Miles Stapleton (d. 4 Dec 1364, "possibly, as the family
historian conjectures, of wounds received in the battle of
Auray"; bur. Ingham, Norfolk) of Bedale and Ingham, eldest
son of Gilbert de Stapleton (d. 1321) and his wife, Agnes (also
called Matilda) FitzAlan (b. 1298) (elder daughter and coheiress
of Bryan FitzAlan, Lord FitzAlan of Bedale); he was the
grandson of Miles de Stapleton (d. 1314); Brian de Stapleton
(d. 1394) was his younger brother; Miles Stapleton
m. (1) [name unknown] and had issue of a son, John (d. 1355);
m. (2) 1350 Joan, second daughter and coheir of Oliver de
Ingham, Baron of Ingham in Norfolk, and widow of Roger
Lestrange of Knockin, by whom he had his heir, Miles de

---

[1] *CP*, Richmond section.
[2] *CP*, Devon section.
[3] *CP*, Grey (of Rotherfield) section; Beltz, pgs. 57–59.
[4] Beltz, pgs. 59–61.

Stapleton, and a daughter, Joan ("their only other issue"), wife of John Plays.[1]

Thomas Wale (d. 26 Oct 1352), son of Thomas Wale and his wife, Lucy, "lady of the manor of Wedon Pinkeney in Northamptonshire"[2]; m. Nicola; no issue. His heirs were Peter Malorre (son of his deceased sister, Margaret), Alice (m. Thomas Chamberlain), and his sister, Juliana.

Hugh Wrottesley (d. 23 Jan 1380/1381), son of William Wrottesley of Wrottesley, co. Stafford; m. (1) Mabel, daughter and coheir of Philip ap Rees, by whom he had his son and heir, John Wrottesley; m. (2) Isabel, daughter of John Arderne of Aldeford, Aderlegh, and Edds.[3]

Nele Loryng (d. 18 Mar 1385/1386; bur. priory of Dunstaple "to which he had been a considerable benefactor"[4]), son and heir of Roger Loryng of Chalgrave, co. Bedford, and his wife, Cassandra (daughter of Reginald Perot), and the grandson of Peter Loryng and Jane Morteyn; m. Margaret, daughter and heir of Ralph Beauple of Cnubeston, Devonshire. He had as his heirs two daughters,[5] Isabel Loryng (d. 21 Aug 1400; bur. Porlock Church, Somerset), who m. (1) William Cogan (d. 1382) of Huntspill, Somerset; m. (2) abt 1383 Robert Haryngton (d. 21 May 1406)[6]; and Margaret Loryng, who m. Thomas Peyvre of Todington, co. Bedford.

John Chandos (d. 31 Dec 1369, Mortemer, from wounds received in an engagement with the French at Lussac; believed bur. Mortemer[7]), son of Edward Chandos and Isabel Twyford

---

[1] Beltz, pgs. 61–62; *DNB*, "Stapleton, Miles de (d. 1364)"; *DNB*, "Stapleton, Brian de (1321?–1394)."

[2] Beltz, pg. 63.

[3] Beltz, pg. 64.

[4] Beltz, pg. 67; Wurts, *Magna Charta*, Part II, pg. 236; *DNB*, "Loryng, Sir Nigel or Nele (d. 1386)."

[5] Beltz, pg. 68; *DNB*, "Loryng, Sir Nigel or Nele (d. 1386)."

[6] *CP*, Harington or Haverington section.

[7] Beltz mentions a monument and cross on the bank of the river Vienne "now [1841] remaining near the ruins of the bridge of Lussac, and which, according to the tradition of the country, commemorate the

(continued...)

(daughter of Robert Twyford) and a descendant of Robert de
Chandos, who served with William the Conqueror. He had
sisters, Elizabeth (d. unm.), [1] Eleanor (m. (1) John Lawton,
"dear friend and companion in arms" of John Chandos;
m. (2) Roger Colyng of Herefordshire), and Margaret.
Margaret's daughter, Isabella, was wife of John Annesley (no
issue). [2] Unm.

James de Audeley (d. 1369, at his estate in Fontenay le
Comte in Poitou; bur. Poitou), Governor of Aquitaine and
Seneschal of Poitou, illegitimate son of James de Audeley [3]
(d. without legitimate issue "shortly before" 1 Mar 1333/
1334 [4]; bur. Langley Abbey, Norfolk) of Stretton Audeley and
Eva Clavering (d. 1369; bur. at Langley Abbey, Norfolk), [5]

---

[7] (...continued)
death of an Englishman of rank..." and since "no other person of
distinction is historically known to have perished on this spot," believes
"these memorials are silent records of [Chandos'] remarkable death."

[1] Silva-Vigiers, *This Moste Highe Prince...John of Gaunt*, pg. 101,
mentions a Sir John Chandos, "mentor and friend of the Black Prince,"
and Elizabeth Chandos, "sister and heir to the famous Sir John
Chandos." This Elizabeth Chandos (liv. 1373), states Silva-Vigiers,
married Peter de la Pole, son of John de la Pole, "named as one of the
unofficial members of the Duke's [John of Gaunt's] council." It is
further stated that the tomb of Elizabeth Chandos and Peter de la Pole is
at Radbourne Hall.

[2] Beltz, pgs. 70–75; *DNB*, "Chandos, Sir John (d. 1370)."

[3] James de Audeley, the father, was brother of Hugh de Audeley
(d. 1347), Earl of Gloucester, who m. Margaret de Clare, daughter of
Gilbert de Clare, Earl of Gloucester, and widow of Piers de Gaveston
(ex. 1312). Hugh and James' sister, Alice de Audeley, as widow of
Ralph de Greystoke (d. 1323), Lord Greystoke, married Ralph Neville
(d. 1367), 2nd Lord Neville. (Beltz, pgs. 75–85; *CP*, Audley section,
Neville section)

[4] *CP*, Audley section.

[5] Eva Clavering's mother was Hawise de Tibetot, daughter of Robert
de Tibetot. Eva Clavering m. (1) Thomas (of Aldithley) de Audeley
(b. 1288; d. bet. 8 Jul and 14 Dec 1307), eldest son of Nicholas
Audeley; no issue; m. (2) bef 2 Dec 1308 Thomas Ufford (k. 24 Jun
1314, Bannockburn) and had issue; m. (4) Robert Benhall. Her third

(continued...)

daughter and heir of John Clavering, 2nd Lord Clavering. No issue.[1]

Otes Holand (d. 3 Sep 1359, Normandy), son of Robert Holand (ex. 7 Oct 1328), 1st Baron Holand, and Maud la Zouche (d. 31 May 1349), and brother of Thomas Holand (d. 1360), Earl of Kent (a First Founder), and Robert Holand (d. 16 Mar 1372/1373, Halse or Hawes, Brackley; bur. St. James's Chapel, Brackley), 2nd Baron Holand.[2] Otho Holand in 1359 was governor of the Channel Islands. No issue.

Henry d'Enne (d. bet. May 1358 and Apr 1360[3]/ d. bef. 23 Apr 1360[4]). "Of the lineage of this knight, and the time and occasion of his entrance into the English service, nothing authenic is known."[5]

Sanchet d'Abrichecourt[6] (d. aft 20 Oct 1345), son of Nicholas d'Abrichecourt, probably the eldest; he had two brothers: Eustace d'Abrichecourt (d. 1 Dec 1372, Evreux) (m. at Wingham in Kent Michaelmas Day/29 Sep 1360 Elizabeth of Kent (d. 6 Jun 1411; bur. Grey Friars, Winchester), daughter of William V, Duke of Juliers, niece of Queen Philippa, and relict of John Plantagenet (d. 26–27 Dec 1352[7]), Earl of Kent); his other brother was Nicholas

---

[5](...continued)
husband, James Audeley (d. 1333/1334), was first cousin of her first husband; however, the Audley section of the *CP* states that because of circumstances not known for certain, she lived with, but did not marry, James Audeley. (Beltz, pgs. 75–84; *CP*, Audley section)

[1] *CP*, Audley section.

[2] *CP*, Holand section; Beltz, pgs. 84–85.

[3] *CP*, Vol. 2, Appendix B, wherein is included a note, "Incorrectly spelt Eam by previous writers."

[4] Beltz, pgs. 86–89.

[5] Beltz, pg. 86.

[6] *CP*, Vol. 2, Appendix B, "The Order of the Garter," offers an alternate spelling—Aubercicourt.

[7] *CP*, Kent section. John Plantagenet was son of Edmund of Woodstock (youngest son of Edward I, King of England) and the brother of Joan the Fair Maid of Kent.

d'Abrichecourt (m. Elizabeth, daughter and heir of Sibilla, the daughter of Thomas de Say). [1]

Walter Paveley (d. 28 Jun 1375; bur. Church of the Friars Preachers, or Blackfriars, London), son of Walter de Paveley (d. 1327/1329) and Maud Burghersh (b. 9 Aug 1304, Roydon, Norfolk) (daughter and heiress of Stephen Burghersh (d. 1309/1310), Baron Burghersh, brother of Bartholomew de Burghersh the elder (d. 1355), Baron Burghersh, and Henry Burghersh (d. 8 Jul 1341), Bishop of Lincoln). His wife's name is unknown, though it is believed she was of the St. Philibert family. He had two sons, Edward (d. 7 Dec 1375) and Walter (d. Dec 1379); however, neither son left issue. [2]

Sources:

Beltz, K. H., George Frederick, *Memorials of the Most Noble Order of the Garter*, William Pickering, London, 1841.

Cokayne, G. E., *The Complete Peerage*, St Catherine Press, London, 1912.

Hallam, Elizabeth, ed., *The Plantagenet Encyclopedia*, Grove Weidenfeld, NY, 1990.

Stephen, Sir Leslie, and Lee, Sir Sidney, eds., *Dictionary of National Biography*, Oxford University Press, London, 1964.

Wurts, John S., *Magna Charta*, Parts I–II, Brookfield Publishing Co., Philadelphia, Pa., 1945.

Thomas
Beauchamp
(d. 1369)
Earl of Warwick

---

[1] Beltz, pgs. 90–92. The death date of Sanchet d'Abrichecourt is uncertain; however, Beltz and the *CP* note that he was succeeded in the Order of the Garter by William FitzWaryn who died 28 Oct 1361.

[2] *DNB*, "Paveley, Sir Walter (1319–1375)"; Beltz, pgs. 93–95.

The Sureties for the Magna Charta

The Magna Charta was signed by King John in June of 1215 in the meadow of Runnymede, near London. Included in the charta was a clause which forced the king to keep the promises stated therein or to face a rebellion by his people and the loss of his possessions. To ensure that this clause was honored, the barons elected twenty-five from among themselves to "receive complaints against the actions of the king or his officials." In effect, the king became "reduced to the role of executive officer of the law under the supervision of a baronial committee." [1]

There are seventeen of those Sureties known to have descendants living to the present day [2]:

William d'Albini (Aubeney) (b. aft 1146; d. 1 May 1236), Lord of Belvoir Castle, Leicestershire, grandson of William de Albini (Brito) (d. 1155/1156); m. (1) Margery de Umfreville, daughter of Odinel de Umfreville; m. (2) Agatha Trusbut.

Roger Bigod (b. abt 1150; d. bef 2 Aug 1220/1221), Earl of Norfolk; m. Ida.

Hugh Bigod (d. Feb 1224/1225), Earl of Norfolk, son of Magna Charta Surety Roger Bigod; m. bef Lent 1207 Maud Marshal [3] (d. 27 Mar 1248 [4]/bet. 1 and 7 Apr 1248 [5]),

---

[1] Warren, *King John*, pg. 239.

[2] From Wurts, *Magna Charta* - Part I, pgs. 30–31, published 1945.

[3] Maud Marshal m. (2) "immediately upon Hugh's death" William de Warenne (d. 27 May 1240), Earl of Surrey. She "styled herself Marshal of England, Countess of Norfolk and Warenne." (*CP*, Norfolk section)

[4] *CP*, Norfolk section.

[5] *CP*, Surrey section.

daughter of William Marshal (d. 1219), Earl of Pembroke, and his wife, Isabel.

Henry de Bohun (b. 1176; d. 1 Jun 1220, on a pilgrimage to the Holy Land[1]), Earl of Hereford, Constable of England; m. Maud FitzGeoffrey (d. 1236), daughter of Geoffrey FitzPiers (d. 1213), Earl of Essex, and his wife, Beatrice de Say.

Richard de Clare (d. bet 30 Oct and 28 Nov 1217), 6th Earl of Clare, Hertford, and Gloucester, son of Roger de Clare (d. 1173), Earl of Hertford; m. Amice FitzRobert (d. 1 Jan 1224/1225), Countess of Gloucester, daughter of William FitzRobert, Earl of Gloucester, and his wife, Hawise de Beaumont.[2]

Gilbert de Clare (b. abt 1180; d. 25 Oct 1230, Penros, Brittany; bur. 10 Nov 1230, Tewkesbury), Earl of Gloucester and Hertford, son of Magna Charta Surety Richard de Clare; m. 9 Oct 1217 Isabel Marshal, daughter of William Marshal (d. 1219), Earl of Pembroke.[3]

John FitzRobert (d. 1240), Lord of Warkworth Castle, Northumberland; m. as his second wife Ada de Baliol (d. 29 Jul 1251, Stokesley[4]), daughter of Hugh de Balliol of Barnard Castle and sister of John de Balliol (who m. Devorgilla of Galloway[5]).

Robert FitzWalter (d. 9 Dec 1235; bur. Dunmow Priory), Lord of Dunmow Castle, Essexshire, Lord of Baynard's Castle, leader of the Magna Charta barons[6]; m. Gunnor (liv. 1207), daughter of Robert of Valognes. The *DNB* states, "it is said"

---

[1] *DNB*, "Bohun, Henry de, first Earl of Hereford (1176–1220)."

[2] *Sureties* 28-1.

[3] *Ancestral* 63-28, 66-27; *CP*, Gloucester section.

[4] *Sureties* 44-1.

[5] Devorgilla and John de Balliol were parents of John de Balliol the younger, King of Scots. (Bingham, *Kings and Queens of Scotland*, Table 3)

[6] *DNB*, "FitzWalter, Robert (d. 1235)."

that FitzWalter had a second wife, Rohese.[1] *Sureties*[2] states
FitzWalter m. Rohese and had issue of Walter FitzRobert
(d. bef 10 Apr 1258), who m. Ida de Longespée, daughter of
William Longespée, Earl of Salisbury and illegitimate son of
Henry II, King of England.

William de Huntingfield (d. bef 25 Jan 1220/1221), a
feudal baron in Suffolk, son of Roger de Huntingfield and Alice
de Senlis[3]; m. by 1194 Isabel (d. 1209), daughter of William
FitzRoger.

John de Lacie (b. 1192; d. 22 Jul 1240), Earl of Lincoln,
Lord of Halton Castle, Cheshire; m. bef 21 Jun 1221 as his
second wife Margaret de Quincy (d. bef 30 Mar 1266),
daughter of Robert de Quincy (d. 1217) and Hawise of Chester
(d. bet 6 Jun 1241 and 3 Mar 1242/1243), Countess of Lincoln.

William de Lanvallei (d. 1217), Lord of Stanway Castle,
Essex; m. a daughter of Alan Basset.

William Malet (d. abt 1217), Lord of Curry-Malet,
Somersetshire; m. Aliva/Alicia Basset, daughter of Thomas
Basset. His two daughters were Mabel and Helewise/Hawise.
Mabel Malet m. Hugh de Vivonia. Hawise Malet (liv. 4 May
1287) m. (1) by 23 Mar 1216/1217 Hugh Poyntz (d. 4 Apr

---

[1] *DNB*, "FitzWalter, Robert (d. 1235)." Robert FitzWalter's first
daughter by his first marriage, Maud, m. (no issue) Geoffrey de
Mandeville (d. 23 Feb 1215/1216), Earl of Essex. His second daughter
by his first marriage, Christina, m. (1) (no issue) William Mandeville
(d. 8 Jan 1226/1227), Earl of Essex, brother of Geoffrey de Mandeville;
she m. (2) (no issue) Raymond de Burgh (d. abt 1 Jul 1230, Nantes).
(*CP*, Essex section)

The *DNB* article states that Robert FitzWalter had a son,
"presumably Robert Fitzwalter, junior," who must have died before his
father and that his heir, Walter FitzRobert (d. 1257), was probably a
younger son or a grandson.

The *CP*, Salisbury section, pg. 381, footnote (k), states that Ida was
"said to have m." (1) Walter FitzRobert ("presumably the Walter
FitzRobert whose wife was Ida in 1256–57") and (2) William de
Beauchamp of Bedford.

[2] *Sureties* 50.

[3] *Sureties* 51-1.

1220); m. (2) Robert de Muscegros (d. 29 Jan 1253/1254).[1]

William de Mowbray (d. by Mar 1223/1224 or
d. abt 1222?/1223/1224, Axholme; bur. Newburgh), Lord of
Axholme Castle, Lincolnshire, son of Nigel/Nele de Mowbray
(d. 1191, Acre, on Crusade) and his wife, Mabel (d. abt 1203)
(perhaps the daughter of Edmund or Roger, Earl of Clare); is
said to have married Agnes de Albini (daughter of perhaps the
second Earl of Arundel) or Avice of unknown parentage. There
was issue of two sons, Nigel/Nele de Mowbray (d. without
issue, prob. 1228/1230, Nantes) and Roger de Mowbray
(d. abt Nov 1266), who became the father of Roger (d. 1298),
7th baron Mowbray.[2]

Saire de Quincey (b. 1155; d. 3 Nov 1219, Damietta;
bur. Acre), Earl of Winchester; m. bef 1173 Margaret de
Beaumont (d. bef 12 Feb 1234/1235), daughter of Robert de
Beaumont (d. 1190, Greece, on returning from pilgrimage to
Palestine[3]), 3rd Earl of Leicester, and his wife, Pernel de
Grandmesnil (d. 1 Apr 1212).[4]

Robert de Roos/Ros (d. bef 23 Dec 1226; bur. Temple
Church, London), nicknamed Fursan, Lord of Hamlake Castle,
Yorkshire; m. at Haddington 1191 Isabel, illegitimate daughter
of William the Lion, King of Scots, by Isabel Avenal, and the
widow of Robert de Brus. They had issue of William de Ros
(d. prob. 1264[5]) and Robert, Baron Ros of Wark (d. 1274).[6]

Geoffrey de Saye (b. abt 1155; d. bef 26 Aug 1230,
Poitou; bur. Hospital of St. Mary, Dover), a feudal baron in
Sussex?; m. Alice, "possibly" daughter of John de Chesney;

---

[1] *Sureties* 57-1, 2; 60-2; *DNB*, "Malet or Mallet, William
(*fl.* 1195–1215)."

[2] *DNB*, "Mowbray, "William de, fourth Baron Mowbray
(d. 1222?)"; *CP*, Mowbray section.

[3] *DNB*, "Beaumont, Robert de, Earl of Leicester (d. 1190), baronial
leader."

[4] *CP*, Winchester section, Leicester section; *Sureties* 74.

[5] *CP*, Ros section.

[6] *DNB*, "Ros, Robert de (d. 1227), surnamed Fursan"; *DNB*, "Ros,
Robert de, Baron Ros of Wark (d. 1274)"; *DNB*, "Ros, William de,
second Baron Ros (d. 1317)"; *CP*, Ros section.

m. (2) Margery, "sis. and coh. of Will. Briwerre, by whom he was divorced." Margery was widow of Eudes de Dammartin (d. 1225).[1]

Robert de Vere (b. aft 1164; d. bef 25 Oct 1221; bur. Benedictine priory at Hatfield), 3rd Earl of Oxford, son of Aubrey de Vere (d. 26 Dec 1194; bur. Colne), 1st Earl of Oxford; m. Isabel (b. abt 1176?; d. 3 Feb 1245[2]; bur. Church of the Preaching Friars, Oxford, which she had founded), daughter of Hugh de Bolbec and widow of Henry de Nonant. They were parents of Hugh de Vere (b. abt 1210; d. bef 23 Dec 1263; bur. Earls Colne), Earl of Oxford.[3]

The eight sureties not known to have surviving descendants:

William de Fortibus (d. 29 Mar 1241, in the Mediterranean), Earl of Aumale, son of Hawise (d. 11 Mar 1213/1214) (daughter of William le Gros, Count of Aumale) and her second husband (m. aft 3 Jul 1190), William de Forz (d. 1195); m. in or aft 1214 Aveline de Montfichet (d. abt Nov 1239; bur. Thornton Abbey), daughter of Richard de Montfichet of Stansted, Essex, and his wife, Milicent.[4]

William de Hardell (d. aft 1216), Mayor of London.

Geoffrey de Mandeville (d. 23 Feb 1215/1216; bur. Trinity Priory within Aldgate), Earl of Essex and Gloucester; m. (1) Maud, daughter of Robert FitzWauter of Woodham Walter, Essex; no issue; m. (2) bet 16 and 26 Jan 1213/1214, Isabelle (or Hadwisa) (d. 14 Oct 1217; bur. Canterbury Cathedral Church), daughter of William FitzRobert, Earl of Gloucester, and the ex-wife of John, King of England; no issue.[5]

William Marshal (b. abt 1190; d. 6 Apr 1231; bur. 15 Apr 1231, Temple Church, London), Earl of Pembroke, son of

---

[1] *CP*, Say section.
[2] *CP*, Oxford section.
[3] *CP*, Oxford section; *DNB*, "Vere, Robert de, third Earl of Oxford (1170?–1221)."
[4] *CP*, Aumale section.
[5] *CP*, Essex section.

William Marshal (d. 1219), Earl of Pembroke; m. (1) Alice
(d. bef 1221; bur. St. Paul's Cathedral, London), daughter of
Baldwin de Bethune, Count of Aumale; no issue; m. (2) 23 Apr
1224 Eleanor, daughter of John, King of England, and Isabelle
of Angoulême; no issue. Eleanor m. (2) Simon de Montfort
(d. 1265), Earl of Leicester.[1]

Roger de Montbegon (d. 1226), Lord of Hornby,
Lancashire.

Richard de Montfichet (d. aft 1258), perhaps a feudal
baron in Essex.

Richard de Percy (b. abt 1170; d. in or bef Aug 1244;
bur. Fountains Abbey), a feudal baron of Yorkshire, son of
Jocelin of Louvain and Agnes de Percy; m. (1) Alice[2];
m. (2) Agnes (d. bef 20 Jul 1293), daughter of Geoffrey de
Neville of Raby.[3]

Eustace de Vesci (d. 1216), Lord of Alnwick,
Northumberland.

Sources:

Bridgwater, William, and Sherwood, Elizabeth J., *The Columbia Encyclopedia*, Columbia University Press, Morningside Heights, New York, 1950.

Cokayne, G. E., *The Complete Peerage*, St Catherine Press, London, 1912.

Stephen, Sir Leslie, and Lee, Sir Sidney, eds., *Dictionary of National Biography*, Oxford University Press, London, 1964.

Warren, W. L., *King John*, University of California Press, Berkeley, 1978.

Weis, Frederick Lewis, *The Magna Charta Sureties, 1215*, Genealogical Publishing Co., Inc., Baltimore, 1982.

Wurts, John S., *Magna Charta* - Part I, Brookfield Publishing Co., Philadelphia, PA, 1945, pgs. 30-31.

---

[1] *CP*, Pembroke section.

[2] Alice was "a sister of William Brewer." (*DNB*, "Percy, Richard de, fifth Baron Percy (1170?-1244)")

[3] *CP*, Percy section.

Tables and Lists
Bibliography and References

The Kings of England 1066–1377

King	Born	Crowned	Reigned	Married	Died
Norman Kings					
William I the Conqueror	Abt 1027/1028	25 Dec 1066	1066–1087	Matilda of Flanders; m. 1051/1053: b. abt 1030/1031; crowned Whitsunday 1068; d. 2 or 3 Nov 1083	9 Sep 1087
William II Rufus	1056–1060	26 Sep 1087	1087–1100		2 Aug 1100
Henry I Beauclerc	Abt Sep 1067/1068/1070	5/6 Aug 1100	1100–1135	(1) Edith Matilda of Scotland; m. 11 Nov 1100; b. 1079/1080; crowned 11 Nov 1100; d. 1 May 1118; (2) Adelaide of Louvain; m. 29 Jan 1121/1122; b. abt 1103/1105; crowned 3 Feb 1121/1122; d. 23 Mar or 23 Apr 1151	1 Dec 1135
Stephen	Abt 1096/1097	22/26 Dec 1135, St. Stephen's Day; 25 Dec 1141	1135–1154	Matilda of Boulogne; m. 1125; b. abt 1103 or 1105; crowned by Easter/22 Mar 1136; d. 3 May 1152	25 Oct 1154

King	Born	Crowned	Reigned	Married	Died
Matilda FitzEmpress	Abt 1102	Was not crowned.		(1) Henry V, Holy Roman Emperor; m. 7 Jan 1114; d. 22/23 May 1125; (2) Geoffrey Plantagenet; m. 22 May 1127; b. 24 Aug 1113; d. 7 Sep 1151	9/10 Sep 1167
Plantagenet or Angevin Kings					
Henry II Curtmantle	5 Mar 1133	19 Dec 1154	1154–1189	Eleanor of Aquitaine; m. 18 May 1152; crowned 19 Dec 1154; b. abt 1122; d. 31 Mar or 1 Apr 1204	6 Jul 1189
Richard I the Lion-Heart	8 Sep 1157	3 Sep 1189	1189–1199	Berengaria of Navarre; m. 12 May 1191; b. abt 1163; crowned 12 May 1191; d. abt 1230	6 Apr 1199
John	24 Dec 1167	27 May 1199	1199–1216	(1) Isabella/Hadwisa, Countess of Gloucester; m. 29 Aug 1189; marriage annulled 1200; d. 14 Oct 1217; (2) Isabella of Angouleme; m. 24 Aug 1200; b. 1186/1188; crowned 8 Oct 1200; d. 31 May 1246	18/19 Oct 1216

King	Born	Crowned	Reigned	Married	Died
Henry III	1 Oct 1207	(1) 28 Oct 1216 (2) 17 May 1220	1216–1272	Eleanor of Provence; m. 14 Jan 1236; b. abt 1217/1223; crowned 20 Jan 1236; d. 24 Jun 1291	16 Nov 1272
Edward I	17 Jun 1239	19 Aug 1274	1272–1307	(1) Eleanor of Castile; m. Oct 1254; b. abt 1244; crowned 19 Aug 1274; d. 28/29 Nov 1290; (2) Marguerite of France; m. 10 Sep 1299; b. 1279; d. 14 Feb 1317	7 Jul 1307
Edward II	25 Apr 1284	23/25 Feb 1308 (deposed 20 Jan 1327)	1307–1327	Isabella of France; m. 25 Jan 1308; b. 1292 or 1295; crowned 23/25 Feb 1308; d. 22 Aug 1358	21 Sep 1327
Edward III	13 Nov 1312	2 Feb 1327	1327–1377	Philippa of Hainault; m. 24 Jan 1328; b. 24 Jun 1311/1314; crowned Mar 1330; d. 14 Aug 1369 Windsor	21 Jun 1377

The Succession 1066–1547

The Normans

1066–1087 William I the Conqueror
1087–1100 William II Rufus
1100–1135 Henry I
1135–1154 Stephen (contested by Matilda "the Empress")

The Plantagenets

1153–1189 Henry II
1189–1199 Richard I
1199–1216 John
1216–1272 Henry III
1272–1307 Edward I
1307–1327 Edward II
1327–1377 Edward III
1377–1399 Richard II

The House of Lancaster

1399–1413 Henry IV
1413–1422 Henry V
1422–1461 Henry VI

The House of York

1461–1483 Edward IV
1483   Edward V
1483–1485 Richard III

The House of Tudor

1485–1509 Henry VII
1509–1547 Henry VIII

The Succession 1066–1377

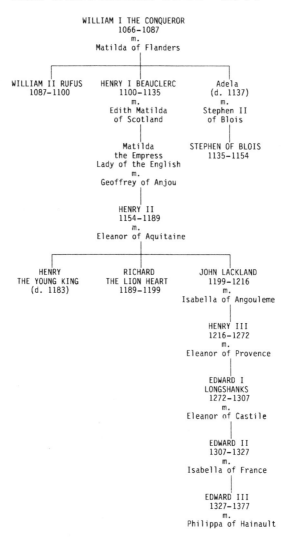

WILLIAM I THE CONQUEROR
1066–1087
m.
Matilda of Flanders

WILLIAM II RUFUS
1087–1100

HENRY I BEAUCLERC
1100–1135
m.
Edith Matilda
of Scotland

Adela
(d. 1137)
m.
Stephen II
of Blois

Matilda
the Empress
Lady of the English
m.
Geoffrey of Anjou

STEPHEN OF BLOIS
1135–1154

HENRY II
1154–1189
m.
Eleanor of Aquitaine

HENRY
THE YOUNG KING
(d. 1183)

RICHARD
THE LION HEART
1189–1199

JOHN LACKLAND
1199–1216
m.
Isabella of Angouleme

HENRY III
1216–1272
m.
Eleanor of Provence

EDWARD I
LONGSHANKS
1272–1307
m.
Eleanor of Castile

EDWARD II
1307–1327
m.
Isabella of France

EDWARD III
1327–1377
m.
Philippa of Hainault

The Main Battles
of the Wars of the Roses

First Battle of St. Albans	22 May 1455
Blore Heath	23 Sep 1459
Northampton	10 Jul 1460
Wakefield	30 Dec 1460
Mortimer's Cross	2 Feb 1461
Second Battle of St. Albans	17 Feb 1461
Towton	29 Mar 1461
Hexham	14 May 1464
Banbury	26 Jul 1469
Stamford	12 Mar 1470
Barnet	14 Apr 1471
Tewkesbury	4 May 1471
Bosworth	22 Aug 1485
Stoke	Jun 1487

Sources:

Alderman, Clifford Lindsey, *Blood-Red the Roses*, Julian Messner, NY, 1971.

Gillingham, John, *The Wars of the Roses: Peace and Conflict in Fifteenth Century England*, Weidenfeld and Nicolson, London, 1993.

Ross, Charles, ed., *Patronage, Pedigree and Power in Later Medieval England*, Alan Sutton, Rowman & Littlefield, 1979.

Kings of France
987-1589

The Capetians

Hugh Capet (987–996)
Robert II the Pious (996–1031)
Henry I (1031–1060)
Philip I (1060–1108)
Louis VI the Fat (1108–1137)
Louis VII the Young (1137–1180)
Philip II Augustus (1180–1223)
Louis VIII the Lion (1223–1226)
Louis IX Saint Louis (1226–1270)
Philip III the Bold (1270–1285)
Philip IV the Fair (1285–1314)
Louis X le Hutin (the Quarrelsome) (1314–1316)
John I (1316)
Philip V the Tall (1316–1322)
Charles IV le Bel (the Fair) (1322–1328)

The House of Valois

Philip VI of Valois (1328–1350)
John II the Good (1350–1364)
Charles V the Wise (1364–1380)
Charles VI the Well-Beloved/Mad (1380–1422)
Charles VII the Well-Served/the Victorious (1422–1461)
Louis XI (1461–1483)
Charles VIII (1483–1498)

The House of Valois-Orleans

Louis XII (1498–1515)
Francis I (1515–1547)
Henry II (1547–1559)
Frances II (1559–1560)
Charles IX (1560–1574)
Henry III (1574–1589)

Sources:

De Castries, Duc, *The Lives of the Kings & Queens of France*, Alfred A.
    Knopf, NY, 1979.
Genealogy of the Kings of France, Artaud Freres Publication, Nantes,
    France.
Hallam, Elizabeth M., ed., *Capetian France 987–1328*, Longman,
    London and New York, 1980.
Morby, John E., *The Wordsworth Handbook of Kings & Queens*,
    Wordsworth Reference, Cumberland House, Hertfordshire, 1994.
Williamson, David, *DeBrett's Kings and Queens of Europe*, Salem
    House Publishers, Mass., 1988.

Kings of Scots
1005–1625

Malcolm II (1005–1034)
Duncan I (1034–1040)
MacBeth (1040–1057)
Lulach (1057–1058)
Malcolm III Canmore (1058–1093)
Donald Ban (1093–1094)
Duncan II (1094)
Donald Ban and Edmund (1094–1097)
Edgar the Peaceable (1097–1107)
Alexander I the Fierce (1107–1124)
David I (1124–1153)
Malcolm IV the Maiden (1153–1165)
William the Lion (1165–1214)
Alexander II (1214–1249)
Alexander III (1249–1286)
Margaret, Maid of Norway (1286–1290)
Interregnum (1290–1292)
John Balliol (1292–1296)
Robert I the Bruce (1306–1329)
David II (1329–1371)
Robert II (1371–1390)
Robert III (1390–1406)
James I (1406–1437)
James II (1437–1460)
James III (1460–1488)
James IV (1488–1513)
James V (1513–1542)
Mary, Queen of Scots (1542–1567)
James VI (1567–1625) (James I of England (1603–1625))

Sources:

Bingham, Caroline, *Kings and Queens of Scotland*, Dorset Press, NY, 1976.
Bold, Alan, *Scotland's Kings & Queens*, Pitkin Pictorials Ltd., London, 1980.
Bridgwater, William, Editor-in-chief, *The Columbia-Viking Desk Encyclopedia*, Viking Press, New York, 1953.
Donaldson, Gordon, *Scottish Kings*, Barnes & Noble Books, NY, 1967.
Ross, Josephine, *The Monarchy of Britain*, William Morrow and Company, Inc., NY, 1982.

Bibliography and References

Adams, Arthur, and Weis, F. L., *The Magna Charta Sureties, 1215*, Genealogical Publishing Co., Baltimore, 1964.

Addison, William, *Essex Worthies*, Phillomore & Co. Ltd., London and Chichester, 1973.

Alderman, Clifford Lindsey, *Blood-Red the Roses*, Julian Messner, NY, 1971.

Anderson, James, *Royal Genealogies: or, the Genealogical Tables of Emperors, Kings and Princes, from Adam to these Times*, Bettenham, London, 1732.

Andrews, Allen, *Kings & Queens of England & Scotland*, Marshall Cavendish Publications Limited, London, 1976.

Andrewes, Patience, *Frederick II of Hohenstaufen*, Oxford University Press, London, 1970.

Angerville, Howard H., comte d', compiler, *Living Descendants of Blood Royal (in America)*, Volume Two, World Nobility and Peerage, London, 1959.

Appleby, John T., *Henry II, the Vanquished King*, G. Bell & Sons, Ltd., London, 1962.

Appleby, John T., *The Troubled Reign of King Stephen 1135–1154*, Barnes & Noble Books, New York, 1995.

Armitage-Smith, Sydney, *John of Gaunt*, Barnes & Noble, Inc., 1964.

Arnstein, Walter L., *Britain Yesterday & Today 1830–Today*.

Ashley, Maurice, *The Life and Times of King John*, Weidenfeld and Nicolson, London, 1972.

Aubrey, W. H. S., *The Rise and Growth of the English Nation: A History of and for the People in Three Volumes*, D. Appleton and Company, NY, 1898.

Bagley, J. J., *The Earls of Derby 1485–1985*, Sidgwick & Jackson, London, 1985.

Barber, Richard, *A Strong Land & A Sturdy*, The Seabury Press, New York, 1976.

Barber, Richard, *The Devil's Crown: Henry II, Richard I, John*, British Broadcasting Corporation, London, 1978.

Barber, Richard, ed., *The Pastons: The Letters of a Family in the Wars of the Roses*, Penguin Books, Middlesex, New York, 1985.

Barlow, Frank, *Edward the Confessor*, University of California Press, Berkeley and Los Angeles, 1970.

Barlow, Frank, *William Rufus*, University of California Press, Berkeley and Los Angeles, 1983.

Barton, John, and Law, Joy, *The Hollow Crown*, The Dial Press, NY, 1971.

Bateman, Somerset, B.A. (London), *Simon de Montfort: His Life and Work*, Cornish Brothers Ltd, Birmingham, 1923.

Belloc, Hilaire, *William the Conqueror*, Peter Davies Limited, Edinburgh, 1933.

Beltz, George Frederick, K. H., *Memorials of the Most Noble Order of the Garter from Its Foundation to the Present Time*, William Pickering, London, 1841 (reprint by AMS Press, Inc., NY, 1973).

Bémont, Charles, *Simon de Montfort, Earl of Leicester 1208–1265*, trans. by E. F. Jacob, Greenwood Press, Publishers, Westport, Connecticut, 1974 reprint of 1930 edition.

Bennett, H. S., *The Pastons and Their England: Studies in an Age of Transition*, Cambridge University Press, Cambridge, 1991.

Bennett, H. S., *Six Medieval Men and Women*, Cambridge at the University Press, Cambridge, 1955.

Bennett, Michael, *Lambert Simnel and the Battle of Stoke*, St. Martin's Press, NY, 1987.

Bennett, Michael, *The Battle of Bosworth*, St. Martin's Press, New York, 1985.

Bentley, James, *Restless Bones: The Story of Relics*, Constable, London, 1985.

Berleth, Richard, *The Twilight Lords: An Irish Chronicle*, Alfred A. Knopf, NY, 1978.

Besant, Walter, *Story of King Alfred*, D. Appleton and Company, 1902.

Bingham, Caroline, *Kings and Queens of Scotland*, Dorset Press, NY, 1976.

Bingham, Caroline, *The Stewart Kingdom of Scotland 1371–1603*, Barnes & Noble Books, New York, 1995.

Bingham, The Hon. D., *The Marriages of the Bourbons*, Vol. 1, AMS Press, NY, 1970.

Bingham, The Hon. Clive D., *The Chief Ministers of England 920-1720*, E. P. Dutton and Co., NY, 1923.

Bisson, T. N., *The Medieval Crown of Aragon: A Short History*, Clarendon Press, Oxford, 1991.

Bold, Alan, *Scotland's Kings & Queens*, Pitkin Pictorials Ltd., London, 1980.

Bowen, Marjorie, *Mary, Queen of Scots*, Sphere Books Limited, London, 1971.

Bridgwater, William, Editor-in-chief, *The Columbia-Viking Desk Encyclopedia*, Viking Press, New York, 1953.

Bridgwater, William, Editor-in-chief, *The Columbia-Viking Desk Encyclopedia*, Viking Press, New York, 1968.

Bridgwater, William, and Sherwood, Elizabeth J., *The Columbia Encyclopedia*, Columbia University Press, Morningside Heights, New York, 1950.

Breasted, James Henry, Huth, Carl F., and Harding, Samuel Bannister, *European History Atlas*, Denoyer-Geppert Company, Chicago, 1957.

Browning, Charles H., *The Magna Charta Barons and their American Descendants*, Genealogical Publishing Co., Inc., Baltimore, MD, for Clearfield Co., 1991.

Bruce, John Collingwood, *The Bayeux Tapestry: The Battle of Hastings and the Norman Conquest*, Dorset Press, New York, 1987.

Bruce, Marie Louise, *Anne Boleyn: A Biography*, Coward, McCann & Geoghegan, Inc., NY, 1972.

Bryan, Thomas R., *The Name and Family of Bryan or Brian*, Shaffer Printing Co., Edgefield, SC, 1970.

Bryant, Arthur, *The Age of Chivalry: The Story of England*, The Reprint Society, London, 1963.

Buck, Sir George, edited by Arthur Kincaid, *The History of King Richard the Third (1619)*, Alan Sutton, Gloucester, 1979.

Burke, Sir Bernard, and Burke, Ashworth P., *A Genealogical and Heraldic History of the Peerage and Baronetage, The Privy Council, Knightage and Companionage*, 69th Edition, Harrison and Sons, London, 1907.

Burke's Peerage, *Burke's Guide to the Royal Family*, Burke's Peerage Limited, 1973.

Burke's Genealogical and Heraldic History of the Peerage: and Baronetage & Knightage, 100th Edition, Burke's Peerage Limited, London, 1953.

Burke, Esq., John, *Extinct and Dormant Baronetcies of England, Ireland, and Scotland*, Genealogical Publishing Co., London, Baltimore, 1985.

Burke, John, *Life in the Castle in Medieval England*, Dorset Press, NY, 1978.

Burke, John Bernard, Esq., *Roll of Battle Abbey*, Genealogical Publishing Co., Baltimore, 1985.

Burke, Sir Bernard, *A Genealogical History of the Dormant, Abeyant, Forfeited, and Extinct Peerages of the British Empire*, (dist. by Heraldic Book Co., Baltimore) London, 1883.

Burton, Elizabeth, *The Pageant of Early Tudor England 1485–1558*, Charles Scribner's Sons, New York, 1976.

Bush, Mrs. Annie Forbes, *Memoirs of the Queens of France with Notices of the Royal Favorites*, Vol. I, Henry Colburn, Publisher, London, 1843.

Butler, Denis, *1066: The Story of a Year*, Anthony Blond Ltd., London, 1966.

Calmette, Joseph, *The Golden Age of Burgundy: The Magnificent Dukes and their Courts*, W. W. Norton & Company, Inc., New York, 1963.

Camp, Anthony J., *My Ancestors Came with the Conqueror: Those Who Did and Some of Those Who Probably Did Not*, Genealogical Publishing Co., Inc., 1990.

Canning, John, ed., *100 Great Kings, Queens, and Rulers of the World*, Taplinger Publishing Co., NY, 1968.

Cannon, John, and Griffiths, Ralph, *The Oxford Illustrated History of the British Monarchy*, Oxford University Press, Oxford and NY, 1988.

Cantor, Norman F., ed., *The Medieval Reader*, HarperCollins Publishers, New York, 1994.

Carpenter, Edward, and Gentleman, David, *Westminster Abbey*, Weidenfeld and Nicolson, London, 1987.

Cartellieri, Otto, *The Court of Burgundy: Studies in the History of Civilization*, Kegan Paul, Trench, Trubner & Co., Ltd., New York, 1929.

Chamberlin, Russell, *The Tower of London: An Illustrated History*, Webb & Bower Limited,1987.

Chambers, Anne, *Eleanor, Countess of Desmond*, Wolfhound Press, Dublin, 1986.

Chaplais, Pierre, *Piers Gaveston: Edward II's Adoptive Brother*, Clarendon Press, Oxford, 1994.

Chapman, Hester, *The Sisters of Henry VIII*.

Chapman, Hester W., *The Last Tudor King: A Study of Edward VI*, The MacMillan Company, NY, 1959.

Chapman, Hester W., *The Challenge of Anne Boleyn*, Coward, Cann & Geoghegan, Inc., NY, 1974.

Chapman, Hester W., *Two Tudor Portraits: Henry Howard & Lady Katherine Grey*, Little, Brown and Company, Boston, Toronto, 1960.

Cheetham, Anthony, *The Life and Times of Richard III*, Cross River Press, New York, 1992.

Chrimes, Ross, Griffiths, eds., *Fifteenth Century England 1399-1509*, Manchester University Press, NY, 1972.

Chrimes, S. B., *Lancastrians, Yorkists, & Henry VII*, MacMillan & Co. Ltd., NY, 1964.

Churchill, Winston S., *The Birth of Britain*, Bantam Books Inc., New York, 1963.

Chute, Marchette, *Geoffrey Chaucer of England*, E. P. Dutton and Co., Inc., NY, 1946, 1958.

Clifford, Esther Rowland, *A Knight of Great Renown*, The University of Chicago Press, 1961.

Clive, Mary, *This Sun of York: A Biography of Edward IV*, Alfred A. Knopf, NY, 1974.

Coffman, Ramon P., *Famous Kings and Queens for Young People*, A. S. Barnes & Company, NY, 1947.

Cokayne, G. E., *The Complete Peerage*, St Catherine Press, London, 1912.

Collins, *The Peerage of England*.

Collis, Louise, *Memoirs of a Medieval Woman*, Harper & Row, NY, 1964.

Cooper, Charles Henry, *Memoir of Margaret, Countess of Richmond and Derby*, Deighton Bell and Co., London, 1874.

Constant, Jean-Marie, *Les Guise*, Hachette litterature, 1984.

Costain, Thomas B., *The Conquerors*, Doubleday & Co., Inc., Garden City, NY, 1949.

Costain, Thomas B., *The Magnificent Century*, Doubleday & Co., Inc., 1951.

Costain, Thomas B., *The Three Edwards*, Doubleday & Company, NY, 1958.

Costain, Thomas B., *The Last Plantagenets*, Popular Library Eagle Books Edition, NY, 1962.

Coulton, G. G., *Chaucer and His England*, Russell & Russell, New York, 1957.

Coward, Barry, *The Stanleys, Lords Stanley and Earls of Derby 1385-1672: The origins, wealth and power of a landowning family*, Printed for the Chetham Society, Manchester, 1983.

Crankshaw, Edward, *The Hapsburgs: Portrait of a Dynasty*, The Viking Press, New York, 1971.

Crawford, Anne, *Letters of the Queens of England 1100-1547*, Alan Sutton Publishing Ltd, Phoenix Mill, 1994.

Crystal, David, ed., *The Barnes & Noble Encyclopedia*, Barnes & Noble Books, New York, 1990.

Dahmus, Joseph, *Seven Medieval Kings*, Doubleday & Company, Inc., Garden City, New York, 1967.

Daniell, Christopher, *A Traveller's History of England*, Interlink Books, NY, 1991.

Davis, R. H. C., *King Stephen 1135-1154*, Longman, London, 1980.

De Castries, Duc, *The Lives of the Kings & Queens of France*, Alfred A. Knopf, NY, 1979.

Delderfield, Eric R., *Kings and Queens of England and Great Britain*, Weathervane Books, New York, 1972.

Delderfield, Eric R., *Kings and Queens of England and Great Britain*, Taplinger Publishing Co., NY, 1970.

Denholm-Young, N., *Richard of Cornwall*, Basil Blackwell, Oxford, 1947.

Dixon, William Hepworth, *Her Majesty's Tower*, Thomas Y. Crowell & Co., New York (Preface dated 1884).

Dockray, Keith, *Three Chronicles of the Reign of Edward IV*, Alan Sutton Publishing, Gloucester, 1988.

Donaldson, Gordon, *Scottish Kings*, Barnes & Noble Books, NY, 1967.

Douglas, David C., *The Norman Fate: 1100–1154*, University of California Press, Berkeley and Los Angeles, 1976.

Douglas, David C., *William the Conqueror*, University of California Press, Berkeley and Los Angeles, 1964.

Duby, Georges, *France in the Middle Ages*, trans. by Juliet Vale, Blackwell, Oxford and Cambridge, 1991.

Duby, Georges, *William Marshal: The Flower of Chivalry*, Pantheon Books, NY, 1984, trans. by Richard Howard, 1985.

Duncan, Jonathan, Esq., *The Dukes of Normandy, from the Time of Rollo to the Expulsion of King John by Philip Augustus of France*, Joseph Rickerby, Sherbourn Land, and Harvey and Darton, Gracechurch Street, London, 1839.

Durant, Will, *The Age of Faith*, Simon and Schuster, NY, 1950.

Ellis, Sir Geoffrey, Bt., *Earldoms in Fee*, The Saint Catherine Press, Limited, London, 1963.

Elton, G. R., *England Under the Tudors*, Methuen & Co., Ltd, London, 1955.

Erlanger, Philippe, *Margaret of Anjou: Queen of England*, trans. by Edward Hyams, Elek Books, London, 1970.

Erickson, Carrolly, *Bloody Mary: The Remarkable Life of Mary Tudor*, Doubleday & Company, Inc., Garden City, NY, 1978.

Erickson, Carrolly, *The First Elizabeth*, Summit Books, NY, 1983.

Ferguson, Charles, *Naked to Mine Enemies*, Vol. II, Time Incorporated, New York, 1958.

Ferguson, John, *English Diplomacy 1422-1461*, Oxford at the Clarendon Press, 1972.

Field, P. J. C., *The Life and Times of Sir Thomas Malory*, St. Edmundsbury Press, Ltd., Bury St. Edmunds, Suffolk, 1993.

Fines, John, *Who's Who in the Middle Ages*, Barnes & Noble Books, New York, 1995.

Fletcher, Ifan Kyrle, *The British Court: Its Traditions & Ceremonial*, Cassell & Company Ltd., London, 1953.

Forester, Thomas, ed. and trans., *The Chronical of Henry of Huntingdon*, Henry G. Bohn, York St., Covent Garden, 1853.

Fraser, Antonia, *The Warrior Queens*, Alfred A. Knopf, NY, 1989.

Fraser, Antonia, ed., *The Lives of the Kings & Queens of England*, Alfred A. Knopf, NY, 1975.

Fry, Plantagenet Somerset, *The Tower of London: Cauldron of Britain's Past*, Quiller Press, London, 1990.

Fuller, Thomas, and Freeman, John, *The Worthies of England*, George Allen & Unwin Ltd, London, 1952.

Fuller, Thomas, and Nuttall, P. A., *Fuller's Worthies of England*, Vol. II, AMS Press Inc., NY, 1965.

Furtado, Peter; Geddes, Candida; Harris, Nathaniel; Harrison, Hazel; and Pettit, Paul, *The Ordnance Survey Guide to Castles in Britain*, W. W. Norton & Company, New York, London, 1987.

Gairdner, James, *Houses of Lancaster and York*, Logmans, Green, and Co., 1887.

Galliou, Patrick, and Jones, Michael, *The Bretons*, Blackwell, Oxford.

Gardner, John, *The Life and Times of Chaucer*, Alfred A. Knopf, NY, 1977.

Gascoigne, Christina, and Bamber, *Castles of Britain*, Thames and Hudson, NY, 1992.

Geldner, Ferdinand, *Konradin*, Meisenbach, Bamberg, 1970.

Gies, Frances, and Gies, Joseph, *Women in the Middle Ages*, Harper Perennial, 1978.

Gillingham, John, *The Wars of the Roses: Peace and Conflict in Fifteenth Century England*, Weidenfeld and Nicolson, London, 1993.

Given-Wilson, Chris, and Curteis, Alice, *The Royal Bastards of Medieval England*, Routledge & Kegan Paul, London, 1984.

Goff, John, *We Never Could Say Their Names: An Account of the Camfield Family of Northamptonshire*, 1975.

Goodman, Anthony, *The Loyal Conspiracy: The Lords Appelant under Richard II*, Routledge & Kegan Paul, London, 1971.

Grand LaRousse Encyclopedia, Librairie LaRousse, Paris, 1964.

Grant, Neil, *The Howards of Norfolk*, Franklin Watts, London and New York, 1979.

Green, J. R., *A Short History of the English People*, Vol. I, Harper & Brothers, Franklin Square, New York, 1893.

Green, John Richard, *England*, Vol. I, Co-Operative Publication Society, NY, London.

Green, Mary Anne Everett, *Lives of the Princesses of England*, Vols. I-III, Henry Colburn, Pub., London, 1849.

Griffiths, Ralph A., *The Reign of King Henry VI: The Exercise of Royal Authority 1422-1461*, Ernest Benn Limited, London, Kent, 1981.

Griffiths, Ralph A., and Sherborne, James, *Kings and Nobles in the Later Middle Ages*, Alan Sutton, Gloucester; St. Martin's Press, New York, 1986.

Griffiths, Ralph A., and Thomas, Roger S., *The Making of the Tudor Dynasty*, St. Martin's Press, New York, 1985.

Grimble, Ian, *The Harrington Family*, Jonathan Cape, London, 1957.

Grinnell-Milne, Duncan, *The Killing of William Rufus: An Investigation in the New Forest*, Augustus M. Kelley Publishers, NY, 1968.

Grove, Henry, *Alienated Tithes In Appropriated and Impropriated Parishes, Commuted or Merged under Local Statutes and the Tithe Acts: Together with all Crown Grants of Tithes, from Henry viii to William iii*, Printed for the Author's Subscribers, London, 1896.

Gunn, S. J., *Charles Brandon, Duke of Suffolk c. 1484-1545*, Basil Blackwell, Oxford, 1988.

Hackett, Francis, *Henry the Eighth*, Garden City Publishing Co., Inc., Garden City, NY, 1929.

Hardy, B. C., *Philippa of Hainault and Her Times*, John Long, Limited, London, 1910.

Haigh, Christopher, *The Reign of Elizabeth I*, MacMillan, 1984.

Hallam, Elizabeth M., ed., *Capetian France 987-1328*, Longman, London and New York, 1980.

Hallam, Elizabeth, ed., *The Plantagenet Encyclopedia*, Grove Weidenfeld, NY, 1990.

Hallam, Elizabeth, ed., *The Plantagenet Chronicles*, Weidenfeld & Nicolson, NY, 1986.

Hallam, Elizabeth, ed., *The Wars of the Roses*, Weidenfeld & Nicholson, NY, 1988.

Hallam, Elizabeth, ed., *Four Gothic Kings*, Weidenfeld & Nicolson, NY, 1987.

Halsted, Carolyn, *The Life of Margaret Beaufort, Countess of Richmond and Derby*, Smith, Elder, and Co., Cornhill, London, 1845.

Hamilton, Martha Frances, *A Study of William de Albini, Earl of Arundel*: A Thesis Presented to the Graduate Faculty of UVA for M.A., 1967.

Hampton, W. E., *Memorials of the Wars of the Roses: A Biographical Guide*, The Richard III Society, Upminster, 1979.

Harris, Barbara J., *Edward Stafford: Third Duke of Buckingham, 1478-1521*, Stanford University Press, Stanford, CA, 1986.

Harriss, G. L., *Cardinal Beaufort: A Study of Lancastrian Ascendancy and Decline*, Clarendon Press, Oxford, 1988.

Harvey, John, *The Plantagenets*, Collins, London, 1948.

Hibbert, Christopher, *The Court at Windsor: A Domestic History*, Harper & Row, NY and Evanston, 1964.

Hibbert, Christopher, *The Tower of London*, Newsweek, NY, 1971.

Hibbert, Christopher, *The Story of England*, Phaidon Press Limited, London, 1992.

Hicks, M. A., *False, Fleeting, Perjur'd Clarence, 1449-78*, Alan Sutton, 1980.

Hiller, Helmut, *Heinrich der Lowe: Herzog und Rebell*, List Verlag Munchen.

History Today Magazine, April 1990, Vol. 40.

History Today Magazine, July 1991, Vol. 41.

Hogrefe, Pearl, *Women of Action in Tudor England: Nine Biographical Sketches*, Iowa State University, Ames, Iowa, 1977.

Hollister, C. Warren, *The Making of England 55 B.C. to 1399*, D. C. Heath & Co., Lexington, Mass., 1966.

Hudson, M. E., and Clark, Mary, *Crown of a Thousand Years: A Millennium of British History presented as a pageant of King and Queens*, Crown Publishers, Inc., New York, 1978.

Hutchinson, Harold F., *King Henry V*, The John Day Co., NY, 1967.

Hutchinson, Harold F., *Edward II*, Stein and Day Publishers, New York, 1972.

Innes, Arthur D., ed., *A Source Book of English History for the Use of Schools*, Cambridge at the University Press, 1912.

Ives, Eric W., *Anne Boleyn*, Basil Blackwell, 1986.

James, John, *The Traveler's Key to Medieval France*, Alfred A. Knopf, NY, 1986.

Jarman, Rosemary Hawley, *Crispin's Day: The Glory of Agincourt*, Little, Brown and Co., Boston, 1979.

Jenkins, Elizabeth, *Elizabeth the Great*, Coward-McCann, Inc., NY, 1959.

Jenkins, Elizabeth, *The Princes in the Tower*, Coward, McCann & Geoghegan, Inc., NY, 1978.

Jenner, Heather, *Royal Wives*, Gerald Duckworth & Co., Ltd., London, 1967.

Jenner, Michael, *Journeys into Medieval England*, Michael Joseph, London, 1991.

Joelson, Annette, *England's Princes of Wales*, Dorset Press, NY, 1966.

Johnson, P. A., *Duke Richard of York 1411-1460*, Clarendon Press, Oxford, 1988.

Johnson, Paul, *The National Trust Book of British Castles*, British Heritage Press, New York, 1979.

Jolliffe, John, ed., *Froissart's Chronicles*, The Modern Library, NY, 1967.

Jones, Michael, *The Creation of Brittany: A Late Medieval State*, The Hambledon Press, London and Ronceverte.

Jones, Michael K., and Underwood, Malcolm G., *The King's Mother, Lady Margaret Beaufort, Countess of Richmond and Derby*, Cambridge University Press, Cambridge, 1992.

Kelly, Amy, *Eleanor of Aquitaine and the Four Kings*, Harvard University Press, Cambridge, Mass., 1950.

Kendall, Paul Murray, *Warwick the Kingmaker*, W. W. Norton & Co., Inc., 1957.

Kendall, Paul Murray, *Richard the Third*, W. W. Norton & Co., Inc., NY, 1955.

Kerr, Nigel and Mary, *A Guide to Medieval Sites in Britain*, Paladin Grafton Books, London, 1989.

Kightly, Charles, and Cyprien, Michael, *A Traveller's Guide to Royal Roads*, Historical Times, Inc., Harrisburg, PA, 1985.

King, Edmund, *Medieval England 1066–1485*, Phaidon Press Limited, Oxford, 1988.

Knowles, C. H., *Simon de Montfort 1265–1965*, The Historical Association, London, 1965.

Labarge, Margaret Wade, *Henry V*, Stein and Day Publishers, NY, 1976.

La Monte, John L., *Feudal Monarchy in the Latin Kingdom of Jerusalem 1100 to 1291*, The Mediaeval Academy of America, Cambridge, Massachusetts, 1932.

Lamb, Harold, *The Flame of Islam*, Doubleday & Company, Inc., NY, 1931.

Lander, J. R., *Crown and Nobility, 1450-1509*, McGille-Queen's University Press, Montreal, 1976.

Lander, J. R., *The Wars of the Roses*, St. Martin.

Lewis, Brenda Ralph, *Kings and Queens of England*, Ladybird Books, Loughborough, Leicestershire, UK, 1986.

Littleton, Taylor, and Rea, Robert R., *To Prove a Villain: The Case of King Richard III*, MacMillan Co., 1964.

Lloyd, Alan, *The Making of the King: 1066*, Holt, Rinehart and Winston, NY, 1966.

Loades, David, *Mary Tudor: A Life*, Basil Blackwell Ltd, Oxford, UK Cambridge, Mass., 1989.

Lodge, Edmund, *The Genealogy of the Existing British Peerage*, Saunders & Otley, London, 1832.

Lofts, Norah, *Queens of England*, Doubleday & Company, Inc., Garden City, NY, 1977.

Lofts, Norah, *Anne Boleyn*, Coward, McCann & Geoghegan, Inc., NY, 1979.

Loyn, H. R., ed., *The Middle Ages: A Concise Encyclopedia*, Thames & Hudson, 1991.

Macauley, David, *Castle*, Houghton Mifflin, Boston, 1977.

Machiavelli, Niccolo, *The Prince and the Discourses*, The Modern Library, New York, 1950.

Mansion, J. E., *Harrap's Standard French and English Dictionary*, Harrap, London, 1989.

Markale, Jean, *Anne de Bretagne*, Hachette litterature, 1980.

Markham, Sir Clements R., *Richard III: His Life & Character*, Russell & Russell, New York, 1968.

Márquez-Villanueva, Francisco, and Vega, Carlos Alberto, eds., *Alfonso X of Castile, The Learned King (1221-1284): An International Symposium, Harvard University, 17 November 1984*, Harvard University, 1990.

Mathew, Gervase, *The Court of Richard II*, John Murray, 1968.

Meade, Marion, *Eleanor of Aquitaine*, Hawthorn Books Publishers, Inc., NY, 1977.

Mears, Kenneth J., *The Tower of London: 900 Years of English History*, Phaidon, Oxford, 1988.

Metcalfe, Carol A., *Alice Chaucer, Duchess of Suffolk, c 1404-1475*.

Michell, John, *The Traveler's Key to Sacred England*, Alfred A. Knopf, NY, 1988.

Mills, Dorothy, and Mann, Sir James, Edward, *The Black Prince: His Tomb and Funeral Achievements in Canterbury Cathedral*, The Canterbury Printers, Ltd., Canterbury, 1987.

Minney, R. J., *The Tower of London*, Prentice-Hall, Englewood Cliffs, NJ, 1974.

Miron, E. L., *The Queens of Aragon: Their Lives and Times*, Brentano's, New York, 1913.

Mitchell, Mairin, *Berengaria, Enigmatic Queen of England*, A. Wright, East Sussex Burwash, 1986.

Moncreiffe of That Ilk, Sir Iain, *Royal Highness: Ancestry of the Royal Child*, Hamish Hamilton, London, 1982.

Moncrieff, M. C., *Kings and Queens of England*, The MacMillan Company, New York, 1966.

Mondadori, Arnoldo, ed., *The Life and Times of Charlemagne*, The Danbury Press, Grolier Enterprises, Inc., 1972.

Montague-Smith, Patrick W., *The Royal Line of Succession*, Pitkin Pictorials Ltd., London, 1968.

Montague-Smith, Patrick W., *The Royal Line of Succession*, Pitkin Pictorials Ltd., London, 1972.

Montgomery, D. H., *The Leading Facts of English History*, Ginn & Company, Publishers, Boston, 1900.

Moore, Olin H., "The Young King: Henry Plantagenet (1155-1183) in History, Literature and Tradition," The Ohio State University, University Studies, Vol. II, No. 12, December 30, 1924.

Morby, John E., *The Wordsworth Handbook of Kings & Queens*, Wordsworth Editions Ltd., Cumberland House, Hertfordshire, 1994.

Morgan, Kenneth O., *The Oxford Illustrated History of Britain*, Oxford University Press, Oxford, NY, 1986.

Morris, Jean, *The Monarchs of England*, Charterhouse, NY, 1975.

Mowry, Arthur May, *First Steps in the History of England*, Silver, Burdett and Company, New York, 1902.

Murray, Jane, *The Kings and Queens of England: A Tourist Guide*, Charles Scribner's Sons, NY, 1974.

Nicolas, Sir Nicholas Harris, edited by William Courthope, *The Historic Peerage of England*, J. Murray, London, 1867.

Neillands, Robin, *The Hundred Years War*, Routledge, London, NY, 1990.

Nelson, Lynn H., trans., *The Chronicle of San Juan de la Peña: A Fourteenth-Century Official History of the Crown of Aragon*, University of Pennsylvania Press, Philadelphia, 1991.

Nelson, Walter Henry, *The Soldier Kings: The House of Hohenzollern*, G. P. Putnam's Sons, New York, 1970.

Nicolas, Sir Nicholas Harris, *The Historic Peerage of England (being a new edition of the Synopsis of the Peerage of England)*, J. Murray, London, 1857.

Noppen, J. G., *Royal Westminster and the Coronation*, Oxford University Press, New York, 1937.

Norgate, Kate, *Minority of Henry III*, London, 1912.

Norman, A. V. B., and Pottinger, Don, *English Weapons & Warfare 449-1660*, Barnes & Noble Books, New York, 1992.

Oman, Charles, *Castles*, Kelly & Kelly, Ltd, London, 1926.

O'Callaghan, Joseph F., *The Learned King: The Reign of Alfonso X of Castile*, University of Pennsylvania Press, Philadelphia.

Packard, Jerrold M., *The Queen & Her Court*, Charles Scribner's Sons, NY, 1981.

Packe, Michael Seaman, ed., *King Edward III*, Routledge & Kegan Paul, London, 1983.

Pain, Nesta, *Empress Matilda, Uncrowned Queen of England*, Weidenfeld and Nicolson, London, 1978.

Painter, Sidney, *William Marshal: Knight-Errant, Baron, and Regent of England*, University of Toronto Press, Toronto, 1982.

Painter, Sydney, *The Scourge of the Clergy: Peter of Dreux, Duke of Brittany*, The Johns Hopkins Press, Baltimore, 1937.

Palmer, Alan, *Princes of Wales*, Weidenfeld and Nicolson, London, 1979.

Parker, K. T., ed., *The Drawings of Hans Holbein at Windsor Castle*, Johnson Reprint Corporation, Harcourt Brace Jovanovich, 1983.

Parry, R. H., ed., *The English Civil War and After 1642-1658*, University of California Press, Berkeley and Los Angeles, 1970.

Parsons, David, ed., *Eleanor of Castile 1290-1990*, Paul Watkins, Lincolnshire, 1991.

Parsons, John Carmi, *Medieval Queenship*, St. Martin's Press, New York, 1993.

Payne, Robert, *The Dream and the Tomb: A History of the Crusades*, Dorset Press, New York, 1984.

Pearsall, Derek, *The Life of Geoffrey Chaucer: A Critical Biography*, Blackwell, Oxford UK and Cambridge USA, 1992.

Phillips, J. R. S., *Aymer de Valence, Earl of Pembroke, 1307-1324*, Oxford at the Clarendon Press, 1972.

Piper, David, *Kings & Queens of England and Scotland*, The Leisure Circle Limited, Middlesex, 1980.

Platt, Colin, *The Abbeys and Priories of Medieval England*, Secker & Warburg, London, 1984.

Plowden, Alison, *Tudor Women*, Atheneum, NY, 1979.

Plowden, Alison, *Elizabeth Tudor and Mary Stewart: Two Queens in One Isle*, Barnes & Noble Books, Totowa, NJ, 1984.

Plowden, Alison, *The Young Elizabeth*, Stein and Day Publishers, NY, 1971.

Plowden, Allison, *The House of Tudor*, Stein and Day, NY, 1976.

Plumb, J. H., and Wheldon, Huw, *Royal Heritage: The Treasures of the British Crown*, Harcourt Brace Jovanovich, 1977.

Pollard, A. J., *Richard III and the Princes in the Tower*, Alan Sutton, Gloucester, 1991.

Pollard, Richard, *The Image of the King*, Atheneum, NY, 1979.

Potter, Jeremy, *Pretenders: Claimants to the Throne*, Constable, London, 1987.

Power, Eileen, edited by M. M. Postan, *Medieval Women*, Cambridge University Press, Cambridge, 1975.

Powicke, F. M., *Medieval England 1066–1485*, Thornton Butterworth, Limited, London, 1931.

Pratt, Fletcher, *The Third King*, William Sloane Associates, Inc., New York.

Prestwich, Michael, *Edward I*, University California Press, Berkeley, 1988.

Previte-Orton, C. W., *The Shorter Cambridge Medieval History*, The University Press, Cambridge, 1962.

Quennell, C. B. and Marjorie, *A History of Everyday Things in England, Part 1, 1066–1499*, B. T. Batsford, Ld., London, 1918.

Radford, L. B., *Henry Beaufort*, 1908.

Ramsay, J. H., *Lancaster and York: A Century of English History (A.D. 1399–1485)*, Vols. I and II, Oxford at the Clarendon Press, 1892.

Ramsay, Sir James H., of Bamff, *Genesis of Lancaster or the Three Reigns of Edward II, Edward III, and Richard II 1307–1399*, Vols. I and II, Oxford at the Clarendon Press, 1913.

Rawcliffe, Carole, *The Staffords, Earls of Stafford and Dukes of Buckingham, 1394-1521*, Cambridge University Press, Cambridge, 1978.

Reeves, A. C., *Lancastrian Englishmen*.

Richard, Jean, *St. Louis, Crusader King of France*, Cambridge University Press, Cambridge, 1983.

Riley-Smith, Jonathan, *The Crusades: A Short History*, Yale University Press, New Haven and London, 1987.

Riley-Smith, Jonathan, *The Feudal Nobility and the Kingdom of Jerusalem, 1174–1277*, MacMillan.

Roberts, Jane, *Holbein*, Bloomsbury Books, London, 1988.

Roche, T. W. E., *The King of Almayne*, John Murray, London, 1966.

Roll, Winifred, *Mary I: The History of an Unhappy Tudor Queen*, Prentice-Hall, Inc., Englewood Cliffs, NJ, 1980.

Ross, Charles, *Edward IV*, University of California Press, Berkeley and Los Angeles, 1974.

Ross, Charles, *Richard III*, University of California Press, Berkeley and Los Angeles, 1981.

Ross, Charles, *The Wars of the Roses: A Concise History*, Thames and Hudson, New York, 1976.

Ross, Charles, ed., *Patronage, Pedigree and Power in Later Medieval England*, Alan Sutton, Rowman & Littlefield, 1979.

Ross, Josephine, *The Monarchy of Britain*, William Morrow and Company, Inc., NY, 1982.

Ross, Stewart, *Monarchs of Scotland*, Facts On File, NY, 1990.

Rothery, Guy Cadogan, *Concise Encyclopedia of Heraldry*, Senate, London, 1994.

Routh, E. M. G., *Lady Margaret*, 1924.

Rowle, John, *Charles the First*, Little, Brown, and Co., Boston, 1975.

Rowling, Marjorie, *Life in Medieval Times*, G. P. Putnam's Sons, New York, 1968.

Rowse, A. L., *The Elizabethans and America*, Harper & Brothers, Publishers, New York, 1959.

Runciman, *A History of the Crusades: Volume Two: The Kingdom of Jerusalem and the Frankish East 1100-1187*, Cambridge University Press, London, 1968.

Runciman, Steven, *A History of the Crusades: Volume Three: The Kingdom of Acre and the Later Crusades*, Cambridge University Press, London, 1966.

Runciman, Steven, *The Sicilian Vespers: A History of the Mediterranean World in the Later Thirteenth Century*, Cambridge at the University Press, London, NY, 1958.

Ryder, Alan, *Alfonso the Magnanimous, King of Aragon, Naples and Sicily, 1396-1458*, Clarendon Press, Oxford, 1990.

Sanford, John L., Townsend, Meredith, *Governing Families of England*, Vol. I, Books for Libraries Press, Freeport, NY, 1972.

Scarisbrick, J. J., *Henry VIII*, University of California Press, Berkeley and Los Angeles, 1968.

Schenk, W., *Reginald Pole, Cardinal of England*, Longmans, Green and Co., London, 1950.

Scofield, Cora L., *The Life and Reign of Edward the Fourth*, Vols. I, II, Frank Cass & Co., Ltd., 1967.

Scott, Ronald McNair, *Robert the Bruce, King of Scots*, Peter Bedrick Books, New York, 1982.

Sedgwick, Henry Dwight, *The Black Prince*, Barnes & Noble Books, New York, 1993.

Sedgwick, Henry Dwight, *A Short History of Italy (476-1900)*, Houghton Mifflin Company, Boston, NY, 1905.

Seton, Anya, *Katherine*, Houghton Mifflin Company, Boston, 1954.

Seton, Monsignor, *An Old Family or the Setons of Scotland and America*, Brentano's, NY, 1899.

Seward, Desmond, *Eleanor of Aquitaine: The Mother Queen*, Dorset Press, NY, 1978.

Seward, Desmond, *Henry V: The Scourge of God*, Viking, NY, NY, 1988.

Seward, Desmond, *The Wars of the Roses Through the Lives of Five Men and Women of the Fifteenth Century*, Viking, New York, 1995.

Seymour, William, *Sovereign Legacy*, Doubleday & Co., Inc., Garden City, NY, 1980.

Sharp, Sir Cuthbert, ed., 1840, *The 1569 Rebellion: The Rising in the North*, Shotton, 1975.

Silva-Vigier, Anil, *This Moste Highe Prince...John of Gaunt 1340-1399*, The Pentland Press, Ltd., Edinburgh, 1992.

Slocombe, George, *William the Conqueror*, GP Putnam's Sons, NY, 1961.

Smallwood, Marilu Burch, comp., *Related Royal Families*, Pub. by author, Storter Printing Co., Gainesville, Fla., 1966.

Smith, Julia M. H., *Province and Empire: Brittany and the Carolingians*, Cambridge University Press, Cambridge.

Smith, Lacey Baldwin, *The Realm of England 1399-1688*.

Smith, Lacey Baldwin, *A Tudor Tragedy: The Life and Times of Catherine Howard*, The Reprint Society, London, 1961.

Snellgrove, Harold S., *The Lusignans in England 1247-1258*, The University of New Mexico Publications in History, Number Two, The University of New Mexico Press, Albuquerque, 1950.

Socarras, Cayetano J., *Alfonso X of Castile: A Study on Imperialistic Frustration*, Ediciones Hispam, Coleccion Blanquerna, Barcelona.

Softly, Barbara, *The Queens of England*, Bell Publishing Company, New York, 1979.

Sorley, Janetta C., *King's Daughters*, Cambridge at the University Press, 1937.

St Clare Byrne, Muriel, ed., *The Lisle Letters*, Penguin Books, 1985.

St. Aubyn, Giles, *The Year of Three Kings 1483*, Collins, London, 1983.

Starkey, David, *The Reign of Henry VIII: Personalities and Politics*, Franklin Watts, NY, 1986.

Starkey, David, ed., *Rivals in Power: Lives and Letters of the Great Tudor Dynasties*, Grove Weidenfeld, New York, 1990.

Stephen, Sir Leslie, and Lee, Sir Sidney, eds., *Dictionary of National Biography*, Oxford University Press, London, 1964.

Stephenson, Carl, *Medieval History: Europe from the Second to the Sixteenth Century*, Harper & Brothers, Publishers, NY, 1951.

Storey, R. L., *End of the House of Lancaster*, Stein and Day, NY, 1967.

Strong, Roy, *Lost Treasures of Britain: Five Centuries of Creation and Destruction*, Viking/Penguin Group, London, 1990.

Strickland, Agnes, *Lives of the Queens of England*, London, 1840-1848.

Stringer, K. J., *Earl David of Huntingdon 1152-1219*, Edinburgh University Press, 1985.

Strong, Roy, *Lost Treasures of Britain*, Viking, London, 1990.

Stuart, Roderick W., *Royalty for Commoners*, Genealogical Publishing Co., Inc., Baltimore, MD, 1992.

Stubbs, W., *The Early Plantagenets*, Scribner, Armstrong & Co., NY, 1876.

Tauté, Anne, compiler, Kings and Queens of Great Britain wall chart, 1990.

Tanner, Lawrence E., *The History and Treasures of Westminster Abbey*, Pitkin, London, 1953.

Tetlow, Edwin, *The Enigma of Hastings*, St. Martin's Press, Inc., New York, 1974.

Tey, Josephine, *The Daughter of Time*, The MacMillan Company, NY, 1952.

Thompson, M. W., *The Decline of the Castle*, Cambridge University Press, Cambridge, 1987.

Trease, Geoffrey, *The Seven Queens of England*, The Vanguard Press, Inc., NY, 1953.

Tuchman, Barbara, *A Distant Mirror: The Calamitous 14th Century*, Alfred A. Knopf, NY, 1978.

Turnbull, Stephen, *The Book of the Medieval Knight*, Villiers House, London, 1985.

Turner, Ralph V., *Men Raised from the Dust: Administrative Service and Upward Mobility in Angevin England*, University of Pennsylvania Press, Philadelphia, 1988.

Turton, Lt.-Col. W. H. Turton, D.S.O., *The Plantagenet Ancestry*, Genealogical Publishing Co., Inc., Baltimore, MD, 1993.

Tyler, William R., *Dijon and the Valois Dukes of Burgundy*, University of Oklahoma Press, Norman.

Tytler, Sarah, *Tudor Queens and Princesses*, Barnes & Noble Books, New York, 1993.

Unstead, R.J., *See Inside a Castle*, Kingfisher Books, London, 1986.

Vale, Malcolm, *The Angevin Legacy and the Hundred Years War 1250-1340*, Basil Blackwell, 1990.

Vaughan, Richard, *Charles the Bold, The Last Valois Duke of Burgundy*, Longman, London, 1973.

Vaughan, Richard, *John the Fearless: The Growth of Burgundian Power*, Barnes & Noble, Inc., New York, 1966.

Vaughan, Richard, *Philip the Bold: The Formation of the Burgundian State*, Longman, London and New York, 1979.

Vaughan, Richard, *Philip the Good: The Apogee of Burgundy*, Barnes & Noble, Inc., New York, 1970.

Vaughan, Richard, *Valois Burgundy*, Allen Lane, 1975.

Virgoe, Roger, ed., *Private Life in the Fifteenth Century: Illustrated Letters of the Paston Family*, Weidenfeld & Nicolson, NY, 1989.

Wahrig, Gerhard, *Das Grosse Deutsche Wörterbuch*, Bertelsmann Lexikon-Verlag, Gütersloh, 1968.

Walker, Leonard, *To Dine With Duke Humphrey*, Ian Henry Publications, Essex, 1987.

Warnicke, Retha M., *The Rise and Fall of Anne Boleyn*, Cambridge University Press, Cambridge, NY, Melbourne, 1989.

Warren, W. L., *Henry II*, University of California Press, Berkeley and Los Angeles, 1973.

Warren, W. L., *King John*, University of California Press, Berkeley, 1978.

Webster's Biographical Dictionary, G. & C. Merriam Co., Publishers, Springfield, Mass., 1962.

Weightman, Christine, *Margaret of York, Duchess of Burgundy 1446-1503*, Alan Sutton, Gloucester, St. Martin's Press, New York, 1989.

Weis, Frederick Lewis, *Ancestral Roots of Sixty Colonists*, Genealogical Publishing Co., Inc., Baltimore, 1976.

Weis, Frederick Lewis, *Ancestral Roots of Sixty Colonists*—6th ed., Genealogical Publishing Co., Inc., Baltimore, 1990.

Weis, Frederick Lewis, *The Magna Charta Sureties, 1215*, Genealogical Publishing Co., Inc., Baltimore, 1982.

Westminster Abbey: Official Guide, Jarrold and Sons Limited, Norwich, 1988.

Whitelock, Dorothy, ed., *The Anglo-Saxon Chronicle*, Rutgers University Press, New Brunswick, NJ, 1961.

Whitlock, Ralph, *The Warrior Kings of Saxon England*, Barnes & Noble, New York, 1993.

Whitfield, Emma Morehead, *Whitfield, Bryan, Smith, and Related Families*, 2 vols., Westminster, MD, 1948-50.

Wilcox, William B., *The Age of Aristocracy 1688-1830*.

Williams, E. Carleton, *My Lord of Bedford 1389-1435, being a life of John of Lancaster, first Duke of Bedford, brother of Henry V and Regent of France*, Longmans, Green and Co., Ltd., London, 1963.

Williams, Daniel, ed., *England in the Fifteenth Century*, The Boydell Press, Suffolk, NHUSA, 1987.

Williams, Neville, *Henry VIII and His Court*, The MacMillan Company, NY, 1971.

Williams, Neville, *Thomas Howard: Fourth Duke of Norfolk*, Barrie and Rockliff, London, 1964.

Williams, Neville, *All the Queen's Men: Elizabeth I and Her Courtiers*, The MacMillan Company, New York, 1972.

Williamson, David, *Debrett's Kings and Queens of Britain*, Dorset Press, New York, 1992.

Williamson, David, *DeBrett's Kings and Queens of Europe*, Salem House Publishers, Mass., 1988.

Wilson, Derek, *The Tower*, Charles Scribner's Sons, NY, 1979.

Wilson, Derek, *The Tower of London*, Constable/Dorset, 1978.

Wilson, Violet A., *Queen Elizabeth's Maids of Honour*, John Lane The Bodley Head Limited, London, 1922.

Wilson, Violet A., *Queen Elizabeth's Maids of Honor and Ladies of Privy Chamber*, John Lane The Bodley Head Limited, London, 1922.

Wise, Terence, *1066: Year of Destiny*, Osprey, London, 1979.

Wismes, Armel de, *Genealogy of the Kings of France*, Artaud Freres Publication, Nantes, France.

Wurts, John S., *Magna Charta* - Parts I-VII, Brookfield Publishing Co., Philadelphia, PA, 1945.

Index

Individuals are listed by surnames whenever possible. The date given pertains to the individual whose name immediately precedes the date. For example, in the entry, *Blanche (d. 1327), da. of John II of Brittany*, the death year identifies Blanche. However, in the entry, *Elizabeth, da. of Richard of York (d. 1460)*, the death date identifies Richard of York.

If a date involves the OS/NS year format, the year has been shortened to the first four digits. Therefore, an individual who died 3 Feb 1287/1288, would be listed as (d. 1287). If an individual died *abt* 1287, for example, he would be listed in the index as simply (d. 1287).

Banner of Richard II, King of England